The Evolution of Human Language

The way language as a human faculty has evolved is a question that preoccupies researchers from a wide spread of disciplines. In this book, a team of writers has been brought together to examine the evolution of language from a variety of such standpoints, including language's genetic basis, the anthropological context of its appearance, its formal structure, its relation to systems of cognition and thought, as well as its possible evolutionary antecedents. The book includes Hauser, Chomsky, and Fitch's seminal and provocative essay on the subject, "The Faculty of Language: What is it, who has it, and how did it evolve?," and charts the progress of research in this active and highly controversial field since its publication in 2002. This timely volume will be welcomed by researchers and students in a number of disciplines, including linguistics, evolutionary biology, psychology, and cognitive science.

RICHARD K. LARSON is Professor of Linguistics at Stony Brook University, New York.

VIVIANE DÉPREZ is Associate Professor of Linguistics at Rutgers University, New Jersey.

HIROKO YAMAKIDO is Assistant Professor of Japanese and Linguistics at Lawrence University, Wisconsin.

Approaches to the Evolution of Language

The evolution of human language is a rapidly growing area of study and research, undertaken from a wide range of perspectives. This new series provides a forum for the very best contributions to this fascinating subject. Taking an interdisciplinary approach, the series as a whole encourages a productive dialogue between those working in linguistics, biology, psychology, anthropology and cognitive science.

Published titles
Language Evolution and Syntactic Theory Anna R. Kinsella

The Evolution of Human Language

Biolinguistic Perspectives

Richard K. Larson

Viviane Déprez

Hiroko Yamakido

CAMBRIDGE UNIVERSITY PRESS

CAMBRIDGE UNIVERSITY PRESS
Cambridge, New York, Melbourne, Madrid, Cape Town, Singapore, São Paulo, Delhi

Cambridge University Press
The Edinburgh Building, Cambridge CB2 8RU, UK

Published in the United States of America by Cambridge University Press, New York

www.cambridge.org
Information on this title: www.cambridge.org/9780521736251

First published 2010

Printed in the United Kingdom at the University Press, Cambridge

A catalogue record for this publication is available from the British Library

ISBN 978-0-521-51645-7 Hardback
ISBN 978-0-521-73625-1 Paperback

Contents

Figures   *page* vii
Contributors   viii
Acknowledgments   ix

Introduction   1

1   The faculty of language: what is it, who has it, and how did it
    evolve?
    MARCD D. HAUSER, NOAM CHOMSKY
    AND W. TECUMSEH FITCH   14

Part I   Language architecture   43

2   Some simple evo devo theses: how true might they be for
    language?
    NOAM CHOMSKY   45

3   Your theory of language evolution depends on your theory
    of language
    RAY JACKENDOFF   63

4   Three meanings of "recursion": key distinctions for biolinguistics
    W. TECUMSEH FITCH   73

5   On obfuscation, obscurantism, and opacity: evolving
    conceptions of the faculty of language
    MARC D. HAUSER   91

Part II   Language and interface systems   101

6   Prospection as a cognitive precursor to symbolic communication
    PETER GÄRDENFORS AND MATHIAS OSVATH   103

7   Did language evolve before speech?
    MICHAEL C. CORBALLIS   115

8   A pragmatic perspective on the evolution of language
    DAN SPERBER AND GLORIA ORIGGI   124

    Part III   Biological and neurological foundations   133

9   Plasticity and canalization in the evolution of linguistic
    communication: an evolutionary developmental approach
    DANIEL DOR AND EVA JABLONKA   135

10 What is language, that it may have evolved, and what is
    evolution, that it may apply to language
    MASSIMO PIATTELLI-PALMARINI   148

11 The creative capacity of language, in what manner is it unique,
    and who had it?
    PHILIP LIEBERMAN   163

12 Genetics and the evolution of language: what genetic studies
    reveal about the evolution of language
    KARIN STROMSWOLD   176

    Part IV   Anthropological context   191

13 A putative role for language in the origin of human consciousness
    IAN TATTERSALL   193

14 On two incompatible theories of language evolution
    DEREK BICKERTON   199

15 On the evolution of language: implications of a new and general
    theory of human origins, properties, and history
    PAUL M. BINGHAM   211

    Notes   225
    References   232
    Index   263

Figures

1.1 Universal genetic organization vs. variable communicative
organization   *page* 15
1.2 Organism-external/-internal factors and the faculty
of language   18
1.3 Research space for investigating the evolution of language   20
1.4 Distribution of imitation in the animal kingdom   30
1.5 Computation of numerosities in humans and nonhumans   35
3.1 Inferential relation between theory of linguistic knowledge
and evolutionary theory   64
3.2 Architecture of Government-Binding Theory   68
3.3 The parallel architecture   68
3.4 Recursion in cognition of a visual array   69
3.5 Architecture of protolanguage   71
12.1 A schema for theories of language evolution   188

Contributors

DEREK BICKERTON, Department of Linguistics, University of Hawaii at Manoa.

PAUL M. BINGHAM, Department of Biochemistry and Cell Biology and College of Human Development, Stony Brook University, New York.

NOAM CHOMSKY, Department of Linguistics and Philosophy, Massachusetts Institute of Technology.

MICHAEL C. CORBALLIS, Department of Psychology, University of Auckland.

DANIEL DOR, Department of Communication, Tel-Aviv University.

W. TECUMSEH FITCH, Department of Neurobiology and Cognition, University of Vienna.

PETER GÄRDENFORS, Lund University Cognitive Science.

MARC D. HAUSER, Department of Psychology, Harvard University.

EVA JABLONKA, Cohn Institute for the History of Philosophy of Science and Ideas, Lester and Sally Entin Faculty of Humanities, Tel Aviv University.

RAY JACKENDOFF, Department of Philosophy, Tufts University, Medford.

PHILIP LIEBERMAN, Cognitive and Linguistic Sciences, Brown University, Providence.

GLORIA ORIGGI, Institut Jean Nicod, Paris.

MATHIAS OSVATH, Lund University Cognitive Science.

MASSIMO PIATTELLI-PALMARINI, Department of Linguistics, Department of Psychology, and Cognitive Science Program, University of Arizona.

DAN SPERBER, Institut Jean Nicod, Paris.

KARIN STROMSWOLD, Department of Psychology, Rutgers University, New Brunswick.

IAN TATTERSALL, Division of Anthropology, American Museum of Natural History, New York.

Acknowledgments

The first Morris International Symposium on Language and Communication, held at Stony Brook University October 14–16, 2005, and upon which this volume was based, was made possible by a grant from the Alice V. and Dave H. Morris Memorial Fund, administered by the New York Community Trust. We are grateful to the Morris Memorial Fund and the New York Community Trust for their generous and enthusiastic support. We thank all original symposium participants (presenter, commentators, and audience) for their contributions to a memorable event, and also students, staff, and faculty of the Stony Brook University Department of Linguistics for organizational assistance. Our special thanks to Dr. Marianne Borroff, one of the principal symposium organizers. Hauser, Chomsky and Fitch (2002) is reprinted here with permission from *Science*, which we gratefully acknowledge.

W. Tecumseh Fitch: I thank Noam Chomsky, Marc Hauser, Arie Verhagen and Gesche Westphal for comments on the manuscript, and Rens Bod, Angela Friederici, Richard Larson, Howard Lasnik, Tim O'Donnell, Geoffrey Pullum, David Raubenheimer, Mark Steedman and particularly Mark Johnson for useful conversations on the topics discussed here. All errors and opinions of course remain my own.

Daniel Dor and Eva Jablonka: We are very grateful to Marion Lamb for her detailed criticism and invaluable suggestions. We also thank Simona Ginsburg, Ehud Lamm and Iddo Tavory for enjoyable discussions and constructive comments on earlier versions of this paper.

Ian Tattersall: I thank Marianne Borroff, Hiroko Yamakido, and Richard Larson for their kind invitation to participate in this volume and the fascinating symposium on which it is based.

Paul Bingham: I am especially grateful to my gifted collaborators in the human uniqueness work (Daijiro Okada; Economics, Rutgers) and in the continued exploration of human evolution and the mind (Joanne Souza; Biology, Stony Brook). Discussions with George Williams, Bob Trivers and David Sloan Wilson were illuminating. I am also especially grateful to my wife and long-time collaborator and colleague, Zuzana Zachar (Biochemistry and Cell Biology, Stony Brook), who has been the source of so many productive discussions and brainstorming sessions over the years. It is not possible to do this kind of work without extensive advice from specialists in many areas. In the particular case of this manuscript, two areas are vital. The first is paleoanthropology. I am grateful to Philip Tobias, Philip Rightmire, John Shea and Jack Stern for especially helpful discussions. The second, of course, is the linguists who have made it possible for a non-linguist to obtain some grasp of our common challenges. On the one hand, I am grateful to the clear-headed, creative, courageous linguists who have written so well and accessibly about the issues that face us, including many of the participants of this Morris Symposium. On the other hand, I am particularly grateful to several Stony Brook colleagues who have kindly shared their expertise – including Mark Aronoff, Ellen Broselow, Susan Brennan, Artie Samuels and Richard Gerrig. As well, conversations with Michael Corballis, Ray Jackendoff, Mark Hauser and Gary Marcus at the Morris Symposium were illuminating.

Introduction

Introduction

This volume is based on a conference the original intent of which was to survey the updated landscape of research directions sparked by Hauser, Chomsky, and Fitch's seminal "The Faculty of Language: What Is It, Who Has It, and How Did It Evolve?", a paper that appeared in *Science* in 2002 and was significant, not only in framing current debates on language evolution within and across disciplines in anthropology, biology, neurosciences, cognitive sciences, philosophy, and, of course, linguistics, and not only for the novel and provocative views it advanced, but also for the controversies it ignited through its focus on recursion as central to the evolution of the language faculty. The chapters in this book present a collection of reflections and further research conducted by top scholars working in the evolution of language, nearly all influenced in one way or another by the Hauser, Chomsky, and Fitch (HCF) paper.

For many, including us, HCF and related efforts have signaled a symbolic lifting of the ban on investigations into the origin of language officially imposed by the Linguistics Society of Paris in 1871. Although this ban is often cited as an example of arbitrary scientific legislation, commanding no real respect, its effects have been surprisingly potent in our own field of linguistics. Whereas anthropology, biology, psychology, and philosophy have happily ignored the Paris ban, addressing evolutionary questions of all sorts, including those that encompass language and its origin, linguistics, as a field, has shown surprising reticence on the topic. Whereas anthropology, biology or anatomy departments routinely treat evolution as a core area meriting specialized faculty, no linguistics department would view language evolution as more than an intellectual sideline, certainly not a core area of specialization in the usual sense.

In view of the dramatic change in the theoretical landscape, with linguists of all theoretical persuasions now active in debates about human language origins, it is interesting to ponder two historical questions. First, why were linguists, and generative grammarians in particular, so little interested in the origins questions that seemed so central to many outside the field? And second, what has changed to justify current interest?

1

The origins question

When addressed by Chomsky in the past, the question of human language origins has been pronounced uninteresting on grounds of being at once too easy and too hard. It appears too easy because there seem to be so few constraints on theorizing in the domain, and no difficulty in coming up with broadly plausible tales of how language began. At the same time, as attested by the childish names labeling the most popular accounts (the "Bow Wow" theory, the "Pooh Pooh" theory, the "Yo He Hoo" theory, etc.), such theorizing does not seem to rise above the level of children's just-so stories in having little empirical or theoretical foundation, and few testable consequences.

On the other hand, the question seems too hard, because it is far from obvious what kind of scientific evidence could, in fact, be brought to bear on the question. As HCF put it, even if we move from the common view of language as a "culturally specific communication system" to the modern linguistic conception of language as "one of the biologically-grounded, internal components of the human mind/brain," potentially meaningful questions like "what components of the human nervous system are recruited in language?" turn out to have answers that are largely meaningless or untestable, such as: "probably most of them." For fruitful research to be possible, scientific questions must be divisible in such a way as to be answerable. Paraphrasing Descartes, we must be able to "divide a problem into parts that admit of separate solution." According to Chomsky, the question of how language evolved simply lacked this divisible character, under even the most scientifically up-to-date conceptions of language of the time, and indeed it is not hard to see why.

The principles and parameters model

In the 1980s, generative models took the language faculty to consist of an intricate set of universal generative "principles and parameters," interacting in modular fashion to yield both the human, biologically unique language faculty, and the variety of its social manifestations. These models were strongly motivated by the twin goals of understanding linguistic diversity and explaining the nature of language acquisition. On the one hand, the considerable apparent variation across the world's languages argued for a language faculty permitting a large space of possible human natural languages. At the same time, the facts of language acquisition – the fact that it seems to occur quickly and reliably in the face of an intrinsically "noisy" and error-filled environment – argued for a language faculty enabling children to select their language effectively within that large space on the basis of minimal input. The model ultimately settled on was one that analogized the language faculty to an electrical device of fixed architecture that included a small set of dials that could assume a finite (and presumably small) number of settings. Linguistic input would allow the learner to determine the "dial settings" appropriate for his or her language. At the end of this "setting acquisition period" the device would simply function. On this picture, the principles of the language faculty constitute its fixed architecture, and the parameters in these principles represent their "tunable" aspects. The set of distinct possible human languages corresponds to the collection of distinct possible dial/parameter settings that yield a functioning language faculty. To achieve a large space of variation from a small number of settings, the principles were assumed to be interactive, so that a particular setting for a parameter would have cascade effects in the ultimate shape of the grammar.

In this period, most of the principles and parameters hypothesized as part of human universal grammar had a character so language-specific that questions about their counterparts in non-linguistic cognitive faculties simply seemed out of place. To take a specific technical example, it would have made little sense at the time to wonder whether the linguistically core notion of 'government' had any counterpart in non-linguistic cognition. Within this framework, the uniqueness of the language faculty to humans appeared to be a matter of its foundational principles and their interactive architecture. Human language was unique because the linguistics "module" was unique in content among all our faculties.

Given this general conception, it comes as no surprise that the question of language origins could gain no empirical or theoretical traction. Faced with principles and parameters of the language faculty so obviously unique in nature, theoretical linguists had little choice but to assume that faculty had evolved all at once, with no precursors in other species, and no counterparts in non-linguistic domains, a view so obviously unsatisfactory that it could only serve to highlight the impasse. Perhaps for these reasons, in this period Chomsky repeatedly pondered in print the biological oddity of language. If evolution is a "tinkerer," as Nobel Prize-winning biologist Francois Jacob put it, then language, as conceived in the principle and parameter framework, seemed at once too unique, too complex, and too perfect a system to be a product of evolution. The situation was therefore a paradox. And a not uncommon (nor unreasonable) strategy when faced with paradox is simply to ignore it until a new perspective can emerge that will allow questions and problems to be parceled out afresh. In our view, this picture accounts not only for earlier lack of interest in questions about the evolution of language, but also for the renewed interest that has emerged.

New beginnings: "minimalism" in linguistic theorizing

A new way of parceling out the problem of language evolution has recently begun to develop as part of an independent theoretical shift in the conception of the language faculty itself, based in particular on a revised view of the core computational mechanisms of language. As noted above, in the principles and parameters framework of the 1980s, the computational mechanisms of language were taken to involve an intricate interaction between complex modules at various levels of representations. In recent years, however, the so-called minimalist program has sought to replace this complexity with a theory consisting of a single, core computational mechanism, *Merge*, embodying the central recursive property of language, and two interfaces to which it links: a sensory-motor interface, and a conceptual-intentional interface. On this picture, human language is conceived as an "interfacing mechanism," linking sensory-motor to conceptual-intentional information in an infinite, recursive manner. The three taken together are referred to by HCF as the "faculty of language broadly construed" (FLB), and the core computational mechanism is referred to as the "faculty of language narrowly construed" (FLN).

Within this broad picture, the two main motivating concerns of the earlier principles and parameters framework – diversity and acquisition – are significantly recast. The invariant architecture of the language faculty is now located in its recursive, hierarchical structuring mechanism, together with principles of efficient computation that govern its operation. "Deep" constraints on linguistic derivations, such as those governing movement (island-hood, superiority, locality), are currently being pursued as issues of computational efficiency and economy in the basic recursive mechanism. By contrast, linguistic variation – the earlier domain of parameters – is now being pursued as an interface phenomenon, arising from how the recursive mechanism interacts with the sensory-motor and conceptual-intentional domains. Thus, word order variation, a primary point of linguistic difference, is viewed as a "linearization phenomenon": an aspect of how the two-dimensional hierarchical structures yielded by core computation are projected into the strings of sequentially pronounced forms required by the sensory-motor system. Languages are assumed to be able to linearize their structures differently. Likewise, variation in expressive relations – how a given notion is lexicalized and subsequently projected – may reflect variation at the conceptual-intentional interface. Thus, in the construction of English motion concepts, manner of motion is incorporated into the verb, while direction is realized in a satellite phrase (*John rolled down the hill*), whereas in other languages, such as French, direction of motion is expressed in the verb, while manner is realized in the satellite (*Le ballon est descendu la colline en roulant* cf. 'John descended the hill rolling'). Such broad differences in lexicalization patterns may well reflect systematic differences in how the linguistic system interfaces with the (presumably pre-existing) domain of motion concepts. Finally, issues of language acquisition – how children are able to achieve rapid, reliable mastery of their language in a noisy, error-ridden environment – also now presumably reduce to interface matters, although intriguing questions remain regarding variation in movement possibilities across languages.

The origins question reconsidered

The conceptual subdivision of language mechanisms into three core components – two interfaces and a recursive link between them – has allowed for a new parceling-out of the problem area from an evolutionary point of view. As HCF have emphasized, when we consider the origins of natural language, and the components comprising it, three core questions may be posed:

1. Is it uniquely human or shared with other species?
2. Was its evolution gradual or saltational?
3. Did it evolve as a unique adaptation for communication or one for another purpose?

As we noted, such questions were difficult to frame and address in earlier stages of linguistic theory. The complex interaction of the components made it difficult to extract a set of properties that could be meaningfully isolated for appropriate investigation. What kind of evidence could be brought to bear on whether Move α – the central transformational component of the computational mechanisms in the principles and parameter model of language – was or was not uniquely human? Such questions can, however, be asked separately of each of the three core components of the newly conceived language faculty: the sensory-motor component, the conceptual-intentional component and the core computational recursive component, and indeed can also in principle be answered differently.

These questions also serve as a useful way of organizing the contributions represented in this volume.

Part 1: Language architecture

Understanding the evolution of language clearly presupposes understanding of what a language is. Only then can we determine what features of it can or should be traced to capacities or structures found in other species, and what (if anything) is truly innovative in it. The authors in this section offer basic views about the language capacity, how it might be studied from a comparative point of view, and what evolutionary expectations might accompany differing theories of it. The volume reprints the original Hauser, Chomsky, and Fitch 2002 *Science* paper "The faculty of language: what is it, who has it, and how did it evolve?" as a convenient reference point for the discussion that follows.

Chomsky begins from a basic view of language as a computational system bridging the human motor-perceptual and conceptual-intentional systems. He surveys the bare conclusions that may drawn about this system, given its empirical properties as revealed by linguistic research, and given the three main factors available to shape it: the experience that forms its input, the genetic factors that encode its specific format, and those principles of design that are known to govern the growth and evolution of biological systems generally (e.g., efficient computation). Chomsky isolates the basic operation of Merge, which "takes structures already formed and combines them into a new structure" as a candidate for what is unique in human language. Chomsky suggests the presence of Merge, together with the assumption of maximally efficient computation, yields the fundamental observed configurations of linguistic structure, including basic thematic Merge (external Merge) and the phenomenon of movement, here analyzed as internal Merge. Chomsky also considers the fascinating question of whether language bears a symmetric relation to its interfaces, or whether one is primary. Based on a range of suggestive evidence, he concludes that the conceptual interface is indeed primary. The picture of language evolution is thus one of the development of recursive Merge in an individual (or small group of individuals) that exploited it initially for its enhanced symbolization and reasoning advantages, and only later deployed it for communication, once its genetic basis had spread to a sufficient number of creatures to make "externalization" adaptively advantageous. Developing this line, Chomsky further suggests that externalization may well be the source of variation in the world's languages: in effect, although natural language has an invariant interface with a single conceptual-intentional system, there may be a multiplicity of ways in which it can interface with motor-perceptual systems.

Chomsky makes a number of closing observations about human symbolic capacity that, superficially at least, appear to complicate our picture of human language evolution and challenge its prospects for success. Specifically, he notes that even if recursive Merge was a key innovation in human language origins, as described above, the conceptual-intentional system with which it interfaces must have already been distinct from that observed in the animal world. As he notes, reference to the world by human language symbols has a mind-dependent quality not found in the communications systems of other animal species. So the picture cannot simply be one of recursive Merge imposed on a system of linguistic/cognitive atoms of the sort found routinely in the animal world. In a certain sense, these atoms must have already been distinct before Merge came upon the scene, leading to separate and intriguing questions about how this particular development might have come about.

Jackendoff's paper presents an interesting counterpoint to Chomsky's, exploring how alternative views of the language capacity and its make-up might generate alternative hypotheses about its evolution. Jackendoff separates four different ways in which a necessary component C of human linguistic capacity might derive: (i) C required no evolutionary innovation and was present in the ancestral lineage in essentially modern form; (ii) C required evolutionary innovation, but its function extended beyond language; (iii) C required evolutionary innovation, but was secured by alteration of an existing non-linguistic feature/capacity; (iv) C required evolutionary innovation, and was secured by something entirely new. Jackendoff advocates "reverse engi-neering" as the best way to study the language capacity in terms of (i)–(iv). That is, one should look at modern human linguistic capacity in terms of normal linguistic evidence, in terms of evidence from other cognitive, perceptual or motor capacities in humans, and in terms of evidence from comparable capaci-ties in other organisms. Jackendoff contrasts two detailed views of the human linguistic capacity with these distinctions as background: what he calls the "syntacto-centric" picture of Chomsky's minimalist program, in which linguis-tic syntax is the source of generative capacity in grammar and cognition, and the parallel architecture that Jackendoff advocates, in which independent genera-tive systems interact.

For Jackendoff, language and cognition are essentially distinct systems with their own atoms and combinatory structures, and mapping relations between them. On his view, linguistic evolution begins with a pre-existing system of combinatory thought that might have been initially externalized in ways not relying on hierarchical structure (cf. Bickerton, this volume), but which ultimately came to incorporate it. This picture, somewhat like the one entertained by Chomsky, shifts important aspects of the question of human language origins to questions about the origins of human concepts, although Jackendoff does not discuss here the mind-dependent aspects of symbolism that Chomsky focuses on.

Fitch's paper provides a detailed look at the property of recursion, identified in HCF as one of (if not the) key innovation in the development of human linguistic capacity. Fitch begins by briefly reviewing the history of HCF and the debate that ensued from it, reiterating the position (echoed in Chomsky's discussion of *Merge*) that recursion is a central feature of human language. Fitch identifies three different meanings/interpretations of recursion employed by the different fields of computer science, linguistics and meta-mathematics. For computer science, a recursive function is one that calls itself during the course of execution. For linguistics, a recursive rule is one that yields self-embedded structures. For meta-mathematics, a partial recursive function is simply a computable function. Fitch shows that unclarity about recur-sion has been a source of confusion in the animal communication literature regarding what species have recursive capacities, and what tests we can do to probe this.

Hauser's contribution has two goals: to address some of the crucial points in HCF that were misunderstood in ensuing debate, and to restate the research program outlined there and its prospects. Hauser reiterates his conviction that the distinction between the faculty of language broadly and narrowly construed (FLB and FLN, respectively) is an important one for guiding research in understanding linguistic evolution, whether or not any particular item is ulti-mately found to inhabit FLN.

Part 2: Language and interface systems

Language interfaces with the conceptual system on the one hand and with the motor-perceptual system on the other. Could non-linguistic cognitive abilities on either end of these interface systems have played a triggering role in the emergence of the human language faculty? In this section, the authors differently explore the cognitive systems that language interfaces with and raise the question of whether and how some of the interface properties interact with language and could be regarded as precursors.

For Gärdenfors and Osvath, a key and unique property of human language is the ability it affords to describe or plan situations that are not present. Working backward from this insight, Gärdenfors and Osvath argue that "anticipatory cognition" is a prerequisite for the action-planning capacity that language allows. They attempt to trace the emergence of this anticipatory cognition in the new feeding habits of prelinguistic Oldowan society; from fruit gatherers, the Oldowan hominins became hunters or scavengers of large carcasses. These changes in feeding habits required, on the one hand, the use of stone tools for butchering activities and, on the other hand, the anticipatory stashing of stone tools in various geographical locations throughout the hunting domain, given that the locations of large animal carcasses cannot be predicted ahead of their discovery. Stashing of stones provides proof of anticipatory cognition, an ability not commonly found in the animal world. Anticipatory cognition, once acquired, can serve as the backdrop of action planning. It allows one to step away from present circumstances and abstractly project oneself in the not-yet-existent future. Plausibly, it represents a precursor of the language-unique ability for displacement and representation of future possible worlds.

Corballis explores the motor interface, arguing that language must have preceded speech in the following sense: gestural communication has its roots in the ability that great apes and humans share for fine-grained movements. Furthermore, both humans and great apes have been shown to exhibit mirror neurons connected to hand and oral gesture. From this basis, it is but a short step to imagine that gestural communication preceded speech and that some of the complexity of language was present even before humans moved to oral communication. As Corballis puts it, speech is essentially "swallowed gestural communication" that resonates via the mirror system in same-species brains. It is thus possible to imagine that language preceded speech, being gestural at first, but possibly with some of its formal properties already in place. It was this gestural communication, Corballis suggests, that underlay the use of speech sound to effect essentially the same type of communication.

Finally, Sperber and Origgi explore the relationship between language and the theory of mind. They make the strong and convincing point that variations in a code, which human languages profusely exhibit in contrast to animals codes, can be evolutionarily advantageous only to beings capable of inferential communication – communication that reflects the speaker's intention to affect the addressee's mental representation, and the addressee's understanding of this intention. Such an inferential system of communication is in turn possible only between beings that share a naïve psychology and possess the ability to attribute to others mental states identical to their own.

Part 3: Biological and neurological foundations

What role do biology, genetics, anatomy, and neurology play in the evolution of language and how are they connected? In this section, the authors address this question from a variety of perspectives rooted in their respective disciplines. The answers offer a diversity of views and provide a stimulating sampling of how divergent conclusions can be drawn from within the very same disciplines. This divergence forcefully illustrates how deeply one's conception of language infuses and frames explorations of the evolutionary problem. Dor and Jablonka, and Piatelli-Palmarini explore the role of biology in language evolution. The former adopts the common-sense conception of language as a culturally specific type of communication, with syntax a minor complication introduced in the course of evolutionary history. By contrast, the latter starts from the Chomskyan notion of I-language (internal language) as a biologically grounded component of the human mind/brain with syntax as its core component. Not surprisingly their perspectives on language evolution arrive at very different views. Lieberman and Stromswold, in contrast, offer rather convergent views, both noting intriguing parallelisms that neurological and biological experimental evidence reveal between the linguistic computational properties of phonology and syntax and those of the motor system.

Dor and Jablonka begin by pointing out how developmental considerations have led to a shift in perspective in the so-called "evo devo" view in biology, bringing new focus on phenotypical development, rather than on genetic variation as the point of departure for evolutionary analysis. They discuss general evo devo concepts and processes centering on plasticity, canalization and genetic accommodation, and offer conjectures about the role that each may have played in the evolution of linguistic communication. The picture they develop envisions the cultural evolution of language as preceding speakers' genetic readiness. On their perspective, language came into being because the human social world evolved to the point where collective inventions became possible. Language results from speaker invention and is a manifestation of humans' exceptional (but not unique) behavioral and neural open-ended plasticity. Invariance of general linguistic properties is attributed to *canalization*, the other side of developmental plasticity. Their perspective, not surprisingly, leads to a picture of gradual evolution: language invention started with the creation of words and gradually complexified, under pressures for communication, to eventually encompass syntax. Why words should have conferred their initial adaptive advantages is, however, largely taken for granted and left unexplained, as are as the specifics of the communication pressures and their importance in shaping language. The picture of language is one of a self-developing process directed by increased canalization, which eventually imparted a certain architectural logic, in turn imposing system constraints on the next innovations. Partial genetic assimilation then started a co-evolutionary spiral in which "language not only adapted to the brains and minds of individual speakers, but the brains and minds of the speakers also adapted themselves to language."

The view of language evolution offered by Piatteli-Palmarini is diametrically opposed to that just sketched. Beginning with general "parables" from the history of physics, demonstrating the fruitfulness of scientific inquiry that places no prior bounds on abstract theorizing, Piattelli-Palmarini forcefully argues for a perspective that takes I-language and its recursive syntax as the relevant object of inquiry for language evolution, and not E-language or linguistic communication. He offers a brief, but pointed demonstration (based on ellipsis phenomena) that syntax and not communication must be recognized as the driving force that shapes language as soon as factual analysis of any depth is attempted. He goes on to argue against views that take language evolution as "the cumulation of a host of smaller steps" and calls for a general reexamination of the notion of evolution, even biological evolution as applied to language. Finally, Piatteli-Palmarini stresses the danger of the subtraction fallacy, which applied to language suggests that word concatenation could be seen as a precursor to fully developed syntactic language. Words, he counters, are not simplex atoms but already highly complex syntactic entities, as demonstrated by Pylkkänen and Marantz (2003), using both linguistic evidence and experimental brain imaging results.

In his contribution, Philip Lieberman offers a broad overview of recent neurological findings ranging from classic aphasia to brain imaging and studies of Parkinson's disease, all highlighting the central role of basal ganglia in both linguistic and non-linguistic cognitive abilities involving reiteration. These findings, Lieberman argues, strongly suggest that the neural circuitry rooted in the basal ganglia should supersede classic neurological models associating core computational components of language and syntax with cortical structures in Broca's area. His survey reasserts the neurological overlap between fine motor skills and linguistic capacities, an overlap also supported by recent genetic findings that identify FOXP2, not as a language-specific gene, but as a gene governing fine motor control, coordination and human reiterative capacities. Lieberman suggests that the capacity for reiteration, which in his view subsumes recursion, is rooted in fine-grained motor control and planning, and is hence neither unique to the language faculty nor to human cognition. On this view, the neural capacity for reiteration, unlike the "narrow faculty of language" hypothesized by HCF, is expressed outside the domain of language, for example, when we change the direction of a thought process or engage in seemingly unrelated activities such as dancing. As such, although it may well underlie syntax and phonology, reiteration is not the basis of the human-unique capacity for language. What is demonstrably unique to humans and moreover clearly language specific, Lieberman counters, is our speech physiology – specifically, the supralaryngeal vocal tract (SVT) that underlies our unique ability to produce quantal vowels. For Lieberman, "the presence of a human SVT in the fossil hominid record can be regarded as an index for the reiterative neural substrate that makes voluntary speech possible." As he puts it, succinctly: "we talk therefore we are." In support of his view, Lieberman notes that the first appearance of the human SVT in the fossil record coincides with the beginning of Klein's "cultural revolution" (Klein 1999). Moreover, although the FOXP2 gene has been recently argued to occur in the Neanderthal genome, the human SVT is demonstrably incompatible with Neanderthal's short neck morphology and thus unique to sapiens.

Finally, Stromswold presents detailed results from genetic studies of language in homozygote vs. heterozygote twins. She argues that genetic factors appear to play a greater role for syntax and phonology than for the lexicon and that the high degree of genetic overlap for oral motor and fine motor skills with that of linguistic abilities supports the idea that the former could be a precursor of the latter.

Part 4: Anthropological context

Theododsius Dobzhansky once famously remarked "Nothing in biology makes sense except from the point of view of evolution." This does not entail, however, that nothing in biology makes sense except from the standpoint of natural selection. The modern understanding of evolution is in fact quite broad, embracing a variety of mechanisms, selection being only one. It is therefore an interesting and highly debated question as to how much of a role selection and adaptation have played in the origin and development of language. The authors in the section provide some sense of the range of views that surround this issue.

Tattersall offers a broad overview of trends in hominid evolution over the last 7 million years, together with some important general reminders of how evolution proceeds and how behavioral and morphological innovation are related. Tattersall points out that over much of hominin history, the human family tree has been "bushy", with numerous species coexisting. Symbolic cognition seems to have arrived late, confined a small population that, in form at any rate, was virtually identical to non-symbolic hominins existing for tens of thousands of years before them. Tattersall notes this as a broad and persistent pattern in hominin evolution, where behavioral innovation does not track differences in morphological form, but rather occurs within an existing form. The intriguing picture that results is one of morphological change opening up potentials for behavioral/cognitive advance that can lie unexploited for very long periods of time until they are "exapted" and recruited for a function quite different than the one that gave rise to them in the first place. This view seems compatible with the general view of HCF wherein language arose suddenly, by recruitment of systems existing for quite independent reasons.

Bickerton rejects the general picture of HCF as overly abstract, as requiring an implausibly "instantaneous" picture of human linguistic development, and as offering no answers to the questions of when, where, how and why human linguistic capacity arose. In its place Bickerton offers a theory integrating current results from human paleontology according to which human language arose gradually from a proto-language by relatively small, incremental steps. Bickerton isolates the crucial property driving early linguistic evolution as "displacement," the ability to speak of things distant from speaker and hearer. He suggests that within the early hominin ecological context, where humans had developed stone tools allowing them to scavenge the carcasses of mega-fauna, but could take advantage of this only in a cooperative mode, ability to recruit scavenging cohorts by linguistic means would have been selectively advantageous. The disagreement between Bickerton and HCF appears in part to be a conflict between a "gradualist" view of evolution, which wants the guiding hand of selection present at each step, and a view of evolution as a more stochastic, more saltative and less selection-driven process.

An interesting suggestion of Bickerton's paper is that modern human language, structured by recursive Merge, could have been anteceded by a proto-language based on a different expression-forming operation: Sequence. The latter joins items in linear, "beads on a string" fashion. Relations among the resulting joined items are determined, not by hierarchical structure, but solely by semantic-pragmatic factors, along (perhaps) with relative linear distance. As an argument for this proposal Bickerton suggests that Sequence is still with us in the assembly of sentences in a discourse: that although structure-based relations obtain within clauses, they do not obtain across the clauses of a discourse. The latter are, Bickerton suggests, bound together only by the looser relations of semantic-pragmatic appropriateness and linear distance found in the hypothetical protolanguage. It is worth observing that this picture of discourse for modern human language is not widely accepted, in either theoretical or computational linguistics. The line of inquiry initiated by Hans Kamp and Irene Heim in so-called "Discourse Representation Theory" (DRT) holds that discourses are in fact hierarchically structured objects the geometric relations of which govern the accessibility of various technical relations; there is a large, on-going industry of work in the DRT framework. Furthermore, a whole line of independent research initiated by Grosz and Sidner in the computational processing of natural language dialogue in the 1980s suggests a similar view. It has been demonstrated, for example, that a view of discourses as structured objects with constituent relations allows predictions of anaphoric reference that are otherwise unavailable. We do not offer these points as contradicting Bickerton's claim of a Sequence operation present in at an antecedent stage of human language, but rather as showing that hierarchical organization is prevalent in modern human language at levels beyond the sentence. Detecting the hypothesized ancestral operation in modern speech is thus perhaps trickier than Bickerton represents.

Bingham is another proposal in an adaptationist line of thinking. Bingham argues for a general selectional approach to human language evolution, citing its adaptive complexity, its elegant engineering, and its historicity, all familiar themes. His view of language is embedded within a broader theory of the unique human adaptation as combining two key features: the existence of "massive, kinship independent social cooperation," and "the capacity for elite remote killing of conspecifics" by throwing. Language is taken to arise within this context as a by-product among a population of humans that had successfully managed conflicts of interest on a large scale; in effect (as we understand it), language of the human sort was always possible, but its deployment was limited by social cooperative factors, which, once removed by the development of elite throwing skills, allowed it to be deployed.

We note that Bingham's proposal is controversial in various respects. The claim that elite throwing was the core innovation responsible for separating late prehumans from their hominoid ancestors clashes directly with recent work on the evolution of hominin shoulder morphology (Larson 2007), which indicates elite overhand throwing to have been a much more recent development, post *Homo erectus*. The latter view is supported by Rhodes and Churchill (2008), who date the appearance of long-range projectile weaponry in the human toolkit at no earlier than 80,000 years ago. It is also interesting to note that modern humans display strong sexual dimorphism with respect to elite overhand throwing: various differences in males versus females conspire to make the former much more effective overhand throwers than the latter. Studies (reviewed in Chimes 2001) show, moreover, that these differences emerge quite early, in children as young as five years old, and steadily increase thereafter. This trajectory differs sharply from that of natural language, which shows no stable, sex-related differences in the acquisition process, and no persisting differences in adults. A natural conclusion from these results is that, far from being a core innovation in the human lineage, elite throwing was in fact a late evolutionary arrival, and one more probably correlated with specialized male social functions (hunting) than with human society generally.

1   The faculty of language: what is it, who has it, and how did it evolve?

Marc D. Hauser, Noam Chomsky and
W. Tecumseh Fitch

We argue that an understanding of the faculty of language requires substantial interdisciplinary cooperation. We suggest how current developments in linguistics can be profitably wedded to work in evolutionary biology, anthropology, psychology, and neuroscience. We submit that a distinction should be made between the faculty of language in the broad sense (FLB) and in the narrow sense (FLN). FLB includes a sensory-motor system, a conceptual-intentional system, and the computational mechanisms for recursion, providing the capacity to generate an infinite range of expressions from a finite set of elements. We hypothesize that FLN only includes recursion and is the only uniquely human component of the faculty of language. We further argue that FLN may have evolved for reasons other than language, hence comparative studies might look for evidence of such computations outside of the domain of communication (for example, number, navigation, and social relations).

If a martian graced our planet, it would be struck by one remarkable similarity among Earth's living creatures and a key difference. Concerning similarity, it would note that all living things are designed on the basis of highly conserved developmental systems that read an (almost) universal language encoded in DNA base pairs. As such, life is arranged hierarchically with a foundation of discrete, unblendable units (codons, and, for the most part, genes) capable of combining to create increasingly complex and virtually limitless varieties of both species and individual organisms. In contrast, it would notice the absence of a universal code of communication (Figure 1.1).

If our martian naturalist were meticulous, it might note that the faculty mediating human communication appears remarkably different from that of other living creatures; it might further note that the human faculty of language appears to be organized like the genetic code – hierarchical, generative, recursive, and virtually limitless with respect to its scope of expression. With these pieces in hand, this martian might begin to wonder how the genetic code changed in such a way as to generate a vast number of mutually incomprehensible communication systems across species while maintaining clarity of comprehension within a given species. The martian would have stumbled onto some

14

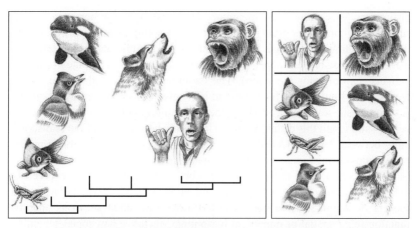

Figure 1.1. The animal kingdom has been designed on the basis of highly conserved developmental systems that read an almost universal language coded in DNA base pairs. This system is shown on the left in terms of a phylogenetic tree. In contrast, animals lack a common universal code of communication, indicated on the right by unconnected animal groups. (Illustration: John Yanson)

of the essential problems surrounding the question of language evolution, and of how humans acquired the faculty of language.

In exploring the problem of language evolution, it is important to distinguish between questions concerning language as a communicative system and questions concerning the computations underlying this system, such as those underlying recursion. As we argue below, many acrimonious debates in this field have been launched by a failure to distinguish between these problems. According to one view (*1*), questions concerning abstract computational mechanisms are distinct from those concerning communication, the latter targeted at problems at the interface between abstract computation and both sensory-motor and conceptual-intentional interfaces. This view should not, of course, be taken as a claim against a relationship between computation and communication. It is possible, as we discuss below, that key computational capacities evolved for reasons other than communication but, after they proved to have utility in communication, were altered because of constraints imposed at both the periphery (e.g., what we can hear and say or see and sign, the rapidity with which the auditory cortex can process rapid temporal and spectral changes) and more central levels (e.g., conceptual and cognitive structures, pragmatics, memory limitations).

At least three theoretical issues cross-cut the debate on language evolution. One of the oldest problems among theorists is the "shared versus unique" distinction. Most current commentators agree that, although bees dance, birds sing, and chimpanzees grunt, these systems of communication differ qualitatively from human language. In particular, animal communication systems lack the rich expressive and open-ended power of human language (based on humans' capacity for recursion). The evolutionary puzzle, therefore, lies in working out how we got from there to here, given this apparent discontinuity. A second issue revolves around whether the evolution of language was gradual versus saltational; this differs from the first issue because a qualitative discontinuity between extant species could have evolved gradually, involving no discontinuities during human evolution. Finally, the "continuity versus exaptation" issue revolves around the problem of whether human language evolved by gradual extension of preexisting communication systems, or whether important aspects of language have been exapted away from their previous adaptive function (e.g., spatial or numerical reasoning, Machiavellian social scheming, tool-making).

Researchers have adopted extreme or intermediate positions regarding these basically independent questions, leading to a wide variety of divergent viewpoints on the evolution of language in the current literature. There is, however, an emerging consensus that, although humans and animals share a diversity of important computational and perceptual resources, there has been substantial evolutionary remodeling since we diverged from a common ancestor some 6 million years ago. The empirical challenge is to determine what was inherited unchanged from this common ancestor, what has been subjected to minor modifications, and what (if anything) is qualitatively new. The additional evolutionary challenge is to determine what selectional pressures led to adaptive changes over time and to understand the various constraints that channeled this evolutionary process. Answering these questions requires a collaborative effort among linguists, biologists, psychologists, and anthropologists.

One aim of this essay is to promote a stronger connection between biology and linguistics by identifying points of contact and agreement between the fields. Although this interdisciplinary marriage was inaugurated more than fifty years ago, it has not yet been fully consummated. We hope to further this goal by, first, helping to clarify the biolinguistic perspective on language and its evolution (2–7). We then review some promising empirical approaches to the evolution of the language faculty, with a special focus on comparative work with nonhuman animals, and conclude with a discussion of how inquiry might profitably advance, highlighting some outstanding problems.

We make no attempt to be comprehensive in our coverage of relevant or interesting topics and problems. Nor is it our goal to review the history of the field. Rather, we focus on topics that make important contact between empirical data and theoretical positions about the nature of the language faculty. We believe that if explorations into the problem of language evolution are to progress, we need a clear explication of the computational requirements for language, the role of evolutionary theory in testing hypotheses of character evolution, and a research program that will enable a productive interchange between linguists and biologists.

Defining the target: two senses of the faculty of language

The word "language" has highly divergent meanings in different contexts and disciplines. In informal usage, a language is understood as a culturally specific communication system (English, Navajo, etc.). In the varieties of modern linguistics that concern us here, the term "language" is used quite differently to refer to an internal component of the mind/brain (sometimes called "internal language" or "I-language"). We assume that this is the primary object of interest for the study of the evolution and function of the language faculty. However, this biologically and individually grounded usage still leaves much open to interpretation (and misunderstanding). For example, a neuroscientist might ask: What components of the human nervous system are recruited in the use of language in its broadest sense? Because any aspect of cognition appears to be, at least in principle, accessible to language, the broadest answer to this question is, probably, "most of it." Even aspects of emotion or cognition not readily verbalized may be influenced by linguistically based thought processes. Thus, this conception is too broad to be of much use. We therefore delineate two more restricted conceptions of the faculty of language, one broader and more inclusive, the other more restricted and narrow (Figure 1.2).

Faculty of language – broad sense (FLB). FLB includes an internal computational system (FLN, below) combined with at least two other organism-internal systems, which we call "sensory-motor" and "conceptual-intentional." Despite debate on the precise nature of these systems, and about whether they are substantially shared with other vertebrates or uniquely adapted to the exigencies of language, we take as uncontroversial the existence of some biological capacity of humans that allows us (and not, for example, chimpanzees) to readily master any human language without explicit instruction. FLB includes this capacity, but excludes other organism-internal systems that are necessary but not sufficient for language (e.g., memory, respiration, digestion, circulation, etc.).

Faculty of language – narrow sense (FLN). FLN is the abstract linguistic computational system alone, independent of the other systems with which it interacts and interfaces. FLN is a component of FLB, and the mechanisms underlying it are some subset of those underlying FLB.

Others have agreed on the need for a restricted sense of "language" but have suggested different delineations. For example, Liberman and his associates (8) have argued that the sensory-motor systems were specifically adapted for language, and hence should be considered part of FLN. There is also a long

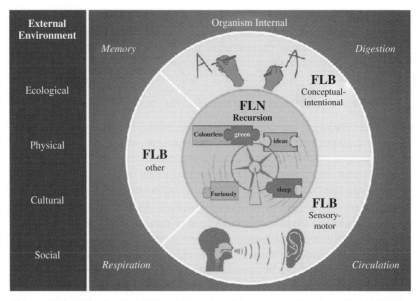

Figure 1.2. A schematic representation of organism-external and -internal factors related to the faculty of language. FLB includes sensory-motor, conceptual-intentional, and other possible systems (which we leave open); FLN includes the core grammatical computations that we suggest are limited to recursion. See text for more complete discussion.

tradition holding that the conceptual-intentional systems are an intrinsic part of language in a narrow sense. In this article, we leave these questions open, restricting attention to FLN as just defined but leaving the possibility of a more inclusive definition open to further empirical research.

The internal architecture of FLN, so conceived, is a topic of much current research and debate (*4*). Without prejudging the issues, we will, for concreteness, adopt a particular conception of this architecture. We assume, putting aside the precise mechanisms, that a key component of FLN is a computational system (narrow syntax) that generates internal representations and maps them into the sensory-motor interface by the phonological system, and into the conceptual-intentional interface by the (formal) semantic system; adopting alternatives that have been proposed would not materially modify the ensuing discussion. All approaches agree that a core property of FLN is recursion, attributed to narrow syntax in the conception just outlined. FLN takes a finite set of elements and yields a potentially infinite array of discrete expressions. This capacity of FLN yields discrete infinity (a property that also characterizes the natural numbers). Each of these discrete expressions is then passed to the sensory-motor and conceptual-intentional systems, which process and elaborate this information in the use of language. Each expression is, in this sense, a pairing of sound and meaning. It has been recognized for thousands of years that language is, fundamentally, a system of sound-meaning connections; the potential infiniteness of this system has been explicitly recognized by Galileo, Descartes, and the seventeenth-century "philosophical grammarians" and their successors, notably von Humboldt. One goal of the study of FLN and, more broadly, FLB is to discover just how the faculty of language satisfies these basic and essential conditions.

The core property of discrete infinity is intuitively familiar to every language user. Sentences are built up of discrete units: There are 6-word sentences and 7-word sentences, but no 6.5-word sentences. There is no longest sentence (any candidate sentence can be trumped by, for example, embedding it in "Mary thinks that ..."), and there is no non-arbitrary upper bound to sentence length. In these respects, language is directly analogous to the natural numbers (see below).

At a minimum, then, FLN includes the capacity of recursion. There are many organism-internal factors, outside FLN or FLB, that impose practical limits on the usage of the system. For example, lung capacity imposes limits on the length of actual spoken sentences, whereas working memory imposes limits on the complexity of sentences if they are to be understandable. Other limitations – for example, on concept formation or motor output speed – represent aspects of FLB, which have their own evolutionary histories and may have played a role in the evolution of the capacities of FLN. Nonetheless, one can profitably inquire into the evolution of FLN without an immediate concern for these limiting aspects of FLB. This is made clear by the observation that, although many aspects of FLB are shared with other vertebrates, the core recursive aspect of FLN currently appears to lack any analog in animal communication and possibly other domains as well. This point, therefore, represents the deepest challenge for a comparative evolutionary approach to language. We believe that investigations of this capacity should include domains other than communication (e.g., number, social relationships, navigation).

Given the distinctions between FLB and FLN and the theoretical distinctions raised above, we can define a research space as sketched in Figure 1.3. This research space identifies, as viable, problems concerning the evolution of sensory-motor systems, of conceptual-intentional systems, and of FLN. The comparative approach, to which we turn next, provides a framework for addressing questions about each of these components of the faculty of language.

The comparative approach to language evolution

The empirical study of the evolution of language is beset with difficulties. Linguistic behavior does not fossilize, and a long tradition of analysis of fossil skull shape and cranial endocasts has led to little consensus about the evolution

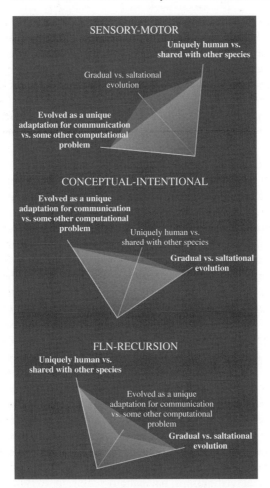

Figure 1.3. Investigations into the evolution of the faculty of language are confronted with a three-dimensional research space that includes three comparative-evolutionary problems cross-cut by the core components of the faculty of language. Thus, for each problem, researchers can investigate details of the sensory-motor system, the conceptual-intentional system, FLN, and the interfaces among these systems.

of language (*7, 9*). A more tractable and, we think, powerful approach to problems of language evolution is provided by the comparative method, which uses empirical data from living species to draw detailed inferences about extinct ancestors (*3, 10–12*). The comparative method was the primary tool used by Darwin (*13, 14*) to analyze evolutionary phenomena and continues to play a central role throughout modern evolutionary biology. Although scholars interested in language evolution have often ignored comparative data altogether or focused narrowly on data from nonhuman primates, current thinking in neuroscience, molecular biology, and developmental biology indicates that many aspects of neural and developmental function are highly conserved, encouraging the extension of the comparative method to all vertebrates (and perhaps beyond). For several reasons, detailed below, we believe that the comparative method should play a more central role in future discussions of language evolution.

An overarching concern in studies of language evolution is with whether particular components of the faculty of language evolved specifically for human language and, therefore (by extension), are unique to humans. Logically, the human uniqueness claim must be based on data indicating an absence of the trait in nonhuman animals and, to be taken seriously, requires a substantial body of relevant comparative data. More concretely, if the language evolution researcher wishes to make the claim that a trait evolved uniquely in humans for the function of language processing, data indicating that no other animal has this particular trait are required.

Although this line of reasoning may appear obvious, it is surprisingly common for a trait to be held up as uniquely human before any appropriate comparative data are available. A famous example is categorical perception, which when discovered seemed so finely tuned to the details of human speech as to constitute a unique human adaptation (*15, 16*). It was some time before the same underlying perceptual discontinuities were discovered in chinchillas and macaques (*17, 18*), and even birds (*19*), leading to the opposite conclusion that the perceptual basis for categorical perception is a primitive vertebrate characteristic that evolved for general auditory processing, as opposed to specific speech processing. Thus, a basic and logically ineliminable role for comparative research on language evolution is this simple and essentially negative one: A trait present in nonhuman animals did not evolve specifically for human language, although it may be part of the language faculty and play an intimate role in language processing. It is possible, of course, that a trait evolved in nonhuman animals and humans independently, as analogs rather than homologs. This would preserve the possibility that the trait evolved for language in humans but evolved for some other reason in the comparative animal group. In cases where the comparative group is a nonhuman primate, and perhaps especially chimpanzees, the plausibility of this evolutionary scenario is weaker. In any case, comparative data are critical to this judgment.

Despite the crucial role of homology in comparative biology, homologous traits are not the only relevant source of evolutionary data. The convergent evolution of similar characters in two independent clades, termed "analogies" or "homoplasies," can be equally revealing (*20*). The remarkably similar (but nonhomologous) structures of human and octopus eyes reveal the stringent constraints placed by the laws of optics and the contingencies of development on an organ capable of focusing a sharp image onto a sheet of receptors. Detailed analogies between the parts of the vertebrate and cephalopod eye also provide independent evidence that each component is an adaptation for image formation, shaped by natural selection. Furthermore, the discovery that remarkably conservative genetic cascades underlie the development of such analogous structures provides important insights into the ways in which developmental mechanisms can channel evolution (*21*). Thus, although potentially misleading for taxonomists, analogies provide critical data about adaptation under physical and developmental constraints. Casting the comparative net more broadly, therefore, will most likely reveal larger regularities in evolution, helping to address the role of such constraints in the evolution of language.

An analogy recognized as particularly relevant to language is the acquisition of song by birds (*12*). In contrast to nonhuman primates, where the production of species-typical vocalizations is largely innate (*22*), most songbirds learn their species-specific song by listening to conspecifics, and they develop highly aberrant song if deprived of such experience. Current investigation of birdsong reveals detailed and intriguing parallels with speech (*11, 23, 24*). For instance, many songbirds pass through a critical period in development beyond which they produce defective songs that no amount of acoustic input can remedy, reminiscent of the difficulty adult humans have in fully mastering new languages. Further, and in parallel with the babbling phase of vocalizing or signing human infants (*25*), young birds pass through a phase of song development in which they spontaneously produce amorphous versions of adult song, termed "subsong" or "babbling." Although the mechanisms underlying the acquisition of birdsong and human language are clearly analogs and not homologs, their core components share a deeply conserved neural and developmental foundation: Most aspects of neurophysiology and development – including regulatory and structural genes, as well as neuron types and neurotransmitters – are shared among vertebrates. That such close parallels have evolved suggests the existence of important constraints on how vertebrate brains can acquire large vocabularies of complex, learned sounds. Such constraints may essentially force natural selection to come up with the same solution repeatedly when confronted with similar problems.

Testing hypotheses about the evolution of the faculty of language

Given the definitions of the faculty of language, together with the comparative framework, we can distinguish several plausible hypotheses about the evolution of its various components. Here, we suggest two hypotheses that span the diversity of opinion among current scholars, plus a third of our own.

Hypothesis 1: FLB is strictly homologous to animal communication. This hypothesis holds that homologs of FLB, including FLN, exist (perhaps in less developed or otherwise modified form) in nonhuman animals (*3, 10, 26*). This has historically been a popular hypothesis outside of linguistics and closely allied fields, and has been defended by some in the speech sciences. According to this hypothesis, human FLB is composed of the same functional components that underlie communication in other species.

Hypothesis 2: FLB is a derived, uniquely human adaptation for language. According to this hypothesis, FLB is a highly complex adaptation for language, on a par with the vertebrate eye, and many of its core components can be viewed as individual traits that have been subjected to selection and perfected in recent human evolutionary history. This appears to represent the null hypothesis for many scholars who take the complexity of language seriously (*27, 28*). The argument starts with the assumption that FLB, as a whole, is highly complex, serves the function of communication with admirable effectiveness, and has an ineliminable genetic component. Because natural selection is the only known biological mechanism capable of generating such functional complexes [the argument from design (*29*)], proponents of this view conclude that natural selection has played a powerful role in shaping many aspects of FLB, including FLN, and, further, that many of these are without parallel in nonhuman animals. Although homologous mechanisms may exist in other animals, the human versions have been modified by natural selection to the extent that they can be reasonably seen as constituting novel traits, perhaps exapted from other contexts (e.g., social intelligence, tool-making [*7, 30–32*]).

Hypothesis 3: Only FLN is uniquely human. On the basis of data reviewed below, we hypothesize that most, if not all, of FLB is based on mechanisms shared with nonhuman animals (as held by hypothesis 1). In contrast, we suggest that FLN – the computational mechanism of recursion – is recently evolved and unique to our species (*33, 34*). According to this hypothesis, much of the complexity manifested in language derives from complexity in the peripheral components of FLB, especially those underlying the sensory-motor (speech or sign) and conceptual-intentional interfaces, combined with sociocultural and communicative contingencies. FLB as a whole thus has an ancient evolutionary history, long predating the emergence of language, and a comparative analysis is necessary to understand this complex system. By contrast, according to recent linguistic theory, the computations underlying FLN may be quite limited. In fact, we propose in this hypothesis that FLN comprises only the core computational mechanisms of recursion as they appear in narrow syntax and the mappings to the interfaces. If FLN is indeed this restricted, this hypothesis has the interesting effect of nullifying the argument from design, and thus rendering the status of FLN as an adaptation open to question. Proponents of the idea that FLN is an adaptation would thus need to supply additional data or arguments to support this viewpoint.

The available comparative data on animal communication systems suggest that the faculty of language as a whole relies on some uniquely human capacities that have evolved recently in the approximately 6 million years since our divergence from a chimpanzee-like common ancestor (*35*). Hypothesis 3, in its strongest form, suggests that only FLN falls into this category (*34*). By this hypothesis, FLB contains a wide variety of cognitive and perceptual mechanisms shared with other species, but only those mechanisms underlying FLN – particularly its capacity for discrete infinity – are uniquely human. This hypothesis suggests that all peripheral components of FLB are shared with other animals, in more or less the same form as they exist in humans, with differences of quantity rather than kind (*9, 34*). What is unique to our species is quite specific to FLN, and includes its internal operations as well as its interface with the other organism-internal systems of FLB.

Each of these hypotheses is plausible to some degree. Ultimately, they can be distinguished only by empirical data, much of which is currently unavailable. Before reviewing some of the relevant data, we briefly consider some key distinctions between them. From a comparative evolutionary viewpoint, an important question is whether linguistic precursors were involved in communication or in something else. Proponents of both hypotheses 1 and 2 posit a direct correspondence, by descent with modification, between some trait involved in FLB in humans and a similar trait in another species; these hypotheses differ in whether the precursors functioned in communication. Although many aspects of FLB very likely arose in this manner, the important issue for these hypotheses is whether a series of gradual modifications could lead eventually to the capacity of language for infinite generativity. Despite the inarguable existence of a broadly shared base of homologous mechanisms involved in FLB, minor modifications to this foundational system alone seem inadequate to generate the fundamental difference – discrete infinity – between language and all known forms of animal communication. This claim is one of several reasons why we suspect that hypothesis 3 may be a productive way to characterize the problem of language evolution.

A primary issue separating hypotheses 2 and 3 is whether the uniquely human capacities of FLN constitute an adaptation. The viewpoint stated in hypothesis 2, especially the notion that FLN in particular is a highly evolved adaptation, has generated much enthusiasm recently (e.g., *36*), especially among evolutionary psychologists (*37, 38*). At present, however, we see little reason to believe either that FLN can be anatomized into many independent but interacting traits, each with its own independent evolutionary history, or that each of these traits could have been strongly shaped by natural selection, given their tenuous connection to communicative efficacy (the surface or phenotypic function upon which selection presumably acted).

We consider the possibility that certain specific aspects of the faculty of language are "spandrels" – by-products of preexisting constraints rather than end products of a history of natural selection (*39*). This possibility, which opens the door to other empirical lines of inquiry, is perfectly compatible with our firm support of the adaptationist program. Indeed, it follows directly from the foundational notion that adaptation is an "onerous concept" to be invoked only when alternative explanations fail (*40*). The question is not whether FLN in toto is adaptive. By allowing us to communicate an endless variety of thoughts, recursion is clearly an adaptive computation. The question is whether particular components of the functioning of FLN are adaptations for language, specifically acted upon by natural selection – or, even more broadly, whether FLN evolved for reasons other than communication.

An analogy may make this distinction clear. The trunk and branches of trees are near-optimal solutions for providing an individual tree's leaves with access to sunlight. For shrubs and small trees, a wide variety of forms (spreading, spherical, multistalked, etc.) provide good solutions to this problem. For a towering rainforest canopy tree, however, most of these forms are rendered impossible by the various constraints imposed by the properties of cellulose and the problems of sucking water and nutrients up to the leaves high in the air. Some aspects of such trees are clearly adaptations channeled by these constraints; others (e.g., the popping of xylem tubes on hot days, the propensity to be toppled in hurricanes) are presumably unavoidable by-products of such constraints.

Recent work on FLN (*4, 41–43*) suggests the possibility that at least the narrow-syntactic component satisfies conditions of highly efficient computation to an extent previously unsuspected. Thus, FLN may approximate a kind of "optimal solution" to the problem of linking the sensory-motor and conceptual-intentional systems. In other words, the generative processes of the language system may provide a near-optimal solution that satisfies the interface conditions to FLB. Many of the details of language that are the traditional focus of linguistic study (e.g., subjacency, Wh- movement, the existence of garden-path sentences [*4, 44*]) may represent by-products of this solution, generated automatically by neural/computational constraints and the structure of FLB – components that lie outside of FLN. Even novel capacities such as recursion are implemented in the same type of neural tissue as the rest of the brain and are thus constrained by biophysical, developmental, and computational factors shared with other vertebrates. Hypothesis 3 raises the possibility that structural details of FLN may result from such preexisting constraints, rather than from direct shaping by natural selection targeted specifically at communication. Insofar as this proves to be true, such structural details are not, strictly speaking, adaptations at all. This hypothesis and the alternative selectionist account are both viable and can eventually be tested with comparative data.

Comparative evidence for the faculty of language

Study of the evolution of language has accelerated in the past decade (*45, 46*). Here, we offer a highly selective review of some of these studies, emphasizing animal work that seems particularly relevant to the hypotheses advanced above; many omissions were necessary for reasons of space, and we firmly believe that a broad diversity of methods and perspectives will ultimately provide the richest answers to the problem of language evolution. For this reason, we present a broader sampler of the field's offerings in table 1.1.

How "special" is speech? Comparative study of the sensory-motor system. Starting with early work on speech perception, there has been a tradition of considering speech "special," and thus based on uniquely human mechanisms adapted for speech perception and/or production (e.g., *7, 8, 47, 48*). This perspective has stimulated a vigorous research program studying animal speech perception and, more recently, speech production. Surprisingly, this research has turned up little evidence for uniquely human mechanisms special to speech, despite a persistent tendency to assume uniqueness even in the absence of relevant animal data.

On the side of perception, for example, many species show an impressive ability to both discriminate between and generalize over human speech sounds, using formants as the critical discriminative cue (*17–19, 49–51*). These data provide evidence not only of categorical perception, but also of the ability to discriminate among prototypical exemplars of different phonemes (*52*). Further, in the absence of training, nonhuman primates can discriminate sentences from two different languages on the basis of rhythmic differences between them (*53*).

On the side of production, birds and nonhuman primates naturally produce and perceive formants in their own species-typical vocalizations (*54–59*). The results also shed light on discussions of the uniquely human structure of the vocal tract and the unusual descended larynx of our species (*7, 48, 60*), because new evidence shows that several other mammalian species also have a descended larynx (*61*). Because these nonhuman species lack speech, a descended larynx clearly has nonphonetic functions; one possibility is exaggerating apparent size. Although this particular anatomical modification undoubtedly plays an important role in speech production in modern humans, it need not have first evolved for this function. The descended larynx may thus be an example of classic Darwinian preadaptation.

Many phenomena in human speech perception have not yet been investigated in animals (e.g., the McGurk effect, an illusion in which the syllable perceived from a talking head represents the interaction between an articulatory gesture seen and a different syllable heard; see *62*). However, the available data suggest a much stronger continuity between animals and humans with respect to speech than previously believed. We argue that the continuity hypothesis thus deserves

Table 1.1. *A sampler of empirical approaches to understanding the evolution of the faculty of language, including both broad (FLB) and narrow (FLN) components.*

Empirical problem	Examples	References
	FLB – sensory-motor system	
Vocal imitation and invention	Tutoring studies of songbirds, analyses of vocal dialects in whales, spontaneous imitation of artificially created sounds in dolphins	(*11, 12, 24, 65*)
Neurophysiology of action-perception systems	Studies assessing whether mirror neurons, which provide a core substrate for the action-perception system, may subserve gestural and (possibly) vocal imitation	(*67, 68, 71*)
Discriminating the sound patterns of language	Operant conditioning studies of the prototype magnet effect in macaques and starlings	(*52, 120*)
Constraints imposed by vocal tract anatomy	Studies of vocal tract length and formant dispersion in birds and primates	(*54–61*)
Biomechanics of sound production	Studies of primate vocal production, including the role of mandibular oscillations	(*121, 122*)
Modalities of language production and perception	Cross-modal perception and sign language in humans versus unimodal communication in animals	(*3, 25, 123*)
	FLB – conceptual-intentional system	
Theory of mind, attribution of mental states	Studies of the seeing/knowing distinction in chimpanzees	(*84, 86–89*)
Capacity to acquire nonlinguistic conceptual representations	Studies of rhesus monkeys and the object/kind concept	(*10, 76, 77, 124*)
Referential vocal signals	Studies of primate vocalizations used to designate predators, food, and social relationships	(*3, 78, 90, 91, 93, 94, 97*)
Imitation as a rational, intentional system	Comparative studies of chimpanzees and human infants suggesting that only the latter read intentionality into action, and thus extract unobserved rational intent	(*125–127*)
Voluntary control over signal production as evidence of intentional communication	Comparative studies that explore the relationship between signal production and the composition of a social audience	(*3, 10, 92, 128*)
	FLN – recursion	
Spontaneous and training methods designed to uncover constraints on rule learning	Studies of serial order learning and finite-state grammars in tamarins and macaques	(*114, 116, 117, 129*)

Table 1.1. (*cont.*)

Empirical problem	Examples	References
Sign or artificial language in trained apes and dolphins	Studies exploring symbol sequencing and open-ended combinatorial manipulation	(*130, 131*)
Models of the faculty of language that attempt to uncover the necessary and sufficient mechanisms	Game theory models of language acquisition, reference, and universal grammar	(*72–74*)
Experiments with animals that explore the nature and content of number representation	Operant conditioning studies to determine whether nonhuman primates can represent number, including properties such as ordinality and cardinality, using such representations in conjunction with mathematical operands (e.g., add, divide)	(*102–106, 132*)
Shared mechanisms across different cognitive domains	Evolution of musical processing and structure, including analyses of brain function and comparative studies of music perception	(*133–135*)

the status of a null hypothesis, which must be rejected by comparative work before any claims of uniqueness can be validated. For now, this null hypothesis of no truly novel traits in the speech domain appears to stand.

There is, however, a striking ability tied to speech that has received insufficient attention: the human capacity for vocal imitation (*63, 64*). Imitation is obviously a necessary component of the human capacity to acquire a shared and arbitrary lexicon, which is itself central to the language capacity. Thus, the capacity to imitate was a crucial prerequisite of FLB as a communicative system. Vocal imitation and learning are not uniquely human. Rich multimodal imitative capacities are seen in other mammals (dolphins) and some birds (parrots), with most songbirds exhibiting a well-developed vocal imitative capacity (*65*). What is surprising is that monkeys show almost no evidence of visually mediated imitation, with chimpanzees showing only slightly better capacities (*66*). Even more striking is the virtual absence of evidence for vocal imitation in either monkeys or apes (*3*). For example, intensively trained chimpanzees are incapable of acquiring anything but a few poorly articulated spoken words, whereas parrots can readily acquire a large vocal repertoire. With respect to their own vocalizations, there are few convincing studies of vocal dialects in primates, thereby suggesting that they lack a vocal imitative capacity (*3, 65*). Evidence for spontaneous visuomanual imitation in chimpanzees is not much stronger, although with persistent training they can learn several hundred hand signs. Further, even in cases where nonhuman animals are capable of imitating in one modality (e.g., song copying in songbirds), only dolphins and humans appear capable of imitation in multiple modalities. The detachment from modality-specific inputs may represent a substantial change in neural organization, one that affects not only imitation but also communication; only humans can lose one modality (e.g., hearing) and make up for this deficit by communicating with complete competence in a different modality (i.e., signing).

Our discussion of limitations is not meant to diminish the impressive achievements of monkeys and apes, but to highlight how different the mechanisms underlying the production of human and nonhuman primate gestures, either vocally expressed or signed, must be. After all, the average high school graduate knows up to 60,000 words, a vocabulary achieved with little effort, especially when contrasted with the herculean efforts devoted to training animals. In sum, the impressive ability of any normal human child for vocal imitation may represent a novel capacity that evolved in our recent evolutionary history, some time after the divergence from our chimpanzee-like ancestors. The existence of analogs in distantly related species, such as birds and cetaceans, suggests considerable potential for the detailed comparative study of vocal imitation. There are, however, potential traps that must be avoided, especially with respect to explorations of the neurobiological substrates of imitation. For example, although macaque monkeys and humans are equipped with so-called "mirror neurons" in the premotor cortex that respond both when an individual acts in a particular way and when the same individual sees someone else act in this same way (67, 68), these neurons are not sufficient for imitation in macaques, as many have presumed: As mentioned, there is no convincing evidence of vocal or visual imitation in monkeys. Consequently, as neuroimaging studies continue to explore the neural basis of imitation in humans (69–71), it will be important to distinguish between the necessary and sufficient neural correlates of imitation. This is especially important, given that some recent attempts to model the evolution of language begin with a hypothetical organism that is equipped with the capacity for imitation and intentionality, as opposed to working out how these mechanisms evolved in the first place (see below; 72–74). If a deeper evolutionary exploration is desired, one dating back to a chimpanzee-like ancestor, then we need to explain how and why such capacities emerged from an ancestral node that lacked such abilities (75) (Figure 1.4).

The conceptual-intentional systems of non-linguistic animals. A wide variety of studies indicate that nonhuman mammals and birds have rich conceptual representations (76, 77). Surprisingly, however, there is a mismatch between the conceptual capacities of animals and the communicative content of their vocal and visual signals (78, 79). For example, although a wide variety of nonhuman primates have access to rich knowledge of who is related to whom, as well as

Figure 1.4. The distribution of imitation in the animal kingdom is patchy. Some animals such as songbirds, dolphins, and humans have evolved exceptional abilities to imitate; other animals, such as apes and monkeys, either lack such abilities or have them in a relatively impoverished form. (Illustration: John Yanson)

who is dominant and who is subordinate, their vocalizations only coarsely express such complexities.

Studies using classical training approaches as well as methods that tap spontaneous abilities reveal that animals acquire and use a wide range of abstract concepts, including tool, color, geometric relationships, food, and number (*66, 76–82*). More controversially, but of considerable relevance to intentional aspects of language and conditions of felicitous use, some studies claim that animals have a theory of mind (*83–85*), including a sense of self and the ability to represent the beliefs and desires of other group members. On the side of positive support, recent studies of chimpanzees suggest that they recognize the perceptual act of seeing as a proxy for the mental state of knowing

(*84*, *86*, *87*). These studies suggest that at least chimpanzees, but perhaps no other nonhuman animals, have a rudimentary theory of mind. On the side of negative support, other studies suggest that even chimpanzees lack a theory of mind, failing, for example, to differentiate between ignorant and knowledgeable individuals with respect to intentional communication (*88*, *89*). Because these experiments make use of different methods and are based on small sample sizes, it is not possible at present to derive any firm conclusions about the presence or absence of mental state attribution in animals. Independently of how this controversy is resolved, however, the best evidence of referential communication in animals comes not from chimpanzees but from a variety of monkeys and birds, species for which there is no convincing evidence for a theory of mind.

The classic studies of vervet monkey alarm calls (*90*) have now been joined by several others, each using comparable methods, with extensions to different species (macaques, Diana monkeys, meerkats, prairie dogs, chickens) and different communicative contexts (social relationships, food, intergroup aggression) (*91–97*). From these studies we can derive five key points relevant to our analysis of the faculty of language. First, individuals produce acoustically distinctive calls in response to functionally important contexts, including the detection of predators and the discovery of food. Second, the acoustic morphology of the signal, although arbitrary in terms of its association with a particular context, is sufficient to enable listeners to respond appropriately without requiring any other contextual information. Third, the number of such signals in the repertoire is small, restricted to objects and events experienced in the present, with no evidence of creative production of new sounds for new situations. Fourth, the acoustic morphology of the calls is fixed, appearing early in development, with experience only playing a role in refining the range of objects or events that elicit such calls. Fifth, there is no evidence that calling is intentional in the sense of taking into account what other individuals believe or want.

Early interpretations of this work suggested that when animals vocalize, they are functionally referring to the objects and events that they have encountered. As such, vervet alarm calls and rhesus monkey food calls, to take two examples, were interpreted as word-like, with callers referring to different kinds of predators or different kinds of food. More recent discussions have considerably weakened this interpretation, suggesting that if the signal is referential at all, it is in the mind of the listener who can extract information about the signaler's current context from the acoustic structure of the call alone (*78*, *95*). Despite this evidence that animals can extract information from the signal, there are several reasons why additional evidence is required before such signals can be considered as precursors for, or homologs of, human words.

Roughly speaking, we can think of a particular human language as consisting of words and computational procedures ("rules") for constructing expressions from them. The computational system has the recursive property briefly outlined earlier, which may be a distinct human property. However, key aspects of words may also be distinctively human. There are, first of all, qualitative differences in scale and mode of acquisition, which suggest that quite different mechanisms are involved; as pointed out above, there is no evidence for vocal imitation in non-human primates, and although human children may use domain-general mechanisms to acquire and recall words (*98, 99*), the rate at which children build the lexicon is so massively different from nonhuman primates that one must entertain the possibility of an independently evolved mechanism. Furthermore, unlike the best animal examples of putatively referential signals, most of the words of human language are not associated with specific functions (e.g., warning cries, food announcements) but can be linked to virtually any concept that humans can entertain. Such usages are often highly intricate and detached from the here and now. Even for the simplest words, there is typically no straightforward word-thing relationship, if "thing" is to be understood in mind-independent terms. Without pursuing the matter here, it appears that many of the elementary properties of words – including those that enter into referentiality – have only weak analogs or homologs in natural animal communication systems, with only slightly better evidence from the training studies with apes and dolphins. Future research must therefore provide stronger support for the precursor position, or it must instead abandon this hypothesis, arguing that this component of FLB (conceptual-intentional) is also uniquely human.

Discrete infinity and constraints on learning. The data summarized thus far, although far from complete, provide overall support for the position of continuity between humans and other animals in terms of FLB. However, we have not yet addressed one issue that many regard as lying at the heart of language: its capacity for limitless expressive power, captured by the notion of discrete infinity. It seems relatively clear, after nearly a century of intensive research on animal communication, that no species other than humans has a comparable capacity to recombine meaningful units into an unlimited variety of larger structures, each differing systematically in meaning. However, little progress has been made in identifying the specific capabilities that are lacking in other animals.

The astronomical variety of sentences any natural language user can produce and understand has an important implication for language acquisition, long a core issue in developmental psychology. A child is exposed to only a small proportion of the possible sentences in its language, thus limiting its data-base for constructing a more general version of that language in its own mind/brain. This point has logical implications for any system that attempts to acquire a natural language on the basis of limited data. It is immediately obvious that given a finite array of data, there are infinitely many theories consistent with it but inconsistent with one another. In the present case, there are in principle infinitely many target systems (potential I-languages) consistent with the data of experience, and unless the search space and acquisition mechanisms are constrained, selection among them is impossible. A version of the problem has been formalized by Gold (*100*) and more recently and rigorously explored by Nowak and colleagues (*72–75*). No known "general learning mechanism" can acquire a natural language solely on the basis of positive or negative evidence, and the prospects for finding any such domain-independent device seem rather dim. The difficulty of this problem leads to the hypothesis that whatever system is responsible must be biased or constrained in certain ways. Such constraints have historically been termed "innate dispositions," with those underlying language referred to as "universal grammar." Although these particular terms have been forcibly rejected by many researchers, and the nature of the particular constraints on human (or animal) learning mechanisms is currently unresolved, the existence of some such constraints cannot be seriously doubted. On the other hand, other constraints in animals must have been overcome at some point in human evolution to account for our ability to acquire the unlimited class of generative systems that includes all natural languages. The nature of these latter constraints has recently become the target of empirical work. We focus here on the nature of number representation and rule learning in nonhuman animals and human infants, both of which can be investigated independently of communication and provide hints as to the nature of the constraints on FLN.

More than fifty years of research using classical training studies demonstrates that animals can represent number, with careful controls for various important confounds (*80*). In the typical experiment, a rat or pigeon is trained to press a lever x number of times to obtain a food reward. Results show that animals can hit the target number to within a closely matched mean, with a standard deviation that increases with magnitude: As the target number increases, so does variation around the mean. These results have led to the idea that animals, including human infants and adults, can represent number approximately as a magnitude with scalar variability (*101, 102*). Number discrimination is limited in this system by Weber's law, with greater discriminability among small numbers than among large numbers (keeping distances between pairs constant) and between numbers that are farther apart (e.g., 7 versus 8 is harder than 7 versus 12). The approximate number sense is accompanied by a second precise mechanism that is limited to values less than 4 but accurately distinguishes 1 from 2, 2 from 3, and 3 from 4; this second system appears to be recruited in the context of object tracking and is limited by working memory constraints (*103*). Of direct relevance to the current discussion, animals can be trained to understand the meaning of number words or Arabic numeral symbols. However, these studies reveal striking differences in how animals and human children acquire the integer list, and provide further evidence that animals lack the capacity to create open-ended generative systems.

Boysen and Matsuzawa have trained chimpanzees to map the number of objects onto a single Arabic numeral, to correctly order such numerals in either an ascending or descending list, and to indicate the sums of two numerals (*104–106*). For example, Boysen shows that a chimpanzee seeing two oranges placed in one box, and another two oranges placed in a second box, will pick the correct sum of four out of a lineup of three cards, each with a different Arabic numeral. The chimpanzees' performance might suggest that their representation of number is like ours. Closer inspection of how these chimpanzees acquired such competences, however, indicates that the format and content of their number representations differ fundamentally from those of human children. In particular, these chimpanzees required thousands of training trials, and often years, to acquire the integer list up to nine, with no evidence of the kind of "aha" experience that all human children of approximately 3.5 years acquire (*107*). A human child who has acquired the numbers 1, 2, and 3 (and sometimes 4) goes on to acquire all the others; he or she grasps the idea that the integer list is constructed on the basis of the successor function. For the chimpanzees, in contrast, each number on the integer list required the same amount of time to learn. In essence, although the chimpanzees' understanding of Arabic numerals is impressive, it parallels their understanding of other symbols and their referential properties: The system apparently never takes on the open-ended generative property of human language. This limitation may, however, reveal an interesting quirk of the child's learning environment and a difference from the training regime of animals: Children typically first learn an arbitrary ordered list of symbols ("1, 2, 3, 4 ...") and later learn the precise meaning of such words; apes and parrots, in contrast, were taught the meanings one by one without learning the list. As Carey (*103*) has argued, this may represent a fundamental difference in experience, a hypothesis that could be tested by first training animals with an arbitrary ordered list.

A second possible limitation on the class of learnable structures concerns the kinds of statistical inferences that animals can compute. Early work in computational linguistics (*108–110*) suggested that we can profitably think about language as a system of rules placed within a hierarchy of increasing complexity. At the lowest level of the hierarchy are rule systems that are limited to local dependencies, a subcategory of so-called "finite-state grammars." Despite their attractive simplicity, such rule systems are inadequate to capture any human language. Natural languages go beyond purely local structure by including a capacity for recursive embedding of phrases within phrases, which can lead to statistical regularities that are separated by an arbitrary number of words or phrases. Such long-distance, hierarchical relationships are found in all natural languages for which, at a minimum, a "phrase-structure grammar" is necessary. It is a foundational observation of modern generative linguistics that, to capture a natural language, a grammar must include such capabilities (Figure 1.5).

Figure 1.5. Human and nonhuman animals exhibit the capacity to compute numerosities, including small precise number quantification and large approximate number estimation. Humans may be unique, however, in the ability to show open-ended, precise quantificational skills with large numbers, including the integer count list. In parallel with the faculty of language, our capacity for number relies on a recursive computation. (Illustration: John Yanson)

Recent studies suggest that the capacity to compute transitional probabilities – an example of a rule at the lowest level of the hierarchy – might be available to human infants and provide a mechanism for segmenting words from a continuous acoustic stream (*111–113*). Specifically, after familiarization to a continuous sequence of consonant-vowel (CV) syllables, where particular trigrams (three CVs in sequence, considered to be "words" in this context) have a high probability of appearing within the corpus, infants are readily able to discriminate these trigrams from others that are uncommon. Although this ability may provide a mechanism for word segmentation, it is apparently not a mechanism that evolved uniquely in humans or for language: The same computation is spontaneously available to human infants for visual sequences and tonal melodies (*113*), as well as to nonhuman primates (cotton-top tamarins) tested with the same methods and stimuli (*114*). Similarly, in the same way that human infants appear capable of computing algebraic rules that operate over particular CV sequences (*115*), so too can cotton-top tamarins (*116*), again demonstrating that the capacity to discover abstract rules at a local level is not unique to humans, and almost certainly did not evolve specifically for language.

Fitch and Hauser (*117*) recently completed a study comparing finite-state and phrase-structure grammar acquisition in human adults and tamarins, using the same subjects and methods as the studies above. The phrase-structure rule tested was AnBn, where A and B were each represented by one of a set of eight different CVs. The rule therefore specified both a set of consistent strings (*n* A's must precede *n* B's) and a set of inconsistent strings; the latter consisted of violations of order (B tokens precede A tokens) or of patterning (alternations of A's and B's such as ABAB). Results showed that human adults rapidly learned this rule implicitly, distinguishing consistent and inconsistent strings. Tamarins, in contrast, failed in three separate experiments testing their ability to acquire this grammar, but they readily mastered a finite-state variant (ABn) implemented with the same stimuli and testing conditions. This suggests that tamarins have a limited capacity to learn the type of long-distance hierarchical dependencies necessary to achieve the class of phrase-structure grammars. If true, this limitation would place severe restrictions on their capacity to learn any natural human language. It is currently unclear whether this limitation generalizes to other animals, and whether it is similarly imposed on humans at different stages of development. Nonetheless, such experiments provide an empirical approach to exploring key differences between humans and animals relevant to FLN.

Our review has stressed the usefulness of animal data for theories about humans, but this exchange need not be one-way. As the research program we have sketched progresses, more general principles about cognitive evolution may emerge. For example, suppose we adopt the conception of hypothesis 3, oversimplifying radically, that the interface systems – sensory-motor and conceptual-intentional – are given, and the innovation that yielded the faculty of language was the evolution of the computational system that links them. The computational system must (i) construct an infinite array of internal expressions from the finite resources of the conceptual-intentional system, and (ii) provide the means to externalize and interpret them at the sensory-motor end. We may now ask to what extent the computational system is optimal, meeting natural conditions of efficient computation such as minimal search and no backtracking. To the extent that this can be established, we will be able to go beyond the (extremely difficult, and still distant) accomplishment of finding the principles of the faculty of language, to an understanding of why the faculty follows these particular principles and not others. We would then understand why languages of a certain class are attainable, whereas other imaginable languages are impossible to learn and sustain. Such progress would not only open the door to a greatly simplified and empirically more tractable evolutionary approach to the faculty of language, but might also be more generally applicable to domains beyond language in a wide range of species – perhaps especially in the domain of spatial navigation and foraging, where problems of optimal search are relevant. For example, elegant studies of insects, birds, and primates reveal that individuals often search for food by an optimal strategy, one involving minimal distances, recall of locations searched, and kinds of objects retrieved (*77, 118, 119*). Only after a concerted, multidisciplinary attack on the problems of language evolution, paralleling forty years of optimal foraging research, will we learn whether such similarities are more than superficial.

Conclusions

We conclude by making three points. First, a practical matter: Linguists and biologists, along with researchers in the relevant branches of psychology and anthropology, can move beyond unproductive theoretical debate to a more collaborative, empirically focused and comparative research program aimed at uncovering both shared (homologous or analogous) and unique components of the faculty of language. Second, although we have argued that most if not all of FLB is shared with other species, whereas FLN may be unique to humans, this represents a tentative, testable hypothesis in need of further empirical investigation. Finally, we believe that a comparative approach is most likely to lead to new insights about both shared and derived features, thereby generating new hypotheses concerning the evolutionary forces that led to the design of the faculty of language. Specifically, although we have said relatively little about the role of natural selection in shaping the design features of FLN, we suggest that by considering the possibility that FLN evolved for reasons other than language, the comparative door has been opened in a new and (we think) exciting way.

Comparative work has generally focused on animal communication or the capacity to acquire a human-created language. If, however, one entertains the hypothesis that recursion evolved to solve other computational problems such as navigation, number quantification, or social relationships, then it is possible that other animals have such abilities, but our research efforts have been targeted at an overly narrow search space (Figure 1.3). If we find evidence for recursion in animals, but in a noncommunicative domain, then we are more likely to pinpoint the mechanisms underlying this ability and the selective pressures that led to it. This discovery, in turn, would open the door to another suite of puzzles: Why did humans, but no other animal, take the power of recursion to create an open-ended and limitless system of communication? Why does our system of recursion operate over a broader range of elements or inputs (e.g., numbers, words) than other animals? One possibility, consistent with current thinking in the cognitive sciences, is that recursion in animals represents a modular system designed for a particular function (e.g., navigation) and impenetrable with respect to other systems. During evolution, the modular and highly domain-specific system of recursion may have become penetrable and domain-general. This opened the way for humans, perhaps uniquely, to apply the power of recursion to other problems. This change from domain-specific to domain-general may have been guided by particular selective pressures, unique to our evolutionary past, or as a consequence (by-product) of other kinds of neural reorganization. Either way, these are testable hypotheses, a refrain that highlights the importance of comparative approaches to the faculty of language.

References and notes

1. N. Chomsky, *Aspects of the Theory of Syntax* (MIT Press, Cambridge, MA, 1965).
2. *Reflections on Language* (Pantheon, New York, 1975).
3. M. D. Hauser, *The Evolution of Communication* (MIT Press, Cambridge, MA, 1996).
4. R. Jackendoff, *Foundations of Language* (Oxford University Press, New York, 2002).
5. L. Jenkins, *Biolinguistics* (Cambridge University Press, Cambridge, 2000).
6. E. H. Lenneberg, *Biological Foundations of Language* (Wiley, New York, 1967).
7. P. Lieberman, *The Biology and Evolution of Language* (Harvard University Press, Cambridge, MA, 1984).
8. A. Liberman, *Speech: A Special Code* (MIT Press, Cambridge, MA, 1996).
9. W. T. Fitch, *Trendsin Cognitive Science* 4, 258 (2000).
10. D. L. Cheney, R. M. Seyfarth, *How Monkeys See the World: Inside the Mind of Another Species* (University of Chicago Press, Chicago, 1990).
11. A. Doupe, P. Kuhl, *Annual Revue of Neuroscience* 22, 567 (1999).
12. P. Marler, *American Scientist* 58, 669 (1970).
13. C. Darwin, *On the Origin of Species* (John Murray, London, 1859).
14. *The Descent of Man and Selection in Relation to Sex* (John Murray, London, 1871).
15. A. M. Liberman, K. S. Harris, H. S. Hoffman, B. C. Griffith, *Journal of Experimental Psychology* 54, 358 (1957).
16. A. M. Liberman, F. S. Cooper, D. P. Shankweiler, M. Studdert-Kennedy, *Psycholical Revue.* 74, 431 (1967).
17. P. K. Kuhl, J. D. Miller, *Science* 190, 69 (1975).
18. P. K. Kuhl, D. M. Padden, *Perception and Psychophysics* 32, 542 (1982).
19. K. R. Kluender, R. Diehl, P. R. Killeen, *Science* 237, 1195 (1987).
20. S. J. Gould, in *Evolution, Brain and Behavior: Persistent Problems*, R. B. Masterton, W. Hodos, H. Jerison, Eds. (Wiley, New York, 1976), pp. 175–179.
21. W. J. Gehring, *Master Control Genes in Development and Evolution: The Homeobox Story* (Yale University Press, New Haven, CT, 1998).
22. R. M. Seyfarth, D. L. Cheney, in *The Design of Animal Communication*, M. D. Hauser, M. Konishi, Eds. (MIT Press, Cambridge, MA, 1999), pp. 391–418.
23. P. Marler, *Journal of Neurobiology* 33, 1 (1997).
24. F. Nottebohm, in *The Design of Animal Communication*, M. D. Hauser, M. Konishi, Eds. (MIT Press, Cambridge, MA, 1999), pp. 63–110.
25. L. A. Petitto, P. Marentette, *Science* 251, 1483 (1991).
26. K. R. Kluender, A. J. Lotto, L. L. Holt, in *Listening to Speech: An Auditory Perspective*, S. Greenberg, W. Ainsworth, Eds. (Erlbaum, Mahwah, NJ, in press).

27. R. Jackendoff, *Trendsin Cognitive Science* 3, 272 (1999).
28. S. Pinker, P. Bloom, *Behavioral and Brain Sciences* 13, 707 (1990).
29. R. Dawkins, *The Blind Watchmaker* (Norton, New York, 1986).
30. D. Bickerton, *Species and Language* (University of Chicago Press, Chicago, 1990).
31. R. Dunbar, *Grooming, Gossip and the Evolution of Language* (Harvard University Press, Cambridge, MA, 1996).
32. D. Kimura, *Neuromotor Mechanisms in Human Communication* (Oxford University Press, Oxford, 1993).
33. N. Chomsky, *Rules and Representations* (Columbia University Press, New York, 1980).
34. M. D. Hauser, in *Language, Brain, and Cognitive Development: Essays in Honor of Jacques Mehler*, E. Dupoux, Ed. (MIT Press, Cambridge, MA, 2001), pp. 417–434.
35. W. Enard *et al.*, *Nature* 418, 869 (2002).
36. J. Maynard Smith, E. Szathmary, *The Major Transitions of Evolution* (Freeman, Oxford, 1995).
37. L. Barrett, R. Dunbar, J. Lycett, *Human Evolutionary Psychology* (Princeton University Press, Princeton, NJ, 2002).
38. D. Buss, *Evolutionary Psychology* (Allyn & Bacon, London, 1999).
39. S. J. Gould, R. C. Lewontin, *Proceedings of the Royal Society of London* 205, 281 (1979).
40. G. C. Williams, *Adaptation and Natural Selection* (Princeton University Press, Princeton, NJ, 1966).
41. N. Chomsky, *The Minimalist Program* (MIT Press, Cambridge, MA, 1995).
42. C. Collins, *Local Economy* (MIT Press, Cambridge, MA, 1997).
43. S. D. Epstein, N. Hornstein, *Working Minimalism* (MIT Press, Cambridge, MA, 1999).
44. L. Haegeman, *Introduction to Government and Binding Theory* (Blackwell, Oxford, 1991).
45. J. R. Hurford, M. Studdert-Kennedy, C. Knight, Eds., *Approaches to the Evolution of Language: Social and Cognitive Bases* (Cambridge University Press, Cambridge, 1998).
46. A. Wray, Ed., *The Transition to Language* (Oxford Univ. Press, Oxford, 2002).
47. A. Liberman, D. H. Whalen, *Trendsin Cognitive Science* 4, 187 (2000).
48. P. Lieberman, *Uniquely Human* (Harvard University Press, Cambridge, MA, 1991).
49. R. J. Dooling, C. T. Best, S. D. Brown, *Journal of the Acoustic Society of America* 97, 1839 (1995).
50. J. M. Sinnott, C. H. Brown, *Journal of the Acoustic Society of America* 102, 588 (1997).
51. M. S. Sommers, D. B. Moody, C. A. Prosen, W. C. Stebbins, *Journal of the Acoustic Society of America* 91, 3499 (1992).
52. K. R. Kluender, A. J. Lotto, L. L. Holt, S. L. Bloedel, *Journal of the Acoustic Society of America* 104, 3568 (1998).
53. F. Ramus, M. D. Hauser, C. T. Miller, D. Morris, J. Mehler, *Science* 288, 349 (2000).
54. W. T. Fitch, *Journal of the Acoustic Society of America* 102, 1213 (1997).
55. J. P. Kelley, *Ethology* 106, 559 (2000).
56. M. D. Hauser, C. S. Evans, P. Marler, *Animal Behaviour* 45, 423 (1993).
57. M. J. Owren, R. Bernacki, *Journal of the Acoustic Society of America* 83, 1927 (1988).

58. M. J. Owren, *Journal of Comparative Psychology* 104, 20 (1990).
59. D. Rendall, M. J. Owren, P. S. Rodman, *Journal of the Acoustic Society of America* 103, 602 (1998).
60. V. E. Negus, *The Comparative Anatomy and Physiology of the Larynx* (Hafner, New York, 1949).
61. W. T. Fitch, D. Reby, *Proceedings of the Royal Society of London Series B* 268, 1669 (2001).
62. J. D. Trout, *Psychological Review* 108, 523 (2000).
63. M. Donald, in *Approaches to the Evolution of Language: Social and Cognitive Bases*, J. R. Hurford, M. Studdert-Kennedy, C. Knight, Eds. (Cambridge University Press, Cambridge, 1998), pp. 44–67.
64. M. Studdert-Kennedy, *Human Neurobiology* 2, 191 (1983).
65. V. M. Janik, P. J. B. Slater, *Animal Behaviour* 60, 1 (2000).
66. M. Tomasello, J. Call, *Primate Cognition* (Oxford University Press, Oxford, 1997).
67. G. Rizzolatti, M. A. Arbib, *Trendsin Cognitive Science* 2, 188 (1998).
68. G. Rizzolatti, L. Fadiga, L. Fogassi, V. Gallese, *Archives of Italian Biology* 137, 169 (1999).
69. T. Chaminade, A. N. Meltzoff, J. Decety, *Neuroimage* 15, 318 (2002).
70. J. Decety, T. Chaminade, J. Grezes, A. N. Meltzoff, *Neuroimage* 15, 265 (2002).
71. M. Iacoboni *et al.*, *Science* 286, 2526 (1999).
72. M. A. Nowak, N. L. Komarova, P. Niyogi, *Science* 291, 114 (2001).
73. M. A. Nowak, N. L. Komarova, *Trendsin Cognitive Science* 5, 288 (2001).
74. M. A. Nowak, J. B. Plotkin, V. A. Jansen, *Nature* 404, 495 (2000).
75. M. A. Nowak, N. L. Komarova, P. Niyogi, *Nature* 417, 611 (2002).
76. C. M. Heyes, F. Huber, *The Evolution of Cognition* (MIT Press, Cambridge, MA, 2000).
77. S. Shettleworth, *Cognition, Evolution and Behavior* (Oxford University Press, New York, 1998).
78. D. L. Cheney, R. M. Seyfarth, in *The Tanner Lectures on Human Values*, G. Peterson, Ed. (University of Utah Press, Salt Lake City, UT, 1998), pp. 173–210.
79. M. D. Hauser, *Wild Minds: What Animals Really Think* (Holt, New York, 2000).
80. C. R. Gallistel, *The Organization of Learning* (MIT Press, Cambridge, MA, 1990).
81. I. M. Pepperberg, *The Alex Studies* (Harvard University Press, Cambridge, MA, 2000).
82. D. Premack, *Gavagai! or the Future History of the Animal Language Controversy* (MIT Press, Cambridge, MA, 1986).
83. G. Woodruff, *Behavioural and Brain Sciences* 4, 515 (1978).
84. D. Premack, A. Premack, *Original Intelligence* (McGraw-Hill, New York, 2002).
85. D. C. Dennett, *Behavioral and Brain Sciences* 6, 343 (1983).
86. B. Hare, J. Call, B. Agnetta, M. Tomasello, *Animal Behaviour* 59, 771 (2000).
87. B. Hare, J. Call, M. Tomasello, *Animal Behaviour* 61, 139 (2001).
88. C. M. Heyes, *Behavioral and Brain Sciences* 21, 101 (1998).
89. D. J. Povinelli, T. J. Eddy, *Monographs of the Society for Research in Child Development* 247 (1996).
90. R. M. Seyfarth, D. L. Cheney, P. Marler, *Science* 210, 801 (1980).
91. W. P. G. Dittus, *Animal Behaviour* 32, 470 (1984).
92. C. S. Evans, P. Marler, in *Comparative Approaches to Cognitive Science*, H. Roitblatt, Ed. (MIT Press, Cambridge, MA, 1995), pp. 241–282.

93. J. Fischer, *Animal Behaviour* 55, 799 (1998).
94. S. Gouzoules, H. Gouzoules, P. Marler, *Animal Behaviour* 32, 182 (1984).
95. M. D. Hauser, *Animal Behaviour* 55, 1647 (1998).
96. C. N. Slobodchikoff, J. Kiriazis, C. Fischer, E. Creef, *Animal Behaviour* 42, 713 (1991).
97. K. Zuberbuhler, D. L. Cheney, R. M. Seyfarth, *Journal of Comparative Psychology* 113, 33 (1999).
98. P. Bloom, L. Markson, *Trendsin Cognitive Science* 2, 67 (1998).
99. P. Bloom, *How Children Learn the Meanings of Words* (MIT Press, Cambridge, MA, 2000).
100. E. M. Gold, *Information and Control* 10, 447 (1967).
101. S. Dehaene, *The Number Sense* (Oxford University Press, Oxford, 1997).
102. C. R. Gallistel, R. Gelman, *Trendsin Cognitive Science* 4, 59 (2000).
103. S. Carey, *Mind Lang.* 16, 37 (2001).
104. S. T. Boysen, G. G. Bernston, *Journal of Comparative Psychology* 103, 23 (1989).
105. N. Kawai, T. Matsuzawa, *Nature* 403, 39 (2000).
106. T. Matsuzawa, *Nature* 315, 57 (1985).
107. K. Wynn, *Cognitive Psychology* 24, 220 (1992).
108. N. Chomsky, *Logical Structure of Linguistic Theory/Excerpted Manuscript* (Plenum, New York, 1975).
109. *IRE Trans. Inform. Theory* 2 (no. 2), 113 (1956).
110. G. Miller, *Inform. Control* 1, 91 (1958).
111. Z. S. Harris, *Language* 31, 190 (1955).
112. J. R. Saffran, R. N. Aslin, E. L. Newport, *Science* 274, 1926 (1996).
113. J. Saffran, E. Johnson, R. N. Aslin, E. Newport, *Cognition* 70, 27 (1999).
114. M. D. Hauser, E. L. Newport, R. N. Aslin, *Cognition* 78, B53 (2001).
115. G. Marcus, S. Vijayan, S. Bandi Rao, P. M. Vishton, *Science* 283, 77 (1999).
116. M. D. Hauser, D. Weiss, G. Marcus, *Cognition* 86, B15 (2002).
117. W. T. Fitch, M. D. Hauser, in preparation.
118. N. S. Clayton, A. Dickinson, *Nature* 395, 272 (1998).
119. C. R. Gallistel, A. E. Cramer, *Journal of Experimental Biology* 199, 211 (1996).
120. P. Kuhl, *Perception and Psychophysics* 50, 93 (1991).
121. P. F. MacNeilage, *Behavioral and Brain Sciences* 21, 499(1998).
122. M. Studdert-Kennedy, in *Approaches to the Evolution of Language: Social and Cognitive Bases*, J. R. Hurford, M. Studdert-Kennedy, C. Knight, Eds. (Cambridge University Press, Cambridge, 1998), pp. 202–221.
123. H. McGurk, J. MacDonald, *Nature* 264, 746 (1976).
124. L. R. Santos, G. M. Sulkowski, G. M. Spaepen, M. D. Hauser, *Cognition* 83, 241 (2002).
125. G. Gergely, H. Bekkering, I. Kiraly, *Nature* 415, 755 (2002).
126. A. N. Meltzoff, M. K. Moore, *Infant Behavior and Development* 17, 83 (1994).
127. A. Whiten, D. Custance, in *Social Learning in Animals: The Roots of Culture*, C. M. Heyes, J. B. G. Galef, Eds. (Academic Press, San Diego, CA, 1996), pp. 291–318.
128. P. Marler, S. Karakashian, M. Gyger, in *Cognitive Ethology: The Minds of Other Animals*, C. Ristau, Ed. (Erlbaum, Hillsdale, NJ, 1991), pp. 135–186.
129. H. S. Terrace, L. K. Son, E. M. Brannon, *Psychological Science* 14, 1 (2003)

130. L. M. Herman, D. G. Richards, J. P. Wolz, *Cognition* 16, 129 (1984).
131. E. S. Savage-Rumbaugh *et al.*, *Monographs of the Society for Research in Child Development* 58 (1993).
132. E. M. Brannon, H. S. Terrace, *Science* 282, 746 (1998).
133. F. Lerdahl, R. Jackendoff, *A Generative Theory of Tonal Music* (MIT Press, Cambridge, MA, 1983).
134. N. Wallin, B. Merker, S. D. Brown, *The Origins of Music* (MIT Press, Cambridge, MA, 2000).
135. R. Zatorre, I. Peretz, *The Biological Foundations of Music* (National Academy Press, New York, 2000).
136. For comments on an earlier draft of the manuscript, we thank D. Cheney, R. Jackendoff, L. Jenkins, M. Nowak, M. Piatelli-Palmerini, S. Pinker, and R. Seyfarth.

Part I

Language architecture

2 Some simple evo devo theses: how true might they be for language?

Noam Chomsky

Study of evolution of some system is feasible only to the extent that its nature is understood. That seems close to truism. One could hardly investigate the evolution of the eye or of insect navigation knowing only that the eye is an "organ of sight" and that navigational skills are a way to return home. The same truism holds for inquiry into the evolution of human language – henceforth simply *language*. Accordingly, a sensible approach is to begin with properties of language that are understood with some confidence and seek to determine how they may have evolved, temporarily putting to the side others that are more poorly understood and the additional problems they might pose. I will try to outline such a course, keeping to a sketch of general directions, hoping at least to sort out various elements of the puzzle and to indicate how they might be addressed – with limited prospects for success, in the judgment of one highly credible commentator.[1]

I will also mention some analogies between "the Evo Devo revolution" in biology and ideas that have been lurking in the background of "biolinguistics" since its origins about half a century ago, and that have been pursued more intensively in recent years. The analogies have been suggestive in the past, and might prove to be more than that in the years ahead.

The term "biolinguistics" was proposed in this context in 1974 by Massimo Piattelli-Palmarini as the topic for an international conference he organized that brought together evolutionary biologists, neuroscientists, linguists, philosophers, and others concerned with language and biology, one of a number of such initiatives. A primary focus of the discussions was the extent to which apparent principles of language are unique to this cognitive system, plainly one of "the basic questions to be asked from the biological point of view" and crucial for the study of development of language in the individual and its evolution in the species. In terminology used more recently, the "basic questions" concern the "faculty of language in the narrow sense" (FLN).[2]

The term "language" as used in this context means *internal language* (I-language, sometimes called "grammar" in one of the uses of this ambiguous term). Under familiar and appropriate idealizations, a person's language is a computational system of the mind/brain that generates an infinite array of hierarchically structured expressions. The language therefore is based on recursive operations that execute this task. Each generated expression can be taken to be a collection of instructions for the *interface* systems with components of the mind/ brain among which the faculty of language is embedded. There are at least two such interfaces: the conceptual/intentional (semantic-pragmatic) systems that make use of generated linguistic expressions for thought, interpretation, and organizing action; and the sensorimotor systems that externalize expressions in production and assign them to sensory data in perception; respectively the C-I and SM systems. A language, so construed, is an internal system that links sound and meaning in a particular way, by means of generated expressions. These are, to first approximation, the most elementary aspects of language.

A basic question for the study of the nature of language and its evolution can, therefore, be posed concisely as follows. To what extent is the thesis T accurate?

(T) Interfaces + Recursion = Language

T – with a question mark – is the title of a recent collection of technical essays exploring the question, which can be sharpened in ways to which we return.[3] The question mark, of course, signals the vast gaps in knowledge and understanding of the intricate phenomena of language, which leave open the prospects for further success in approaching T.

At the time of the 1974 conference, it seemed that the language faculty must be rich, highly structured, and substantially unique to this cognitive system. Hence T seemed so remote from reality that it would have been pointless even to formulate the thesis as a guideline to inquiry (had the question even arisen). In particular, that conclusion followed from considerations of language acquisition. The only plausible idea seemed to be that language acquisition is rather like theory construction. Somehow, the child reflexively identifies certain sensory data as language-related – not a trivial achievement in itself – and then uses the constructed linguistic experience as evidence for a theory that generates an infinite variety of expressions, each of which contains the information about structure, sound, and meaning that underlies the myriad varieties of language use.

To give a few of the early illustrations for concreteness, the internal theory more or less shared by English speakers determines that the sentence (1) is three-ways ambiguous, and that the ambiguities are resolved in the corresponding interrogative form (2):

(1)   Mary saw the man walking to the bus station
(2)   which bus station did Mary see the man walking to?

The three interpretations of (1) are roughly paraphrased as (1')–(1'''):

(1')   Mary saw the man as she was walking to the bus station
(1'')   Mary saw the man who was walking to the bus station
(1''') Mary saw the man walk to the bus station

The interrogative counterpart (2) has only the interpretation (1'''), analogous to "which bus station did Mary see the man walk to."

The explanation appears to rely on computationally plausible principles of generation and minimal search, for which there is a good deal of independent evidence. To form the interrogative expression (2), the phrase "which bus station" is generated in the position in (1) in which its semantic role is determined,[4] then located by minimal search and raised to the position where it is pronounced in (2), and interpreted as an operator taking scope over a variable in its original position. The sentence therefore means, roughly, "for which x, x a bus station, Mary saw the man walking to x." The variable is silent in the phonetic output, but must be there for interpretation. Of the three underlying structures that yield the triple ambiguity, only one permits the raising operation, by virtue of general search conditions (so-called "island conditions"), so the ambiguity is resolved in the interrogative.

It is perhaps worth noting that the structure and meaning of expressions of one's (I-)language may not be accessible without reflection or even hints. For example, the sentence "John had a book stolen" is three-ways ambiguous, but most people find it difficult to discover these facts about their knowledge of language. And it goes without saying that the processes involved are commonly as inaccessible to consciousness as the "rigidity principle" that determines that we see successive impoverished visual presentations as a rigid object in motion.

To take a second example, consider the sentence "John ate an apple." We can omit "an apple," yielding "John ate," which we understand to mean "John ate something or other." Now consider (3):

(3) a. John is ready to eat an apple
     b. John is too angry to eat an apple

We can again omit "an apple," yielding (4):

(4) a. John is ready to eat
     b. John is too angry to eat

By analogy to "John ate," we would expect the expressions (4) to mean "John is ready (too angry) to eat something or other," and so they do. But there is also a second meaning: "John is ready (too angry) for someone or other to eat him, John," similar to the natural interpretation for the structurally analogous expressions "the pie is ready to eat," "John is too angry to invite." The explanation lies in the fact that one of the options underlying the phrase "ready (too angry) to eat" includes a substructure analogous to the structure underlying (2): an operator-variable construction, formed in this case by movement of a phonetically invisible operator O, yielding (5):

(5)   John is ready (too angry) [O [to eat x]]

The operator O has no content and is silent, unlike "which bus station" in (2). The expression therefore has a free variable, hence is a predicate combining with *ready* (*angry*) and holding of *John*. The raising of the empty operator meets the same island conditions as in (2). Thus we can say (6) and (7) but not (8) and (9):[5]

> (6)   which bus station did Mary expect us to walk to
> (7)   Mary is too angry to expect us to talk to
> (8)   which bus station did Mary meet someone who walked to
> (9)   Mary is too angry to meet someone who talked to

There is substantial independent evidence supporting the conclusions, for a variety of constructions.

In both constructions (2) and (4), then, general computational principles yield the required interpretations as an operator-variable construction, with the variable unpronounced in both cases and the operator unpronounced in one. The pronounced forms in themselves tell us little about the structures of the expressions and their range of interpretations. That is quite normal. For such reasons, it has been understood from the earliest work in generative grammar that efforts to approximate what appears in a corpus or to predict what might come next are of only marginal interest. They do not even deal with the relevant data, such as the interpretations of (1)–(9). Accordingly, they do not address basic questions of the study of language: What is the language that a person masters? How does it generate internal expressions that yield information of the kind just illustrated? How is it acquired and used? How did it evolve?

Even the most elementary considerations yield similar conclusions. In the earliest work in generative grammar over fifty years ago, it was assumed that words can be detected by study of transitional probabilities (which, surprisingly, turns out to be false, recent work has shown). Methods were proposed with an information-theoretic flavor to assign such words to categories.[6] But it was evident that even the simplest lexical items raise fundamental problems for analytic procedures of segmentation, classification, statistical analysis, and the like. A lexical item is identified by phonological elements that determine its sound along with morphological elements that determine its meaning. But neither the phonological nor morphological elements have the "beads-on-a-string" property required for elementary computational analysis of a corpus. Furthermore, rather as in the case of the constructions (1)–(9), even the simplest words in many languages have phonological and morphological elements that are silent. The elements that constitute lexical items find their place in the generative procedures that yield the expressions, but cannot be detected in the physical signal. For such reasons, it seemed – and seems – that the language acquired must have the basic properties of an internalized explanatory theory. These are elementary properties that any account of evolution of language must deal with.

Quite generally, construction of theories must be guided by what Charles Sanders Peirce a century ago called an "abductive principle," genetically determined, which "puts a limit upon admissible hypotheses," so that the mind is capable of "imagining correct theories of some kind" and discarding (in fact, not even imagining) infinitely many others consistent with the evidence.[7] For language development, the format that limits admissible hypotheses must, furthermore, be highly restrictive, given the empirical facts of rapidity of acquisition and convergence among individuals. The conclusions about the specificity and richness of the language faculty seemed to follow directly. Plainly such conclusions pose serious barriers to inquiry into how the faculty might have evolved, matters discussed inconclusively at the 1974 conference.

A few years later, a new approach crystallized that suggested ways in which these barriers might be overcome. This "Principles and Parameters" (P&P) approach is based on the idea that the format consists of invariant principles and a "switch-box" of parameters that can be set to one or another value on the basis of fairly elementary experience. A choice of parameter settings determines a language; the diversity of languages would then be reduced to parameter settings. The approach largely emerged from intensive study of a range of languages, but it was also suggested by an analogy to early evo devo discoveries, specifically François Jacob's ideas about how slight changes in regulatory mechanisms might yield great superficial differences – between a butterfly and an elephant, and so on.[8] The model seemed natural for language as well: slight changes in parameter settings might yield superficial variety, through interaction of invariant principles with parameter choices. One illustration is Mark Baker's demonstration that languages that appear on the surface to be radically different – his primary example is Mohawk vs. English – turn out to be remarkably similar when we abstract from the effects of a few choices of values for parameters with a hierarchic organization that he argues to be universal.[9]

The approach stimulated highly productive investigation of languages of great typological variety. It opened entirely new questions, sometimes providing answers; and reinvigorated neighboring fields, particularly the study of language acquisition, reframed as inquiry into setting of parameters in the early years of life, with very fruitful results.

The P&P approach also had implications for the study of evolution of language, removing a major conceptual barrier. With the divorce of principles of language from acquisition, it no longer follows that the format that "limits admissible hypotheses" must be rich and highly structured to satisfy the empirical conditions of language acquisition. That might turn out to be the case, but it is no longer an apparent conceptual necessity. Similarly, it provided a new perspective to undermine the long-standing though implausible belief that languages can "differ from each other without limit and in unpredictable ways," the conclusion of a prominent theoretician summarizing (with some exaggeration, but not too much) what he called "the Boasian" approach, pretty much received opinion in the mid-1950s.[10] Similar views were familiar in biology as well. Thus until quite recently it appeared that variability of organisms might be so great as to constitute "a near infinitude of particulars which have to be sorted out case by case."[11]

The problem of reconciling unity and diversity has constantly arisen in the study of language as well as in general biology. The linguistic theory that developed within the seventeenth-century scientific revolution distinguished universal from particular grammar, though not quite in the contemporary sense. Universal grammar was taken to be the intellectual core of the discipline; particular grammars were regarded as accidental instantiations of the universal system. With the flourishing of anthropological linguistics, the pendulum swung in the other direction, towards diversity, well articulated in the "Boasian" formulation I quoted. In general biology, the issue arose sharply in the famous debate between Georges Cuvier and Geoffroy St. Hilaire in 1830. Cuvier's position, emphasizing diversity, prevailed, particularly after the Darwinian revolution, leading to the conclusions about near infinitude of particulars that have to be sorted out case by case. Perhaps the most quoted sentence in biology is Darwin's final observation in *Origin of Species* about how "from so simple a beginning, endless forms most beautiful and most wonderful have been, and are being, evolved." I do not know if the irony was intended, but these words were taken by Sean Carroll as the title of his introduction to "the new science of Evo Devo," which seeks to show that the forms that have evolved are far from endless, in fact are remarkably uniform.

Recent discoveries tend to reinforce the general approach of D'Arcy Thompson and Alan Turing on the principles that constrain the variety of organisms. In Turing's words, the true science of biology should regard "living organisms as a special kind of system to which the general laws of physics and chemistry apply," sharply constraining their possible variety and fixing their fundamental properties.[12] The perspective may sound less extreme today after the discovery of regulatory mechanisms and organizing principles, deep homologies, master genes, conservation of fundamental mechanisms of development, and much else, perhaps even restrictions of evolutionary/developmental processes so narrow that "replaying the protein tape of life might be surprisingly repetitive," in the words of a study of feasible mutational paths, recalling Steven Gould's famous image.[13] Michael Sherman argues that a "Universal Genome that encodes all major developmental programs essential for various phyla of Metazoa emerged in a unicellular or a primitive multicellular organism shortly before the sudden explosion of complex animal forms during Cambrian period"; and, further, that the many "Metazoan phyla, all having similar genomes, are nonetheless so distinct because they utilize specific combinations of developmental programs."[14] According to this conception, there is one multicellular animal from a sufficiently abstract point of view – the point of view that might be taken by a scientist from a much more advanced civilization viewing events on earth. Superficial variety would result from various arrangements of an evolutionarily conserved "developmental-genetic toolkit," as it is sometimes called.

If ideas of this kind prove to be on the right track, the problem of unity and diversity will be reformulated in ways that would have surprised recent generations of scientists.

The uniformity had not passed unnoticed in Darwin's day. The naturalistic studies of Darwin's close associate and expositor Thomas Huxley led him to observe, with some puzzlement, that there appear to be "predetermined lines of modification" that lead natural selection to "produce varieties of a limited number and kind" for each species. The conclusion is reminiscent of earlier ideas of "rational morphology," a famous example being Goethe's theories of archetypal forms of plants.[15]

Over the years, in both general biology and linguistics the pendulum has been swinging towards unity, yielding new ways of understanding traditional ideas. Research programs that have developed within the P&P framework have some similarity to conclusions of the evo devo revolution that "the rules controlling embryonic development" interact with other physical conditions "to restrict possible changes of structures and functions" in evolutionary development, providing "architectural constraints" that "limit adaptive scope and channel evolutionary patterns."[16]

Evidently, growth of language in the individual ("language learning") must involve the three factors that enter into development of organic systems more generally: (i) genetic endowment, which sets limits on the languages attained; (ii) external data, which select one or another language within a narrow range;[17] (iii) principles not specific to the language faculty. The theory of the genetic endowment is commonly called "universal grammar" (UG), adapting a traditional term to a new context. The study of evolution of language is specifically concerned with UG and its origins. For a generative system like language, one would expect principles of efficient computation to be of particular significance in the third factor category. We can regard an account of some linguistic phenomena as *principled* insofar as it derives them by efficient computation satisfying interface conditions. As principled explanation is approached over a wider range, the hypothesized role of UG declines, and the task of accounting for its evolution is correspondingly eased.[18]

Inquiry into these topics in recent years has come to be called "the minimalist program," but it should be recognized that the program has traditional roots and is largely theory-neutral. The serious study of language has always sought to discover what is distinctive about language, implicitly abstracting from third factor effects. And whatever one's beliefs about design of language may be, the questions of the minimalist research program arise, though some theories may be preferred over others on minimalist (that is, principled) grounds. Contrary to much misunderstanding,[19] there is nothing controversial about the minimalist program itself (though there naturally is, and should be, controversy about various implementations). One may or may not be interested in the questions raised, but there is nothing further to debate about the program. For those concerned with evolution of language, the minimalist program must surely be a central concern.

Let us turn to the approach I mentioned at the outset, beginning with the properties of language that are understood with some confidence, the only reasonable approach for inquiry into the evolution of any system. The internal language, again, is a computational system that generates infinitely many hierarchically structured internal expressions, each of which underlies an array of instructions to the interface systems, SM and C-I (semantic/pragmatic). Thus we can reasonably inquire into the validity of the thesis T, repeated here, and can seek to refine it:

(T) Interfaces + Recursion = Language

One crucial question has to do with the nature of the recursive operations that enter into the computational system of language. How intricate are they? The minimalist program asks how closely they approximate the simplest form possible, perhaps even reaching this limit.

Any generative system, natural or invented, incorporates in some manner an operation that takes structures X and Y already formed and combines them into a new structure Z. Maximally efficient computation will leave X and Y unchanged (the No-Tampering Condition), so we can take Z to be simply {X, Y}. Call this operation *Merge*. Applying without bounds to a *lexicon* of conceptual/lexical "atoms," Merge yields a discrete infinity of structured expressions. In the simplest case, then, unbounded Merge is the sole recursive operation within UG – part of the genetic component of the language faculty, a product of the evolution of this "cognitive organ."

A very strong thesis, sometimes called "the strong minimalist thesis" SMT, is that language keeps to the simplest recursive operation, Merge, and is perfectly designed to satisfy interface conditions. Proceeding beyond T, we therefore can inquire into the validity of SMT:

(SMT) Interfaces + Merge = Language

The associated question mark is even more forceful than before, since SMT reduces the options for recursion. In fact it bars almost everything that has been proposed in the course of work on generative grammar.[20] Any stipulated device beyond Merge carries a burden of proof: the complication of UG must be based on empirical evidence. A significant result of minimalist inquiries has been to show that many complications thought essential are superfluous. As far as I am aware, it is now fair to say that the burden of proof for richer recursive mechanisms has not been credibly met. If so, we may tentatively adopt the assumption that Merge is the sole recursive operation.

Though it has no bearing on the minimalist program for language, one may raise the factual question of whether the basic properties of language, notably recursive generation, are unique to the language faculty or are found elsewhere. If the latter, there still must be a genetic instruction to adopt Merge (or some more complex recursive operations) to form infinitely many structured linguistic expressions satisfying the interface conditions. Nonetheless, it is interesting to ask whether such an operation is language-specific. We know that it is not. The classic illustration is the system of natural numbers. That brings up a problem posed by Alfred Russell Wallace 125 years ago: in his words, the "gigantic development of the mathematical capacity is wholly unexplained by the theory of natural selection, and must be due to some altogether distinct cause," if only because it remained unused.[21] One possibility is that the core element of this capacity, arithmetic, is derivative from language. It is not hard to show that, if the lexicon is reduced to a single element, then Merge will yield a form of arithmetic. Speculations about the origin of the arithmetical capacity as an abstraction from linguistic operations are familiar, as are criticisms, some based on dissociation with lesions and diversity of localization. The significance of such phenomena, however, is far from clear; they relate to use of the capacity, not its possession. For similar reasons, as Luigi Rizzi has observed, dissociations do not show that the capacity to read is not parasitic on the language faculty.

Suppose the single item in the lexicon is a complex object, say some visual array. Then Merge will yield a discrete infinity of visual patterns, but this is simply a special case of arithmetic, and therefore tells us nothing new about recursion beyond language. The same would be true if we add another instance of Merge to form an infinite lexicon, on the model of some actual (if rather trivial) lexical rules of natural language. This is still just a more elaborate form of arithmetic, raising no new issue. If these and other cases fall under the same general rubric, then Merge is not only a genetically determined property of language, but also unique to it.

Either way, evolution of language required some innovation to provide instructions for Merge to operate, forming structured expressions accessible to the two interface systems. There are many proposals involving precursors with a stipulated bound on Merge: for example, an operation to form two-word expressions from single words, perhaps to reduce memory load for the lexicon; then another operation to form three-word expressions; etc. Clearly, there is no empirical evidence from the historical or archeological record for such stipulations, and no obvious rationale for them either, since it is still necessary to assume that at some point unbounded Merge appears. It is no easier to move from seven-word sentences to unbounded Merge than from single words. Hence the assumption of earlier stages seems superfluous. The same issue arises in language acquisition. The modern study of the topic began with the assumption that the child passes through a two-word stage, etc. Again the assumption lacks a rationale, because at some point unbounded Merge must appear. Hence the capacity must have been there all along even if it only comes to function at some later stage. There does appear to be evidence for postulation of earlier stages: namely, observation of what children produce. But that carries little weight. What children understand at the early stages far exceeds what they produce, and is quite different in character as well. At the "telegraphic stage" of speech production, for example, children understand normal speech with the function words in the right places but are baffled by telegraphic speech.[22] Hence for both evolution and development, there seems to be little reason to suppose that there were precursors to unbounded Merge.

Suppose X is merged to Y. Evidently, either X is external to Y or is part of Y: *external* and *internal* Merge, respectively, the latter sometimes called *Move*. A well-designed language, lacking arbitrary stipulations, will allow both cases. Internal Merge yields the familiar phenomenon of displacement, as in the examples (1)–(9) discussed earlier. It yields, for example, a question of the form "what did John see [what]," with two occurrences of "what." The structurally more prominent one is pronounced in sentence-initial position while the bracketed one is deleted by rules mapping to the SM interface. As discussed earlier, the full internal expression is interpreted at the semantic interface as an operator-variable construction, with "what" given the same semantic role it has when it is not displaced, as in "who saw what." Deletion of all but the most prominent element restricts computational load, since the deleted elements do not have to be "spelled out"; the reduction is quite substantial in real cases. No comparable problem arises at the C-I interface.

In a well-designed language, the two kinds of Merge will have different interface properties. That appears to be true. They correlate with the well-known duality of semantics that has been studied from various points of view. External Merge yields argument structure: agent, patient, goal, predicate, etc. Internal Merge yields discourse-related properties such as topic and distinctions of old/ new information, also scope and other non-argument semantic properties. The correlation appears to be very close, and as more is understood it might be discovered to be perfect (perhaps in some refined form).

The exposition so far has taken the relation of internal language to the two interface systems to be symmetrical, adopting the traditional assumption that language is a mechanism for linking sound and meaning. But the symmetry assumption can be questioned. At the 1974 symposium, a number of participants suggested that the relation is not symmetrical; rather that the primary relation is to the semantic interface, to systems of thought. Salvador Luria was the most forceful advocate of the view that communicative needs would not have provided "any great selective pressure to produce a system such as language," with its crucial relation to "development of abstract or productive thinking." The same idea was taken up by his fellow Nobel laureate François Jacob, who suggested that "the role of language as a communication system between individuals would have come about only secondarily, as many linguists believe ... The quality of language that makes it unique does not seem to be so much its role in communicating directives for action" or other common features of animal communication, but rather "its role in symbolizing, in evoking cognitive images," in "molding" our notion of reality and yielding our capacity for thought and planning, through its unique property of allowing "infinite combinations of symbols" and therefore "mental creation of possible worlds." Such ideas trace back to the cognitive revolution of the seventeenth century, which in many ways foreshadows developments from the 1950s.[23]

Generation of expressions to satisfy the C-I interface yields a "language of thought." If the assumption of asymmetry is correct, then the earliest stage of language would have been just that: a language of thought, available for use internally. It has been argued that an independent language of thought must be postulated. I think there are reasons for skepticism, but that would take us too far afield.[24]

The empirical question of asymmetry can be approached from the study of existing languages. We can seek evidence to determine whether they are optimized to satisfy one or the other interface system. There is, I think, mounting evidence that the thought systems are indeed primary in this respect. We have just seen one illustration: the properties of internal Merge. The No-Tampering Condition, a third factor property of computational efficiency, entails that the internally generated expression should include the initial and final occurrences of the internally merged item, and all intermediate occurrences. This is correct at the semantic interface; I mentioned a simple case, but it is true far more generally, in quite interesting ways. It is, however, clearly not true at the SM interface, where all but the hierarchically prominent position are deleted (with interesting exceptions not relevant here). Why should this be? Here conditions of computational efficiency and of ease of communication are in conflict. Computational efficiency yields the universally attested facts: only the hierarchically most prominent position is pronounced. But that leads to comprehension problems. For parsing programs, and perception, major problems are to locate the "gaps" associated with the element that is pronounced, problems that would largely be overcome if all occurrences were pronounced. The conflict between computational efficiency and ease of communication appears to be resolved, universally, in favor of computational efficiency to satisfy the semantic interface, lending support to speculations about its primacy in language design. There are other cases of computational efficiency leading to problems of comprehension or articulating thoughts: for example, structural ambiguity, "garden path" sentences, islands (insofar as they can be explained in computational terms).

The same conclusion about asymmetry is suggested by discoveries about sign languages in recent years, which provide substantial evidence that external-ization of language is modality-independent. There are striking cases of inven-tion of sign languages by deaf children exposed to no linguistic evidence and by communities of deaf people who developed a sign language. In the known cases, sign languages are structurally very much like spoken languages, and follow the same developmental patterns from the babbling stage to full com-petence. They are also distinguished sharply from the gestural systems of the signers, even when the same gesture is used both iconically and symbolically, as Laura Petitto discovered. She and her colleagues have also studied children raised in bimodal (signing-speaking) homes, and have found no preferences or basic differences. Her own conclusion is that even "sensitivity to phonetic-syllabic contrasts is a fundamentally linguistic (not acoustic) process and part of the baby's biological endowment," and that the same holds at higher levels of structure. Imaging studies, Pettito concludes, lend further support to the hypoth-esis that "there exists tissue in the human brain dedicated to a *function* of human language *structure* independent of speech and sound." Studies of brain damage among signers has led to similar conclusions, as has comparative work indicat-ing that the SM systems of earlier hominids were recruited for language, perhaps with no special adaptation. Reviewing the evolution of the "human capacity" – Alexander Marshack's term for the "elusive quality that makes humans so distinctive" – Ian Tattersall concludes that "the peripheral equipment that allows articulate speech had been around for several hundred thousand years [prior to the 'invention of language'], having emerged for other purposes entirely"; "a vocal tract capable of articulate speech had thus been achieved among humans well over half a million years before we have any independent evidence that our forebears were using language or speaking."[25]

Investigation of the second interface, systems of thought, is of course much harder. Relevant evidence is far harder to obtain. Positioning the C-I interface within the network of cognitive systems raises subtle questions about which aspects of thought might be language-independent, including questions of argument structure (so-called "theta roles"), the status of propositions and propositional attitudes, determination of event structure, and much else. Challenging questions arise, for example, in determining the place of principles of interpretation of referential dependence and variable-binding; or phonetic-semantic interactions, as in establishing focus and presupposition, or even the declarative-interrogative distinction. Detailed linguistic work sheds consider-able light on such questions, and in principle, comparative work might do so as well – but it too is difficult, though proceeding in interesting ways.[26] It seems that much of what takes place in these cognitive domains is human-specific, in part language-specific, hence part of UG, posing problems for study of evolution of language that are difficult even to formulate seriously today.

The same seems to be true even for the "atoms" of computation and interpretation – concepts and lexical items (to the extent that they differ – again, far from a simple question). Even at this level, where the core questions of traditional semantics arise, there seem to be critical differences between human conceptual systems and symbolic/representational systems of other animals. Crucially, even the simplest words and concepts of human language and thought lack the relation to mind-independent entities that appears to be characteristic of animal communication. The latter is held to be based on a one-one relation between mind/brain processes and "an aspect of the environment to which these processes adapt the animal's behavior," to quote C. R. Gallistel. According to Jane Goodall, for chimpanzees "the production of a sound in the *absence* of the appropriate emotional state seems to be an almost impossible task."[27] The symbols of human language and thought are sharply different. Their use is not automatically keyed to emotional states, and they do not pick out mind-independent objects or events in the external world, matters explored in interesting ways by seventeenth- and eighteenth-century British philosophers, developing ideas that trace back to Aristotle.

In general, there appears to be no *reference* relation in human language and thought in the technical sense of Frege, Peirce, Tarski, Quine, and contemporary "externalist" philosophy of language and mind. Referring is an action, and the internal symbols that are used to refer do not pick out mind-independent objects. On investigation, it turns out that what we understand to be a house, a river, a person, a tree, water, and so on, is not a physical construct of some kind. Rather, these are creations of what seventeenth-century investigators called our "cognoscitive powers," which provide us with rich means to interpret and refer to the outside world from certain perspectives. The entities of discourse are individuated by mental operations that cannot be reduced to a "peculiar nature belonging" to what we are talking about, as Hume summarized a century of inquiry. In this regard, internal conceptual symbols are rather like the phonetic units of mental representations, such as the syllable [ba]; every particular act externalizing this mental entity yields a mind-independent entity, but it would be idle to seek a mind-independent construct that corresponds to the internal syllable. Communication is not a matter of producing some mind-external entity that the hearer picks out of the world the way a physicist could. Rather, speech communication is a more-or-less affair, in which the speaker produces external events and hearers seek to match them as best they can to their own internal resources. Words and concepts appear to be similar in this regard, even the simplest of them. Communication relies on shared cognoscitive powers, and succeeds insofar as shared mental constructs, background, concerns, presuppositions, and so on, allow for common perspectives to be (more less) attained. These properties of lexical items seem to be unique to human language and thought, and have to be accounted for somehow in the study of their evolution. How, no one has any idea. The fact that there even is a problem has barely been recognized, as a result of the powerful grip of the doctrines of referentialism.[28]

Reformulating the tasks in different terms, among the many puzzling questions about language, two are salient: First, why are there any languages at all? Second, why are there so many languages? According to what seems to be a fairly general scientific consensus, the questions are very recent ones in evolutionary time. Roughly 100,000+ years ago, the first question did not arise, because there were no languages. By about 50,000 years ago, the answers to both questions had been settled. By then our ancestors began to leave Africa, soon spreading over the entire world. The evidence is compelling that since then the language faculty has remained essentially unchanged – which is not surprising in such a brief period. An infant from a stone age tribe in the South Pacific, if brought to Boston, will be indistinguishable in linguistic and other cognitive functions from children born in Boston who trace their ancestry to the first English colonists; and conversely. The actual dates are uncertain, and do not matter much for our purposes. The general picture appears to be roughly accurate.

At some time within this narrow window, so the archeological record reveals, there was an emergence of creative imagination, language and symbolism generally, mathematics, interpretation and recording of natural phenomena, intricate social practices and the like, yielding what Wallace called "man's intellectual and moral nature," Marshack's "human capacity." In a review of current thinking about these matters, Ian Tattersall writes that he is "almost sure that it was the invention of language" that was the "sudden and emergent" event that was the "releasing stimulus" for the appearance of the human capacity in the evolutionary record – the "great leap forward" as Jared Diamond called it. Presumably some genetic event rewired the brain, providing the mechanisms for language, with the rich syntax that yields the modes of expression of thought that are a prerequisite for social development and the sharp changes of behavior that are revealed in the archeological record and presumably occasioned the trek from Africa, where anatomically modern humans had apparently been present for hundreds of thousands of years. It appears that human brain size may have reached its current level recently, perhaps about 100,000 years ago, which suggests to some specialists that "human language probably evolved, at least in part, as an automatic but adaptive consequence of increased absolute brain size" (neuroscientist George Striedter).[29]

With regard to language, Tattersall concludes that "after a long – and poorly understood – period of erratic brain expansion and reorganization in the human lineage, something occurred that set the stage for language acquisition. This innovation would have depended on the phenomenon of emergence, whereby a chance combination of preexisting elements results in something totally unexpected," presumably "a neural change … in some population of the human lineage … rather minor in genetic terms, [which] probably had nothing whatever to do with adaptation" though it conferred advantages, then proliferated. "We have to conclude that the appearance of language and its anatomical correlates was not driven by natural selection, however beneficial these innovations may appear in hindsight." Perhaps it was a side effect of increased brain size, as Striedter suggests, or perhaps some chance mutation. Sometime later came further innovations that led to behaviorally modern humans, the crystallization of the "human capacity," and rapid spread of humans around the world. Like Luria and Jacob, Tattersall takes language to be "virtually synonymous with symbolic thought," implying that externalization is a secondary phenomenon, ideas that I think are supported by other evidence, as I mentioned. Elsewhere he suggests that human intelligence more generally is an "*emergent* quality, the result of a chance combination of factors, rather than a product of Nature's patient and gradual engineering over the eons."[30]

If this picture is basically accurate, then SMT has considerable initial plausibility, if only because of the narrow window of the "sudden emergence," which would lead one to expect something more like a snowflake than the outcome of extensive Jacobian "tinkering" over a long period.[31]

Putting these thoughts together, we can suggest what seems to be the simplest speculation about the evolution of language. Within some small group from which we are all descended, a rewiring of the brain took place in some individual, call him *Prometheus*, yielding the operation of unbounded Merge, applying to concepts with intricate (and little understood) properties. Guided very likely by third factor principles, Prometheus's language provides him with an infinite array of structured expressions with interpretations of the kind illustrated: duality of semantics, operator-variable constructions, unpronounced elements with substantial consequences for interpretation and thought, etc. Prometheus had many advantages: capacities for complex thought, planning, interpretation, and so on. The capacity would then be transmitted to offspring, coming to predominate (no trivial matter, it appears, but let us put that aside). At that stage, there would be an advantage to externalization, so the capacity might come to be linked as a secondary process to the SM system for externalization and interaction, including communication – a special case, at least if we invest the term "communication" with some substantive meaning. It is not easy to imagine an account of human evolution that does not assume at least this much, in one or another form. Any additional assumptions carry an empirical burden of proof (ignorance, which abounds, leaves the questions open).

Still to be addressed is the second of the salient puzzling questions: Why are there so many languages? That seems curious, and a violation of the spirit of SMT. There have been suggestions over the years, ranging from sociological/ cultural to possible minimax optimization. None seem compelling. Asymmetry of interface relations suggests an alternative: perhaps it is not a matter of evolution of language at all.

Externalization is not a simple task. It has to relate two quite distinct systems: one is an SM system that appears to have been basically intact for hundreds of thousands of years; the second is a newly emerged computational system for thought, which approaches perfect design insofar as SMT is correct. We would expect, then, that morphology and phonology – the linguistic processes that convert internal syntactic objects to the entities accessible to the SM system – might turn out to be intricate, varied, and subject to accidental historical and cultural events: the Norman conquest, teen-age jargon, and so on. Parametrization and diversity too would be mostly – maybe entirely – restricted to external- ization. Though it is contested, that may include linearization, which appears to play no role in syntax and the C-I interface,[32] and the options for linearization. Something like that is approximately what we seem to find, insofar as current understanding reaches: a computational system efficiently generating expres- sions that provide the language of thought, and complex and highly varied modes of externalization, which, furthermore, readily adapt to disruptive acci- dental contingencies.

The processes of externalization (morphology, phonology, and their various aspects) have been intensively studied within the framework of generative grammar, and had been the primary topic of investigation in the study of language that traces back millennia. The reasons for this focus of attention are clear. They are concerned with phenomena that are readily observable, and they also have general human interest, precisely because they are complex and highly varied. A child acquiring English, or an adult trying to learn English, has to find out about irregular verbs, but does not learn the properties of (1)–(9) (and can't be taught them, except in the context of linguistic theory). For the semantics of natural language there is virtually no evidence available, apart from such superficial phenomena as the arbitrary pairing of sound and meaning. The subtleties of each of the paired elements is a topic of scientific inquiry. They are not learned, but are derived "by the original hand of nature," in Hume's phrase: UG, in our terms. For syntax too, evidence is thin, as (1)–(9) illustrate, so a similar conclusion is in order. But for phonetic properties and surface morphology there is extensive direct evidence, and the variability requires that they be acquired or consciously learned.

We would nevertheless expect to find that the cognitive problem of external- ization is solved by each child in an optimal way. The child is typically confronted with confused linguistic data of many kinds, obviously not sorted into I-languages. The task for its language faculty is to construct the optimal account to deal with these chaotic phenomena, making use of whatever resources are available: specifically, the restrictions on search space provided by UG (Peirce's "limit upon admissible hypotheses") and "third factor" elements, among them general learning strategies and principles of computational efficiency. But this kind of optimization in problem-solving is not to be confused with evolutionary processes of optimization – those that lead, for example, to optimal forms of neural wiring.[33]

We may then have a way to unravel the second of the two basic puzzles: Why are there so many languages? The reason might be that the problem of externalization can be solved in many different and independent ways, either before or after the dispersal of the original population.

Solving the externalization problem may not have involved an evolutionary change – that is, genomic change. It might simply be a problem addressed by existing cognitive processes, in different ways, and at different times. There is sometimes a misleading tendency to confuse literal evolutionary change with historical change, two entirely distinct phenomena. As already noted, there is very strong evidence that there has been no relevant evolution of the language faculty since dispersal from Africa some 50,000 years ago, though undoubtedly there has been a great deal of change, even invention of modes of externalization (as in sign language). Confusion about these matters could be mitigated by replacing the metaphorical notions "evolution of language" and "language change" by their more exact counterparts: evolution of the organisms that use language, and change in the ways they do so. In these terms, emergence of the language faculty involved evolution, while historical change (which goes on constantly) does not.

Again, these seem to be the simplest assumptions, and I do not know of any reason to reject them. If they are generally on the right track, it follows that externalization may scarcely have evolved at all; rather, it might have been a process of problem-solving using existing cognitive capacities. Evolution in the biological sense of the term would then be restricted to the mutation that yielded the operation Merge along with whatever residue resists explanation in terms of the strong minimalist thesis, and UG constraints on parameter-setting in externalization insofar as these cannot be explained independently. Accordingly, any approach to evolution of language that focuses on communication, or the SM system, or statistical properties of spoken language, and the like, may well be seriously misguided.

An important qualification is necessary, however. The intensive linguistic study of externalization has revealed what appear to be significant constraints on the process: it is far from "anything goes." Only certain kinds of systems of rules (filters, and other devices) and substantive elements appear to be available for externalization of syntactic objects. Some of the constraints might derive from third factor considerations of optimal computation, issues that have been investigated from the origins of generative grammar (sometimes under the rubric of "simplicity considerations" and "evaluation measures"), and that arise in various ways in earlier work as well: for example the search for symmetrical patterns in structuralist phonology.[34] But that still leaves such principles as those determining the form and permissible ordering of rules, the ways prosodic structures are assigned to syntactic objects, and other aspects of externalization. Perhaps these constraints, at least some of them, are derived from cognitive capacities independent of language. Insofar as they fall within UG, they pose yet another problem for the study of evolution of language.

Returning finally to the basic questions, we have some suggestions about how it came about that there is even one language, and about why languages appear to vary so widely – the latter partly an illusion, much like the apparent limitless variety of organisms. Taking T – or better, if possible, SMT – as a guideline, the basic tasks are to account for: (i) recursion – optimally just Merge;[35] (ii) the lexical/conceptual items that are the "atoms" of computation; (iii) the properties of the SM and C-I interfaces insofar as they fall within UG/ FLN; (iv) the interpretive mechanisms that map syntactic objects into a form interpretable at C-I (with many fundamental open questions about where operations apply in the overarching cognitive system): (v) the secondary process of externalization, insofar as it is shaped by UG constraints; (vi) whatever resists principled explanation in the sense outlined earlier. In each case, deeper understanding of third factor effects and comparative evidence could well turn out to be informative.

If all properties of language could be given principled explanation, then we would conclude that language is perfectly designed to satisfy C-I conditions, and that the various mappings to the SM interface are maximally efficient solutions to cognitive problems. That is too much to expect, but recent work seems to me to show that the ideal is considerably less remote than would have been imagined not long ago, offering possible avenues to gain new insight into evolution and development of language.

3   Your theory of language evolution depends on your theory of language

Ray Jackendoff

This paper is more about the questions for a theory of language evolution than about the answers. I'd like to ask what there is for a theory of the evolution of language to explain, and I want to show how this depends on what you think language is.

So, what *is* language? Everybody recognizes that language is partly culturally dependent: there is a huge variety of disparate languages in the world, passed down through cultural transmission. If that's all there is to language, a theory of the evolution of language has nothing at all to explain. We need only explain the cultural evolution of langua*ges*: English, Dutch, Mandarin, Hausa, etc. are products of cultural history.

However, most readers of the present volume probably subscribe to the contemporary scientific view of language, which goes beneath the cultural differences among languages. It focuses on individual language users and asks:

Q1: (Structure and acquisition of language competence) What is the structure of the knowledge that individual language users store in their brains, and how did they come to acquire this knowledge?

The question of acquisition leads to an important corollary question:

Q2: (Structure of capacity to learn language) What is the structure of the knowledge/ability in the child that makes language acquisition possible?

This latter knowledge is independent of what language the child actually learns in response to the environment. It is closer to what is generally called the language capacity (or the language instinct or universal grammar or the language acquisition device). Because it's prior to learning, it has to be built into the brain by something in the genetic code, plus standard processes of biological development – which of course we don't understand very well. Ultimately, then, a theory of language evolution has to account for the presence of the genetic code that is responsible for the development of the language capacity in every normal human.

Figure 3.1 summarizes this chain of causal and theoretical dependence between the process of evolution and the linguistic competence of native speakers. The structure of adult knowledge of language is a product of a learning process, and therefore the theory of the learning process ultimately

63

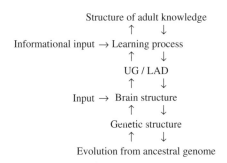

Figure 3.1. Inferential relation between theory of linguistic knowledge and evolutionary theory

has to account for how the adult knowledge is structured. The learning process is based on two sources: (a) information the child takes in from the environment, and (b) the child's prior knowledge about how to structure and generalize that information, coming from the innate universal grammar. Therefore a theory of the learning process constrains the theory of universal grammar: the latter had better be rich enough to account for learning.

In turn, universal grammar is the product (or functional realization) of innate brain structure. Therefore our theory of brain structure has to be rich enough to account for the ability to learn and process language. The language learner's brain structure is a consequence of developmental processes that arise from the inter-action of the human genome with environmental input such as nutrition and informational stimulation. Our theory of the genome and its role in the devel-opmental process has to be sufficient to account for the brain structure that supports language learning. And finally, the human genome is a product of evolutionary processes acting on ancestral species, and our account of these evolutionary processes must be sufficient to account for the presence of the brain structure that supports language acquisition. Thus there is a long chain of reasoning between evolutionary processes and modern-day speakers' use of language.

Another dimension of the problem is not addressed by figure 3.1:

Q3: (Special vs. general) What aspects of the language capacity in the mind/brain are special for language, and what aspects make use of more general capacities?

For any aspect of the language capacity, there are four logical possibilities, which for reasons of terminological neutrality I'll call Departments 1, 2, 3, and 4.

Department 1 contains things necessary to language that have required *no* changes from the ancestral genome. Examples would be the lungs and the basic auditory system, which as far as I know are pretty much unchanged from primate prototypes.

Department 2 consists of innovations in the human lineage that are essential to language or language acquisition but that serve purposes more general than language. Examples might be the use of pointing for drawing attention, the capacity for detailed imitation of others' actions, and a fully developed theory of mind (that is, the ability to conceptualize the beliefs and intentions of others, including their beliefs about one's own beliefs and intentions). At least according to my reading of the literature (e.g. Povinelli 2000; Tomasello *et al.* 2005), these are all unique to humans, but not restricted to use in language or language acquisition.

Department 3 contains aspects of language that are unique to humans, that are used exclusively for language or language acquisition, and that resulted from some alteration or specialization of preexisting primate structures or capacities. A clear example would be the shape of the human vocal tract and the neural structures used for controlling it in speech.

Department 4 consists of aspects of language that require something altogether new and unprecedented in the primate lineage.

Roughly, Departments 1 and 2 are what Hauser, Chomsky, and Fitch (2002) call the broad faculty of language; Department 4 is their narrow faculty of language. It is not clear to me where Department 3 falls according to their criteria (see discussion in Jackendoff and Pinker 2005).

This division is crucial for a theory of the evolution of language. Other things being equal, a theory of language that puts more in Departments 1 and 2, less in Department 3, and as little as possible in Department 4 is preferable on evolutionary grounds, because this gives evolution less work to do to get to the present stage.

Given all these dependencies and possibilities, and the near absence of any telling evidence in the archeological record, how are we to study the evolution of language? To me, the most productive methodology seems to be to engage in reverse engineering.

We attempt to infer the nature of universal grammar and the language acquisition device from the structure of the modern language capacity, using not only evidence from normal language, but also evidence from language deficits, language acquisition, pidgins/creoles (Bickerton 1981; DeGraff 1999), and language creation à la NSL (Kegl, Senghas, and Coppola 1999) and Israeli Bedouin Sign Language (Sandler *et al.* 2005). This is what linguists and psycholinguists normally do.

We can correlate this with comparative evidence from other cognitive capacities to separate the special parts of language from the more general parts. To do this properly, we need to have analyses of other capacities in sufficient detail that we can compare them to language to see what's more general. At present there is little in the way of such analyses. My work with Fred Lerdahl on music (Lerdahl and

Jackendoff 1983; Jackendoff and Lerdahl 2006) is the only comparable analysis that I know of; David Marr's approach to vision (Marr 1982) was on the right track but has been largely abandoned; Jackendoff 2007 offers a sketch of the structure of complex action that may show some promise. This means that cross-capacity comparison, though in principle valuable, cannot be very telling right now.

We can correlate what is known about language and other human capacities with comparative evidence from other organisms, in order to separate what is uniquely human from what is more general across organisms, especially apes, and to see which of the uniquely human aspects of cognition are specializations of preexisting capacities and which are total innovations. This is the program of research advocated by Hauser, Chomsky, and Fitch (2002). To do this properly, we need analyses of animal capacities comparable to our best analyses of language; here I think the situation is even worse than comparing language to other *human* capacities.

After all this comparative work, it might turn out that Departments 3 and 4 are null: that all aspects of language acquisition can be accounted for in terms of more general human cognitive capacities, with no further tuning of existing capacities and no unprecedented innovation. If this is the case, then there's nothing *special* needed for evolution of language, just evolution of more general capacities. And in principle this would be a fine result if we could bring it off. Many people think this is the way it will turn out. For example, those who think language is purely a cultural phenomenon (e.g. Tomasello 2005) are in effect taking this view – though they still have to account for the evolution of human *culture*. Even some linguists, such as Joan Bybee (e.g. Bybee and McClelland 2005) and Adele Goldberg (2005), say "There's nothing innate about language," meaning "There's nothing innate that's *special* for language." Some people – I think Terrence Deacon (1997) and Michael Arbib (2005) might fall into this class – think that the only thing specific to language is the capacity for symbolic use of sound and/or gesture; Departments 3 and 4 are otherwise empty.

Towards a more detailed attempt to sort this out, let's first consider *phonology*. Phonological representations require a digitization of the auditory signal into sequences of discrete speech sounds grouped into syllables. In turn, speech sounds themselves are digitized into a discrete structured space of phonological features. This aspect of phonology is clearly adaptive for language: it is what makes possible a very large number of distinguishable signals – that is, a large vocabulary, an essential feature of human language. We can ask two questions.

First, would the acquisition of phonological representations be possible with *no* special capacities in the brain beyond precise vocal imitation (which itself seems fairly special to language and perhaps music)? That is, is phonological structure just a cultural invention (as Arbib claims), or do children come specially prepared to detect digitized vocal signals?

Second, if children do come with such special preparation, are there antecedents elsewhere in human or animal cognition for digitization of sounds either in sequences or in the structuring of the sound repertoire, and if so, how and when did these antecedents arise? There are two different cases to consider: first, in close human relatives, indicating possible homology and little or no evolution in the descent of humans from primate lineage – this looks unlikely. Second, it might be found in distant species such as birds or whales, indicating independent evolution. Here I suppose the jury is out. (See Yip 2006 for a summary of questions and results on animal counterparts of phonology.)

Now let's turn to *syntax* and *semantics*. An important part of the innate language capacity has to be the overall architecture of language, since the child can't be expected to discover whether language has a structure along the lines of, say, the standard theory, the minimalist program, lexical-functional grammar, cognitive grammar, or some correct theory we haven't thought of yet. I want to contrast two sorts of possible architectures for language, which differ particularly in how syntax and semantics are articulated, to see what questions each raises for the evolution of the language capacity. These two architectures are:

1. A *syntactocentric* architecture – the architecture assumed by mainstream generative grammar (e.g. Chomsky 1965, 1981, 1995b);
2. A *parallel* architecture, which is developed in my books *Foundations of Language* (Jackendoff 2002) and *Simpler Syntax* (Culicover and Jackendoff 2005).

Let me take them up briefly in turn.

In a syntactocentric architecture, the generative capacity of language is localized in the syntactic component. Lexical items are associations of phonological, syntactic, and semantic features, and they are embedded into a syntactic structure in the course of derivation. The combinatorial properties of sound and meaning are derived from or read off of different levels or stages or phases of a syntactic derivation. Because everything is read off of syntax, there can be no correspondences between phonology and semantics without some sort of syntactic mediation. Figure 3.2 shows an overall flow diagram for one version of this architecture, Government-Binding Theory of the 1980s and early 1990s (Chomsky 1981).

A parallel architecture, by contrast, incorporates independent principles of combinatoriality in phonology, syntax, and semantics, each restricted to its proprietary structure. The structures from the three components are linked with each other by *interface rules*, which are of the form "Substructure X in level L1 may correspond to/be linked to substructure Y in level L2." Lexical items are still associations of phonological, syntactic, and semantic features, but in this architecture, these associations are an active part of the interfaces among the three types of structure, rather than being passively manipulated by syntactic derivations. Also among the interface rules may be rules that accomplish direct

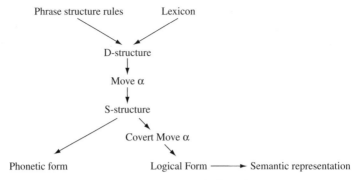

Figure 3.2. Architecture of Government-Binding Theory

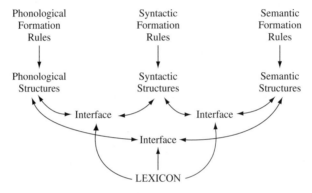

Figure 3.3. The parallel architecture

linkages between phonology and semantics, independent of syntax. Figure 3.3 lays out the organization of the parallel architecture.

Of course, I have a strong preference for the parallel architecture, but I acknowledge that there are numerous proponents of the syntactocentric theory in the world. This is not the place to argue about which theory is correct on grounds internal to linguistics. I've presented my side in fairly gory detail in Jackendoff (2002) and Culicover and Jackendoff (2005). Here I only want to ask:

Q4: What are the implications of these opposing theories for evolution of language?

At least as I understand it, the implication of syntactocentrism is that the combinatorial structure of human thought is derived from (or is a consequence of) the combinatoriality of syntactic structure. Thus syntactic structure is what makes thought/reasoning possible, at least reasoning that involves concepts that cannot be expressed in a single word. In addition, syntax provides the vehicle for connecting thought with vocalization, since it is a necessary link between semantics and phonology. In a way, this is a very Cartesian view, tying together the human capacities for language and reason.

In terms of evolution, though, it is hard to think of any sort of preadaptation on top of which this sort of language capacity could have been an innovation. The whole generative syntactic system and the mappings to phonetic and logical form have to spring into existence more or less out of the blue – though once they come into existence they're obviously adaptive. This theoretical situation therefore creates a motivation for theorists to try to reduce the evolution of the language capacity to a single step. For example, Hauser, Chomsky, and Fitch (2002), assuming a version of the syntactocentric theory, speculate that all that was needed to get the language capacity up and running was the insertion of recursion into a preexisting system. This preexisting system was either the standard-issue ape cognitive capacity or some more general-purpose cognitive innovation in humans; that is, these aspects of language would belong to Departments 1 or 2. Recursion, in contrast, is for them a uniquely human innovation, possibly *sui generis* (Department 4) or possibly a borrowing from some non-communicative cognitive capacity such as navigation, in which case it would fall into Department 3. Culicover and Jackendoff (2005) and Pinker and Jackendoff (2005) show that recursion is in fact a component of visual cognition, as illustrated by the array in Figure 3.4, which is perceived as built recursively out of elementary x's and o's, assembled into lines of five elements, which are then assembled into nine-element squares. These are arranged into rows of three, and the three rows together form a rectangle which could be further embedded. Thus the answer is that recursion belongs to Department 3.

However, Hauser, Chomsky, and Fitch's proposal does not address the evolutionary source of the lexicon, where all the features specific to particular languages are coded. These features of course include phonological features. As I mentioned earlier, phonological structure is digitized in two respects, and therefore at least on

```
XXXXX OOOOO XXXXX  XXXXX OOOOO XXXXX XXXXX OOOOO XXXXX
OOOOO XXXXX OOOOO OOOOO XXXXX OOOOO OOOOO XXXXX OOOOO
XXXXX OOOOO XXXXX XXXXX OOOOO XXXXX XXXXX OOOOO XXXXX

XXXXX OOOOO XXXXX XXXXX OOOOO XXXXX XXXXX OOOOO XXXXX
OOOOO XXXXX OOOOO OOOOO XXXXX OOOOO OOOOO XXXXX OOOOO
XXXXX OOOOO XXXXX XXXXX OOOOO XXXXX XXXXX OOOOO XXXXX

XXXXX OOOOO XXXXX XXXXX OOOOO XXXXX XXXXX OOOOO XXXXX
OOOOO XXXXX OOOOO OOOOO XXXXX OOOOO OOOOO XXXXX OOOOO
XXXXX OOOOO XXXXX XXXXX OOOOO XXXXX XXXXX OOOOO XXXXX
```

Figure 3.4. Recursion in cognition of a visual array

the face of it, phonology differs from the structure of vocal signals in other species, in particular those of our closest relatives. Thus these features seem to belong to Departments 3 or 4, requiring some special innovation in our species.

Lexical entries also include syntactic features, which determine possibilities for syntactic combinatoriality – feature complexes such as *transitive verb*. Since these are specifically syntactic features, practically by definition they belong to Department 4, since there aren't nouns, verbs, prepositions, tense markers, agreement markers, or case markers in any other cognitive capacity. These syntactic aspects of the lexicon are cognitively useful only if there are syntactic trees to insert lexical items into, so it is hard to imagine why or how they should have evolved prior to the advent of syntax. The other possibility, that syntactic categories and syntactic features emerged automatically with the introduction of recursion, seems equally hard to imagine, since syntactic features are neither properties of the sensorimotor interface nor properties of the conceptual-intentional interface (though some of them are *related* to the latter – see Jackendoff (2002), section 5.9; Culicover and Jackendoff (2005), section 5.6 for my take on this). Of course, I'll be the first to admit that finding something hard to imagine doesn't make it false. On the other hand, it's also hard to imagine how syntax could work without these features, so it looks like they have to join recursion as part of the proposed single step.

I might point out as well that some people, including some linguists, think all these syntactic features either don't exist or arose through cultural innovation (see references above). This would make life better for the syntactocentric view of evolution, but on the other hand most practitioners of the syntactocentric view would fervently reject such a view of syntactic features.

Consider now the parallel architecture. In this architecture, semantic/conceptual structure is the product of a combinatorial capacity that is independent of syntax. This allows the possibility that thought was highly structured in our prelinguistic ancestors – they just couldn't express it. Such combinatorial thought could serve as a crucial preadaptation for the evolution of combinatorial expression: our ancestors had combinatorial thoughts that it would be useful to share. Moreover, the parallel architecture permits correspondences to be established directly between phonology and semantics, without syntactic mediation. It therefore leaves open the possibility of a hominid paleo- or protolexicon, storing associations of pieces of thought to vocal or gestural expression, without a syntactic component at all. Such a mechanism would not necessarily have to be digitized in the modern sense, but it would create the opportunity for evolution to discover the modern digitized form.

Such a system would lend itself to the production of multiple vocalizations to express combinatorial thought. (It is not clear to me whether such a development would require additional mutations, or whether it might be just a consequence of training up working memory.) An elaborate modern syntax is not

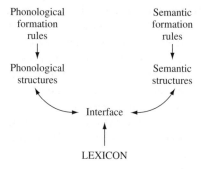

Figure 3.5. Architecture of protolanguage

necessary for this: since such vocalizations are necessarily in some linear order, the opportunity is present for using linear order to crudely express semantic relations, for example agents first, and modifiers adjacent to what they modify. This sort of organization is arguably found in present-day pidgins, which may lack any hierarchical organization of concatenated words. The system at this stage, roughly Bickerton's (1990) "protolanguage", looks like figure 3.5: the parallel architecture minus the syntactic component and its interfaces.

One can then see syntactic structure as the final capstone innovation, providing a more regimented way to conventionalize semantic relations among words, where the semantic relations and the words are already present in the pre-existing system, unlike in the syntactocentric theory.

In other words, with the parallel architecture, one can imagine various scenarios in which the language capacity evolves in stages, each adding an increment to the system's communicative efficiency and flexibility. There is a fair amount in Departments 3 and 4, but it is motivated by its incremental adaptivity. And the stages I've mentioned here can be articulated into still more gradual stages, as I've proposed in Jackendoff (2002). Some of these stages may be cultural inventions, but others, such as the digitization of phonology, the adaptation of headed hierarchical structure for syntactic purposes, and probably the capacity for dividing words into syntactic categories, seem to require fundamental innovations in the brain's representational capacity.

Thus the two theories of the architecture of language not only have important differences in how they account for the modern language capacity. They also lend themselves to quite different hypotheses about the evolution of language. Again, though, it's worth stressing that these hypotheses are more along the lines of plausibility arguments than evidence for one approach over the other.

What sort of evidence would one seek to help make these stories more than plausibility arguments? One issue I would see as crucial is the degree to which other animals can be shown to exhibit combinatorially structured thought. This need not be anything especially elaborate, such as recursive theory of mind. It just has to be complex enough to require some embedding and to allow some flexibility of behavior. Places I would be inclined to look for such a capacity would be in spatial cognition (as we've seen in figure 3.4), in action planning (Whiten 2002), and especially in social cognition, which involves fairly sophisticated integration of factors such as group membership, dominance, kinship, alliance, and history of reciprocation and conflict (Seyfarth and Cheney 2003). To the extent that combinatorial thought is possible in an organism without language, we might be correspondingly skeptical of the assumption that syntactic generativity is the source of thought.

Another question to ask is whether there are analogues elsewhere in human or animal cognition for the lexicon, which is an extensive store of associations of different types of structure. A possibility in human cognition is our vast knowledge of artifacts and how to use them – everything from buttons and doorknobs to steering wheels, tennis rackets, computer keyboards, and guitars. This involves an integration of visual and motor representations. Should this or some other capacity prove to be analogous to the lexicon, we can then ask if there are principles that permit the combination of its elements into larger complexes of thought and action. If so, are these principles more like the principles of mainstream generative grammar, which derive structures by rules extrinsic to the lexicon, or are they more like those of the parallel architecture, in which lexical items are an integral part of the interface components? Again, if a clear answer emerges, it tells us something about the overall texture of cognitive capacities. To the extent that the texture of the language capacity falls in with the other capacities, its components are at worst in Department 3, rather than in Department 4. And perhaps this other capacity will offer clearer clues about the course of *its* evolution that will shed some light on the evolution of language. You never know.

I note yet again that these are not questions that can be answered from the paleontological record. They are strictly arguments from reverse engineering. Maybe someday, when we understand more fully how genes build brains, we will be able to tighten the argument further. But for the moment I think the best we can do is set a direction, be clear about the questions, and not succumb to premature confidence or discouragement. What I hope to have shown here is that depending on what your theory of syntax and semantics and rules and lexicon looks like, you're going to seek different sorts of comparative evidence, both across the rest of human cognition and across the animal kingdom.

4   Three meanings of "recursion": key distinctions for biolinguistics

W. Tecumseh Fitch

Introduction

There has recently been a resurgence of scientific interest concerning the importance of various types of phrase structure in human language, and their potential presence in other species (Hauser, Chomsky, and Fitch 2002; Fitch and Hauser 2004; Everett 2005; Fitch, Hauser, and Chomsky 2005; Pinker and Jackendoff 2005; Gentner *et al.* 2006). Following Hauser, Chomsky, and Fitch (2002, HCF hereafter), many of these recent discussions have used the term "recursion," but the term has rarely been defined explicitly. There are several possible interpretations of this word, which is used somewhat differently in different disciplines, without there being one universally accepted scientific definition. With the recent advent of intense inter-disciplinary discussion of these issues, it has become clear that several different interpretations of the term are being used interchangeably. We seem to have reached a point where serious misunderstandings are in danger of propagating through the literature. The main purpose of this paper is to clarify these different meanings, and in the process to examine the implications of recent and ongoing experiments for different types of grammars in animals and humans.

My main research interest is in understanding the types of rules that structure acoustic signals and cognition in a wide variety of different vertebrate species, with the hope that this will provide a better basis for understanding the biology and evolution of the computational subsystems involved in human language. This should, in turn, provide a more focused behavioral foundation for neuro-scientific investigations, ultimately helping to uncover the types of neural computation necessary for human language. Although one component of such an investigation is to determine which of these mechanisms are unique to humans and/or unique to language, this is not my primary goal. In contrast, some researchers seem primarily concerned with discovering the key "mark" of language, the factor or factors that separate language, and humans, from all other systems. I personally find this question of little intrinsic interest, because I think language must be considered as a suite of mechanisms, no one of which is primary. Each component has its own biological basis and evolutionary past (Fitch 2005). Recursion, however defined, is but one of these components.

Why recursion?

The central theme of the HCF paper was the need for a broad and multi-component approach to language (which led to the FLB/FLN distinction: the faculty of language in broad and narrow senses), and the value of a comparative approach. Adopting a multi-component perspective first requires some specification of the mechanisms in question, and second a consideration of which of the many mechanisms involved in language are independent from other systems of cognition and communication. Recursion arose immediately as a core operation, appearing in many guises in syntax and semantics, for which there is little evidence in animal communication. Many of the other oft-cited differentiators of language from animal communication systems (Hockett 1960) could be plausibly supposed to follow from the combination of a recursive subsystem with preexisting conceptual structures, conditioned by the exigencies of a serializing phonological component. Furthermore, previous arguments for recursion in other cognitive domains such as music (Hofstadter 1979) remain empirically unconvincing. Recursion might be the language-specific mechanism that potentially differentiated language both from other human cognitive domains, and from known communication systems in animals. Surprisingly, recursion emerged as the only mechanism we could think of that was both crucially involved in language and at least arguably unique to it. All the other candidates were either disqualified by the existing data, or it seemed to us, plausibly subsumed under recursion combined with interface constraints. In HCF terms, this suggests that recursion is part of FLN. We considered other possibilities, especially theory of mind, but this may be shared with other cognitive domains (and indeed central to all aspects of human social and cultural behavior), and may also be present, based on new experimental data, in animals (Hare, Call, and Tomasello 2001). Peripheral specializations like a permanently descended larynx had recently been discovered in other species, and core components of language such as vocal imitation were well-known ingredients of other animal communication systems (Fitch 2000a; Fitch and Reby 2001).

Does the conclusion we reached imply that "language is recursion," as the "recursion-only hypothesis" that has been attributed to us (Pinker and Jackendoff 2005) supposedly claims? Of course not – neither we nor any other reasonable person would ascribe to this obviously false claim. HCF gives a long list of separate mechanisms involved in language. Theory of mind is clearly a prerequisite for proper pragmatic inference, as is imitation for a shared signal repertoire. Indeed a host of more basic cognitive capacities such as various forms of memory, auditory processing and motor control are all crucial, indispensable components of human language. Perhaps some phonetic specificities of the human auditory system and vocal tract are important for speech – though the evidence remains weak (Hauser and Fitch 2003) – but these don't apply to signed language. Few critics have challenged the idea that recursion is *a* crucial component of human language, and no one suggests that it is the *only* component. The most prominent critique, that of Pinker and Jackendoff (2005), is focused on their distaste for the minimalist approach to syntax, which was essentially unmentioned in our paper, rather than any fundamental disagreement about the nature, or the importance, of recursion.

So while I regret certain editorial decisions that perhaps made our argument more opaque than desirable (the paper, although long by *Science* standards, had to be cut to about half its original length), I stand by the focus on recursion in the original paper. Indeed, once various confusions and possible mis-interpretations are cleared up, I think the hypothesis that recursion is a uniquely powerful aspect of the human mind, brought crucially and uniquely into play in human language, remains a provocative and strong (in the sense of falsifiable) hypothesis. However, if this hypothesis *is* falsified (as most strong hypotheses eventually are in science), it will be by empirical study, not by clever argument. The remainder of this paper will thus be an attempt to, first, forestall further misinterpretation by clarifying several distinct uses of the term "recursion," and second, to explore some of the empirical issues involved in determining its presence in other cognitive domains or species. Such experiments are possible, though non-trivial, and a few on human subjects are already in progress. I hope it will also become clear why this hypothesis should be of interest to those interested in how the human mind and brain function.

Three interpretations of recursion

Recursion is one of the most critical and powerful concepts in mathematics and computer science. Like Oroboros, the mythical snake which, biting its own tail, represents the endless round of existence, recursive functions take their own past output as their next input, and potentially allow (in the absence of process-ing limitations) indefinitely complex output from even the simplest of functions. This basic idea – a simple route to boundlessly complex computation – is the aspect of recursion that binds all uses of this term together. However, there are some important subtle differences in usage, each potentially relevant to recent discussions in biolinguistics. These three interpretations (from computer sci-ence, linguistics, and meta-mathematics) do not exhaust the possibilities, but they provide three solid anchors in the space of possibilities. For more detail, textbooks are cited in the appropriate places below. An accessible introduction to recursion in its many guises can be found in Hofstadter (1979); its relevance to meta-mathematics is explored in Penrose (1989), Chaitin (2006) and to computer programming in Rohl (1984). I will give a brief discussion of some other variant interpretations after the main three. The computer science interpretation of recursion is the one I present first, and suspect most scholars would take to be canonical.

Computer science (CS) interpretation

A recursive function is one which calls itself (that is, where a command to run function x appears within the definition of function x itself).

By the definition above, recursiveness is determined by a particular aspect of its implementation (its definition in the programming language code). Recursiveness cannot be determined by the input-output behavior of the function alone, because there are typically many different ways to write a function that performs a particular task, only a subset of which are recursive.

For example, here is a recursive function definition in pseudocode:

```
define function Tree():
    ... do various things ...
    Tree(); // a recursive call to the same function
    ... do other things
```

Note that there seems a danger here of an infinite regress, where the function "Tree" calls itself *ad infinitum* and never ends. Programmers avoid this by having at least one situation in which the procedure does not call itself any more: it "bottoms out" with a non-recursive return value. After such a "termination condition" has executed, the overall program can work its way back out of the chain of recursive function calls, and finally finish up and return a value. For example:

```
define function Tree(variable):
    if variable = n
        then return(x) // termination condition
    else
        Tree(); // a recursive call
    ... do other things
```

As a more concrete example, here is a recursive function defining A^nB^n for all n greater than zero (the reason for choosing this particular function will become clear later):

```
define function AnBn(n) :
   if n is 1
        then return "AB"
   else
        return ("A" + AnBn(n-1) + "B"); // recursive call
```

Given some n, the function will call itself with n-1, n-2, etc until this variable finally reaches one. At this point, the function will bottom out and begin retracing its steps, finishing off the remaining work left by all of the previous calls. This ability to retrace a "stack" of function calls must be specifically designed into the programming language and hardware. Although some early computer languages did not allow recursion, today support for recursion is considered a necessity for any "real" programming language (Raymond 2004).

From a structural point of view, we might say that this function produces "center embedded strings", so-called because they embed "AB" strings in the middle of other "A_B" strings. However, the code *itself* contains no representation of structure (there are no trees representing the connections between various A and B components). Any embedded structure remains implicit in the stack of calls, not explicit in the function definition.

In contrast, here is an equally-intuitive non-recursive "iterative" function defining A^nB^n strings for all $n > 0$

```
define function AnBn(n) :
integer counter i;
A_section = "A";
B_section= "B";
if n > 1 then {
   for (i = 2) to (i = n)
        A_section = A_section + "A";
        B_section = B_section + "B";
   end
}
return A_section + B_section
```

Here, we never call the function A^nB^n within the function itself. Instead we use a counter that simply marches from 1 to n, adding A's and B's to the end of their respective strings, and finally returns both of them strung together. Here we might consider the structure to be of two "flat" trees, each of length n, connected into one larger A+B unit. But again, this structure remains implicit, and is not actually present in the data structure underlying the string.

These two programs will behave identically from the viewpoint of an outside program. Either program called with AnBn(3) will return AAABBB, either called with AnBn(4) will return AAAABBBB; and so on. In each case the realities of computers are that there will be some practical limit to how large n can be: in the recursive case this limit is the depth of the calling stack, while in the iterative case it is the maximum value of the integer i. These might be the same, but they are more likely to be different, and there is no a priori reason that one or the other should be larger. Thus, an outside programmer using someone else's compiled $A^n B^n$ function has no way of knowing which definition has been used to create that function. The only way to know is to look inside the function definition (to look at the source code), or perhaps to examine the lower-level behavior of the hardware that implements the function, by probing registers and logic gates with measurement devices.

Although the type of example above, where a function calls itself directly, provides the prototypical instance of recursion in computer programming, two other variants are worth mentioning. First, recursion is still present if function A calls function B, and then, before finishing, function B calls function A again. Such function pairs can be termed "mutually recursive". More complex variants are also possible, with three or even more functions calling each other recursively. Another less important variant, termed "tail recursion," is where the recursive call occurs at the end of the function (leaving no "unfinished business" behind to be completed). Although tail recursion may be elegant and useful for certain tasks (e.g. reversing a string of symbols), it is in some sense a degenerate case of recursion, in the sense that such functions can be automatically and mechanically rewritten non-recursively (this is what an optimizing compiler might do). Finishing off a stack of tail recursive calls simply entails reading off their already stored results, and the work done by each run of the function does not depend on the results returned by the self-embedded function calls.

It is worth noting that computer scientists will sometimes rewrite recursive functions as non-recursive functions, or vice versa, for reasons of clarity or speed. Iterative functions may execute faster than their recursive counterparts, and modern optimizing compilers may even replace a recursively defined function with its iterative equivalent. However, there are many algorithms that cannot be automatically rewritten iteratively,[1] and there are many problems in computer science (particularly those dealing with open-ended tree structures) where the recursive definition is preferable because it is more flexible and concise, or even the only practically viable option. Again, there is no a priori reason that non-recursive or recursive functions should be favored: it depends on the problem to be solved. However, if one wants to be able to deal flexibly with a variety of hierarchically structured data and programming constructs, recursion is an essential tool for the modern computer scientist (see, e.g., Knuth 1973; Skiena 1998; Raymond 2004).

Linguistic interpretation

A recursive rule is one which has the property of self-embedding, that is, in which the same phrase type appears on both sides of a phrase structure rewrite rule. So

S -> A S B; //an example of a recursive rule, while
S -> AB ; //is a non-recursive rule

Note that the two of these rules, together, can define the A^nB^n language (much as in the recursive computer example given above). Crucially, by the standard interpretation of phrase structure rules as generating not just strings ("weak" generation), but tree structures that reflect the process giving rise to those strings ("strong" generation), this definition generates structures properly termed "center embedded."

Two common examples of rules widely thought to be recursive in natural languages are the rules for generating embedded Sentences (S) and complex Noun Phrases (NP). For example, (abbreviating the definition of noun phrase for concision):

NP -> {"the dog," "the cat," "the tree," "the lake"}
NP -> NP + "beside" + NP

The latter recursive rule generates NPs like "the dog beside the cat," "the cat beside the tree beside the lake," and so on.

Repeatedly applying these two simple rules, we can, in principle, generate an infinite number of noun phrases. Note that despite a common misconception, the strings making up this infinite set are not themselves of "infinite length" (whatever that would mean). Each of the noun phrases produced is made up of a strictly finite number of words. The principle is simply that for any proposed "longest string" we can automatically generate an even longer one by simply adding "the dog beside" onto the front, or "beside the dog" to the end. This is exactly analogous to the uncontroversial mathematical fact that there is no largest integer, but each particular integer is finite (so we never need more than a finite (if astronomical) number of digits to specify any of them).

Thus far, linguistic recursion is directly analogous to the CS-interpretation. The key difference, alluded to above, is that the linguistic definition entails a self-embedded *structure* being specified (*strong* generation), in addition to the computed output string itself (*weak* generation). One can easily create computer programs that generate self-embedded recursive structures, so these two interpretations are not incompatible: algorithms including a "strong" structural component, in just this linguistic sense, and are part of the arsenal of any practicing computer scientist (most algorithms over trees are of this sort) (Rohl 1984; Skiena 1998). But a problem often arises if we hope to determine "from the outside" whether a system is or is not recursive in this linguistic sense. As for the computer example, the linguistic definition depends on the presence of self-embedding in the *implementation* of a recursive rule (e.g., the phrase structure rule S -> A S B;). The fact that this self-embedding rule additionally entails a self-embedded structure is an additional linguistic stipulation.

Empirical tests of linguistic recursion   Since at present we have no way to peer at the "source code" of our internal language faculty, what basis do we have for deciding if it involves recursion or not? Specifically, how can we determine if the crucial condition of *self*-embedding has been satisfied? One answer is based on our combined intuitions about whether a given string is grammatical or not, and whether the units are of the same type of referent. As language users, we know that "John is angry" is a sentence, and we know that "Mary thinks that John is angry" is also a sentence. We can then generalize the conclusion to say that any sentence can be preceded by the phrase "Mary thinks that ..." and it will still be an English sentence. That is, we have an independent way to cash out the claim that S can appear on both sides of the sentence-building rule: this fits the native speaker's intuition about what "counts" as a sentence and how one builds such sentences. Thus, the additional element of *semantic* structure is a crucial component of our judgment about recursion in natural language (in the strong linguistic sense).

Unfortunately this approach is of little use for exploring the computational capacities of other species, since it is far from obvious how one might ask a mockingbird or a humpback whale whether a given string is both grammatically acceptable and contains multiple members of the same class (e.g., "sentence," "moan phrase," etc.). Indeed a fictitious cetacean linguist interrogating a human might trenchantly ask us to *prove* that two constructs we term "sentences" and denote with the *S* symbol are both "the same". We would be left defending this claim based on our intuition, rather than on any objective facts about the strings themselves. We cannot prove, using finite data sets, that the underlying rule system is not non-recursive, as follows:

NP -> {the dog, the cat, the tree, the lake}
NP2 -> NP1 + "beside" + NP
NP3 -> NP2 + "beside" + NP1
NP4 -> NP3 + "beside" + NP2
etc ...

This rule system involves a new type of structure at the output of each rule, labeling each type of NP as different, and thus none of these rules are recursive. To any finite *n*, we can define a set of structures NP1 to NP *n* and do the job without using recursion. Inefficient and inelegant perhaps, but possible, and if our cetacean researcher insisted on this interpretation we would have little way to refute it without (as in the computer science example) looking at the underlying implementation, which in this case is in the brain rather than a computer program (or chip). Given our current state of technology and understanding in neuroscience, this might seem like the end of the (empirical) road for the study of recursion in humans.

Meaning as an empirical indicator of structure   Fortunately there is another possibility. In language, strings are not just combinations of meaningless characters, but map in a systematic way onto meanings. This suggests that we could use the correct *interpretation* of the meaning to probe the underlying structures assigned by the rule system. Thus, while there is nothing in the strings themselves which can tell us definitively whether the underlying rule system is recursive or not, if we have some independent empirical way to investigate the *conceptual structures* assigned to those strings by a language user, we can in principle exclude all reasonable non-recursive possibilities. We can use an orthogonal domain (meaning) to triangulate on the structure assigned to strings, and thus obtain behavioral evidence about the self-embedded nature of these structures (or lack thereof). We do not have to simply wait for neuroscience to mature in order for this question to be further explored (although the ultimate empirical test will still be at this implementation level). While not trivial, such experiments can be done today, and indeed may help neuroscientists by providing some behavioral tasks entailing recursive cognitive processing.

Given the facts just described, this is the interpretation of recursion that seems most relevant to human language. "Recursion" in this slightly more specialized sense refers to a recursive mapping between signals and their meanings. "Mapping" here denotes the bidirectional process by which particular meanings are assigned to particular signals, and vice versa. We can use this additional consideration to infer that a mapping procedure is recursive when it takes an unbounded set of meanings (object specifiers like "the dog," "the dog beside the tree," etc.) and assigns them to the same type of string (e.g. noun phrase: a specific noun with modifier). Note that syntactic nouns can be identified in meaning-independent fashion, so we can avoid tautology. For example, many singular noun phrases in English are identified by starting with a determiner, which thus provides a first-pass indicator of noun-phraseness. In other languages nouns might be syntactically defined by their ability to bear some inflectional marker such as gender or animateness.

Fortunately, the extra empirical purchase allowed by an additional dimension of meaning is not necessarily limited to language, but applies to any system where structure-dependent meanings or interpretations can be reliably assigned to signals. For instance in mathematics a person familiar with algebra knows that "$y = 4 \times 3$" is not only a complete and well-formed formula (unlike, say, "4 3 = +" or "= y + 3 4"), but also that this formula implies that "$y = 12$." Together, grammaticality judgments *and* value assignments of a string can obtain the dual purchase we need to investigate such recursion. Although there can be little question of the necessity for linguistic-style recursion in our interpretation of mathematical formulae, there also is little doubt that this ability is not an independent part of our biological endowment (indeed it is very likely directly parasitic on our linguistic capacities). Nonetheless, investigations of formula interpretation could prove quite useful for investigating recursion in a non-linguistic abstract domain, and for exploring its neural basis.

Similarly, in music one might use the fact that listeners make a key assignment to a short sequence of notes (e.g. interpreting the sequence "C E G" as implying a chord, and key of C) to probe for recursion in musical sequences which modulate (change key). Such a test is implied by Hofstadter (1979) in his discussion of recursion in Bach, though he proposed no experiments to test the suggestion. Bach, with the aid of his pen and paper, certainly kept the original key of a piece in mind when modulating (he "pushed the key onto the stack" to be popped off the stack later in reverse order), and obeyed a Baroque rule stipulating that one should end in the same key one started in. (Perhaps a better interpretation is that this constraint is a self-imposed challenge, since Bach seemed to delight in getting himself into difficult musical corners and then finding his way back out.)

However, this compositional constraint is little more than a mathematical trick unless *listeners* mirror this stack-pushing process, intuitively feeling that a piece must end in the original key, in order to be "complete" or "well-formed" or "grammatical." Perhaps the skilled and experienced listener to Baroque music would show this effect – but even here we must await experimental evidence, one way or another, before making any judgment on the matter. Again, such experiments are possible, but not trivial. In any case, much contemporary popular music modulates but does *not* return to the original key, and I am thus skeptical about whether Baroque modulation conventions show that "music is recursive" in any broadly shared, biologically meaningful sense. Outside of Western music, even the question of what constitutes a musical "grammaticality judgment," independent of key, remains difficult (one might consider the metrical framework as a possibly orthogonal syntactic system). The question of musical recursion thus, to my knowledge, remains empirically open.

In conclusion, the addition of a structural element to the linguistic interpretation of "recursion" extends it in an important way from the computer science interpretation, "upgrading" recursion from a question of weak (string-oriented) to strong (structure-oriented) generative power. In the case of language (or mathematical formulae), the addition of meaning provides more empirical purchase than would otherwise be available. In HCF the phrase "recursion and the mapping to the interfaces" implies this linguistic interpretation. In retrospect this was apparently not clear to many readers (perhaps "recursive mapping between signals and meanings" would have been more transparent). Such mappings crucially allow linguistic recursion to be something, in principle, that we can test for behaviorally in our own species. In animals the more direct neuroscientific route, mapping out the neurophysiology and connectional anatomy, probably remains our best bet at present. Recursion, in the linguistic sense, but applied to non-linguistic domains, allows for behavioral testing, unlike the CS-interpretation.

A meta-mathematical interpretation: "recursive function theory"

In general, mathematicians use the term "recursion" in much the same way as computer scientists, canonically to designate proofs "by induction." In this type of proof, a function f is defined at some particular value x using its own, previously defined, value at some other values (e.g. $f(x-1)$), again with a single value or simpler function providing the non-recursive ground condition. This usage is directly analogous, *mutatis mutandis*, to the two usages already discussed, and the corresponding *operation* of "primitive recursion" is an indispensable tool in mathematical proof.

However, in the rarified branch of meta-mathematics known as "recursive function theory" (developed by such pioneers as Peano, Gödel, Church, Post and Kleene), another usage of "recursive" has come into use, based upon, but far more general than, any of the previous ones (for reviews see Davis 1958; Cutland 1980; Epstein and Carnielli 2000). The terminological problem is that the class of "recursive functions," as defined here, includes some functions *that do not use the recursion operation in their definition*. Thus, for instance, a function giving all of the even numbers is termed a "recursive function," even though it can be implemented with simple iteration. This terminological infelicity arises because the aim of this branch of mathematics is to reach to the outermost limits of what formal mathematics (and computers) can grasp, and indeed to go beyond it. Because this goal is quite different from, and far more abstract than, that of the previous two disciplines, it has led to a potentially confusing terminological difference that I will attempt to clarify further.

In meta-mathematics, "(partial) recursive" has come to denote a class of functions, essentially synonymous with "computable," and thus to encompass virtually all algorithmically specifiable functions. Two other categories, "primitive recursive" and "m-recursive" (a.k.a. "general recursive") are subsets of this class of functions, but each is still vast in extent, and includes many functions which do not make use of the primitive recursion operator at all. All of these classes include any function made up of some basic functions (zero, successor, and projection) combined using certain operations (composition and primitive recursion for "primitive recursive", and additionally "least search" for "partial" and "general recursive") (my terminology follows Epstein and Carnielli 2000). Since any of the functions so created are termed "primitive/partial/general recursive," even the lowly zero function ($f(x) = 0$ for all x) is "general recursive", as is any composition of, say, the zero and successor functions.

By this terminology, the simple "increment" operator (for example a counter function that says, "add 1 to a value") already yields a "primitive recursive" function, and virtually any algorithm, program or calculation would count as recursive. Thus the C or Java statement x++ means add one to x. As an example, the successor function implemented in a simple iterative loop:

```
define function successor{while i > 0 : print i++}
```

will, when seeded with i=1, print the string of integers forever (or at least as long as the computer keeps working). While not involving recursion in the CS or linguistic senses, by the meta-mathematical definition this function is a member of the class of "general recursive functions" as well as "primitive recursive functions." Thus, the interpretation of "recursive," as embodied by the mathematician's terms, differs considerably from the two earlier interpretations. This is because the terminology arose as part of the larger foundational concerns of meta-mathematics, in the context of a very different and difficult task: attempting to define and delineate the notion of "effectively computable." "Recursion" in the ordinary sense of self-referential inductive proof is, in this context, just a simple but powerful tool in this much wider endeavor, hardly in need of terms and distinctions of its own.

The historical circumstances leading to the adoption of this terminology in pure mathematics are explored in detail by Soare (1996), which I recommend. For now, it suffices to say that this well-established mathematical usage of "recursive function theory" is neither universally accepted (indeed Soare and others decry it), nor in keeping with usage of "recursion" in other disciplines. It also appears to be in decline, with the term "computability theory" apparently replacing the older name. Neither computer scientists nor linguists would generally consider a simple iterative function with a fixed bound to be recursive in any sense, despite it being a member of the meta-mathematical class of primitive recursive functions. However, because these specific terms are well established in the branch of mathematics concerned with the theory of algorithms and computation, one might well encounter these definitions, and perhaps even think they are somehow more basic or correct than the computer science or linguistic definitions. I flag the existence of this body of terminology for those who encounter it and, like myself, find it confusing.

Technical terms are of course simply tools that we can define and use as we like, and polysemy is only dangerous when it goes unrecognized. As far as I can tell, these broader all-inclusive definitions are never intended when linguists or computer scientists use the term "recursive," so there is typically little room for ambiguity in these fields. However, in that merger of mathematics and linguistics called formal language theory, all three of these definitions have some chance of coming up, and it becomes crucial to specify which meaning is intended. If necessary, we could distinguish the normal computer science usage as "self-calling recursive functions" and the usage above as "iterative recursive functions," though it is difficult for me to see why the term recursion should be applied, at all, to bounded loops. It is true that one could write x++ in some computer languages as x = x + 1; with a superficial appearance of recursion. Perhaps this might (mis)lead one to apply the term "recursive" to such functions. But of course, in pure mathematical terms, this formula is always false, as there is no number x that is the same if you add one to it, and the example trades on the polysemy of the "=" symbol in computer programming, which can signify both the assignment of a value, or a Boolean comparison in logic. This quirk of programming syntax should not in general lead to any deeper confusion between iteration and recursion.

Other uses of the term "recursive": "recurrence"

The three examples above provide anchors in the semantic space occupied by the term "recursion," but still do not exhaust the possibilities. One occasionally encounters uses of "recursive" in engineering for any circuit involving feedback (where "feedback" is the more standard and appropriate term, or where other terms such as "infinite impulse response" are used to denote recurrence of vectors rather than of single numbers). There is a mostly extinct thread of tradition in neural modeling which uses the term "recursive" for any network which feeds back signals into itself (e.g., Kamp and Hasler 1990). Given such variant uses, we clearly need to distinguish between those feedback systems that are "truly" recursive, in the sense of self-calling or self-embedding, from those that simply feed back a signal and lose the results of prior computation at each timestep.

A simple feed-forward net takes its inputs, maps them through zero or more internal or "hidden" layers, and then produces an output, with no backwards interactions. However, many networks today take the output signal and feed it back (at least partially) into the input layer (Medsker and Jain 2000). Such networks are more typically called *recurrent* (as in Elman's "simple recurrent networks" or SRNs), rather than recursive. For such systems the term "recurrent" is well suited and widely used. The crucial distinction between recurrent and recursive systems concerns whether the system preserves the structure of the signal fed back at each timestep, so that the system must be able to cope with arbitrarily complex input structures. In recurrent systems all past inputs are averaged or otherwise combined; while in recursive systems they remain potentially distinct. In linguistic recursion, the structure providing new input at each timestep grows ever more complex, and this complex structure is represented and preserved. This is also the case in many computationally recursive implementations, particularly those manipulating tree structures, which require a stack of unbounded storage capacity to achieve this. In contrast, an SRN or similar network *always* has the same number of input units, regardless of how many iterations of feedback it receives, and cannot handle more complex input. The structure of the network itself thus provides a sharp limit to the complexity of the fed-back signal that it can deal with (in fact this same argument applies in greater force to the use of "recursion" for iteration, where, in a fragment of computer code like $x=x+1$, there is only a single value through which the feedback can occur). This distinction between recurrent and recursive is respected in almost all modern treatments of connectionist networks (Medsker and Jain 2000), particularly those that deal with language, where true recursion, rather than simple recurrence, is of the essence (e.g., Stoianov 2000).

If a researcher interested in language wishes to preserve their usage of the term "recursion" for simple loops involving feedback or iteration (in my opinion perversely, as it will hinder rather than aid clear communication), they should at least signal this crucial distinction between self-embedding, structure-preserving recursion (in either the CS or linguistic senses) and other forms of feedback. Recurrence is a ubiquitous element of the vertebrate nervous system (e.g. in spinal reflex arcs), and the recurrence implemented in many neural nets mirrors a prominent aspect of the mammalian neocortex, which has substantial and elaborate feedback connections among cortical areas. Given this ubiquity, virtually any aspect of human cognition is neurally recurrent, and language certainly makes use of recurrence as well (particularly at the sensorimotor interface, in vocal motor control). Recurrence is thus a widely shared element of the faculty of language in a broad sense. Equally clearly, a circuit which "remembers" past structures only for a single computational time-step is not capable of representing or processing arbitrarily complex structures, and recurrence will not by itself provide a mechanism for expressing indefinitely complex thoughts.

Discussion

Despite the relative consistency of usage within each of these separate fields, there is ample room for confusion and miscommunication once interdisciplinary discussions begin. This is clearly evidenced by recent discussions of recursion (or lack thereof) in animal signal perception and grammar induction.

Recursion and the Chomsky hierarchy

A prominent current confusion results from the mistaken idea that success in parsing the A^nB^n grammar discussed above is a litmus test for recursion. The first place I saw this misinterpretation was, to my dismay, a commentary on Fitch and Hauser (2004), written by David Premack, appearing in the same issue of *Science*: "In a paper on page 377 of this issue, Fitch and Hauser (4) report that tamarin monkeys are not capable of recursion. Although the monkeys learned a nonrecursive grammar, they failed to learn a grammar that is recursive. Humans readily learn both" (Premack 2004: 318). In fact, our paper did not mention recursion, because A^nB^n is not a test for recursion. However, a later paper by Perruchet and Rey (2005) apparently assumed that we shared Premack's assessment of our experiment, disputing our "claim" about A^nB^n "generating center-embedded sentences." Most recently, Gentner *et al.* (2006) concluded that starlings are able, with training, to master the A^nB^n grammar, and titled their paper "Recursive syntactic pattern learning by songbirds." The abstract states that A^nB^n is a "recursive, self-embedding, context-free grammar." The accompanying commentary by Gary Marcus continues the error, asserting that "The A^nB^n language ... is generally assumed to be recursive" (p. 1117).

This notion that A^nB^n requires recursion is incorrect, and appears to reflect an inadequate grasp of computer science and formal language theory (e.g., Sipser 1997; Gersting 1999; Hopcroft, Motwani, and Ullman 2000; Linz 2001). In formal language theory, A^nB^n is generally accepted (at least since Chomsky 1957) as a canonical grammar beyond finite-state capabilities, and nothing else. Although one *could* implement A^nB^n recursively, one can also implement it iteratively without recursion (as the code snippets in section 2.1 above illustrate). Furthermore, a finite-state system like the $(AB)^n$ grammar used in Fitch and Hauser (2004) could *also* be implemented recursively. Here are the two rules that do so, the first recursive:

$S ->$ "AB" $+ S$;
$S ->$ "AB"

Therefore, the question of recursive implementation is orthogonal to the analysis of grammatical power embodied in the Chomsky hierarchy, and specifically to the finite-state/context-free distinction, for which A^nB^n *is* a valid test, as a system indisputably beyond the finite-state level.

For these reasons, Fitch and Hauser (2004) did not suggest the A^nB^n grammar as a test for "recursion" – indeed the word will be found nowhere in that paper – but as a particular grammar that, because it is beyond finite-state capabilities, can be used experimentally to distinguish the weak generative power of grammars in formal language theory. The crucial factor distinguishing A^nB^n (and similar e.g. mirror grammars) from any finite-state grammar is that it requires some additional memory mechanism(s) to keep track of "n." A function capable of distinguishing A^nB^n from A^nB^m (where *n* and *m* are different) must be able to compare the counts across the two "phrases" – and it is this comparison that is beyond finite state capabilities. The memory that allows this could be implemented via a push-down stack, a persistent counter or increment variable (as in my non-recursive code snippet), or other possibilities (e.g. a queue-based memory generating structure *beyond* the context-free level). *Any* of these possibilities puts A^nB^n beyond the reach of a finite-state grammar; but none of them is necessarily recursive. Only if we knew the *structure* assigned to strings from a grammar could we begin to determine, behaviorally, if it involved a recursive implementation, as I have stressed above. (Our choice of a center-embedded structure in the figure illustrating an A^nB^n string may have implied recursion to some readers (e.g., Perruchet and Rey 2005), but it is only one of several possible structures that could be assigned).

Thus, for either of the two main interpretations above, it is an error to see success at recognizing strings from A^nB^n (as for starlings) as indicating recursion, or to see failure at the same task (as for tamarins) as necessarily implying a lack of recursion. Determining if recursion is used requires either "looking under the hood" (that is examining the source code, or the hardware implementation – the domain of neuroscience) or some independent behavioral means of evaluating structure (as discussed above for music or mathematics). Is there perhaps a sense in which success at recognizing the stringset defined by A^nB^n could indicate recursion in the mathematician's sense discussed last? It appears not. Although that sense would entail that A^nB^n is "primitive recursive," it also entails that the much simpler $(AB)^n$ language is "recursive" in this same sense. Thus, I can see no valid sense in which the finding of Gentner *et al.* – that starlings can recognize A^nB^n – justifies a claim that starlings have recursion, or "challenges" HCF. What Gentner *et al.* have shown may nonetheless be quite important: it suggests that starlings can master a language beyond finite state (context-free, or perhaps beyond), and this opens the door to both further behavioral testing as well as neuroscientific investigation. Can birds also succeed on a mildly context-sensitive language, of the sort believed to be necessary for certain aspects of human language (Joshi, Vijay-Shanker, and Weir 1991; Stabler 2004)? Someday, we may find that starlings indeed solve the A^nB^n task recursively (though I wouldn't bet on it). But until the neuroscientific work is done, the findings neither demonstrate, nor even strongly imply, that starlings solve the A^nB^n recognition task recursively.

Are there languages that lack recursion?

Another issue that has garnered considerable attention in recent discussions is field linguist Daniel Everett's claim that Pirahã, a language of the southwestern Amazonian Basin, lacks recursion (Everett 2005). For several reasons this claim is difficult to evaluate. First, virtually all Pirahã are monolingual, and none of them are linguists – so we currently lack any reports from a native speaker about their grammar. There are only two non-native but reasonably fluent speakers of Pirahã with linguistic training – Daniel and Keren Everett – and they disagree (in personal communication) about this and many other questions about Pirahã linguistics. Finally, Daniel Everett's own earlier work freely discusses, and gives many examples, of complex phrasal embedding in Pirahã (e.g., Everett 1986; Everett 1991) and these data have been effectively used to challenge Everett's more recent arguments (Nevins, Pesetsky, and Rodrigues 2007). Thus, until other linguists become competent enough in Pirahã to evaluate Everett's most recent claims, they remain unconvincing, based on Everett's own prior authority. Certainly, as Everett concurs in personal communication, Pirahã speakers can construct and communicate recursive thought structures like any other human group, and thus they must have self-embedding of *conceptual* constructions. The remaining question, concerning the linguistic mapping of such structures onto phonological surface form via embedding vs. parataxis, does not concern any underlying cognitive or neural competence. The relevance of the Pirahã to the discussion in HCF thus seems exaggerated (cf. Fitch, Hauser, and Chomsky 2005), and the overall arguments in Everett (2005), like those of Pinker and Jackendoff (2005), primarily concern differing opinions about how linguistic research should be conducted, rather than about recursion *per se*.

The future: why recursion matters

One might well ask, given the confusion surrounding the term "recursion," whether one should continue to find this ability interesting, and worthy of scientific pursuit. The answer is definitely "yes," and the reason is quite simple: the core idea of recursion is clear and unambiguous, and it is the simplest and most powerful route to the type of unbounded expressive power that is a crucial feature of mathematics or language. To see this, imagine a "protolanguage" equipped with vocal imitation (and thus an open-ended shared vocabulary) and a basic finite-state level syntax that combined nouns and verbs (Bickerton [1990, 2000] has developed such a speculative protolanguage in considerable detail). This system would allow its users to express (to themselves and others) a wide range of useful concepts and could even instantiate Hockett's "design features" of duality of patterning and displacement, along with other more basic semantic attributes like predication.

What such a system would *not* be able to do is generate or parse constructions beyond a pregiven canonical level of specificity or generality. Recursive embedding of phrases within phrases is an important tool allowing language users to express *any* concept that can be conceived, to whatever degree of accuracy or abstraction is needed. The achievements of human science, philosophy, literature, law, and of culture in general depend, centrally, upon there being no limit to how specific (or how general) the referents of our linguistic utterances can be. Without this capacity, language might be a useful concrete communication system, perhaps even adequate for the majority of day-to-day social communication that modern humans engage in. But such a system would obviously be sharply limited, compared to the system we actually have, as a system for expressing thought. A protolanguage lacking a flexible and unbounded means of expressing any concept would be stuck at a prosaic, predetermined level of description and representation. Useful and adaptive, perhaps, but a pale shadow of the endlessly expressive language that we all have, and mostly take for granted.

Surely, then, the distinction between language as it actually exists, and a hypothetical non-recursive "protolanguage" is an important one. And equally surely, the means by which our finite brains achieve this unfettered potential expressivity is a fascinating open question for scientists in all branches of cognitive science, and especially for cognitive neuroscientists. Whether linguistic recursion, in the sense clarified above, turns out to be unique to language or shared with (say) music or vision remains another open and interesting empirical question, as does the question of whether it such a capacity is shared with other animals. But it is the computational *power* recursion grants us that is the central issue, not its uniqueness or lack thereof.

I am a pluralist with respect to the "interesting questions" in biolinguistics, and have nothing but encouragement for the biolinguist who finds other questions more interesting, or more empirically tractable, than those discussed here. There are certainly enough fascinating open issues in human language to keep many busy tilling these fields for many decades to come, for example concerning the mechanisms underlying vocal imitation, social learning, or the biology and evolution of theory of mind (some are discussed further in Fitch (2005, in press)). But further scientific inquiry into linguistic recursion – how it is implemented neurally, how the implementation is coded genetically, and how it evolved – will be an important component of any future science of biolinguistics. Studying recursion empirically poses some challenges, but they are not insurmountable once potential confusions are cleared up. Thus, in my opinion, it would be perverse to deny the importance of recursion as it is employed in human language, given that it is at the heart of one of the characteristics that makes language so precious and irreplaceable for our species: what Humboldt aptly termed "the infinite use of finite means."

5   On obfuscation, obscurantism, and opacity: evolving conceptions of the faculty of language

Marc D. Hauser

Let me start out with an experience that I assume is relatively familiar. You have just landed in a foreign country, speak only the most minimalist version of the local language, and try to get by, generating telegraphic utterances about toilets, banks, and places to eat. Largely, you feel deeply misunderstood and frustrated, but occasionally enjoy the novelty of your experiences, including the people you meet along the way and the attention you sometimes receive. The response to my paper on the evolution of the language faculty with Chomsky and Fitch (2002) has left me in a similar state. Sometimes I think, based on the confusion surrounding our paper, that we must have been speaking an utterly foreign language. At other times, paraphrasing one of my favorite Dawkins-isms, I think there is a wanton eagerness to misunderstand, misconstrue, or fabricate. Sometimes I yield to a more charitable view and assume that we failed to make our position clear because of a telegraphic attempt to articulate a complicated set of arguments and proposals for both the prior history of work on this topic as well as potentially fruitful directions for the future. And sometimes I think that the state of play in the study of language evolution is doomed to endless obfuscation, obscurantism, and opacity! This feeling was reinforced when our follow-up attempt to clarify the original arguments (Fitch, Hauser, and Chomsky 2005) in response to the critical paper by Pinker and Jackendoff (2005) failed as well, at least by my own sampling of several commentaries, in print (Bickerton 2007; Everett 2005; Gentner *et al.* 2006; Goldberg 2003; Tomasello 2004; Treves 2005), online (Dessalles 2004) and in spoken conversation during conferences and colloquia. I only had one recourse: find the nearest pub and drink heavily.

Time has passed. Lest we leave the interested reader thinking that we are martians from another planet, I hope to set the record straight here on some of the critical distinctions raised in the original paper, and why I think they are critical for an empirically anchored research program on the evolution of language.

Warning: Before you read further, everything that follows pertains to my own particular views, and is not necessarily shared by either Chomsky or Fitch.

In so far as they agree, I am delighted. In so far as they disagree, I am sure they will let me know.

Setting the record straight

The following comments are in response to either printed publications or to discussions following my own or a colleague's lectures.

I am not an anti-adaptationist

I fully adhere to the Darwinian research program, and use it whenever I can (e.g., Palleroni, Miller, Hauser and Marler 2005). That I am also interested in mechanisms, and sometimes don't see how the adaptationist perspective yields novel insights for language, is a different issue. To date, I don't find that natural selection theory provides any guidance with respect to empirical research on the evolution of linguistic structure. That is, it is not entirely clear how thinking about selection and adaptive design gives us any leverage on such problems as why "Why" moves to the front of a sentence in English but not overtly in Chinese, why only some languages have a singular–plural distinction, why there are dependencies between certain semantic structures but not others, and why particular aspects of a phrase structure are dominant. By making this claim, I am not rejecting out of hand the possibility of a Darwinian approach to these features of language, but I am not optimistic. Instead, I have used the comparative method to explore commonalities and differences among animals, humans included, focusing on the three core components of the language faculty (syntax, semantics, phonology) and their interfaces. On this note, I must note a puzzling point made by Bickerton (2007) in a commentary on our original paper. He introduces the discussion by stating that the paper's "magisterial tone was surprising, considering how little work any of its authors had previously produced in the field." I can't think of a definition of "little work" that makes any sense here. Speaking for myself, prior to the 2002 publication of Hauser, Chomsky, and Fitch, I had published a 750-page book on the evolution of communication (Hauser 1996), linking animal and human work, a paper in *Science* on rhythm discrimination in monkeys and human infants (Ramus *et al.* 2000), a paper on statistical learning with leading psycholinguists (Hauser, Newport, and Aslin 2001), a paper on fundamental frequency declination, and much more; and prior to Bickerton's commentary, many more papers emerged, including another in *Science* with Fitch on finite and phrase structure processing (Fitch and Hauser 2004). Fitch (see this volume) had published many other high-profile papers as well, focused on issues of speech production and perception. And Chomsky (see this volume) had written a number of articles on how insights from evo devo may illuminate current work in linguistics, especially in terms of physical constraints and optimal design on syntactic structure and computation. I guess these don't count, or perhaps they count as just a *little work*. Oh well.

I did not say that language has nothing to do with communication

I think everyone will agree that to say that language is simply another form of communication, perhaps more powerful than other animal forms, is to diminish some of the most interesting aspects of human language. The computations underlying language are involved in communication, and other aspects of non-communicated thought. Empirically, I am interested in both those computations that are involved in language and enter into communication, as well as those computations that may never see the communicative light of day, at least in other animals. That is, I want to leave open the possibility that some of the computations that are involved in human language and communication are only involved in non-communicative functions in other animals. It is also logically possible that some of the computations involved in human language are not involved in human communication.

The take-home message is not that the study of animal communication is irrelevant

Given point 2 above, I can see how it is possible to interpret our paper as a flat-out rejection of all work on animal communication – either the communicative signals that emerge naturally or what we can learn from training animals with artificial systems. This inference is incorrect. I continue to do work on animal communication (Egnor, Iguina, and Hauser 2006; Egnor, Wickelgren, and Hauser 2007; Miller, Dibble, and Hauser 2001; Miller, Iguina, and Hauser 2005), and have great respect for and interest in the work of others in this area (Bradbury and Vehrencamp 1998; Cheney and Seyfarth 2005; Searcy and Nowicki 2005). That said, the arguments developed in our paper opened the door to a different set of relevant findings. Specifically, by recognizing the possibility that some of the computations underlying human language may be present in other animals, but not operative in their communicative systems, we opened the door to looking at other kinds of behavior and other kinds of animal systems. In particular, and as we alluded to in the original paper and our follow-up, some of the computations that underlie spatial navigation (e.g., path integration and minimal search) may be, in some sense, analogous or even homologous to computations in language and yet never enter into these species' communicative systems. These arguments have recently been picked up, albeit somewhat generally, by other researchers, most notably Wolpert, Doya, and Kawoto (2003) in their discussion of motor control.

The statement that our sensory-motor system is homologous or analogous with other animals' systems was not stated as fact, but as a hypothesis

Scientific claims are only as good as the empirical evidence. This is not to say that theories are uninteresting if they lack empirical support. Empirically, naked theories can be extremely interesting. I have proposed, both alone (Hauser 2001), and in papers with Fitch (Fitch and Hauser 2002) and Chomsky (Fitch, Hauser, and Chomsky 2005), that the current empirical evidence supports the hypothesis that many of the sensory-motor systems that underlie phonological computation are homologous or analogous to sensory-motor systems in other animals. That this empirical foundation is thin, with many interesting phenomena yet to be explored, is both true and irrelevant with respect to a test of the hypothesis. The sensory-motor system covers a vast and rich set of processes, including especially the phonological system (Yip 2006), but of those explored (e.g., formant production and perception, categorical perception, rhythmic discrimination), a substantial proportion are present in other animals.

The hypothesis is not *recursion only!*

First, a mea culpa for an unfortunate cutting of corners in the abstract of Hauser, Chomsky, and Fitch (2002). In that abstract, we did state, as a working hypothesis, that recursion represents the critical ingredient in what makes human language unique. What we later clarified, both in the original paper and in our response to Pinker and Jackendoff, is the more completely developed hypothesis: what is unique to human language are the computations underlying narrow syntax as they interface with semantics and phonology; the mappings are critical as they may well represent what is in FLN, that is, distinctively human and linguistic. Further, these mappings or interfaces are likely to cover up a good deal of complicated machinery, including translational devices that enable distinctively phonological representations to contact distinctively semantic representations, generating lexical entries. This hypothesis may turn out to be false. It also may turn out to be true that recursion alone is the critical ingredient that sparked the evolution of the language faculty, leaving plenty of room for subsequent modifications.

I am not *a closet minimalist*

A bit of history here. The motivation for the original paper was straightforward. Chomsky had just given the Teuber lecture at MIT on "Language and the Brain" and, during his presentation, raised many points concerning language evolution and specifically, some of the ideas I had floated many years back in my book *The Evolution of Communication* (1996). Following the presentation, we corresponded a good deal over email, including three-way exchanges with Fitch, including discussions of prior history, especially the apparently mistaken views on both sides of the divide between linguistics and biology. The emails were rich. Following these discussions, we decided to write something together, attempting to flesh out one perspective on the faculty of language, its core components, and potential evolutionary history and uniqueness as a domain of knowledge. As important, from our perspective at least, was an attempt to diffuse some of the acrimonious debates of the past, and showcase possible avenues for future research, carried out collaboratively, with linguists helping animal biologists and psychologists to target crucial aspects of the faculty, and animal scientists in turn, showing linguists what is possible and how such work can inform current linguistic theory. At the time of the writing, Fitch and I had little understanding of the minimalist program. We developed the ideas and wrote the paper with minimal understanding of minimalism, and with only a nod to a few potentially relevant citations. Let me be very clear: our original paper may well have been music to those who adhere to the minimalist program, but I personally had no intention of writing their libretto.

One more bit of history: when we sent in our initial response to Pinker and Jackendoff's critique, we had a section responding to their comments on minimalism. Due to space constraints imposed by the journal, this section was unfortunately cut out; for those interested in this response, it has been posted on my website as "Appendix. The Minimalist Program: www.wjh.harvard. edu/~mnkylab/publications/recent.htm.

What is the difference between FLB and FLN and why you should care

One of the biggest sources of confusion in the literature, and in conversation, appears to be that between the faculty of language in the broad sense, or FLB, and the faculty of language in the narrow sense, or FLN. Here is how I see the distinction. FLB represents all those organism-internal capacities that are necessary to support language. Memory is one such capacity. Memory plays a critical role in both language production and comprehension, but it is not specific to language, entering into many other domains of thought and representation. What is in FLB are those processes that are neither unique to humans nor unique to language. FLN, in contrast, represents those organism-internal capacities that are both unique to humans and unique to language. What we proposed was "in" FLN, repeating the definition above, are those computational capacities supporting narrow syntax (including recursion) as they interface with the systems of semantics and phonology.

Several points of clarification. As stated, our definition of FLN (as opposed to the hypothesis regarding what it entails) has two critical comparative ingredients, specifically, comparative in a taxonomic or phylogenetic sense and comparative in a domains of knowledge sense. What this means strategically, at least in terms of empirical work, is that if someone finds evidence in a nonhuman animal of a capacity that enters into human linguistic processing in a non-trivial and non-derivative sense, then this capacity is automatically eliminated from FLN, and moved into FLB; that is, the capacity enters into language processing, but is not specific to it or to our species. In contrast, if a fairly exhaustive comparative search fails to find evidence for a capacity that enters into language processing in humans, this does not automatically enter it into FLN. At this point, it is necessary to explore other domains of knowledge. Thus, we know that at some level, recursive operations enter into language, music, mathematics, and vision. These may, however, all be derivative of language. Though determining what is or is not derivative will not be easy, one can take something like orthography as an example of a human specific ability that is entirely derivative of language. More importantly, for operations such as the combinatorics that enable the limitless expressive capacity of language, what may be in FLN is how this computation interfaces with domain-specific representations such as those in semantics and phonology. What may be in FLN, then, are the interfaces alone (i.e., the mechanisms that enable cross-talk between different representational systems), making the three core components of language (computational rules, semantics, phonology), on their own, part of FLB; needless to say, I am not committed to this possibility, and think that it is quite likely that certain kinds of conceptual representations are uniquely human and unique to language, and most certainly, the distinctive features of phonology are likely to be as well. There is also a final possibility that we did not make explicit in the original paper: FLN may be completely empty. It is logically possible that none of the computations that enter into language, either on their own or as interfaces, are uniquely human and unique to language.

Given my personal interests in comparative studies of animals, as well as comparative studies of other domains of knowledge such as music (Hauser and McDermott 2003) and morality (Hauser 2006), I find the flavor of the FLB-FLN to be a useful guide. Whenever I think about critical tests in animals or humans, I immediately appeal to this distinction, thinking about how tests of other species, both closely and distantly related, may help flesh out the comparative phylogenetic claim. I also think about how comparable tests could be run across different domains of knowledge in our own species. I hope I am not alone in finding this distinction useful, at least as a guide to empirical research.

The future looks bright, so don't wear shades

In collaboration with many terrific students and colleagues, I have had the pleasure of watching and contributing to a new subdiscipline that I have called *evolingo* (Hauser, Barner, and O'Donnell 2007), modeled on evo devo (Caroll 2005; Kirschner and Gerhart 2005), and framed to explore the possibility that a significant set of core computations underlying human language are present in other animals, but without the requisite interfaces to systems of sensory-motor output or conceptual-intentional representations. These attempts have been greatly bolstered by a number of other experimenters and labs (Arnold and Zuberbuhler 2006; Toro and Trobalon 2005; Toro, Trobalon, and Sebastian-Galles 2003; Toro, Trobalon, and Sebastian-Galles 2005; Watanabe, Yamamoto, and Uozumi 2006), generating findings of considerable significance to our understanding of language evolution. Of course, all of these findings are both of great interest and open to alternative accounts (I include my own), but in most cases, with relatively clear paths ahead. To illustrate, a few words on my paper with Fitch (Fitch and Hauser 2004) in which we set out to test pieces of what some have called the *Chomsky hierarchy*. The basic idea, initially, was to design an experiment that would be of direct relevance to those working in formal linguistics, especially syntax, and which, irrespective of the outcome of the work, would provide insights into some of the potentially shared or unique components of the language faculty. We tested cotton-top tamarins on two artificial grammars – $(AB)^n$, which is an example of a finite state grammar, and A^nB^n, which is an example of a (context-free) phrase structure grammar. We used a familiarization-discrimination method in which the A category was associated with one set of speech syllables whereas B was associated with a second set of highly distinctive speech syllables. Under these test conditions, tamarins successfully extracted the $(AB)^n$, but failed on the A^nB^n. We concluded the paper by suggesting that tamarins may be hindered by a "specific and fundamental computational limitation on their ability to spontaneously recognize or remember hierarchically organized acoustic structures … Thus, the acquisition of hierarchical processing ability may have represented a critical juncture in the evolution of the human language faculty." We also pointed out that further confirmation of this hypothesis would require tests with other species, grammars, and methods.

I think this paper was an important start, reinforced in part by ensuing commentary and follow up studies in other species and with other methods (Friederici 2004; Gentner *et al.* 2006). But the negative commentaries, offline discussions with colleagues, and two papers that I have written with colleagues as co-authors (O'Donnell, Hauser, and Fitch, 2005; Rogers, Pullum, and Hauser in review), has made me appreciate some problems with this initial study, as well as many of the others on artificial grammar learning. Without going into the details, which can be read elsewhere, A^nB^n was not the best choice for at least one good reason: success on the A^nB^n grammar leaves open many different possible mechanisms underlying this competence. Thus, even if the tamarins had successfully extracted this grammar (showing discrimination between grammatical and ungrammatical test exemplars), the results would not provide specific information about the mechanism used, because there are different ways to generalize from the initial, familiarization input, to the novel test trials. In other words, a success with A^nB^n would certainly indicate that tamarins have access to computational resources that, with respect to expressive power, exceed those classically associated with finite state grammars. A success would not, however, pinpoint the specific computation in play.

The problem inherent in A^nB^n is not unique to this grammar. Artificial language learning experiments are notoriously difficult to design and interpret. The next phase of exploration will involve studies carefully designed to anticipate possible alternative accounts that control for low-level cues (or testing their impact), using a variety of methods, including developmental studies involving looking time, brain imaging experiments of adults, and a variety of approaches to testing animals. Only with converging results from different techniques and different species can we expect this research paradigm to yield valuable results. Concerning the issue of design, my students and I have begun exploring the quite large space of computations covered by the finite state languages, and in particular, those that can be explicated by tapping the riches of formal language theory (Rogers, Pullum, and Hauser in review). For example, my students and I are currently testing starlings, tamarins, rhesus monkeys and chimpanzees on a rather simple stringset called *some-B*, in which strings (tokens of this class) include As and Bs, and either begin with a B or include an AB pair. Thus, for example, in a habituation-discrimination paradigm with rhesus monkeys, we would use their vocalizations as exemplars to represent A and B, such as A->grunt and B-> coo. In habituation, they would hear stimuli consisting of multiple exemplars of a grunt with one coo vocalization (i.e., the B sound) placed somewhere in the string of grunts. In the test-discrimination trials, subjects would hear new "grammatical" strings consisting of new string lengths or positioning of the coo, and "ungrammatical" strings that are identical in string length to the grammatical stimuli, but lack a coo. If subjects have extracted some-B from the habituation material, then they should respond more to ungrammatical strings lacking a coo (i.e., no B).

Concerning methods, though we initially made considerable use of the looking time procedure using both speech and, more recently, species-specific vocalizations, we have now embarked on the implementation of new methods, some involving operant training, others tapping more ethologically natural behaviors such as the antiphonal calling responses of cotton-top tamarins to patterned input (Egnor *et al.* 2007). The broad comparative sweep that includes comparative in the phylogenetic sense as well as comparative in the methodological sense is essential to the potential success of this line of questioning. In particular, it is only by testing a broad range of species that we will both learn how something evolved, as well as whether claims of uniqueness are justified.

Further, by implementing a broad range of methods we not only increase our confidence in the robustness of our findings by triangulating on a problem from different angles, but we can take advantage of the different methods to explore how a capacity is not only acquired but implemented and maintained. Thus, for example, the overwhelming majority of the phenomena explored by linguists are not taught in schools and at some level, appear innately specified. That said, if animal researchers attempt to explore whether other organisms have the capacity to generate or understand such phenomenon, it is important to distinguish between a spontaneously available capacity and one that involves considerable training or experience to express. If nonhuman animals share with humans a capacity that is implemented by the language faculty, then it is certainly not uniquely human or unique to language. But if these animals can only acquire or express this capacity following substantial training, then the difference lies in mechanisms of learning as they interface with the linguistically relevant computations.

Let me end where I started, but on a more positive note. Though I have expressed frustration with the reception of our paper, I feel as did Oscar Wilde who noted that it is better to be criticized than ignored. I also sense that the study of language evolution has entered into a new phase, with different theoretical approaches, experimental procedures, and test populations, and significantly, far less speculation and far more empirical evidence. I hope these clarifications help. If not, let me know and I will return to the pub for consolation.

Part II

Language and interface systems

6   Prospection as a cognitive precursor to symbolic communication

Peter Gärdenfors and Mathias Osvath

What are the significant forces behind the evolution of language?

Explaining how language evolved involves answering two quite distinct scientific questions (Bickerton 2003; Tomasello 2003). The first is why humans have developed a system of *symbolic* representation as a basis for much of their communication. The second is why this system has acquired the structural characteristics of the *syntax* of extant human languages. In this paper, we focus on the first question.

Homo sapiens is the only species we know to have a symbolic language. If one believes that language has come into existence according to the principles of evolutionary theory, there should be some selective advantage that has promoted the development of language among humans. Recently, a popular approach has been that language arose as a result of increased *social interaction*, for example as a consequence of increasing group size (Dunbar 1996) or as some form of ritualization (Deacon 1997; Knight 1998b).

However, despite all the merits of these proposals, they have problems explaining why humanlike symbolic language has *not* evolved among other apes or animals (Bickerton 2002: 209; Gärdenfors 2004: 237; Johansson, Zlatev, and Gärdenfors 2006). As a matter of fact, the social interaction among many species is highly developed. Bickerton (2002: 210) argues: "When a complex and unique development occurs in only one species, the most logical conclusion is that the selective pressure driving that development must have been unique to that species. Thus the strength of social intelligence in other primates argues against, not for, social intelligence as the force behind the emergence of language."

The upshot is that some other evolutionary forces behind the evolution of language must be identified – forces that have only applied to the hominin line. One factor that has been surprisingly neglected in the discussions of the evolution of language is the difference in the *ecology* of the early hominins and the other apes (Bickerton 2002). Partly following Osvath and Gärdenfors (2005), we shall argue that the Oldowan culture, 2.6–1.5 million years ago, constituted an eco-logical niche containing evolutionary forces that generated symbolic cognition. The long-ranging character of this culture made the use of prospective cognition, that is the skill to plan for future events and needs, beneficial. The second step of our argument is that advanced prospective cognition made communication about future goals advantageous for the hominins. The evolutionary gain of being able to communicate about referents that are not yet present is that collaborative forms of long-term planning become possible. Symbolic communication is an efficient way of solving problems concerning cooperation about future goals – more efficient than iconic miming, as we shall argue.

The basis for our hypothesis is the notion of prospective cognition. This will be the topic of the following section. In the section after that, we outline the Oldowan culture and explain why this culture contained the selective pressures for evolving a symbolic language. The next section discusses the new possibil-ities for cooperation, in particular cooperation about future goals, which open up once prospective cognition is present. Cooperation is enhanced by commu-nication, and in the final section we argue that a symbolic system is required for efficient cooperation about future goals.

Prospective cognition

One way to understand the functions of most of the higher forms of cognition is to analyze how humans and other animals represent various things and states, in particular the surrounding world and its possibilities. There is an extensive debate in the literature on what is the appropriate meaning of "representation" in this context (see e.g., Roitblat 1982; Vauclair 1990; Humphrey 1993; Gärdenfors 1996, 2003; and Grush 1997). In order to give intelligible descrip-tions of many phenomena in animal and human cognition, it is useful to distinguish between two kinds of mental representations: *cued* and *detached* (Gärdenfors 1996, 2003).

A *cued* representation stands for something that is present in the current external situation of the representing individual. In general, the represented object need not be actually present in the situation, but it must have been triggered by something in a recent situation. Also delayed responses, in the behaviorist's sense, are based on cued representations according to this charac-terization. When, for example, a particular object is categorized as food, the animal will then act differently than if the same object had been categorized as a potential mate. We are not assuming that the individual is, in any sense, aware of the representation, only that there is some generalizing factor that determines its behavior.

In contrast, *detached* representations may stand for objects or events that are neither present in the current situation nor directly triggered by some recent external situation. A memory of something that can be evoked independently of the context where the memory was created would be an example of a detached representation. For example, consider a chimpanzee who performs the following sequence of actions: walks away from a termite hill, breaks a twig, peels its leaves off to make a stick, returns to the termite hill, and uses the stick to "fish" for termites. This behavior seems very difficult to explain unless it is assumed that the chimp has a detached representation of a stick and its use. A detached representation is something the individual can utilize regardless of whether what it represents is present or not.

A detached representation can even stand for something that does not exist at all. For example, our imaginative worlds are full of centaurs, unicorns, elves, and trolls – about which we easily communicate – although they do not truly correspond to any sensory impressions we have received. Being able to use a detached representation requires that one can suppress the sensations one has at the moment; otherwise they will come into conflict with the representation (Glenberg 1997). This capacity places new demands on mental capacities. The suppression of information appears to be managed by the frontal lobes of the brain, which are the parts that have expanded most rapidly during the evolution of the hominins. The frontal lobe is believed to be crucial for skills such as planning and fantasizing and for the so-called "executive functions" of self-control (Hughes, Russell, and Robbins 1994).

This notion of detachment is related to Hockett's (1960) "displacement" which is one of the criteria he uses to characterize what constitutes a language. But the notion of a detached representation is not identical with his. The reason is that the definition of "displacement" (Hockett 1960: 417) includes the following: "Any delay between the reception of a stimulus and the appearance of the response means that the former has been coded into a stable spatial array, which endures at least until it is read off in the response." This description has a clear behaviorist ring to it, and it means that every signal that is not an immediate reaction to a stimulus would be counted as an example of "displacement" according to this criterion.

The collection of all detached representations of an organism and their interrelations will be called *the inner world* of the individual. There are strong indications that humans have more complex inner worlds than other animals (Gärdenfors 2003). Gomez (2004: 20) argues that the prolonged immaturity in the children of apes and in particular humans results in a greater flexibility in forming representations which in turn leads to greater cognitive and behavioral flexibility.

The ability to envision various actions and their consequences is a necessary requirement for an animal to be capable of *planning*. Following Gulz (1991: 46), we will use the following criterion: An organism is planning its actions if it has a representation of a goal and a start situation and it is capable of generating a representation of partially ordered set of actions for itself for getting from start to goal. This criterion presupposes representations of (1) goal and start situations, (2) sequences of actions, and (3) the outcomes of actions. The representations of the actions must be detached, otherwise the organism has no choice. According to our characterization, planning therefore presupposes an inner world.

There are several clear cases of planning among primates and in other species (see e.g., chapters 5, 7, 8 and 9 in Ellen and Thinus-Blanc 1987; Gulz 1991: 58–61; Byrne 1995; Suddendorf and Corballis 1997; and Hauser 2000). The termite-fishing chimpanzee mentioned earlier is one such example. It is important to distinguish between immediate planning for present needs and prospective planning for future needs Gulz (1991) calls prospective planning anticipatory planning, a term that we also used in Gärdenfors (2003) and Osvath and Gärdenfors (2005)). The crucial distinction is that for an individual to be capable of prospective planning it must have a detached representation of its *future needs*. In contrast, immediate planning only requires a representation of the current need.

It has been commonly argued that the prospective skill for planning for future needs is exclusive to humans (e.g. Gilbert and Wilson 2007; Köhler 1921, 1925; Premack 2007; Roberts 2002, 2006; Suddendorf and Corballis 1997, 2007; Tulving 2005). This is sometime called the Bischof-Köhler hypothesis. However this hypothesis can no longer be upheld in the light of recent findings. Great apes are not only able to select tools for future use (Mulcahy and Call 2006), but also to save tools that have currently been used to satisfy a desire (Osvath 2009a). Even tool making for future needs has been documented in chimpanzees (Osvath 2009b). Perhaps most importantly, great apes are able outcompete current drives in favor of future ones as well as being able to envision future events (Osvath and Osvath 2008). Interestingly enough, this ability to plan for future needs also seems to have evolved independently in the avian taxon of corvids (Correia, Dickinson, and Clayton 2007; Raby *et al.* 2007).

It is notoriously difficult to obtain unequivocal observations of such prospective planning behaviors in the wild. However, this difficulty should not be confused with the absence of the cognitive skill. Rather, the lack of observations might be a result of the complexity of the situations in the wild involving factors we cannot control for. Hence it is most often appropriate to give leaner interpretations of behaviors seen in the wild than to ascribe the animal a skill for planning for future needs. On the basis of this we want to make two general points. The first is that the most reliable sources of information we have about planning for future needs are the artifacts surrounding future-oriented behaviors. These are found in abundance when it comes to humans, but are very scarce when it concerns non-hominin species. Given the findings of great ape and corvid planning abilities, this indicates that the skill for planning for future needs did not start evolving as an answer to an artifactual culture (as we have argued elsewhere: Osvath and Gärdenfors 2005). It is not unlikely that prospective cognition indeed has its roots in advanced social life (Osvath and Gärdenfors 2007). This leads to the second point: The skill for future planning was to substantial extent already present in the first hominins as they shared their last common ancestors with the rest of the great apes. This means that when the ecological situation changed, this skill could be exploited in the survival strategies of the hominins.

Oldowan: a long-ranging culture

The appearance of the first sharp-edged stone tools in the archeological record roughly coincides with a series of other relevant events in the human evolution. Ice sheets started to grow in the northern parts of the world and Africa experienced deforestation and expanding savannahs. The increased grasslands reduced the floral food resources for the hominins, as the savannah is only about half as productive as a tropical forest. On the other hand, the production of herbivores on the savannah is almost three times as high, yielding a markedly larger mammal biomass (Leonard and Robertson 1997, 2000). These ecological changes resulted in selective pressures on the hominins that lead them to change their diet from predominantly vegetarian to more protein and fat based. The resulting culture is associated with the finds at Oldowan (Isaac 1982, 1984). The sharp stone edge appears to be a direct answer to this shift as even the earliest finds of Oldowan technology are associated with butchering (de Heinzelin et al. 1999; Semaw et al. 2003). It is also likely that the stone tools were used for woodworking and processing plant materials, as is indicated by a microwear analysis of 1.5 million-year-old Koobi Fora stone artifacts (Keeley and Toth 1981). Bickerton (2002: 213–214) argues that the savannah conditions forced the hominin to use a wider variety of food sources than the other primates and that these food sources were more transient and scattered than the predominantly vegetarian food sources exploited by the other primates. From this he concludes that the day ranges of the early hominins must have been larger than those of extant apes.

There is clear evidence that *transport* of the artifacts (at least the stone tools) was an important trait of the Oldowan culture (Toth 1985). Another important and distinctive feature in the new increased meat eating lifestyle is the accumulation of tools and bones (hominin meal leftovers) at certain places in the plio-pleistocene landscape. Although these accumulations have been interpreted in numerous ways, some assumptions are fairly undisputed: Stone tools or their raw material as well as pieces of carcasses were transported to these locations from kilometers away (Toth 1985; Plummer 2004).

Plummer (2004) summarizes the main components of the Oldowan culture as: (1) the manufacturing and use of stone tools; (2) the transport of artifacts (at least the stone tools); (3) the transport of pieces of carcasses; and (4) the use of accumulation spots. The most significant advantage of this culture is that it enabled a much wider exploitation of species that provided meat. The conglomerate of cultural and other environmental factors and their implications, behavioral and others, were causally intertwined in complex and intricate ways. It is not quite clear who manufactured the Oldowan tools, but Plummer (2004: 127) concludes his analysis by saying that *Homo habilis* was probably the maker between 2.3 and 2.0 million years ago and *Homo ergaster* between 2.0 and 1.6 million years ago.

The Oldowan lifestyle was in a way signified by an extension in time and space. For example, there were long delays between the acquisition and the use of the tool, as well as considerable geographical distances between the sources of tool raw material sources and killing sites. The fitness of the hominins in this niche would increase with adaptations for long ranging, as shown in the morphological remains. These morphological adaptations must also have been related to behavioral adaptations. We submit that the behavioral adaptations relied on prospective cognition. This cognition was most likely within the capacity of these hominins, because extant great apes also display such abilities. However, we submit that these cognitive skills became more important for the Oldowan hominins and had an obvious ecological use.

Our first example supporting this concerns the curated technology (Toth 1985) that is represented by the Oldowan culture. Plummer (2004) summarizes the curated characteristics as follows: "Oldowan was not simply an expedient technology: the repeated carrying of artifacts for use at different points on the landscape may reflect pressure to curate or economize, based on a current or projected need for stone." There certainly seem to have existed projected, that is, detached, needs within the Oldowan culture. It is not possible to know exactly where the next fresh kill will be found; it might be several kilometers away from nearest raw material source. Without sharp-edged stone tools in the immediate vicinity, a carcass would lose much of its value for a hominin. The big predators and scavengers would probably not allow enough time for the hominins to locate the nearest tool source, not to mention all the extra energy that would be lost in a non-planned search for tools. This problem could be solved by habitual stone carrying.

However, just carrying tools is a strategy that lacks flexibility. If a hominin can envision which area it is going to patrol, then it can decide if it has to bring raw material for tools or not. Transporting something that would not be needed is uneconomic. The strategy of accumulating stones of the preferred raw material in areas where no stones can be found is beneficial, since long periods of haphazard transports are avoided. This strategy becomes even more effective if one keeps track of the resources available in a given accumulation spot: neither letting it run out of stones nor wasting energy by carrying stones to an already abundant supply. Prospective cognition would solve this task swiftly. Another aspect of Oldowan culture seems to be the saving of a tool (or a core) after it has been used once. It is needless to point out the great economy in such behavior. With prospective cognition one "knows" that there will be a need for the tool in the future as well. Prospective cognition opens up a very flexible selectivity that can be used with high precision and efficiency depending on one's current imagined goal related to a future need.

Our second example of prospective thinking that had selective effects concerns division of labor. This form of prospective cognition could in fact be used to turn the group of hominins into a virtual Swiss army knife, which would benefit every individual within the group. A division of labor within the group could solve a multitude of needs at once. Some individuals might carry throwing stones, some might carry sharp edges and others could carry water or wooden tools. It is a way of optimizing the carrying resources of the group, which is probably already burdened with carrying infants. Such cooperation requires a shared goal outside the scope of the immediate drive state, and, more importantly, it is dependent on an advanced form of communication.

Another form of division of labor associated with the *Homo ergaster/erectus* is a sexual division in foraging. Scavenging or hunting was arguably mainly a male concern. One of the simple reasons for this is that hominin children could not maintain the speed and endurance of the adults in the presumed patrolling activities, as children are less energy efficient (see e.g., Plummer 2004) and of course slower and weaker. Children were most probably close to their mothers, who must have been somewhat more stationary due to care of their infants. And among other things, the bipedal foot of hominin infants (and the loss of bodily hair) makes it impossible for them to cling to their mothers. Unlike other primates, the hominin mothers therefore had to use their arms to carry their babies (see e.g., Savage-Rumbaugh 1994). Females would thus have been engaged in a "slower" foraging, such as gathering high quality plant food. This kind of division is a common foraging strategy in modern tropical foraging societies where males provide most of the energy and protein to the diet (Kaplan *et al.* 2000).

The modern human form of hunting and gathering is highly dependent on prospective cognition. The individual must in some sense be able to imagine other individuals currently outside his or her immediate sensory scope doing their part of the job. The strategy does not allow the individual an immediate consumption of all the obtained food, even if there is a drive state that signals hunger. Individuals must also at some times ignore high-energy food and focus on their task, hunting or gathering (a standard procedure for most hunter-gather foragers), in order to achieve the main goal – a variable and nutritious meal.

These examples present some reasons why complex prospective cognition was beneficial within the Oldowan culture. Once the period of Acheulean tools is reached, beginning about 1.5 million years ago, it is apparent that prospective cognition was in full use. Overall, it could be said that prospective cognition fits well with the lifestyle of the hunter/scavenger-gathering and highly energy-consuming *Homo ergaster/erectus* (Plummer 2004: 128). Hominins used an already existing cognitive capacity to cope with the changing ecological requirements. It is not unlikely that the new demands chiseled out a more fine-tuned and complex prospective cognition. However, it should be noted that the prospective skill is obviously not a cognitive necessity when dealing with savannah conditions. Many animals use different kind of strategies. Nevertheless, it seems that the most efficient adaptation for these primates was to use prospection and planning.

Collaborating for future goals

Humans as well as some animals cooperate in order to reach common goals. There are many ways of cooperating, some of which are not cooperation in the literal sense of the word. Among these one may count more or less instinctive coordination of behavior, such as it emerges among termites building hills or honeybees gathering food. At the opposite side of the scale, we find human cooperation, depending on elaborate long-term planning and negotiation (Gärdenfors 2007).

The hominin life on the savannah opened up for many new forms of cooperation for future goals. For example, Plummer (2004: 139) writes: "Given that body size often predicts rank in the carnivore guild, an individual *Homo habilis* would likely not have fared well in a contest with many of its contemporary carnivores. Competition with large carnivores may have favored cohesive groups and coordinated group movements in *Homo habilis*, cooperative behavior including group defense, diurnal foraging (as many large predators preferentially hunt at night) with both hunting and scavenging being practiced as the opportunities arose, and the ability (using stone tools) to rapidly dismember large carcasses so as to minimize time spent at death sites."

For many forms of cooperation among animals, it seems that representations are not needed. If the common goal is present in the actual environment, for example food to be eaten or an antagonist to be fought, the collaborators need not focus on a joint representation of it before acting. If, on the other hand, the goal is detached, that is, distant in time or space, then a *common representation* of it must be produced before cooperative action can be taken. For example, building a shared dwelling requires coordinated planning of how to obtain the building material and advanced collaboration in the construction. In general terms, cooperation about future goals requires that *the inner worlds of the individuals be coordinated*.

To show the evolutionary importance of cooperation for future goals, Deacon (1997: 385–401) suggests that the first form of symbolic communication is marriage agreements, that is, deliberate commitments to pair bonding. He argues that there was strong evolutionary pressure in hominin societies to establish relationships of exclusive sexual access. He says (Deacon 1997: 399) that such an exclusive sexual bond "is a prescription for future behaviors." Even though we do not know of any evidence that marriage agreement was the first form of symbolic communication, we still find this example interesting in the discussion of early prospective cognition. A detached pair-bonding agreement implicitly determines which future behaviors are allowed and not allowed. These expectations concerning future behavior do not only include the pair, but also the other members of the social group who are supposed not to disturb the relation by cheating. Anybody who breaks the agreement risks punishment from the entire group. Thus in order to maintain such bonds, they must be linked to social sanctions. With the aid of some form of ritual, one can mark out that there exists a loyalty bond for the rest of the group and that the appropriate sanctions are now in function. It should also be noted that episodic memory is required to be able to *refer* to the established loyalty bond later on, by miming or by speech, and to remind group members of the sanctions (Atran 2002: 159–160).

A marriage is a special case of a *contract*. Creating contracts is an advanced form of cooperating for future goals so it is no wonder that it is a uniquely human activity. The reason for this that a contract presumes that both partners have a "theory of mind": If we agree that I shall deliver a duck tomorrow in exchange for the axe you have given me now, I believe that you believe that I will deliver the duck and you believe that I believe that our agreement will then be fulfilled, etc. Furthermore, a contract depends on the possibility of *future* sanctions: If I don't deliver the duck, you or the society will punish me for breeching the agreement.

The need for symbols in communication about future goals

Symbolic language is the primary tool by which agents can make their inner worlds known to each other. In previous work (Brinck and Gärdenfors 2003; Gärdenfors 2003, 2004; Osvath and Gärdenfors 2005), it has been proposed that there is a strong connection between a lifestyle dependent on prospective cognition and the evolution of symbolic communication. In brief, the argument is that symbolic language makes it possible to efficiently *cooperate about future goals*.

Language is based on the use of representations as stand-ins for entities, present or just imagined. Use of such representations replaces the use of environmental cues in communication. If somebody has an idea about a goal she wishes to attain, she can use language to communicate her thoughts. In this way, language makes it possible for us to *share visions* about the future. The question that has to be answered is why symbolic communication is necessary for this kind of communication.

Tomasello (2003: 95) defines symbolic communication as the process by which "one individual attempts to manipulate the attention of, or to share attention with, another individual. In specifically linguistic communication ... this attempt quite often involves both (a) reference, or inviting the other to share attention to some outside entity (broadly construed), and (b) predication, or directing the other's attention to some currently *unshared* features or aspects of that entity." As we shall see below, we cannot fully accept this definition. One aspect that is missing in his characterization is that, depending on the character of the "outside entity," different cognitive demands on the individual whose attention is manipulated will be relevant. To understand the differences, one must distinguish between (1) entities that are present in the shared environment, (2) entities that are not present in time or space but about which there is some common knowledge, and (3) entities that are unknown to the other individual. Communication about future goals often involves entities of the third kind.

Depending on which type of entity is communicated about, different minimal forms of communication are required. It becomes very natural to map the three kinds of entities to be communicated about to Peirce's (1931–1935) triad of index, icon and symbol:

(1) If the entity is present, then *indexical* communication, for example pointing, is sufficient. In general, animal communication consists of signals, referring to what is present at the moment in the environment, be it food, danger or a mate. This form of communication does not presume that the signaler ascribes any mental representation of the communicated object in the mind of the receiver. It is important to note that this kind of communication does not require any form of symbols. (This is why we do not fully accept Tomasello's definition presented above.) Consequently, as long as all communication concerns present entities, there will be no evolutionary pressures for the use of symbols.

(2) If the communicated entity is not present, direct signaling will not work. If I want to refer to a deer that I saw down by the river yesterday, merely pointing will not help, nor will a call signal. This form of communication clearly requires detached representations. *Iconic miming* may establish the reference, but only if the signaler and receiver have sufficient *common knowledge* about the indicated entity and there are sufficient cues from previous communication or the environment to make it possible for the receiver to identify the object. (This would be a case of what is called triadic miming in Zlatev, Persson, and Gärdenfors 2005). When the relevant entity is an action, this form of communication works particularly well. By using icons, one agent can show another how to act in order for the two of them to reach a common goal. Icons can work as an imperative, urging the receiver to "Do like this!" (Brinck and Gärdenfors 2003).

(3) The most difficult type of communication concerns *novel* entities that do not yet exist. Collaboration about future goals may often fall within this category. Here the signaler can neither rely on common knowledge about the entity, nor on cues from the environment. Iconic communication might work in exceptional cases, but we submit that it is for this

kind of communication that *symbols* prove their mettle. For example, if I have come up with an idea about how to build a new kind of defense wall around our camp, it is very difficult to see how this can be communicated by miming alone. In particular, if the communication involves the predication of Tomasello's definition above, that is, directing the other's attention to some currently unshared features or aspects of that entity, symbols seem to be crucial (see also Dessalles [2007]). Such a predication process will also require the productivity and compositionality of a symbolic system.

In this characterization we use "symbolic communication" in a basically Peircian way, meaning that the act is conventional and breaks up compositionally into meaningful sub-acts that relate systematically to each other and to other similar acts (Deacon 1997; Zlatev, Persson, and Gärdenfors 2005). This form of communication is, as far as we know, uniquely human. In this context it should be noted that Tomasello's (2003: 95) definition of symbolic communication that was presented above also covers what we call indexical and iconic cases.

An important feature of the use of symbols in cooperation is that they can set the cooperators free from the goals that are available in the present environment. Again, this requires that the present goals can be suppressed, which hinges on the executive functions of the frontal brain lobes. The detached goals and the means to reach them are picked out and externally shared through the symbolic communication. This kind of sharing gives humans an enormous advantage concerning cooperation in comparison to other species.

Again, we can refer to the role of contracts. Agreeing on a contract involves a form of prospective cognition. For example, when promising to give you a duck tomorrow in exchange for the axe you are offering me now, I must consider the possibility of future punishment. A contract is therefore a kind of cooperation about the future. Forming the agreement that constitutes the basis of a contract involves an advanced form of communication that may be difficult to achieve without using symbols.

We view the advantages provided by cooperation about future goals to be a strong evolutionary force behind the emergence of symbols. More precisely, our thesis is that there has been a co-evolution of cooperation about future goals and symbolic communication (cf. the "ratchet effect" discussed by Tomasello [1999: 37–40]). However, without the presence of advanced prospective cognition, the selective pressures that resulted in symbolic communication would not have emerged.

Conclusion

Prospective cognition is a key feature in the cognition of humans and is essential for language and other behaviors identified as unique for our species. This cognitive trait is fundamental in cooperation for future goals as well as for symbolic communication. We have argued for the use of prospective planning in the Oldowan culture, partly based on transport over extended space and time.

The second part of the argument is that the new ecological factors within the Oldowan artifactual culture together with the use of prospective cognition opened up for new forms of cooperation involving future goals concerning non-existing entities. Such cooperation has resulted in selective advantages for the individuals within cooperative hominin groups. The new forms of cooperation created a need for a communication in order to share visions about the future goals. We have argued that the required form of communication is symbolic since this form makes it much more efficient to communicate about detached needs and goals. In support of this, Peirce (1931–1935: 4.448) writes: "The value of a symbol is that it serves to make thought and conduct rational and enables us to predict the future."

The evolutionary relationships between cooperation, symbolic communication, and prospective cognition are probably intertwined in complicated co-evolutionary processes. The pre-Oldowan hominins were probably on the brink of symbolic communication. Most of the cognitive prerequisites were in place due to previous selective pressures. Merely a push in the symbolic direction was needed. Such a nudge was facilitated by the conditions of the Oldowan culture. Coherent with evolutionary theory, this suggests that there was a gradual shift into symbolic cognition, in contrast to explanations relying on discontinuity (e.g. Bickerton 1990).

7   Did language evolve before speech?

Michael C. Corballis

It is generally agreed that language is uniquely human, at least in the narrow sense of a recursive, generative structure that can convey an unlimited variety of different meanings (e.g., Hauser, Chomsky, and Fitch 2002; Jackendoff 2002; Pinker 1994). This implies that language must have evolved at some time since the hominid lineage split from that leading to modern chimpanzees. There is conflicting evidence as to the precise date of this occurrence, with a recent suggestion that there was an initial split some 7 million years ago, followed by a period of hybridization, then a second split some time after 6.3 million years ago (Patterson *et al.* 2006). The distinguishing characteristic of the hominids was bipedalism.

Nevertheless it was not until the emergence of the genus *Homo*, from around 2 million years ago, that there is evidence of a shift from ape-like mentality toward more human-like cognition. Stone tool industries have been dated from about 2.5 million years ago in Ethiopia (Semaw *et al.* 1997), and tentatively identified with *Homo rudolfensis*. However these tools, which belong to the Oldowan industry, are primitive, and some have suggested that *H. rudolfensis* and *H. habilis*, the hominid traditionally associated with the Oldowan, should really be considered australopithecines (e.g., Wood 2002). The true climb to humanity probably began with the emergence of the larger-brained *Homo erectus* around 1.8 million years ago, and the somewhat more sophisticated Acheulian tool industry dates from around 1.5 million years ago (Ambrose 2001).

It therefore seems likely that language evolved, perhaps from a more prim-itive, agrammatical "protolanguage" (Bickerton 1995), during the past 2 million years. There is nevertheless conflicting opinion as to precisely when language would have reached its present level of syntactic complexity. In this chapter I contrast two scenarios: An early scenario in which language evolved gradually over the past 2 million years, and a late scenario in which language emerged only with or after the appearance of our own species, *Homo sapiens*, some 200,000 years ago. I review the evidence for these different scenarios, and go on to suggest that they can be reconciled if it is supposed that language itself evolved gradually, but that it was based in the first instance on manual gestures, with gradually increasing vocal involvement. Hence it was not language itself that emerged with *Homo sapiens*, but rather the capacity for autonomous speech.

An early scenario

It is commonly assumed among evolutionary psychologists that the human mind was largely shaped during the Pleistocene (Tooby and Cosmides 2000). This epoch is formally dated from 1.81 million years ago to 11,500 years ago, although it has been argued that it should be dated from as early as 2.58 million years ago (Suc *et al*. 1997), which corresponds more closely to the emergence of the genus *Homo*. Although there is doubt as to the status of *rudolfensis* and *habilis*, there can be little doubt that important changes were heralded with the emergence of *Homo ergaster* in Africa and *ergaster*'s cousin *Homo erectus* in Asia. First and foremost, there was a rapid increase in brain size from some 2 million years ago to around 1 million years ago. According to estimates based on fossil skulls, brain size increased from an average of a chimpanzee-level 457 cc in *Australopithecus africanus*, to 552 cc in *habilis*, to 854 cc in early *H. erectus* (also known as *H. ergaster*), to 1016 cc in later *H. erectus*. Thereafter there was a more gradual increase to 1552 cc in *H. neanderthalensis*, and back to 1355 cc in *H. sapiens* (Wood and Collard 1999).

This very rapid increase in brain size over the first million years of the genus *Homo* may have been driven by the global shift to cooler climate after 2.5 million years ago, when much of southern and eastern Africa probably became more open and sparsely wooded (Foley 1987). This left the hominids not only more exposed to attack from dangerous predators, such as saber-tooth cats, lions, and hyenas, but also obliged to compete with them as carnivores. The solution was not to compete on the same terms, but to establish what Tooby and DeVore (1987) called the "cognitive niche," relying on social cooperation and intelligent planning for survival. The pattern of activity probably changed from simple foraging to hunting and gathering. The increase in brain size may therefore have been driven by selection for such cognitive characteristics as theory of mind and mental time travel (Suddendorf and Corballis 1997; 2007), requiring more complex computational ability.

It is highly likely that communication during this period evolved from a simple protolanguage to a form of true language involving increasingly sophisticated grammar. As Pinker (2003: 27) put it, it became increasingly important to encode, and no doubt express, propositions as to "who did what to whom, what is true of what, when, where, and why." Given the complexity of human language, it also seem reasonable to suppose that it evolved relatively gradually, through natural selection, rather than as the result of some sudden mutation (Pinker and Bloom 1990). Consistent with such a scenario, Jackendoff (2002) has outlined the series of steps by which true language might have evolved.

A late scenario

Despite these considerations, there has been a persistent view that true language did indeed emerge suddenly, with or even after the appearance of *Homo sapiens*. This so-called "big bang" theory is often attributed to Bickerton, who wrote that "true language, via the emergence of syntax, was a catastrophic event, occurring within the first few generations of Homo sapiens sapiens." (1995: 69)[1] Even more radically, Crow (2002) has proposed that a genetic mutation gave rise to the speciation of *Homo sapiens*, along with such uniquely human attributes as language, cerebral asymmetry, theory of mind, and a vulnerability to psychosis. There is perhaps an echo of Descartes in these views, and a hint of the miraculous.

Indeed Chomsky (1975b) once even questioned whether language was a product of natural selection at all, suggesting that it may have arisen simply as a consequence of possessing an enlarged brain, without the assistance of natural selection:

We know very little about what happens when 10^{10} neurons are crammed into something the size of a basketball, with further conditions imposed by the specific manner in which this system developed over time. It would be a serious error to suppose that all properties, or the interesting structures that evolved, can be 'explained' in terms of natural selection (Chomsky 1975b: 59).

This assertion might also be taken to mean that language emerged relatively suddenly, perhaps when the brain reached some critical size. If this were the case, one would expect language to be present in the Neanderthals as well as in *Homo sapiens*, since the Neanderthals had slightly larger brains.

The late scenario is based in part on fossil evidence that the anatomical requirements for speech were not complete until the emergence of *Homo sapiens*. For example, the hypoglossal nerve, which passes through this canal and innervates the tongue, is much larger in humans than in great apes, probably because of the important role of the tongue in speech. Fossil evidence suggests that the size of the hypoglossal canal in early australopithecines, and perhaps in *Homo habilis*, was within the range of that in modern great apes, while that of the Neanderthal and early *H. sapiens* skulls contained was well within the modern human range (Kay, Cartmill, and Barlow 1998), although this has been disputed (DeGusta, Gilbert, and Turner 1999). A further clue comes from the finding that the thoracic region of the spinal cord is relatively larger in humans than in nonhuman primates, probably because breathing during speech involves extra muscles of the thorax and abdomen. Fossil evidence indicates that this enlargement was not present in the early hominids or even in *Homo ergaster*, dating from about 1.6 million years ago, but was present in several Neanderthal fossils (MacLarnon and Hewitt 2004).

The adaptations for articulate speech may have been incomplete even in the Neanderthals of 30,000 years ago, and therefore presumably in the common ancestor of modern humans and the Neanderthals of some 400,000 years ago. According to P. Lieberman (1998) the lowering of the larynx necessary for the full range of speech sounds was incomplete in the Neanderthals. This work remains controversial (e.g., Gibson and Jessee 1999), but there is other evidence that the cranial structure underwent changes subsequent to the split between anatomically modern and earlier "archaic" *Homo*, such as the Neanderthals, *Homo heidelbergensis*, and *Homo rhodesiensis*. One such change is the shortening of the sphenoid, the central bone of the cranial base from which the face grows forward, resulting in a flattened face (D. E. Lieberman 1998). D. E. Lieberman speculates that this is an adaptation for speech, contributing to the unique proportions of the human vocal tract, in which the horizontal and vertical components are roughly equal in length. This configuration, he argues, improves the ability to produce acoustically distinct speech sounds, such as the vowel [i] (P. Lieberman 2002). It is not seen in Neanderthal skeletal structure. Another adaptation unique to *H. sapiens* is neurocranial globularity, defined as the roundness of the cranial vault in the sagittal, coronal, and transverse planes, which is likely to have increased the relative size of the temporal and/or frontal lobes relative to other parts of the brain (D. E. Lieberman, McBratney, and Krovitz 2002). These changes may reflect more refined control of articulation and also, perhaps, more accurate perceptual discrimination of articulated sounds.

The evidence from Neanderthal therefore raises doubts as to whether articulate speech had evolved by 400,000 years ago, and recent genetic evidence suggests an even more recent date. A mutation of the FOXP2 gene in some members of an English family known as the KE family has resulted in a quite severe deficit in vocal articulation (Watkins, Dronkers, and Vargha-Khadem 2002). Although highly conserved in mammals, the FOXP2 gene underwent two mutations since the split between hominid and chimpanzee lines, and it has been estimated that the more recent of these occurred "not less than" 100,000 years ago (Enard *et al.* 2002), although the error associated with this estimate makes it not unreasonable to suppose that it coincided with the emergence of *Homo sapiens* around 170,000 years ago. It is also of interest that members of the KE family affected by the mutation, unlike their unaffected relatives, show no activation in Broca's area while covertly generating verbs (Liégeois *et al.* 2003). This might be taken to mean that the FOXP2 gene in humans is involved in the cooption of vocal control by Broca's area (Corballis 2004a).

Reconciliation: the gestural theory

For the most part, the evidence for the late scenario has to do with speech rather than language itself. If follows that language may have evolved well before it became autonomously vocal. If so, then the most likely form of early language was manual, and perhaps facial, rather than vocal.

The idea that language may have originated in manual gesture has a long if intermittent pedigree (e.g., Arbib 2005; Armstrong 1999; Armstrong, Stokoe and Wilcox, 1995; Armstrong and Wilcox 2007; Condillac 1971; Corballis 2002; Critchley 1975; Hewes 1973; Rizzolatti and Arbib 1998; Wundt 1921). Great apes have proven unable to acquire speech (e.g., Hayes 1952), but have developed vocabularies of several hundred "words," and some primitive gram-mar, using manual signs (e.g., Gardner and Gardner 1969), including pointing to symbols on a keyboard. (Savage-Rumbaugh, Shanker, and Taylor 1998). While these exploits fall well short of fully grammatical language, they strongly suggest that, at the time of the split from the apes, the hominids would have been much better pre-adapted to acquire a language system based on manual signs than one based on vocal calls.

Nevertheless the gestural theory of language origins has not received wide-spread acceptance. One of the reasons for this has been well expressed by the linguist Robbins Burling: "[T]he gestural theory has one nearly fatal flaw. Its sticking point has always been the switch that would have been needed to move from a visual language to an audible one" (Burling 2005: 123). This argument can be overcome, at least to some extent, if it is proposed that the switch was a gradual one, with facial and vocal elements gradually introduced into a system that was initially primarily manual, although perhaps punctuated by grunts. Through this gradual process, autonomous speech was eventually possible, although even today people characteristically augment their speech with manual gesture (Goldin-Meadow and McNeill 1999). The arguments for a gradual, more or less seamless switch are discussed next.

A gradual switch?

One argument in favor of a gradual switch has to do with the discovery of the so-called "mirror system" in the primate brain, which underlies manual gesture. In the human brain, this system also seems to mediate speech. In particular, area F5 in the monkey brain includes some neurons, called mirror neurons, that respond both when the animal makes a grasping movement and when it watches another individual making the same movement. Area F5 is also thought to be the homolog of Broca's area in the human brain, leading Rizzolatti and Arbib (1998) to propose that speech grew out of manual gestures.

Neurophysiological investigation has also shown close connections in the systems involved in manual and orofacial movement. For example, Rizzolatti, *et al.* (1988) recorded from neurons in area F5 in the monkey that fire when the animal makes movements to grasp an object with either the hand or the mouth. Petrides, Caddoret, and Mackey (2005) have identified an area in the monkey brain just rostral to premotor area 6, also considered a homologue of part of Broca's area that is involved in control of the orofacial musculature. Neurons in the mirror system also respond to both to certain movements, such as tearing paper or cracking nuts, onto the sounds of those movements (Kohler *et al.* 2002). There is still no evidence from nonhuman primates, though, that vocalization itself is mapped onto vocal production. Indeed, vocalization in nonhuman primates appears to be primarily under limbic control, whereas incorporation of vocal control into the pyramidal system, providing the level of intentional control necessary for speech, is unique to humans (Ploog 2002).

The neural links between hand and mouth may be related to ingestive behaviour rather than communication, but later adapted for gestural and finally vocal language. The F5 neurons that respond to grasping movements with either hand or mouth may be functionally involved in preparing the mouth to grasp the object when the hand grasps it, thereby encoding the goal of the action (taking possession of the object) (Rizzolatti *et al.* 1988). The connection between hand and mouth can also be demonstrated behaviorally in humans. Gentilucci *et al.* (2001) showed that when subjects were instructed to open their mouths while grasping objects, the size of the mouth opening increased with the size of the grasped object, and conversely, when they open their hands while grasping objects with their mouths, the size of the hand opening also increased with the size of the object.

Grasping movements of the hand also affect the kinematics of speech itself, in mirror-like fashion: Varying the size of objects that are grasped or brought to the mouth induces changes in parameters of lip kinematics and voice spectra of syllables pronounced simultaneously with the actions in both the person performing these actions, and in someone observing the same actions (see Gentilucci and Corballis 2006 for review). The relationship between representations of actions and spoken language is further supported by neuroimaging studies, which show activation of Broca's area when people make meaningful arm gestures (e.g., Decety *et al.* 1997), or even imagine them (Gerardin *et al.* 2000; Grafton *et al.* 1996; Hanakawa *et al.* 2003).

As Rizzolatti and Arbib (1998) recognized, the mirror system operates according to the same principles as postulated earlier by the motor theory of speech perception (Liberman *et al.* 1967), which holds that speech sounds are perceived in terms of how they are produced, rather than as acoustic elements. This has led to what is known as articulatory phonology (Browman and Goldstein 1995), in which speech itself is understood as comprised of gestures (see also Studdert-Kennedy 1998). These gestures are produced by six articulatory organs: the lips, the velum, the larynx, and the blade, body, and root of the tongue. In the context of speech understood as gesture, then, the incorporation of vocal control into the mirror system may have been a relatively small step.

It is possible that the manual origins of speech are recapitulated in ontogeny, since it is becoming increasingly apparent that manual gesture plays a critical role in the development of speech in infants (e.g., Iverson and Goldin-Meadow

2005). Even in adults, speech is characteristically accompanied by manual gestures, and the close coupling of these gestures with speech has led McNeill to conclude that they derive from the same production system. Speech itself also retains a strong visual component. This is illustrated by the McGurk effect (McGurk and MacDonald 1976), in which dubbing sounds onto a mouth that is saying something different alters what the hearer actually hears. That is, the viewer/listener often reports what the speaker is seen to be saying rather than the speech sound itself, or sometimes a blend of the two. Deaf people often become highly proficient at lip-reading, and even in individuals with normal hearing the brain areas involved in speech production are activated even they view speech-related lip movements (Calvert and Campbell 2003; Watkins, Strafella, and Paus 2003).

An evolutionary scenario

A possible evolutionary scenario might run as follows. Given the specialization of the primate mirror system for manual action, intentional communication probably began as a manual system. Given that the hominids, who split from the apes some 6 million years ago, were bipedal, the freeing of the hands would have allowed the cumulative development of a manual system of communication for some 4 million years. There is little evidence for cognitive advancement during this period, suggesting that communication probably did not yet incorporate syntax.

The emergence of the genus *Homo* from some 2 million years ago probably signaled pressure for more complex communication, leading to incremental development of syntax. At the same time, tool manufacture would have increased competition for the use of the hands, creating pressure for a switch from the hands to the face, and ultimately to voiced speech. The relatively slow development of manufacture suggests, however, that language may have retained a strong manual element at least until the emergence of *Homo sapiens*, when technology suddenly blossomed. In any event, it is likely that there was continual pressure to relieve pressure on the hands, with increasing emphasis on the face, perhaps throughout the Pleistocene. Incorporation of mouth movements, in particular, would be facilitated by preexisting neural connections, documented above, having to do with the role of the hands in bringing food to the mouth. Thus there may have been increasing pressure for the tongue, lips, and vocal tract to assume more of the communicative burden. Since the tongue, velum, and larynx are for the most part invisible, there may have been pressure to add sound, so that gestures of the mouth were rendered accessible. Adding voicing to the gestures also provides for the distinction between voiced and unvoiced sounds, adding to the possible repertoire. In this view, speech itself may be considered to be facial gesture, half swallowed.

Although manual and vocal language can be considered linguistically equivalent, there are other more practical advantages to vocalization. For one thing, speech is much less energy-consuming than manual gesture. Anecdotal evidence from courses in sign language suggests that the instructors require regular massages in order to meet the sheer physical demands of sign-language expression. In contrast, the physiological costs of speech are so low as to be nearly unmeasurable (Russell, Cerny, and Stathopoulos 1998). In terms of expenditure of energy, speech adds little to the cost of breathing, which we must do anyway to sustain life.

A switch to autonomous vocalization would not only have freed the hands from necessary involvement in communication, but also allowed people to speak and use tools at the same time, or speak while pointing out aspects of the environment. These developments led perhaps to pedagogy (Corballis 2002). Speech is less attentionally demanding than signed language; one can attend to speech with one's eyes shut, or when watching something else. Speech also allows communication over longer distances, as well as communication at night or when the speaker is not visible to the listener. The San, a modern hunter-gatherer society, are known to talk late at night, sometimes all through the night, to resolve conflict and share knowledge (Konner 1982). Boutla *et al.* (2004) have shown that the span of short-term memory is shorter for American Sign Language than for speech, suggesting that voicing may have permitted longer and more complex sentences to be transmitted – although the authors claim that the shorter memory span has no impact on the linguistic skill of signers.

Although the switch from manual to vocal language may have been gradual, the final step to autonomous speech may have had a relatively sudden and decisive impact, perhaps even defining the human condition – a small step on the genome perhaps, but a giant step for mankind. If the mutation of the FOXP2 gene was indeed instrumental in this final step, then it may at least partly explain what has been termed the "human revolution" (Mellars and Stringer 1989), and subsequent emergence of modern human behavior. The human revolution was manifest in the dramatic appearance of more sophisticated tools, bodily ornamentation, art, and perhaps music, which made their appearance from some 40,000 years ago in Europe. Some have argued that the human revolution actually began in Europe (e.g., Klein *et al.* 2004), but others have suggested that modern human behaviors and technology were assembled in Africa from perhaps 100,000 years ago and exported from there to Europe and other regions of the world (McBrearty and Brooks 2000).

The evidence now suggests that there was an exodus of *Homo sapiens* from Africa, heading east around the coastlines of southern Asia, with one group diverging north into Europe by around 40,000 to 45,000 years ago, and the other continuing into Australasia. Mellars (2006) suggests that the original migration out of Africa occurred between 40,000 and 60,000 years ago, but Oppenheimer (2003) suggests a much earlier date of 83,000 years ago. Some recent evidence supports the earlier date; stone assemblages on the Indian subcontinent suggestive of modern human inhabitants have been dated to both before and after the eruption of Mt. Toba, which occurred 74,000 years ago (Petraglia *et al.* 2007), and there has been controversial dating of *Homo sapiens* in Australia as early as 62,000 years ago (Adcock *et al.* 2001). Signs of advanced technology can now be traced to some 100,000 years ago or earlier, prior to the African exodus (e.g., Henshilwood *et al.* 2001; Vanhaeren *et al.* 2006; Yellen, Brooks, Cornelissen, Mehlman *et al.* 1995), and are also found along the routes taken by that exodus (Oppenheimer 2003). These events are consistent with the possibility that autonomous speech emerged in Africa perhaps 100,000 years ago, or even more recently, after the emergence of *Homo sapiens* but before the migration from Africa, and led to increasing sophistication in technology and manual crafts. The final conversion to autonomous speech may have been an invention (Corballis 2002) or, as suggested above, it may have resulted from the FOXP2 mutation (Corballis 2004b).

The development of what we are pleased to call civilization often depends on advances in communication. The emergence of grammatical language was itself a major step, and part of a transition to a degree of social complexity that effectively defines our genus. The emergence of autonomous speech perhaps led to the final transition toward modern behavior (Corballis 2004b). But subsequent advances in communication, including writing, telephone, radio, television, and the Internet, have each exerted profound influences on the way we think, act, and build our lives. Although the switch from manual to vocal language may have been gradual, the final accomplishment of autonomous speech (albeit with some residual gesturing) may have had a similar impact.

To conclude, given the practical advantages of speech over manual gesture, it may be useful to recapitulate the reasons for postulating the manual phase at all. One reason is that the primate brain was much better pre-adapted for manual action, at least with respect to intentional communication. This is well illustrated by the failure to teach great apes an effective intentional vocal system, and the comparative success in teaching forms of manual systems that have at least some of the hallmarks of language. Another reason is that language is computationally complex, and must surely have evolved relatively slowly, through natural selection (Pinker and Bloom 1990). Yet, as reviewed earlier, the evidence suggests that the anatomical adjustments necessary for articulate speech emerged late in hominid evolution, and possibly not until the arrival of our own species, *Homo sapiens*. It therefore seems necessary to conclude that language itself was evolving as a manuofacial system before articulate speech became possible.

8   A pragmatic perspective on the evolution of language

Dan Sperber and Gloria Origgi

Suppose you overhear someone of whom you know nothing say, "It was too slow." You have no problem understanding the sentence, but how much does that help you understand what the speaker means in uttering it? Very little. You don't know what the pronoun "it" refers to, what time span is indicated by this use of past tense "was," and from what point of view "it" was "too slow." The speaker might have uttered this sentence in order to convey an indefinite variety of meanings, for example, that the chemical reaction in the lab that afternoon had been too slow compared to what she had expected, that the decrease in unemployment had been too slow in France when Jospin was Prime Minister to help him win the presidential election, or that Jack's car was too slow (and so, last weekend, they had borrowed Peter's).

"It was too slow" is an ordinary sentence. Most – arguably all – sentences of any human language likewise underdetermine their interpretation. The grammar of a language, even if taken to include not only syntax but also phonology and semantics, does not, by itself, provide a sufficient basis for understanding utterances. To do this, humans do not just associate a linguistic meaning to the sound of a sentence; they also use information on the speech situation, the interlocutors, their past interactions, the background knowledge they share, and so on. Without this contextualization, an utterance provides just fragments of meaning without a definite import.

A new branch of linguistics, pragmatics, has developed over the past forty years (see, for instance, Atlas 2005; Carston 2002; Ducrot 1972; Horn 1989; Grice 1989; Levinson 1983, 2000; Recanati 2004; Sperber and Wilson 1986; Stalnaker 1999; Szabo 2005). It studies the interpretation of utterances in context. Work in pragmatics has at least established that contextual factors play a major role in the interpretation of every utterance both at the explicit and implicit levels. Realizing the high dependence of interpretation on context leads one to rethink the role of language in linguistic communication. Such rethinking has a variety of implications in related fields, semantics in particular. Here we discuss the implications of a pragmatic perspective for the evolution of language.

Two models of communication

Two models of linguistic communication stand in sharp contrast: the classical model of communication, or "code model," and the much more recent "inferential model." According to the code model, sentences of a language are sound-meaning pairs. In order to convey her meaning, all the speaker has to do is encode it into a sound structure that is paired to it in the language, and all the hearer has to do is decode the sound back into the meaning. According to the inferential model, based on the work of the philosopher Paul Grice (1957, 1989) and developed in particular in Relevance Theory (Carston 2002; Sperber and Wilson 1986), the linguistic decoding of an utterance provides just a semantic structure that falls quite short of determining the meaning intended by the speaker, and that serves rather as a piece of evidence from which this meaning can be inferred.

Both the code and the inferential models agree that human languages are codes which, through a recursive grammar, pair phonetic and semantic structures. It is a common observation that, thanks to their grammar and their huge lexicons, human languages are incomparably richer codes than the small repertoires of signals used in animal communication. Another striking difference – but one hardly ever mentioned – is that, *qua* codes, human languages are quite defective. Every signal in an optimal code must be paired with only one message, so that the receiver of the signal can unambiguously recover the initial message. Typically, animal codes (and artificial codes too) contain no ambiguity. Linguistic sentences, on the other hand, are full of semantic ambiguities, referential indeterminacies, and do not at all encode many other aspects of the meaning they serve to convey. This does not mean that human languages are dysfunctional. What it strongly suggests, rather, is that the function of language is not to encode the speaker's meaning, or in other terms, that the code model of linguistic communication is wrong.

According to the inferential model, understanding the speaker's meaning is an inferential process that uses as premises on the one hand the fact that the speaker has uttered a given sentence to which the grammar of the language assigns semantic properties, and on the other hand, contextual information. Grice (1957) first suggested such a perspective by reanalyzing the notion of speaker's meaning. Speaker's meaning, in Grice's analysis, is a complex communicative intention that must be recognized by the hearer in order to be fulfilled. It is an intention to achieve a certain effect upon the mind of the hearer by means of the hearer's recognition of the very intention to achieve this effect.

Seen this way, communication depends upon the ability of human beings to attribute mental states to others; that is, it depends upon their "naïve psychology" or their "theory of mind." This ability has been the subject of considerable work in developmental psychology and in the study of the evolution of social behavior (e.g. Baron-Cohen, Tager-Flusberg, and Cohen 2000; Byrne and Whiten 1988; Carruthers and Smith 1996; Leslie, Friedman, and German 2004; Whiten and Byrne 1997). Humans spontaneously interpret one another's behavior, not as simple bodily movements, but as the belief-guided fulfillment of intentions. Living in a world inhabited not only by physical objects and living bodies, but also by mental states, humans may want to act upon these mental states. They may seek to change the desires and beliefs of others. Such action can be carried out unbeknownst to the person one seeks to influence. It can also be performed overtly – one makes it manifest that one is trying to cause one's audience to believe or desire something – and this is communication proper. Communication is achieved by giving the hearer evidence of the meaning one intends to communicate. This evidence can be of any sort – gestures, mimicry, demonstrations – and it can be coded or not. What matters is that the evidence provided together with the context allows the addressee to infer the communicator's meaning.

In inferential communication, the communicator seeks to fulfill her intention by making it manifest to the hearer. Such a procedure carries a clear risk: the addressee, recognizing that the communicator intends to act upon his mental states, can easily foil this intention. On the other hand, inferential communication, because of the very fact that it is overt, has two advantages that make it generally much more powerful than all the other ways of acting upon people's mental states. While a mistrustful hearer may refuse to be influenced, a hearer who trusts the communicator's competence and honesty will make an effort to understand a message that he assumes is relevant and is disposed to accept. More importantly still, whereas the manipulation of the mental states of others by non-communicational means is relatively cumbersome and always imprecise, overt communication, where both the communicator and the addressee are intent on comprehension, makes it possible to transmit at very little cost contents as rich and precise as one wants.

The role of language in inferential communication is to provide the communicator with evidence, as exact and complex as she wishes, of the content she wants the hearer to accept. For this, it is not necessary that the utterance encode this content *in extenso* and unambiguously. Quite commonly, a fragmentary, ambiguous and loose coding is sufficient, in the context, for indicating a complete and unequivocal meaning. In this respect, inferential comprehension is not different from any other cognitive process of non-demonstrative inference that draws relatively reliable conclusions from fragmentary evidence open to multiple interpretations by relying upon both empirical regularities and context. The main task of pragmatics is to explain how such a process of inference is carried out in the particular case of linguistic communication: what empirical regularities guide the process? How are the linguistic properties of the utterance, on the one hand, and contextual information on the other, put to use? Although different pragmatic theories (see Horn and Ward 2004) give different answers to these questions, they share two basic assumptions: comprehension is inferential, and, by drawing on both the sentence meaning and the context, it aims at discovering the meaning intended by the speaker.

The evolution of language and the two models of linguistic communication

Clearly, the classical code model and the inferential model developed in pragmatics assign different functions to language in linguistic communication. To different functions there should correspond, in the species' history, different selective pressures and hence different hypotheses regarding the biological evolution of language. Scholars working on the evolution of language, however, have generally paid little or no attention to pragmatics (Dessalles 2000 is an exception). A few who are aware of pragmatic aspects of language use (e.g. Pinker 1994: ch. 7; Jackendoff 2002) treat them as marginal and, in practice, accept the code model as a very good approximation. Many, in fact, consider the evolution of language without worrying much about its specific properties, be they grammatical or pragmatic. For some, it is because their contribution consists in explaining the emergence of language on the basis of some biological function that could be fulfilled by any language-like system, whatever its precise properties (e.g. Dunbar 1996). For others (see Kirby 2002 for a review), it is because their work on modeling the possible evolutionary emergence of codes in a population of artificial agents is progressing so satisfactorily at the formal level that they tend to take its empirical relevance as self-evident.

Coded communication functions best when emitter and receiver share exactly the same code. Any difference between the emitter's and the receiver's codes is a possible source of error in the communication process. In animal communication where, in most cases, the code is genetically specified, a mutation affecting an individual's code is likely to produce a mismatch between its signals and those of its conspecifics. Such a mismatch compromises the individual's ability to act as an emitter or as a receiver of information and is counter-adaptive.

More generally, since a code must be shared by a population in order to be advantageous, evolution cannot easily "experiment" with modifications that not only have a very low chance of being advantageous (as the effect of any random mutation), but the advantageousness of which, moreover, begins only when the modification is sufficiently widespread in the population to be of use, that is one or several generations after the initial mutant. The most plausible modifications to a genetically transmitted code are additions of new signals (for example, a signal of alarm for a new species of predators in the environment) – additions that do not modify the structure of the preexisting code. The small size of codes in animal communication suggests that these additions are themselves quite rare. Indeed, animal communication codes which, unlike human languages, really function according to the code model, are typically tiny, without syntax, and highly stable within a given species. The great majority of them involve no learning (and when learning is involved, as in the case of songbirds, it usually concerns only a single signal that serves to distinguish local populations of the same species and that therefore cannot be fully genetically specified).

In the case of inferential communication, the situation is quite different. The success of inferential communication does not require that the communicator and audience have the same semantic representation of the utterance (or of other types of communicative behaviors). It is enough that the utterance, however they may represent it, be seen as evidence for the same conclusion. Take, for example, the following trivial dialogue:

> *John*:   I'm beat!
> *Lisa*:   Ok, let's go back home.

It is of little importance whether the meaning that John and Lisa associate with the word "beat" is the same. It may be that, for John, "beat" means extreme fatigue, while for Lisa, "beat" is simply a synonym of "tired". In any event, John says, "I'm beat," not in order to indicate a degree of fatigue that this term might encode, but in order to indicate contextually both his wish to return home and the reason for it, namely his fatigue. The level of fatigue that may justify one's desire to return home depends on the situation: it is not the same at a party among friends, while taking a stroll, or at work. In John's utterance, then, "beat" indicates not a level of fatigue encoded by the word, but the level of fatigue which, in the situation of the utterance, is relevant in that it justifies John's wish. This ad hoc meaning is contextually constructed. If, in John's lexicon, "beat" encodes extreme fatigue, then he is using the term hyperbolically. If, in Lisa's lexicon, "beat" is simply a synonym of "tired," she understands John's use of it literally. All the same, John and Lisa communicate successfully. Classifying usages as literal, loose, or figurative plays no part in the real-time comprehension process.

As we just illustrated, it is not necessary that the codes between interlocutors be identical. It is not sufficient, either. Consider the following dialogue:

> *John*:   Can you fix my watch?
> *Watchmaker*:   That will take some time.

The semantics of "will take some time" is trivial (or in any case, let us suppose that it is, and in the same manner, for John and the watchmaker): everything that has non-zero duration takes time. Yet, in uttering this truism, the watchmaker sets John along the way to a non-truistic and relevant interpretation. Repairing the watch will take not just any amount of time, but an amount of time to which it is relevant to draw John's attention. If John expects that the time for repair will be at least one week, he will understand "It will take some time" as meaning that the repair will take several weeks. If the watchmaker, for her part, thinks that John expects the repair to be done the same day, she will express herself as she did in order to convey that the repair will be a matter of days rather than hours. That the words "to take," "some" and "time" have the same meaning in their lexicon does not protect John and the watchmaker from the possibility of misunderstanding.

According to the inferential model, the near identity of the interlocutors' codes is neither necessary nor sufficient in order for them to communicate effectively. In these conditions, a mutation affecting the language faculty and causing the mutant's grammar to diverge from that of her interlocutors is not necessarily detrimental to her ability to communicate. As we will now show, such a mutation may even be advantageous.

In particular, a language faculty leading to the internalization of a grammar that attributes more structure to utterances than they superficially realize (one that, for example, projects onto them unexpressed constituents) could facilitate inferential comprehension.

Imagine a protolanguage having only word-size sound-meaning pairs, without any syntactic structure. The word "drink" in this protolanguage designates the action of drinking and nothing else (it is not, unlike the word "drink" in English, a two-place predicate); the word "water" designates the substance and nothing else, and so on. With such a limited code, a hearer's decoding of the meaning associated with the word pronounced by the speaker would not suffice to assure communication between them. The hearer who associates with the utterance "water" the concept of water is not thereby informed of anything whatsoever. Even a concatenation of expressions in such a language, for example, "drink water," would not be decoded as we spontaneously tend to do on the basis of our comprehension of English. "Drink water" does not denote, in this protolanguage, the action of drinking water. One only has two concepts, that of drinking and that of water, which are activated without being grammatically or semantically linked. The mental activation of one or several concepts having no semantic linkage between them does not denote a state of affairs nor an action associating these two concepts; and it falls even shorter of expressing an attitude such as belief or desire.

In these conditions, such a protolanguage could be of use only to beings capable of inferential communication. For such individuals, activation by decoding, even of only a single concept, could easily provide them with evidence sufficient for reconstructing a full-fledged meaning, the speaker's meaning. Imagine two speakers of this protolanguage, let us call them *John* and *Lisa*, walking in the desert. John points to the horizon and utters, "Water." Lisa correctly infers from this that he means something like, *There is water over there*. Just when they reach the water hole, John, exhausted, collapses and mutters, "Water." Lisa correctly infers that he means something like, *give me some water*. With the signals of animal communication – communication that is fully coded – such a range of interpretive constructions is not possible.

Imagine now that Lisa was in fact a mutant whose language faculty, more complex than that of her fellow creatures, had allowed her as a child to analyze the words of the protolanguage that she was in the process of acquiring, either as arguments or as one- or two-place predicates. She had thus categorized "drink" as a two-place predicate, "water" as an argument, and so on. When Lisa the mutant hears parched John mutter, "water," what is activated in her mind is not only the concept of water, but a syntactic structure with an unexpressed predicate capable of taking water as an argument. Her decoding thus goes beyond what was in fact encoded by John. He is not a mutant and therefore expresses himself in the rudimentary language of their community, without mentally adding to it an underlying syntactic structure. This mismatch between John's and Lisa's representation of the utterance is not, however, detrimental to communication. Even if she weren't a mutant, in order to interpret what John meant Lisa would have had to mentally (but not linguistically) represent not only water but also the action that had water as an object. Lisa the mutant is immediately set along the right path thanks to the syntactic structure she falsely, though usefully, attributes to John's utterance.

When she speaks, Lisa the mutant encodes, by means of signals that are homonymous to those of her community, not only atomic concepts but also predicate-argument structures. When she says, "water," her utterance also encodes the unexpressed place-holder of a predicate for which "water" would be the argument. When she says "drink," her utterance encodes the unexpressed place-holder of the two arguments of "drink." When she says "drink water," her utterance encodes not only the two concepts *drink* and *water*, but also the complex concept *drink some water* (plus the unexpressed place-holder of the argument-subject of "drink"). Lisa's interlocutors do not recognize these under-lying structures in her utterances, but they arrive at the intended interpretations all the same by a linguistically less prepared inferential path.

Now, if Lisa is a second-generation mutant, having among her interlocutors brothers and sisters who are also mutants and who therefore speak and com-prehend as she does, then she and her co-mutants communicate more effectively than the other members of their community. They communicate, in fact, by means of a language whose utterances, phonologically identical to those of the non-mutants' language, are syntactically and semantically more complex and hence easier to deal with pragmatically. In the language of these mutants, new linguistic signs may emerge and stabilize by a process of grammaticalization that is inaccessible to non-mutants. For example, pronouns could come to take the place of unspecified arguments.

This imaginary example illustrates the way in which a more advanced language faculty, which leads individuals possessing it to internalize a code that is richer than that of their community, may emerge and evolve. It only occurs this way in a system of inferential communication. In a system of code-based communication, every departure from the common grammar will be disadvantageous or at best neutral, but it will never be advantageous.

These considerations apply to all possible stages of the evolution of the language faculty as well as to its initial emergence. Being disposed to treating uncoded communicative behavior as a coded signal may facilitate inferential comprehension of the communicator's intentions and lead to the stabilization of this kind of behavior as a signal.

Conclusions

The human mind is characterized by two cognitive abilities having no real equivalent in other species on Earth: language and naïve psychology, that is, the ability to represent the mental states of others. We have suggested here that it is because of the interaction of these two abilities that human communication was able to develop and acquire its incomparable power (cf. Origgi 2001; Origgi and Sperber 2000; Sperber 2000; Sperber and Wilson 2002). From a pragmatic perspective, it is quite clear that the language faculty and human languages, with their richness and flaws, are only adaptive in a species that is already capable of naïve psychology and inferential communication. The relatively rapid evolution of languages themselves and their relative heterogeneity within one and the same linguistic community – these two aspects being associated – can only be adequately explained if the function of language in communication is to provide evidence of the speaker's meaning and not to encode it.

In these conditions, the study of the evolution of the language faculty must be closely associated to that of the evolution of naïve psychology. Likewise, the study of the evolution of languages must systematically take into account their pragmatic dimension.

Part III

Biological and neurological foundations

9 Plasticity and canalization in the evolution of linguistic communication: an evolutionary developmental approach

Daniel Dor and Eva Jablonka

Introduction

In the last decade, the introduction of a developmental framework into the core of evolutionary theory has brought about a radical change in perspective. In the emerging synthesis, known as "evolutionary developmental biology" (or "evo devo"), the development of the phenotype, rather than the genetic variant, assumes a primary theoretical position, and is the point of departure for evolutionary analysis. Changes in development which lead to changed phenotypes are primary and the organism exhibiting an altered phenotype is the target of selection. Genes, as West-Eberhardt (2003) succinctly has put it, "are followers in evolution": changes in gene frequencies follow, rather then precede, phenotypic changes that mainly arise as reactions to environmental changes. The focus of developmentally informed studies of evolution is therefore on processes of development that can generate evolutionary innovation, on the constraints and generic properties of developmental systems, on the architecture of developmental networks, and on the evolution of the ability to develop and learn (Gilbert 2003). It is clear today that in order to explain the evolution of a new trait – be it morphological, physiological, or behavioral – it is necessary to explain the evolution of the developmental processes that contribute to its construction during ontogeny. Therefore, processes leading to developmental flexibility and sensitivity to environmental variations on the one hand, and to the buffering of environmental and genetic "noise" on the other hand, are important subjects of empirical and theoretical research. Moreover, an account of the origins of novelty, new morphological and physiological characteristics that are clearly not variations on an existing theme, as well as the regulatory architecture of the developmental system that imposes constraints and affordances on innovation production, are central to the development-oriented research project (Wagner 2000). This developmental framework can be used to study the evolution of behavior, and we apply it to the evolution of linguistic communication.

In a series of papers (Dor and Jablonka 2000, 2001, 2004), we developed and presented a social-developmental, innovation-based theory of the evolution of language. At the core of the theory lies the understanding that language itself, the socially constructed tool of communication, culturally evolved before its speakers were specifically prepared for it on the genetic level. Language was, from the very beginning, a collective invention. It came into being not because its speakers already had genes specifically selected for language, but because their social world evolved to the point where collective inventions (not just of language, but of other cultural tools too) became possible. As language gradually developed, and as it became a more and more important element in the social lives of its speakers, the speakers found themselves locked in a new evolutionary spiral: they came to be selected on the basis of their linguistic performance. The invention of language, and the cultural process of further development and propagation, thus launched a process of selection in which genetic variants that contributed to linguistic ability were selected. The selection of genes whose effects are made visible because of a change in the environment is known as genetic accommodation, and we suggested that during the evolution of language new types of genetic variability were exposed, and new types of genetically based capacities (for learning, for communicating and so on), were selected.

The evolution of language is particularly difficult to study because one needs to address processes at three levels: at the level of the social and linguistic structures, at the ontogenetic, individual level, and at the genetic population level. In this paper we would like to discuss certain aspects of the relation between the three levels and suggest that an evolutionary developmental perspective can open up new frontiers for the study of the evolution of language. Our point of departure is the behavioral plasticity of humans, which is the basis for the evolution of language.

Developmental-behavioral plasticity

Behavioral flexibility in humans is probably the most dramatic example of behavioral plasticity in the living world, and it is based on the remarkable learning ability of humans. It asserts itself in the foundational fact that children learn different languages, in the fact that language acquisition takes place under variable social and psychological conditions, in the attested variability in the onset and duration of the acquisition process, and in the strategies adopted by different children throughout the process. However, developmental flexibility is not necessarily behavioral and is not specific to humans. It is one of the defining properties of biological organisms, and biologists call it *plasticity*. Plasticity is defined as the ability of a single genotype to generate, in response to different environmental circumstances, variable forms of morphology, physiology, and/or behavior. These phenotypic responses can be reversible or irreversible, adaptive or non-adaptive, active or passive, continuous or discontinuous (West-Eberhard 2003). The repertoire of alternative adaptive plastic responses to new conditions may be limited and predictable, as with seasonal changes in the coloration and patterns of butterflies' wings, or it can be large and relatively open-ended including unpredictable, novel adaptive responses. This is evident when we consider how we learn a new skill (for example, learning a to ride a bike or learning to read and write), or when we consider morphological adjustments in bones and muscles that are the results of changes in mechanical pressures brought about by new modes of movement (for example, when a mammal needs to use its hind legs in an unusual way). These are environmentally induced developmental reorganizations that were never specifically selected for, and that are based on the general potentialities and plasticity mechanisms of the preexisting genotype.

A good example of a novel phenotypic response, based on relatively open-ended plasticity mechanisms is provided by the linguistic capacity that the bonobo Kanzi (Savage-Rumbaugh, Shanker, and Taylor 1998) managed to achieve in the lab. Symbolic communication is not part of the behavioral repertoire of his species, yet Kanzi now efficiently uses the communication system invented by the humans around him. His mind is plastic enough for that. The conditions within which he grew up have reorganized preexisting components of his developmental systems (behavioral and neurological) in a new and adaptive way.

But what are the mechanisms allowing for the open-ended plasticity underlying Kanzi's amazing communicative behavior, and the extraordinary variability of human linguistic behaviors? *Exploration and selective stabilization* mechanisms are the most prominent mechanisms that lead to open-ended plasticity. They may occur at the cellular, physiological, behavioral, and social levels. All are based on a similar principle – the generation of a large set of local variations and interactions, with only a small subset eventually being stabilized and manifested. Which output is realized depends on the initial conditions, the ease with which developmental trajectories can be deflected, and the number of possible points around which development can be stably organized. Following convention, we refer to these points as "attractors," since they are stabilizing end-states towards which the system seems to "strive." Selective stabilization thus involves both the constraining of certain aspects of the response, and extensive plasticity (output variability) *within this range*.

An example of a cellular mechanism of selective stabilization is the mechanism underlying spindle formation during mitosis, where there is "dynamic instability" involving the opposing and random processes of growth and breakdown of microtubules polymers. A growing fiber stabilizes only when it incidentally (yet inevitably) reaches the kinetochore of a chromosome (the attractor) thus forming the spindle fibers. This process leads to a very reliable spindle formation despite many initial conditions and variable developmental paths for reaching the attractor (Gerhart and Kirschner 1997). Another example is provided by the selective stabilization of synaptic connections during development and learning (Changeux, Courrege, and Danchin 1973; Edelman 1987). At the behavioral level, any learning that involves elements of trial-and-error can be described as exploration followed by the stabilization of a selected behavior.

Although *how much* learning is involved in language-acquisition is a controversial issue, exploration and selective stabilization mechanisms are obviously associated with the process. The entire language out there, which is spoken by the adults around the child, is the "attractor," and in order for the child to be able to reach the attractor, the child must explore – at all levels: the child must try different ways of communication, different ways of usage of language, different interpretations for the utterances heard around him/her. Moreover, the child's brain goes through a whole series of explorational and selective stabilization processes, in which neural pathways, allowing for successful comprehension and production, are stabilized.

The other side of the developmental plasticity coin is invariance, stability in the face of perturbations, which biologists refer to as *canalization*. Canalization is defined as "the adjustment of developmental pathways by natural selection so as to bring about a uniform result in spite of genetic and environmental variations" (Jablonka and Lamb 1995: 290). In other words, canalization produces a situation where the output is stable *despite* changes in inputs and/or in developmental trajectories. It leads to robustness and stability in a "noisy" world, in which both the genetic milieu and the external environment are constantly changing. We must note, however, that there may be properties of the developing system that lead to uniform results, which are *not* the result of natural selection for constancy. For example, they may be the inevitable effects of the regulatory structure of the developmental network (Hermisson and Wagner 2004). In such cases, the explanation of the origins of the buffering properties that lead to the system's stability in terms of natural selection is unwarranted, although natural selection may eventually contribute to the *maintenance* of the canalized state.

Some features of language and linguistic communication seem to be stable across languages, and across ontogenies, despite the facts of environmental, developmental, cultural, and genetic variation (for partially converging lists of features see Vouloumanos and Werker 2004; Pinker and Jackendoff 2005). Although there is no consensus, most linguists agree that all speakers of all languages share the ability, which becomes manifest relatively early during development, to attend to, imitate, remember, and generate components and patterns of linguistic structure. Most linguists also agree that all spoken languages have constrained ranges of phonemes that are organized in a combinatorial manner (as in bird songs), and form theoretically unlimited phoneme-strings.

Canalization and plasticity seem to be opposites, and for a particular level of phenotypic description they indeed are – a phenotypic response may be either invariant because of canalization (i.e., it may have a single stable output despite many inputs and developmental contexts), or plastic (i.e., context-sensitive with several outputs). The relationship between canalization and plasticity, however, is much more interesting. Almost every case of canalized development (in the face of genetic and environmental "noise") requires plasticity at underlying or overlying levels of organization. Thus, for example, the increase in the number of red blood cells at high altitudes can be seen as a plastic response if we look at the number of red blood cells (which changes), but it is an illustration of canalization if we look at the concentration of oxygen in the blood (which remains constant). It is the plasticity at the level of adjusting the number of red blood cells that allows the stability at the level of oxygen concentration. Similarly, although all normal children acquire the languages of their communities there is plasticity in that the *particular* routes of linguistic development differ, as does the *specific* output – the individual idiosyncrasies of one's language production. Different children come to the world with different genetic makeups, different learning capacities and different embryological histories, and they are exposed to different sets of linguistic inputs. The very fact that they eventually manage to zoom in on the target language and produce a relatively invariant behavior means that they must manifest great plasticity at the neural level. Looking at the brains of different speakers we therefore expect to find a lot of variability at the brain physiology level, and we expect this to be true even of identical twins who have identical genotypes. In fact, it is the ability to generate neurological variability (which is inevitable given genetic differences, anatomical differences between brains, differences among ontogenies, and differences of processes of linguistic socialization) that allows for the construction of different developmental trajectories that lead to something that everyone recognizes as language.

The open-ended plasticity mechanisms at the behavioral and the neural levels are the point of departure of our account of the evolution of language. As we argue below, the evolution of language is incomprehensible without the assumption of such open-ended behavioral plasticity, which enables individuals to explore communicative possibilities and generate communicative novelties. Innovating organisms are, we argue, genetically prepared for the search for behaviors that break the genetic mold of the regular patterns of their lives. The innovations themselves emerge from the search process, which almost always requires a certain amount of luck.

The cultural evolution of language/s

Our account of the evolution of language begins with the cultural history of linguistic innovation, the gradual process in which exploratory communicative behaviors came to be stabilized and conventionalized as part of the linguistic system. From the first prototype (or prototypes) of language back in the past, until today, individual speakers everywhere have been trying to solve new communicative problems (or found themselves accidently doing so) by means that were not yet part of their linguistic arsenal. Speakers have been inventing words for things that have not yet been named by their language; using existing words for new meanings; arranging their words in new ways to express new relational meanings; producing more complex messages; finding new ways to reduce ambiguity; using language for functions that have not been thought of before, and so on. Some of the inventors, at different points in time, might have been by their cognitive nature already more adapted to language, but this is definitely not necessary: Some of them might have actually been those who found language more difficult to learn and to use, and were thus looking for ways to streamline it and arrange it in ways that were easier for them to learn (we will get back to this topic later). Much more important than the variations in the cognitive capacities of the inventors, however, were the functional and contextual conditions of the inventions: The nature of the communicative problems that required solutions, the developmental state of the language at the time of the invention, and the social and communicative circumstances. Throughout the process, new communicative problems kept emerging, and new functional solutions were required, simply because society, communication, and the realities of life kept changing. Language played a crucial role in directing the process of its own development, for a double reason: first, many of the problems that required a functional solution emerged as systemic consequences of the development of the language. Second, as more and more elements came to be canalized, and the language came to assume a certain architectural logic, the logic gradually imposed system constraints on what the next viable innovation could be.

Throughout the process of cultural evolution, the community gradually sophisticated its common world-view, adding new linguistic categories and allowing more successful linguistic communication. Each time a new invention became part of the language, the "attractor" for language acquisition has changed and developed. In the process of cultural evolution, however, language also developed into a more constrained communication system, a system of rules. This was a type of "cultural canalization" because it led to greater stability of linguistic production and comprehension among speakers, despite increases and changes in lexicon and additions of new grammatical elements. This stability did not lead to reduced variability of linguistic production or comprehension. On the contrary: by being subject to rules, plasticity increased within its bounded domain.

The social and communicative circumstances at the time of the invention were important for several different reasons, mostly because the success of the explorative communicative behavior, and then its stabilization, required other people, apart from the innovative speaker, to understand what the speaker tried to do. Innovative speakers may achieve nothing in the absence of attentive and innovative listeners. The same is true of the entire process of stabilization. For a linguistic innovation to be adopted into the language, it has to propagate throughout the community, and be accepted by many of those who did not, or could not, invent it themselves. This process is highly dependent on the relevant social conditions (including the relations of power and the politics of identity in the community).

Cultural evolution, however, did not just involve the effort to allow for cooperative mutually beneficial communication. Language-related struggles may have also contributed to the process of language evolution. As groups became large, it was inevitable that different subgroups would develop their own communicative interests, which might have included, at some point, the concealment of information from members of other groups. Secrecy, in this case, would be advantageous to the members of the "secretive" group. Access to this secret information would, however, be of value to the excluded group members, so there was a clear conflict of interest: members of the excluded group would engage in an attempt to decipher the secret information, which would lead to a ciphering-deciphering arms-race (Dor and Jablonka 2004). If such conflicts have indeed been important during the evolution of linguistic communication, they could have participated in interesting processes taking place at different levels. They may help explain why languages seem to have a wider vocabulary and a more complex structure than is expected from simple utility considerations; they may also help explain the emergence of stratification within languages, including the phenomena of jargon and slang. Hide-and-seek linguistic games may have also contributed to processes of social differentiation (including the extreme case of castes) and division of labor within groups, since linguistic differentiation is likely to enhance social differentiation.

The evolution of speakers

Everything that has ever happened to humans in their evolution as speakers was driven by the social process of the cultural evolution of language. When the first prototype of language was invented, the new tool opened for its users new horizons of communication. Precisely because the new tool proved so efficient, it also presented the speakers with a new and pressing learning challenge: they had to learn to use language, to use it efficiently and in coordination with the other members of the community. In the exploration process that ensued, different individuals recruited capacities of different kinds, and found different strategies to cope with the challenge. Some of them, at the same time, kept developing the language, finding new ways to enhance its expressive power. Every progressively more complex version of language that came to be adopted as a result of a complex social process of negotiation and struggle, made the learning challenge more difficult and more complex. Every enhancement in the expressive power of language made it more important, and eventually virtually necessary, for everybody to learn to use the language – because it gradually changed the entire social world in which they lived.

Cultural selection for the most effective communicators inevitably involved selection for individuals with cognitive features that assisted the development of the now essential linguistic learning. Natural selection favors these organisms in a population which can respond in an effective functional manner to the new inducing or learning conditions. Those genetic changes that stabilize a functional phenotypic response (i.e., make it more reliable and precise), and/or that ameliorate detrimental side-effects, were selected. West-Eberhard terms such genotypic change *genetic accommodation* (2003: 140, 146). Selection of genes is possible only because alleles become selectively relevant as a result of phenotypic adjustments to new environments. Variation is "unmasked." Genetic accommodation therefore follows phenotypic adjust-ments: changes in gene frequencies follow rather than lead in the evolutionary process.

A special case of genetic accommodation, which probably was important in the evolution of language, is *genetic assimilation* which occurs when selection at the genetic level leads to a more canalized response. It arises through the replacement by natural selection of a physiological or behavioral response, which was originally dependent on an environmental stimulus or learning, by a response that is fully or partially independent of external induction or learning. A behavioral response that was probably fully assimi-lated is the fear of the smell of lions shown by hyena cubs before they have ever encountered a lion. A response that depended on an external stimulus has become independent of the external stimulus through natural selection. This case is an example of full and complete assimilation, but this is an extreme case of a more general process. Usually, genetic assimilation is partial, leading to the ability to produce the response with decreased exposure to the stimulus (e.g. a smaller number of learning trials, a shorter induction period, a lower threshold, etc.) (Avital and Jablonka 2000).

Partial genetic assimilation may result not only in a more facile response but may also lead to the sophistication of behavior through a process which Avital and Jablonka (2000) called the *assimilate-stretch* principle. By decreasing the number of trials necessary to learn one aspect of behavior, the individual may be able to learn additional things. In other words, by making some learned acts easier, more things can be learned *with the same cognitive resources*, and the result will be an increase of learned behavioural outputs. Hence, genetic assimilation can lead to the sophistication of behavior and may explain many complex sequences of actions, which are otherwise baffling from an evolutionary point of view. In addition, learning to do one thing readily can be a scaffolding for learning other things. For example, if we learn to communicate about the difference between now and not-now, we may also advance our ability to distinguish more sharply between before-now and after-now, then learn to communicate about this distinction, and so on and so forth.

Partial genetic assimilation also leads to the sophistication of behavior by another route – via the construction of broad categories. While complete assimilation leads to a fixed response that does not require any learning (just a single input-trigger), partial assimilation does require learning and hence is inherently plastic. Partial assimilation of communication categories may thus lead to the ability to think about the world, to further communicate about the world, and to respond to the world in terms of categories (for example one/more-than-one, etc). Probably what happens is that certain connections between different parts of the brain become strengthened, or some parts of the brain become "recruited" for a new function. Developmentally this may come at the expense of other functions, or as a substitute for them, and this may lead to increased dependence on the new connections.

What kinds of cognitive capacities were recruited, and eventually genetically accommodated (or partially assimilated) during the evolution of language? Since the task at hand has always been a learning task, individuals with greater general learning capacities must have been selected over the others: the social evolution of language thus played an important driving role in the long process in which humans developed their unprecedented capacities for general learning. Bigger brains, with bigger areas dedicated to associative learning, better long- and short-term memories, better skills of social engagement and learning, including more sophisticated versions of a theory of mind, better imitation skills – all these were gradually emerging as some of the resulting characteristics of the minds of more advanced humans. In other words, the genetically accommodated minds were, first of all, more plastic. Plasticity, of course, has made the entire process possible from the very beginning: as we noted earlier, the bonobo Kanzi is able to communicate well beyond the ability of non-tutored members of his species. However, it is as important to note that he does not seem to be capable of learning our full-fledged languages. This indicates that we have evolved cognitive linguistic plasticity far beyond Kanzi and the other primates.

Increase in general learning ability, however, could not have been the only genetically accommodated and assimilated trait. Individual members of speaking communities must have also been selected for any and every type of capacity they managed to recruit which helped them cope not just with the general learning task – but with different elements of the task that had to do with the *specific* properties of language itself. Certain individuals, at different points in the evolution of language, and regardless of their general learning achievements, found it easier than the others to produce well-demarcated linguistic sounds (and to do it more quickly), to distinguish linguistic sounds from noise in the course of comprehension and analyze them phonetically and phonologically, to learn and remember more signs, to understand the semantic relations between the signs and their relations to the world, to construct and communicate more complex messages, to understand the speakers' pragmatic intent in comprehension, to apply logical analysis to quantifiers – and so on. Genetic accommodation may have been accelerated through positive assortative mating, in which individuals with better linguistic ability chose similar individuals as mates (Nance and Kearsey 2004).

It is not clear whether conflicts between encipherers and decipherers contributed to the genetic accommodation of linguistic plasticity. Hide-and-seek linguistic conflicts probably led to better linguistic memory and attention to linguistic forms, and enhanced the usage of words as objects of play and deliberate manipulation (i.e., encourage linguistic wit). A lot of evidence from child-language, especially in relation to language games, indicates that exploratory behavior has been extended into the linguistic realm. These effects all seem to reflect increased plasticity at the neural and behavioral levels, and were obviously the consequence of the cultural and genetic evolution of language. Genetic accommodation could lead to features that further allow for the development of the hide-and-seek linguistic games, only if such games characterized human societies for a long time, and made systematic fitness differences. If there was systematic selection of those individuals whose cognitions are more suited for inventing, learning, and using rapidly changing "codes," this would have selected for further increase in linguistic capacity.

The co-evolutionary spiral

The evolution of speakers did not just follow the evolution of languages – it also reciprocated by influencing the way the languages evolved. As we stressed, the process was driven throughout by the social and communicative dynamics: The communicative problems that had to be solved, the emerging system constraints of language itself, the social fabric of communication – all these were throughout the dominant factors. But the cognitive capacities of individual speakers played a constitutive role in three complementary ways. First, as humanity advanced, technologically and epistemologically (partly because of language), human minds kept changing, both in terms of content and process: humans came to know things about the world that they did not know before (and probably forgot certain things too); they came to see the world in spatial and temporal directions that were closed to them in the past; their thoughts, fears and ambitions kept changing; they were capable of doing things in very different ways – and all these required changes in language, for information sharing, cooperation and social communication (and also for deceiving and hiding information). Importantly, changes of this type were introduced into the language, as innovations, by individuals who thought and felt certain things (about the world, about society, about communication) that were not yet communicable by language, and *also felt the need* to communicate them. The ways the minds of these individuals worked thus did have an impact on the evolution of language: to the extent that they managed to stabilize their innovations, they actually dragged language closer to their minds. The other members eventually learned about these things through language. In this sense, then, language was partially directed in its evolution by the specific properties of its innovators as cognitive agents.

Second, some of the innovators probably managed to do what they did because they had some very particular capacities that were not generally shared by the others. The first humans who began to explore the possibility of investing meaning in word order, for example, and were thus among the first to start developing what eventually became syntax, were probably much more sensitive – because of the particularities of their developmental history – to linear order on the one hand, and to the complexities of their (very rudimentary) semantics, on the other. They may have otherwise been very competent with language, but on the other hand, they may have launched the explorations precisely because they were lacking in their pragmatic capacities and thus found it much more difficult to cope with ambiguity. This way or the other, languages eventually came to reflect something about the way their minds worked.

Finally, all the innovations, on their way to stabilization, had to be accepted by the others, and in order to be accepted, they had to be *learnable*. There was thus an upper limit on the complexity of innovations: they had to be simple enough, easy enough to learn for the others. To a certain extent, then, the evolution of language itself was constrained by the general learning capacity of the population. The importance of this constraint, however, should not be overestimated for three complementary reasons. First, the fact that the innovation was already out there, as an object for learning, implies that many of those who could not invent it (because they lacked some specific cognitive capacity) could now rely on their general cognitive plasticity, and their social learning capacities, in the course of learning it. Second, for a specific innovation to be accepted and stabilized, it did not have to be learnable by *everybody*. Usage of the tools of language is never evenly distributed across the population. Third, many individuals may have been able to learn some of the innovation, to approximate its usage in a way that enabled them, for example, to understand it when used by others, but not to use it themselves. Linguistic production is always more difficult than comprehension (for the same level of complexity). There may have been linguistic innovators who were too far ahead of their times, so to speak, whose innovations were too complicated for the others to learn. But all in all, this constraint most probably played a positive auxiliary role in the evolution of language, in the sense that it gave an edge (other things being equal) to simpler innovations over complicated ones, and thus contributed to the general streamlining of the entire system.

Conclusions

The general idea that the evolution of language involved a complex interaction between genes and culture was suggested by scholars from different theoretical camps, including Pinker and Bloom (1990), Maynard Smith and Szathmáry (1995), Jablonka and Rechav (1996), Deacon (1997), Kirby (1999), Briscoe (2003), and many others. Pinker and Bloom on the one hand and Deacon on the other seem to represent two extreme views of the co-evolutionary view. Pinker and Bloom suggested that specific linguistic properties – as they are defined in the generative literature – may have appeared as part of the social evolution of language, and then been genetically assimilated. Deacon objected: he claimed that languages are simply too varied, too different from each other, for any particular property of any of them to have been universally internalized, in an identical way, by all humans. Deacon thus concluded that only properties of general cognition could be assimilated. Language emerged from the general cognitive capacities that all humans share (including the capacity for symbolic thinking), and evolved together with a gradual rise in these general capacities.

In spite of the differences between their positions, some ideas are shared by both sides to the debate. Chomsky's foundational idea, that our genetic endowment for language is universally spread among all human beings obviously informs Pinker and Bloom, but it is also accepted by Deacon albeit in a different way. Deacon rightly rejects the idea that *languages* are universal, and concludes that genetic assimilation of linguistically specific properties was therefore impossible. Nevertheless, both sides agree that languages are the way they are because our minds are universally the way they are. For Pinker and Bloom, this implied linguistic specificities universally encoded in our genes. For Deacon, it implied linguistic specificities locally shaped (in different ways) by the universal human capacity for symbolic thought. Both sides also agree that the entire process of the evolution of language was essentially driven by human cognition – not by the social activity of innovation. Elements of language were indeed invented, but the elements that survived and were eventually established in language were those which adapted themselves to the structures of our minds and brains.

Our analysis, couched as it is within the evolutionary-developmental framework, offers a different solution, and removes what seems to us like the last serious objection, voiced by Deacon, to the idea of partial genetic assimilation. It bases itself on the understanding that the evolution of language has always been first and foremost a socially driven process. Brain plasticity allowed for phenotypic adjustments through learning, and then for the partial genetic accommodation, of language-learning; our general learning capacities might have ruled out some structures that were too complex, but the structures of our brains and minds were never the primary attractors around which humans had to organize their developmental pathways. The primary attractors have always been the languages of the communities. Language not only adapted to the brains and minds of individual speakers, but the brains and minds of the speakers had to adapt themselves to language. And since human brains and minds have always been somewhat different from each other, they had to adapt themselves to language in somewhat different ways. Nothing was *fully* internalized on the way: no grammatical rules or meta-rules. Our minds and our brains as modern humans, however, are much more sensitive, much more attuned, to linguistic particularities than the minds and brains of our ancestors. We are much better prepared for language then they were, but we are still, each and every one of us, somewhat differently prepared. Variability, at all levels, is an inevitable driver and outcome of the logic of the evolution of language.

10   What is language, that it may have evolved, and what is evolution, that it may apply to language

Massimo Piattelli-Palmarini

Linguistics and biology are both witnessing such a rapid and ground-breaking progress that I think it wise to step back a moment and reconsider the very issue of the evolution of language at its roots. I wish to start with two real-life parables, drawing some important lessons from each. The first is from physics, the second from biology.

Parable 1. The Italian physicist Gabriele Veneziano is acknowledged to have been the first inventor/discoverer of the core idea behind string theory. Veneziano had not realized, back in 1968, where his idea was leading. Initially, his "dual resonance models" were only an elegant way of summarizing several apparently scattered facts and hypotheses and of solving some inconsistencies of the standard theory. In the fullness of time, it turned out that the consequence of that initial idea, and of the mathematical formalism used to express it, was that the world of elementary particles is the projection onto our four-dimensional space of modes of vibration and oscillation of microscopic uni-dimensional strings in a space with eleven dimensions. String theory is, for the moment at least, so many steps removed from experimental observation that its partial success has to be gauged by indirect confirmation of some of its secondary predictions. This is, understandably, far from deterring physicists, and work in string theory is in full swing.

One lesson here (Lesson 1 – L1) is that good scientists may well embark on intellectual ventures the nature, conceptual contents, boundaries and interpretations of which are only dimly perceptible to them at the very start. The hairsplitting conceptual analysis on which certain philosophers so eagerly embark can often be an exercise in futility. Only the full unfolding of a scientific enterprise will reveal what the meaning of certain scientific concepts is.[1] Modern physics has taught us that, even when conceptual analysis manages to lay bare some hidden inconsistencies, the remedy consists in improving and radicalizing the theory, possibly making of these inconsistencies a virtue, not in freezing all inquiry until those concepts are duly sanitized under a shower of educated commonsense.

The second lesson (Lesson 2 – L2) is: No limit should be imposed on the degree of abstraction that may be needed in order to turn observations and careful descriptions into genuine explanations.

The new fields of mathematics that string theory has engendered, and the apparently dead ones it has revamped and redeveloped (such as, for instance, enumerative geometry) are so rich and beautiful that some mathematicians do not care very much whether the theory is actually "true" of the physical world. Hence:

(L3): it is typical of innovative scientific theories to generate also problems they cannot solve, but that would have remained invisible without them. Such theories typically allow to observe facts that would otherwise have gone undetected, and they frequently generate new methods that find applications well beyond the theories themselves.

Parallels with linguistics

I think that a few clear examples will suffice to show how basic theoretical notions required modification, as linguistic inquiry developed and deepened. One prominent example is, of course, the very notion of *language*. The pre-theoretical notion, the one we are all familiar with (instances of which are English, French, Swahili and so on) is an extensional one: a corpus of utterances existing "out there," produced by a certain community of speakers, analyzable in terms of a rule-governed combinatorics of morphemes, words, and idioms. Classical structuralism, focusing on the distributional analysis of linguistic forms in large corpora and offering Phrase-Structure rewriting rules, refined this common-sense notion, but substantially adopted it (Harris 1986/1951). However, upon a deeper analysis, the apparently unproblematic idea of languages as "common treasures" of expressions turned out to be fraught with difficulties, nay, arguably, to be irremediably inconsistent (Chomsky 1986b). In fact, since its inception, generative grammar made the notion of grammar (a finite object) primary, and the notion of language (an infinite object generated by that grammar) derived.

Moreover, witnessing the sharpness of the native speaker's grammaticality judgments for a potentially infinite set of sentences never encountered before, it became inevitable that the central object of inquiry shifted from finite corpora and from the speaker's linguistic "behavior" (performance) to the speaker's tacit knowledge of language (competence). More precise terms were introduced by Chomsky later on, but in hindsight it is clear that already at the beginning of the generative enterprise the central theoretical notion was that of I-language (individual, internal, intensional) not that of E-language (external, extensional, public). Avoiding the identification of I-languages with strictly individual idiolects, but aiming at a characterization of the speaker's tacit knowledge as (somehow, intuitively) capturing a specific E-language (or E-dialect), the distinction between a stable "core grammar" and a mutable "periphery" was introduced. As the theory progressed, the notion of I-language became that of an internal computational-derivational system exhaustively characterized, in its final adult state, by a complete set of values for the syntactic parameters of the ambient language, as chosen by the local linguistic community out of a finite repertoire of theoretical possibilities.

Further progress led to conjecture that all inter-linguistic parametric variation was to be localized in the phonology, the morphology, and the lexicon, dispensing with all syntactic and semantic parameters. A crucial distinction was, thus, traced between a genuinely universal computational-derivational system (Narrow Syntax – NS) and its complex interactions at the interface with two other systems: the perceptual-articulatory one and the conceptual-interpretive one. All inter-linguistic variation is, thus, localized at these interfaces (for an exhaustive exposition and historical reconstruction of these ideas, see Lasnik, Uriagereka, and Boeckx (2005). The abstract concept so central to the present model is quite different from the initial, pre-theoretical, externalistic concept of "language". Whence:

(L4): I-languages are what one has to attempt to reconstruct the evolution of, when dealing with language evolution.

From constituents to phases

The case of phrasal constituents is also illuminating. Traditional grammars already countenanced Noun Phrases, Verb Phrases, Adjectival Phrases and Prepositional Phrases (Graffi 2001). The founding intuition is that certain substrings of words within sentences strictly belong together and constitute a relevant subunit. Those grammars had ascertained that the inventory of such units is extremely reduced, and that they are, at a deep level of analysis, the same in all languages, the world over. Textbook criteria do exist for singling out phrasal constituents and for making their linguistic reality more transparent (conjunction, coordination, extraposition, adjunction, the perceived naturalness of pauses between – but not inside – constituents, shifts of intonation, etc.). None of these superficial criteria is, however, exceptionless, nor are they entirely reliable even when applied together. Split constituents are especially hard to capture in this way. Traditional grammars also identified, under various terminologies, more prominent elements (heads) and less prominent ones (complements) within the same constituent. It became clear, early on, that syntactic principles have quintessentially to be formulated with reference to constituents (head-complement and head-head relations, c-command, constraints on syntactic movement created by specific nodes in the internal structure of constituents, etc.). No syntactic principle applies directly to words as such, nor does it apply directly to superficial word ordering. In fact, the paradigm case of an impossible syntactic rule is one that applies, say, to the third or fourth word in each sentence (for a recent confirmation of this impossibility by means of brain imaging see Musso *et al.* (2003).

The logic of linguistic inquiry led to the postulatation of other kinds of phrasal constituents, of a more abstract nature, not countenanced by traditional grammars (the so-called functional ones, for instance Complementizer Phrase, Inflectional Phrase, Tense Phrase). Some constituents were nested within other constituents, and these in turn were nested within yet other constituents, recursively. In the early 1990s their proliferation had become almost an embarrassment. It was a standard joke to ask generative linguists how many functional heads there are in the sentence *John saw Mary.* The minimalist program changed all this, reinterpreting an embarrassment of riches as the multifarious consequences of the recursive, cyclic application of just two elementary operations: Merge and Move. The more abstract and more basic concept of *phases* was developed.

Phases are self-contained derivational domains, characteristically nested one into the other, that are simultaneously sent to the two interfaces in strict succession, without any possibility of backtracking or looking-ahead. There are strict constraints of correspondence between the features of phases in a same sentence. Only the "edge" (roughly, the left periphery) of a phase remains momentarily open to modification, until the phase is sent to the two interfaces.

Phases have a theoretical status of their own, but they also map onto two kinds of older phrasal constituents (essentially CP, and vP), not without some problems, though (Carnie 2008). The phase edges are the loci of the transmission, checking, and matching of features. Edge features and their derivation, in the present reinterpretation, embody the specific kind of recursiveness that is at the core of natural language. In a recent lecture at MIT (July 2005) Chomsky suggested that the evolution of language must be reconceptualized as, basically, the evolution of an apparatus capable of dealing with edge features. We will come back to this important suggestion at the very end.

The upshot of these considerations, therefore, is:

(L5): Every inquiry into the evolution of language must be an inquiry into the evolution of the computational brain machinery capable of carrying out edge-features operations.

Parable 2. In the first thirty years or so of the twentieth century a scientific program called mathematical biology (or, alternatively, physical biology) was developed, and it appeared, at first sight, quite promising. The long-forgotten (but in recent years more and more frequently cited) work by D'Arcy Wentworth Thompson on "The Laws of Form" (Thompson and Bonner 1917/ 1992) was centered on the thesis that biologists of his day had overemphasized the role of evolution, and underemphasized the roles of physical and mathematical laws in shaping the form and structure of living organisms. Best known are his graphic, formally simple, topological transformations to which differences in the forms of related animals could be attributed. In those same years, the Italian Vito Volterra and the American Alfred J. Lotka independently, but convergently, developed their now famous universal equations of population dynamics. These could indifferently capture the stability/instability of predator-prey ecosystems, of mutually inhibiting/reinforcing chemical reactions, of viral infections, all the way up to the cyclically oscillating equilibria and "fixed points" ascertained in populations of lynxes and hares in the Hudson Bay Valley.

In the words of Lotka, the key of this mathematical biology was:

a viewpoint, a perspective, a method of approach … a habit of thought … which has hitherto received its principal development and application outside the boundaries of biological science … Namely: the study of fundamental equations whereby evolution is conceived as redistribution of matter. (Lotka 1924/1956: 41–42).

Lotka's dense and immensely erudite 1924 treatise offers many interesting insights on sustainable rates of growth, birth and mortality rates, equilibria between species, biochemical cycles, and rates of energy transformations, even on the evolution of human means of transportation. But there is no doubt that the immense progress in biology we have witnessed since the mid-1950s *could not* have come from these general mathematical analyses. The revolution in genetics and in biology was marked by the advent of the *age of specificity* (Piattelli-Palmarini 1981). Biophysics and bio-mathematics became micro-structural and, powerfully boosted by the quantum revolution in physics, turned their attention to the various kinds of chemical bonds in biological macro-molecules, to the X-ray diffraction of crystals of nucleic acids and proteins, the generation and conduction of the nerve impulse, the modeling of motor control and motor planning, and later on, to the logical modeling of neuronal networks.

The lesson here is:

(L6): The legitimate desire to capture mathematical, formal and physical invariants in biology could not be satisfied by those equations and by D'Arcy Thomson's topological shears.

Real progress in this direction is presently coming from elsewhere. In order to capture the physical and mathematical invariants in biological systems we have to capitalize on all the microstructural data we have, on what we reliably know about genetic evolution, and on the calculus of optimizations at a microscopic and developmental level (Cherniak, Mokhtarzada, Rodriguez-Esteban and Changizi 2004; Cherniak 2009; Fodor and Piattelli-Palmarini in press). The key to the laws of form is in a different look at specific microstructures, at biochemical and molecular evolution (Kauffman 1993). We will come back to this in a moment.

The age of specificity in cognition

General equations of learning and mathematical learning curves were also, at the beginning of the twentieth century, the core of experimental psychology, especially of behavioral psychology, and they stayed that way until, roughly, the late 1950s. The slow, progressive demise of behaviorism came from insuperable internal predicaments (Gallistel 2000, 2002) and from an increasing awareness of the importance of data from ethology, i.e. data on different innate species-specific repertoires of spontaneous behaviors and different innate species-specific learning potentials. The early success of abstract neural modeling (McCulloch and Pitts 1943) and of developmental neurobiology (Lettvin et al. 1959; Hubel and Wiesel 1959, 1962) also began to change the picture. A radically new perspective was to emerge from the study of language and language acquisition, and, on a different front, from the experimental study of the impact of top-down processing on perception and reasoning (Bruner and Postman 1949; Bruner, Goodnow, and Austin 1956; Bruner 1973). Cognitive science as we now know it and love it is ultimately the offshoot of this change of perspective (Nadel and Piattelli-Palmarini 2003).

The coming of the age of specificity in cognition has given us generative grammar, the modularity of mind, visual cognition, special attention to specific brain lesions and the corresponding cognitive pathologies, a sound developmental psychology and the progressive ascertainment of the awesome subtlety and abstraction of bottom-up mental processing (which also characterizes the most interesting parts of the domain of Judgment and Decision Making (Kahneman 2003). In this long and complex story, however, I wish to stress the much-resisted ascent of specificity in the domain of language.

Formal inquiries into different classes of languages, natural and artificial, based on the theory of automata, were remarkably productive as a mathematical enterprise (Chomsky 1956; Bar-Hillel 1953a, 1953b, 1954; Schutzemberger 1961). The Chomsky hierarchy identified a new mathematically well-defined class of automata (pushdown automata), corresponding to an interesting class of output languages (context-free languages – CFLs) and could establish, on the basis of rigorous proof, that natural languages belong in a more powerful class than CFLs. Consequently, the even less powerful class of finite-state languages (notably statistical grammars, and in-frame-substitution grammars, quite popular in those years) could be ruled out on principled grounds. To this day, however, it remains uncertain, from a purely formal point of view, where natural languages exactly lie. They are situated higher than CFLs and lower than Universal Turing Automata, but it's hard to characterize them more precisely (Stabler 2009). Possibly the right formal characterization still eludes us, or possibly there cannot be any such purely formal characterization, because of inherent bio-evolutionary contingencies. Be that as it may, since the very beginning (ever since "The Logical Structure of Linguistic Inquiry" and "Syntactic Structures") (Chomsky 1955, 1957) real progress in the study of human languages has been made by supplementing the formal analysis with specific plausible considerations and constraints of a cognitive-linguistic nature (introducing unpronounced linguistic components, accounting for equivalences and contrasts that are obviously clear to every speaker, applying learnability constraints, avoiding ad hoc stipulations, and the duplication of rules and principles, etc.).

This style of theorizing (strictly in terms of the speaker-hearer's tacit knowledge of her I-Language) has progressively (and I suspect irreversibly) supplanted formal analyses. To the point that, with the possible exception of an earlier impact of E. M. Gold's mathematical results (Gold 1967; Pinker 1979, 1984) on learnability theory before principles and parameters (Wexler and Culicover 1980), the recent rebirth of formal linguistics with claimed consequences on language evolution (Nowak, Plotkin, and Jansen 2000; Komarova and Nowak 2001; Nowak, Komarova, and Niyogi 2001, 2002), whatever its merits, is isolated both from linguistic theory proper and from the quest for the genetic and neural bases of language evolution.

In summary, from the mid-1950s onwards the age of specificity has conquered linguistics too. It became progressively more and more evident that there was little gain of understanding to be derived from a study of language seen as a special application of general principles of cognition (exemplary in this respect still is, I think, the whole of the Piaget–Chomsky debate at Royaumont, now over thirty years old) (Piattelli-Palmarini 1980). Not everyone agreed then, nor does everyone agree now. In fact, it is still frequently the case that generic explanations of the workings of language are tried and retried, up to exhaustion, *before* any specificity of the language system is admitted or even contemplated. As rightly underlined by Chomsky and Sperber at the Royaumont debate (Piattelli-Palmarini 1980), *any* future, yet unspecified *possible* explanation was judged by some participants (notably Piaget, Céllérier, Papert, and Wilden) preferable to an actual, detailed, and satisfactory explanation, offered there and then, based on the specificity and the autonomy of syntax.[2] Contrary to a frequent misunderstanding, the specificity of language *still* is at the core of the minimalist program. Narrow syntax is the optimal solution to the problem posed by the interaction with two quite specific interfaces (the phonatory-perceptual one and the conceptual one) and the model as a whole still has no revealing analogies with other cognitive systems (visual, motor, pragmatic, ratiocinative etc.).[3]

The minimalist program invites us to explore the possibility that the design of the narrow language faculty (Narrow Syntax) is more akin to that of an optimal physical system than to that of a contingent species-specific juxtaposition of modules shaped by evolutionary tinkering (as it was still largely the case with the Theory of Government and Binding). But the broad faculty of language (as defined in (Hauser, Chomsky, and Fitch 2002), is still specific, and does not resemble other cognitive systems. In this domain too, the answer lies not in any of the older generalist strategies (Piaget's auto-equilibration, thematization, reflexive abstraction etc., nor the modern versions offered by connectionists). This leads to:

(L7): It would be ill advised to deny or belittle any bit of insight that the age of specificity has brought us. The point is to explain all these insights in a compact way, not to explain them away.

Some limits of the "age of specificity" outlook in biology

In the title of his Croonian Lecture of 1908 and of his later book *Inborn Errors of Metabolism* (1909/1923), Regius Professor of Medicine at Oxford, Archibald E. Garrod, coined a revealing expression, and one destined to stay.[4] In hindsight, it was inevitable that the first instances of a causal connection between genetic mutations and defective phenotypes were those of genes possessing very high penetrance, that is, cases in which the probability of the metabolic error, given the presence of the altered gene, is close to one, regardless of endo-environmental and exo-environmental variations.

Garrod's list has not ceased to expand. Any modern textbook of human genetics offers ample and detailed reviews of such cases, duly explaining dominance, recessivity, homo-and hetero-zygosis, gene regulation and so on. However, in recent years, even textbook cases à la Garrod, such as cystic fibrosis, have been reexamined, because data on a wide range of different severities of the syndrome have disclosed more subtle, less penetrant, genetic influences. Any attempt even at a rapid review of these conceptual changes and the data that have prompted them would be utterly out of place here. Nonetheless, I wish to point out that the picture is changing. The textbook picture only applies to a quite restricted subset of all the pathologies that have genetic causes. The classical Garrodian picture is real, and important, and those high-penetrance pathological cases are often, alas, lethal. But it now appears quite likely that the majority of gene-caused pathologies are not of that kind.

Once DNA and RNA were identified as the carriers of genetic information, and the protein-synthesizing machinery of the cell (ribosomes, t-RNAs etc.) was adequately characterized, arbitrary strings of nucleic acids could be inserted into this machinery, even in artificial in vitro preparations, and the corresponding polypeptide chains were systematically obtained. Thanks to this ingenious method, with artful variations, (insertions and deletions of chemical bases into chains of nucleic acids), the genetic code was eventually deciphered (for a detailed historical account, see Judson 1979/1986). Though our understanding of the whole process has witnessed momentous refinements (RNA editing, quality control, chaperonines, the histone code, etc.), the overall picture remains substantially unmodified in the eyes of a majority of biologists.

Biological evolution is still today conceived as driven by random mutations, followed by the synthesis of the corresponding modified protein (or proteins), followed by a developing organism that expresses the consequences of possessing those altered proteins. As the story goes, the ensuing reproductive potential of the mutants, in competition with other variants, decides who will survive and leave progeny and who will not. The process is blind, mechanistic, gradual and it eventually produces better and better organisms. Most attempts developed so far to account for the evolution of language follow this path, including recent speculations about the evolutionary role of FOXP2. I am suggesting that this picture requires radical expansion. I am a member of a scientific generation that was educated within the (now) standard textbook picture. I love every bit of it, and I am still persuaded that it has been a vast, deep, and healthy scientific revolution. The molecular-genetic revolution has pushed biology as a whole out of scientific pre-history into scientific history. But now the time has come to expand this picture, to start a further revolution.

A host of other factors, *all perfectly* mechanistic (one has to insist on this point) have recently come to enrich it (Fodor and Piattelli-Palmarini in press).

A quick summary

There are macroevolutionary changes that are caused by single point mutations in regulatory genes (for a quite dramatic instance see Ronshaugen, McGinnis, and McGinnis 2002)). These changes may well affect several organs and several functions at once, for instance the testes, the liver and the cerebral cortex (Simeone *et al*. 1992). The existence and the evolutionary impact of "spandrels" (Gould and Lewontin 1979; Lightfoot 2000) are corroborated at a strictly molecular, mechanistic level. At the price of repeating the obvious, if a function A (say, connectivity in the cortex) is driven by the selective pressures on another function B (blood filtering by the kidneys) because they are *both* under the control of a same regulatory gene, then there is no gain in understanding if we construct an adaptive story *only* for A.

Repeated genes and transposable elements give a whole new perspective on evolution (Juan Uriagareka and I have developed this story, and its plausible impact on language evolution in recent papers (Piattelli-Palmarini and Uriagereka 2004, 2005, 2008, in press). At least one clear case of a major new biological function brought about by transposable elements exists: adaptive immunity (Agrawal, Eastman and Schatz 1998).

Epigenetics, the genetic regulatory effects of subtle environmental factors, sometimes inheritable at least two generations down the line, is a crucial new dimension to be reckoned with (Petronis 2001; Gibbs 2003; Grewal and Moazed 2003; Jaenisch and Bird 2003; Pray 2004; True, Berlin, and Lindquist 2004). The functional evolutionary connection between the differential spread of repeated sequences in different species (for instance chimps and humans, as we have learned quite recently) and epigenetic regulation is being actively investigated as we speak (Vercelli, Martinez, and Chandler, personal communication). There is little doubt that *some* connection exists and that its impact on evolutionary reconstructions can hardly turn out to be secondary.

The pervasiveness, through evolutionary quite distant organisms, of certain regulatory genes shows that different parameters of the internal environment can differently switch a same gene towards the production of quite different forms. The PAX6 genetic system is substantially the same from the fruit fly all the way up to humans, but it gives rise to predictably different kinds of eyes, depending on the signals it receives from the tissues that surround it. *Pace* François Jacob, the eye was not independently invented five times by evolution. Rather, the same set of developmental genes can give rise to five different kinds of eye, under five different kinds of signals. The effects of evolutionary tinkering à la Jacob are everywhere to be found in biology, but one should not overextend the power of tinkering. There are, in biology at large, also instances of discrete variations, piloted by a discrete number of possible assemblies of biochemical and structural parameters. And there are bona fide optimal solutions to be found in biological systems (Cherniak *et al.* 2004; Cherniak in press). Contrary to the still prevailing wisdom, it may well *not* be the case that *all* the sub-optimal solutions have been tried out in the course of evolution, to be then discarded by selection. When optimal invariants are found across many orders of magnitude and across evolutionarily wildly scattered species it is more likely that they are the result of a regimentation by physico-chemical factors than of the eleventh-hour filtering of innumerable independent blind trials.

Finally, a host of subtle, context-dependent, dynamic and cross-chromosomally coordinated, gene regulations has been revealed. This also adds a new dimension not only to embryological development, but ultimately to biological evolution more generally. The cumulative lesson here is, in my opinion:

(L8): Many current attempts to reconstruct the evolution of every biological trait in terms of gradualistic, piecemeal, functionally driven cumulative changes are doomed to fail. The biological picture is becoming so complex and multi-faceted that one has to start afresh, with different assumptions and models.

So, what about language?

Some fifteen years ago, summarizing and combining insights I owed to Chomsky, Gould, and Lewontin, I launched a detailed challenge to all explanations of the evolution of language in terms of communicative needs. The linguistic examples (some already well known at the time) that I had collected, organized, and laid out in that paper showed how unlikely it was (to put it mildly) that the communicative function could have shaped the structure of language, of syntax in particular (Piattelli-Palmarini 1989). Steven Pinker and Paul Bloom rose to the occasion and did their best to counter that move, offering *other* linguistic material and suggesting hypotheses that could, they claimed, reconcile linguistics with an evolution driven by the communicative function (Pinker and Bloom 1990). I have not been moved by their (or anyone else's) attempt. Juan Uriagereka, in a whole very fine book (Uriagereka 1998), and David Lightfoot in a crisp article (Lightfoot 2000), joined forces with me. Our central point was, and still is, that a vast collection of data on syntax from a variety of languages, patiently collected and analyzed over decades, defies all communication-based, praxis-based and motor-control-based explanations.

Fragments, sluicing and deletions

To the heap of syntactico-semantic facts expounded in the papers and the book I just mentioned (in fact, in the whole of the formidable literature in generative grammar of the past fifty years or so), I want to add here another challenge for the functionalists. If language had been shaped by communicative needs, one would expect a paradigmatic confirmation of this alleged fact in truncated expressions, when whole parts of sentences are elided, yet every speaker-hearer clearly understands what is being said, given the context of the utterance. The following are canonical and well-studied examples:

Q: Who did Mary see?
A: John   FRAGMENT
Mary met someone, but I do not know who.   SLUICING
Q: Who was Peter talking with?
A: *Mary*   FRAGMENT w. PREPOSITIONAL STRANDING
Mary bought a book, and Bob did too. VP-ELLIPSIS

In each of these cases some sentential component has been elided, left as tacitly understood, because considered (and correctly so) redundant, obvious and not essential. The rub, for the functionalist, is that these fragments must obey, in every language, very precise syntactico-semantic constraints. For instance, in languages that have manifest case, both *Who* in the question and *John* in the truncated answer will have Case (accusative or dative, or whatever case the verb assigns). In languages that, unlike English, do not allow prepositional stranding, such as Italian and Spanish, one cannot answer with a bare noun (*Mary*), but must repeat the preposition (*with Mary*). More subtle syntactic constraints apply to the truncated expressions in more complicated constructions, in perfect agreement with the syntactic specificities of the various languages. There is indeed, as Jason Merchant insightfully states, "a syntax of silence" (Merchant 2001, 2004; Fox and Lasnik 2003).

Interestingly enough, such truncations are *not* always possible. Superficially similar sentences reveal a clear contrast in this respect. The asterisks here below indicate such impossibility.

> She was reading, but I don't know what.
> *She was wearing, but I don't know what.
> *She is bathing, but I don't know who(m).

Many corresponding examples have been collected from a variety of languages (Merchant 2004), showing that there are strict syntactic constraints even on such fragments. The boundaries of what can be elided, where and how, neatly match the syntactic differences between languages. The lesson here is (borrowing an expression from Alec Marantz).

(L9): There is no escape from syntax, not even when it would seem that mere isolated words or mere fragments of sentences could suffice to communicate.

This kind of virtual reverse engineering shows that, once a brain has been built to handle full-blown languages, you cannot shut off this capability, not even temporarily or episodically, not even when the subtleties of the whole grammar are a hindrance to communication (Lightfoot 2000).

Similar considerations apply to idioms (Marantz 1997), i.e. something one would have supposed to come as close as anything fully linguistic can to a list of arbitrary, non-compositional, sign-meaning pairs. Finally (for the present discussion) the full weight of syntax is also present in codeswitching, that is, when words and expressions from one language are naturally inserted by a multilingual speaker into sentences of another language. Several syntactic and morpho-lexical constraints apply (MacSwan 2005; van Gelderen and MacSwan 2008). Since codeswitching entails the union of at least two (lexically encoded) grammars, but ordering relations are not preserved under union, codeswitching within one component of Phonological Form is not possible. For instance,

English *eat* and Spanish *comer* cannot be inserted with the other language's morphemes for verb inflection

> * Juan *com-* ed *Juan esta *eat-* iendo
> Auxiliaries cannot be mixed either
> The students had seen *il film italiano*
> But
> * The students had *visto il film italiano*

Restrictions to switching apply also to agreement, closed class words, functional words, determiners, and quantifiers.

Summing up so far: Some authors have described grammar as "the servant of language, not the master" (Minsky 1986: 266), as a later social construct (Arbib 2005), a remedy for ambiguity (for an effective counter, see Uriagereka 1998) or somehow a byproduct of semantics and pragmatics (for instance Piaget, in Piattelli-Palmarini 1980, and Tomasello 2000).

The lesson here is that communication as mere speech minus syntax is not an option, lest we fall into the fallacy of subtraction. Various conjectures about a protolanguage in our ancestors instantiate this fallacy, in my opinion.

Protolanguage and/as the fallacy of subtraction

Words are fully syntactic entities and it's illusory to pretend that we can strip them of all syntactic valence to reconstruct an aboriginal non-compositional protolanguage made of words only, without syntax (see for instance Arbib 2005). It's very hard to even *define* words in the absence of a full panoply of phonological, morphological, and syntactic criteria (Di Sciullo and Williams 1978). Intuitively, pre-theoretically, words are sub-sentential and sub-phrasal linguistic units, but there is great variation across languages as to what constitutes a single word.[5] No single phonological, morphological, syntactic, or semantic criterion applies in all cases, for all languages. As soon as inquiry deepens, more refined technical notions have to be introduced (listemes, lexemes, vocables, etc.).

Words typically possess a rich internal structure, not only in terms of phonemes, syllables, and morphemes, but also in terms of syntactic valence. The clearest example is the rich internal structure of verbs, with their full complement of arguments, light verbs (pronounced or unpronounced), power to assign Case, to select their subject and object and to select their auxiliary. But it has been argued that determiners (*a, the, all, some*, etc.) are relevantly similar to verbs (Larson 1991; Larson and Yamakido 2005), also having internal arguments. Prepositions head Prepositional Phrases and assign Case. Nominals derived from verbs preserve at least some of the rich internal structure of the verb (the most famous example in the generative literature being *destroy/ destruction*) (Chomsky 1972).

In some versions of linguistic theory (lexicalism), syntactic structures simply *are* the projection of lexical internal structures. In other versions (constructivism) independently existing syntactic structures constrain the insertion of lexical structures into specific nodes, and meaning is the result of the match between these structures (Hale and Keyser 1993, 2002). Minimalism has fully developed a suggestion that was already present, in a weaker form, in previous versions of the theory: parts of words (morphemes, or more abstract features) move as such, are checked and matched as such, and possess their own syntactic reality. The very idea behind IP (Inflectional Phrases) already was that inflectional traits are the head of a whole phrasal constituent, with systematic parametric differences (rich versus poor inflection) between languages. The very idea of a distributed morphology (Halle and Marantz 1993) and then the minimalist theory of feature-checking, of probe-goal relations and feature-deletion, make it very hard to disentangle the concept of word from a host of structures within words, and from the compositional potentials of words (internally available links with other words).

In the light of all this (and much besides I cannot go into for reasons of space), it is as illegitimate to conceive natural language as {words + syntax} as it is to conceive, say, the color system as {something visible + hue + saturation + brightness}. What would the "something visible" be, once you strip a given color of its hue, saturation, and brightness? What would a non-compositional protolanguage be, once you strip words as we know them from their internal structure and their compositional valence (Piattelli-Palmarini 2008)? We have what Quine has called the fallacy of subtraction (for a crisp warning against falling into this fallacy in a different case, see Fodor 2003). The no-escape-from-syntax lesson and the other lessons I have selected above should redirect a more productive inquiry into the evolution of language.

Conclusion: tentative redirections

Let's adopt the view that the evolution of language may not be the result of a cumulation of a host of smaller steps (this is akin to the view offered by Hauser, Chomsky, and Fitch 2002 and at odds with the one offered by Jackendoff 2002 and Pinker and Jackendoff 2005). And let's adopt the hypothesis that communication may not have been *at all* the driving force behind language. We have just seen that contemporary biology offers cases of major anatomo-functional discontinuities resulting from atomic events in the genome (point mutations in regulatory genes). As I have said above, cases of the evolution of one trait as a result of selective pressures on a functionally (though not genetically) totally different trait have also been documented. If we keep looking only at communication we may miss the discovery of the trait whose selective pressures may actually have driven language evolution.[6]

Memory facilitations for the growth of a syntax-free lexicon, whatever that may be, do not seem a promising avenue (contra claims by Nowak, Komarova, and Niyogi, 2002). Recursion is undoubtedly a centerpiece of the story (arguably *the* centerpiece) and there cannot be, on logical grounds, a fraction of recursion.[7] Not any kind of recursion will do, however. We do not speak in numbers, nor in LISP. Chomsky's suggestion that the derivation and checking of edge features (EFs) is *exactly* the kind of recursive, discrete, compositional computation that characterizes natural language deserves close attention.

Phases are of two kinds. To put it simply, they are predicational units (vP) or introducers of propositional attitudes (CP). Complementizer Phrases (CPs) stand at the pinnacle of the syntactic hierarchy, because they introduce the sentence as a whole, and the relation of the speaker to the proposition (the thought) that the sentence expresses. In a first approximation, C (the Complementizer) can be represented as a (mostly tacit) equivalent of "that ..." It's the highest functional head of the sentence. The other kind of phase (vP) is constituted by a verb and all its complements. Again in a first approximation, it expresses what is being predicated of what, and what modifies what.

It stands to reason that predication is embedded, sometimes deeply embedded, within a propositional attitude, and that one predication may be embedded within another. Predications are kinds of judgments, we grasp what is being predicated of what. The carriers of predicates must lie within the scope of the predication, which in turn can lie within the scope of another predication, and ultimately must lie within the scope of the propositional attitude introduced by C.

There is a crucial consideration which goes all the way back to Immanuel Kant but seems to be ignored by many who suggest scenarios for language evolution (Jerry Fodor has been relentless, over the years, and rightly so, in reminding us of this sharp divide. Most recently in Fodor 2003.) One thing is a relation between perceptions or between mental representations (say, perceptions or representations may be similar or causally interrelated), quite another is the perception, or the mental representation, *that* there is a similarity out there, *that* A is causally linked to B. The similarity (the causality, the coincidence, the difference, etc.) must be itself *in the scope* of the sensation, or the mental representation. Pace the empiricists of yesterday and of today, no number of repetitions of similar sensations caused by A and B, no number of occurrences of mental representations prompted by C being followed by D, can *by themselves* generate the judgment *that* A is similar to B, the representation *that* C is the cause of D. The current state of linguistic theory suggests that only a brain/mind equipped with the capacity to handle CPs and vPs recursively *can* make this transition. Relations of identity, co-reference, and the tracking of what is being predicated of what, of what modifies what (Ike-uchi 2003) become crucial only for a brain/mind so equipped. Words and their meanings become permeated through and through by these dependencies. All reference is only to objects and events *under a description*, objects and events are presented to the mind by language always *from a certain mental point of view* (Chomsky 1995a; Pietroski 2005).

Intensionality becomes both inescapable and primary, while extensionality is derived. The recursive handling of edge features is *precisely* what allows all this. To the best of our present knowledge, nothing else can. This is why it makes a lot of sense that we should care to reconstruct the evolution of *this* capacity, if we care at all to reconstruct the evolution of language.

11 The creative capacity of language, in what manner is it unique, and who had it?

Philip Lieberman

Introduction

Humans have the ability to effortlessly acquire thousands of words, which are each associated with a wide range of semantic references. Other species share this ability to a limited degree. Chimpanzees who have acquired the ability to communicate by means of manual sign language or other manual systems have 150 word productive vocabularies and can coin new words. They appear to think in terms of words, signing the names of objects as they look at picture-books (Gardner and Gardner 1980). Chimpanzees, both "common" (Gardner and Gardner 1980) and bonobos (Savage-Rumbaugh *et al.* 1986) can comprehend distinctions in meaning conveyed by the syntax of simple sentences and aspects of the morphology of ASL. Although present-day chimpanzees are not identical to the common ancestor of humans and apes who lived some six or seven million years ago, they in many ways are living hominoid fossils and any capacity present in chimpanzees most likely was present in our common ancestor. Likewise, any aspect of human linguistic ability that is absent in chimpanzees is a "derived" feature that evolved in the course of human evolution.

The derived properties of language that will be discussed here are speech and syntax. Chimpanzees cannot talk, although they could form many of the phonetic distinctions that convey human language (Lieberman 1968). Non-human primates lack the neural capacity that allows humans to produce a potentially limitless number of words from a finite set of motor gestures. This neural capacity, which I will denote with the term "reiteration," also allows humans to produce a potentially infinite number of sentences from a large, but finite, number of words and syntactic processes. Reiteration subsumes the recursive properties of syntax that have often been noted by linguists, but unlike the hypothetical "narrow faculty of language" proposed by Hauser, Chomsky, and Fitch (2002), which they claim is specific to syntax, the neural capacity for reiteration is expressed outside the domain of language when we change the direction of a thought process as well as in seemingly unrelated activities such as dancing. Indeed, central to my argument are the findings of current studies that suggest that the neural bases of reiteration derive from brain mechanisms originally adapted for motor control. In the course of evolution these neural mechanisms were modified to allow animals to respond flexibly to external events and ultimately were modified to confer human cognitive flexibility, expressed as reiteration in the domain of language and other endeavors. In this, I claim no original insight; the credit goes to Karl Lashley, who in 1951 proposed that neural mechanisms originally adapted for motor control are the basis for human creative behavior. I shall note recent anatomical data that suggest that, though a degree of cognitive creative ability must have been present far earlier than the Upper Paleolithic, the appearance of species-specific human speech-producing anatomy in that period, some 50,000 years ago, is an index for fully human creative capacities.

Reiteration and recursion

Although linguists generally distinguish between the creative properties of phonology and syntax, the difference appears to result from theory-specific constraints. Reiteration is the process wherein a hierarchical structure can be formed within which elements having nested hierarchical structures. A sentence such as, *The boy who was talking fell down*, has within the framework of the sentence the relative clause, *who fell down*. Generative grammars since Chomsky (1957) have claimed that the relative clause derives from a sentence node "S" inserted into the hierarchical framework of a hypothetical "underlying" sentence. In the 1957 system, transformational rules acted on the underlying sentence to yield the sentence that might be uttered or written. In Chomsky's (1995b) current "minimalist" grammar, the syntactic rule "Merge" recursively inserts sentences and other syntactic units into the framework of a carrier sentence; the minimalist rule "Move" then rewrites the resulting string of words to yield the sentence that one actually hears or reads. The terminology shifts in different versions of generative grammar, but they all claim that an underlying phrase marker exists, that through syntactic operations yields the sentences or semi-sentences present in any real data base. Recursion in expositions such as Hauser, Chomsky, and Fitch (2002) and their subsequent papers involves the insertion of identical elements, usually sentences, into a phrase marker. However, this definition is theory-specific, based on hypothetical underlying phrase markers and the requisite hypothetical syntactic operations (rules). The process of reiteration instead generates the sentences and semi-sentences that can be observed in real life by inserting relative clauses, prepositional clauses, adverbials, adjectives, and other elements of complex sentences without the torturous and often arbitrary operations of traditional generative theories.

The reiterative function of the basal ganglia that will be discussed below includes reordering and replicating cognitive pattern generators (Graybiel 1997). The cognitive pattern generator that elicits the relative clause, *who fell down*, would simply be inserted into the frame of the carrier sentence. In short, reiteration is in my view a general property of human creative capabilities deriving ultimately from motor and cognitive flexibility, manifest in the domain of linguistics in both syntax and phonology.

The Broca-Wernicke model

An understanding of the evolutionary roots of human reiterative ability and its relation to other aspects of human behavior first requires pointing out the deficiencies of the traditional Broca-Wernicke theory. Phrenology (Spurzheim 1815) is usually dismissed as a quack science, but although the predictions of its proponents, were tested and refuted, it lives on in the traditional "language organ" theory of the brain. The traditional Broca-Wernicke theory identifies these regions of the neocortex as the "seats" of language. The Broca-Wernicke theory is based on the study of "experiments-in-nature," patients suffering brain damage that resulted in "aphasia" – the permanent loss of linguistic abilities. Paul Broca (1861) studied the speech deficits of a patient "Tan," who had suffered a series of strokes. The strokes had caused extensive brain damage, including "the third frontal convolution," an anterior (front) area of the cortex. Broca noted that Tan could only utter the syllable "tan," and, influenced by phrenological theories that mapped complex behaviors to discrete parts of the skull, concluded that damage to this cortical region (which includes Broca's area) caused the patient's speech deficit. Broca, however, overlooked Tan's extensive subcortical damage and non-linguistic motor impairments. Wernicke in 1874 found that patients who had suffered damage in the posterior left hemisphere had difficulty comprehending speech. Wernicke localized receptive linguistic ability to this area. Since vocal communication involves both comprehending and talking, Lichtheim (1885) proposed a cortical pathway linking Broca's and Wernicke's areas. According to the traditional model, speech is perceived in Wernicke's area, a posterior temporal region associated with auditory perception. A hypothetical cortical pathway then transmits information to Broca's region, which is adjacent to cortical motor control areas.

Although the Broca-Wernicke model is simple, it is wrong. Current studies show that the behavioral deficits of Broca's aphasia are not limited to speech production; they include difficulty comprehending distinctions in meaning conveyed by syntax and recalling words (Blumstein 1995). Cognitive deficits, outside the domain of language also occur. Kurt Goldstein (1948) characterized Broca's aphasia as "loss of the abstract capacity," including difficulties in adapting to changing circumstances. It, moreover, has been apparent for more than twenty years that permanent loss of language does not occur absent subcortical damage, even when Broca's or Wernicke's areas have been destroyed.

The probable subcortical locus of aphasia was proposed in the early years of the twentieth century; computer aided tomography (CT) scans and magnetic resonance imaging (MRI) confirm that aphasia does not occur unless sub-cortical damage is present (Stuss and Benson 1986; Dronkers *et al.* 1992; D'Esposito and Alexander 1995). Patients having extensive damage to Broca's or Wernicke's areas generally recover unless subcortical damage also occurs. As D'Esposito and Alexander in their study of aphasia conclude, it is apparent that a purely cortical lesion cannot produce Broca's or Wernicke's aphasia (1995: 41). Moreover, damage to subcortical structures, sparing cortex, can produce aphasic syndromes; subcortical damage that leaves Broca's area intact can result in Broca-like speech production and language deficits (e.g. Naeser *et al.* 1982; Benson and Geschwind 1985; Alexander, Naeser, and Palumbo 1987).

Alexander and his colleagues (1987), for example, reviewed nineteen cases of aphasia that resulted solely from subcortical lesions. The aphasic deficits ranged from fairly mild impairment in a patient's ability to recall words, to "global aphasia" in which a patient produced very limited speech. The severest language deficits occurred in patients who had suffered the most extensive subcortical brain damage. Damage to the basal ganglia, peri-ventricular path-ways from the basal ganglia to cortical targets, and the internal capsule (which contains nerve fibers that project to the cortex) was present in aphasic patients. Subsequent studies rule out damage to the internal capsule causing aphasia because surgical lesions of the internal capsule aimed at mitigating obsessive-compulsive behavior do not induce aphasia (Greenberg, Murphy, and Rasmussen 2000). Impairment of neural circuits involving the basal ganglia appears to be the root cause of Broca's aphasia.

Neural circuits

Complex brains contain many distinct neuroanatomical structures that perform local operations such as processing tactile, visual, or auditory stimuli. Other structures and cortical regions perform local operations such as regulating aspects of motor control or holding information in short-term (working) mem-ory, etc. (e.g. Marsden and Obeso 1994; Mirenowicz and Schultz 1996; Monchi *et al.* 2001; Polit and Bizzi 1978; Sanes *et al.* 1995). However, an isolated structure or cortical area usually does not by itself regulate a complete complex behavior. Instead a particular neural structure may support many anatomically segregated groups, "populations," of neurons that carry out a similar "local" operation. Each neuronal population is linked to, "projects" to, an anatomically distinct neuronal population in another region of the brain. A series of linked neuronal populations form a neural "circuit." The resulting neural circuit, linking local operations in different parts of the brain, appear to be the basis for complex observable aspects of behavior, such as walking, talking, dancing, processing the syntax of a sentence, and so on.

Moreover, within a given neural structure, distinct anatomically segregated neuronal populations may occur that each project to neurons in different brain structures, forming multiple circuits that each regulates some other behavior. This is the case for the basal ganglia, reflecting its evolutionary history and accounting for its role in conferring human creative "reiterative" ability.

Cortical-Striatal-Cortical Circuits

A class of neural circuits involves linkages between areas of the cortex and subcortical striatal structures. The basal ganglia are subcortical structures located deep within the brain. They can be traced back to anurans similar to present-day frogs (Marín, Smeets, and González 1998). The striatal component of the basal ganglia includes the caudate nucleus and the lentiform nucleus. The lentiform nucleus itself consists of the putamen and globus pallidus. The putamen receives sensory inputs from most parts of the brain. The globus pallidus is an output structure receiving inputs from the putamen and caudate nucleus. The caudate nucleus, putamen, and globus pallidus are interconnected and form a system with close connections to the substantia nigra, thalamus, other subcortical structures and cortex. The thalamus, in turn, connects to different cortical areas. The connections with cortex are complex (Alexander, Delong, and Strick 1986; Parent 1986; Alexander and Crutcher 1990; Delong 1993; Marsden and Obeso 1994; Middleton and Strick 1994).

Disruptions in behavior seemingly unrelated such as obsessive-compulsive disorder (Greenberg, Murphy, and Rasmussen 2000), schizophrenia (Graybiel 1997) and Parkinson's Disease (Jellinger 1990) derive from the impairment of neural circuits linking cortical areas with the basal ganglia. Behavioral changes usually attributed to frontal lobe cortical dysfunction can be observed in patients having damage to basal ganglia (e. g., Cummings and Benson 1984; Flowers and Robertson 1985; Alexander, Delong, and Strick 1986; Lange, Robbins, Marsden, James et al. 1992; Delong 1993). Cummings in his 1993 review article identifies five parallel basal ganglia circuits which are involved in motor control, cognition, attention and other aspects of behavior. Current tracer and neuroimaging studies confirm the role of basal ganglia circuits to the dorsolateral and ventrolateral prefrontal regions of the prefrontal cortex (a frontal region of the cortex) in regulating cognitive behavior.

Traditional tracer studies entail injecting substances into living animals that attach themselves to the outputs of neurons projecting to other neurons forming neural circuits. Post-mortem sectioning, staining, and microscopic examination then reveal the neural pathways. Tracer studies of monkey brains confirm that the caudate nucleus and putamen support independent circuits that project to cortical areas associated with motor control and cognition (Alexander, Delong, and Strick 1986; Middleton and Strick 1994; Graybiel 1995, 1997). Non-invasive Diffusion Tensor Imaging (DTI) techniques, that are based on MRI technology, confirm the presence of similar neural circuits in humans (Lehericy *et al.* 2004).

Neurodegenerative Diseases

Parkinson's (PD) constitutes an experiment-in-nature that allows isolating the contribution of the basal ganglia to complex behaviors. PD damages the basal ganglia, mostly sparing cortex (Jellinger 1990). The primary deficits of PD are motoric; tremors, rigidity, and movement disruptions occur. Speech production deficits occur similar in nature to those occurring in Broca's aphasia. Speech slows down as vowel durations increase. Difficulties occur in sequencing the rapid lip, tongue, and laryngeal maneuvers necessary to produce "stop" consonants. Stop consonants are produced by momentarily obstructing the SVT with the lips (for [b] and [p]) or tongue (for [d], [t],[g] and [k]). The lips or tongue then open the SVT, producing a momentary "burst," an abrupt acoustic signal. The larynx must then produce phonation keyed to the burst. Phonation must occur within 20 msec. from the burst for the English "voiced" stops [b], [d], and [g] (the initial consonants of the words "bad," "dab," and "god"). Phonation must be delayed, usually for at least 60 msec. for the English "unvoiced" stops [p], [t], and [k] (the initial consonants of "pad," "tab," and "cod"). This phonetic distinction, which entails controlling the sequence of gestures between tongue or lips and the muscles of the larynx, was termed "voice-onset-time" (VOT) by Lisker and Abramson (1964).

Similar VOT distinctions differentiate the stop consonants of all human languages analyzed to date. (Many languages also differentiate words by means of "prevoiced" stops in which voicing starts before the burst.) A breakdown in regulating VOT is the most symptomatic speech deficit of Broca's aphasia (Blumstein *et al.* 1980; Baum *et al.* 1990) and in PD (Lieberman *et al.* 1992; Lieberman, Ross, and Ravosa 2000). In contrast, formant frequency patterns that reflect SVT maneuvers are generally preserved in both Broca's aphasia and PD (Blumstein 1994; Lieberman 2006). Broca's aphasics (Blumstein 1995) and PD patients can have difficulty producing and comprehending sentences that have complex syntax (e.g., Illes *et al.* 1988; Lieberman, Friedman, and Feldman 1990; Lieberman *et al.* 1992; Natsopoulos *et al.* 1993; Grossman *et al.* 1991, 1993; Lieberman 2000; Hochstadt 2004). As PD progresses, dementia occurs, different in kind from Alzheimer's (Cummings and

Benson 1984). Afflicted patients retain semantic and real-world knowledge but are unable to readily form or change cognitive sets (Flowers and Robertson 1985; Cools *et al.* 2001). These seemingly unrelated deficits derive from the "local" operations performed by the basal ganglia.

Local basal ganglia operations

The local basal ganglia operations characterized by Marsden and Obeso (1994) and Graybiel (1995, 1997, 1998) provide an explanation for the reiterative capacity conferred by cortical-striatal-cortical circuits. In the era before medication with Levadopa was used to treat Parkinson's Disease, thousands of operations were performed. The effects were reviewed in a seminal paper by Marsden and Obeso (1994). They note that the basal ganglia have two different motor control functions.

First, their normal routine activity may promote automatic execution of routine movement by facilitating the desired cortically driven movements and suppressing unwanted muscular activity. Secondly, they may be called into play to interrupt or alter such ongoing action in novel circumstances … they respond to unusual circumstances to reorder the cortical control of movement. (Marsden and Obeso 1994: 889)

Marsden and Obbeso conclude that,

Perhaps the basal ganglia are an elaborate machine, within the overall frontal lobe distributed system, that allow routine thought and action, but which responds to new circumstances to allow a change in direction of ideas and movement. Loss of basal ganglia contribution, such as in Parkinson's disease, thus would lead to inflexibility of mental and motor response …" (1994: 893)

Electrophysiologic and imaging studies

Electrophysiologic studies that monitor brain activity in monkeys and other species by means of exceedingly fine "microelectrode" probes confirm these local operations (reviewed in Graybiel 1995, 1997, 1998). When the basal ganglia of rats are destroyed they are able to execute the individual submovements that when linked together would constitute a grooming sequence (Berridge and Whitshaw 1992), but they cannot perform the complete grooming sequence. Electrophysiologic studies of the rodents' basal ganglia neurons show firing patterns that sequentially inhibit and release submovements to the motor cortex, thereby stringing them into a grooming sequence (Aldridge *et al.* 1993).

Brain imaging studies of neurologically intact human subjects such as the event-related functional magnetic resonance imaging (fMRI) study of Monchi *et al.* (2001) confirm the role of basal ganglia in conferring human cognitive flexibility. Brain activity was monitored in neurologically intact subjects in the Wisconsin Card Sorting Test (WCST), which evaluates a person's ability to form and shift cognitive criteria. Subjects had to sort cards by matching the images on them to the colors, shapes, or number of images on "match" cards. As predicted, neural circuits involving prefrontal cortex and basal ganglia were activated throughout the test. Bilateral activation was observed in prefrontal cortex, basal ganglia, and thalamus.

Dorsolateral prefrontal cortical areas were active at the points where the subjects had to relate the current match with earlier events stored in working memory. A cortical-striatal circuit involving a different cortical area, (the mid-ventrolateral prefrontal cortex, including Broca's area), caudate nucleus, putamen and thalamus was active when subjects had to shift to a different matching criterion. Increased activity occurred in the putamen during these cognitive shifts. Stowe *et al.* (2004) used PET imaging of neurologically intact subjects in a sentence comprehension study that involved a form of set shifting. The basal ganglia to dorsolateral prefrontal cortex circuit was active when subjects have to change their interpretation of an ambiguous sentence, confirming that basal ganglia cognitive set shifting also manifests itself in language. Other neuro-imaging studies show basal ganglia as well as cortical activity during sentence comprehension and word retrieval tasks (Klein *et al.* 1994; Kotz *et al.* 2003; Rissman, Eliassen, and Blumstein 2003).

In short, the basal ganglia act in concert with cortical areas of the brain to carry out motor, cognitive and linguistic tasks (Lieberman 2006). Cortical areas in both hemispheres of the cortex are active in these tasks, including Broca's and Wernicke's areas, their right hemisphere homologues and prefrontal areas that are not traditionally associated with language (Just *et al.* 1996). The imaging studies noted above and many other studies show that Broca's area is active when a person listens to speech, when a person recalls a word as well as the meaning of a sentence or when a listener identifies the emotional content of a sentence The absence of basal ganglia activity in other imaging studies may reflect "region of interest" (ROI) procedures that did not look for subcortical activity during linguistic tasks.

FOXP2, motor control and human reiterative capabilities

As Theodosius Dobzhansky (1973) put it, "Nothing in biology makes sense except in the light of evolution." And as Darwin (1859) first observed, organs initially adapted to control one function take on "new" tasks. Seen in this light, the local motor sequencing operations of the subcortical basal ganglia appear to be precursors for similar operations in cognitive domains. As noted above, the basal ganglia can alter a motor act when circumstances dictate by switching from one "motor pattern generator" to another more appropriate one. During a thought process they can switch from one "cognitive pattern generator" to another (Graybiel 1997), including syntactic operations. The roots of human creative ability expressed in reiteration thus stretch far back in time. The question is when and how the enhanced human reiterative capabilities evolved.

The FOXP2 regulatory gene clearly is not the only gene involved in the evolution of human language, but it has provided some insights concerning this question. As Fisher and Marcus (2006) emphasize, FOXP2 is not a "language" gene. FOXP2 is a regulatory gene that turns on other genes during embryonic development. It enters into the development of lung tissue and other aspects of anatomy and appears to have a role in facilitating learning and precise motor control in humans and other species. Some of the effects of FOXP2 on human behavior have been revealed through the sustained study of a large extended family marked by a genetic anomaly. A "syndrome," a suite of speech and orofacial movement disorders, and cognitive and linguistic deficits occurs in afflicted members of the KE family who have an anomalous version of FOXP2 (Vargha-Khadem *et al.* 1995; Vargha-Khadem *et al.* 1998; Lai *et al.* 2001; Watkins *et al.* 2002). These individuals have severe orofacial apraxia ; afflicted members of the KE family are not able to protrude their tongues while closing their lips and have difficulty repeating two word sequences. On intelligence tests, they have significantly lower scores than their non-afflicted siblings. Some afflicted individuals had higher non-verbal IQ scores than unaffected members of the KE family. However, intelligence derives from the interaction of many neural systems and the environment, and the low-mean 86 non-verbal IQ of the affected members versus a mean of 104 for unaffected family members suggests FOXP2 anomalies being responsible for generally lower intelligence.

MRI imaging of affected family members shows that the caudate nucleus is abnormally small bilaterally, while the putamen, globus pallidus, angular gyrus, cingulate cortex and Broca's area are abnormal unilaterally (Vargha-Khadem *et al.* 1995, 1998). Watkins *et al.* (2002) found that reduced caudate nucleus volume was "significantly correlated with family members' performance on a test of oral praxis, non-word repetition, and the coding subtest of the Wechsler Intelligence Scale." fMRI studies that compare afflicted members of the KE family with both their normal siblings and age-matched controls show that under-activation occurs in the putamen, Broca's area and its right homolog (Liégeois *et al.* 2003), which is what would be expected in neural circuits connecting the striatum and Broca's area (Lehericy *et al.* 2004). The pattern between neural anomalies and behavioral deficits is similar to those seen in individuals afflicted with PD, focal lesions in basal ganglia, and oxygen deficits, which also result in basal ganglia dysfunction (Lieberman *et al.* 2005).

These neural anomalies and behavioral deficits results from a dominant point mutation mapped to chromosome 7q31 in the FOXP2 gene (Fisher *et al.* 1998; Lai *et al.* 2001). The regulatory gene releases a protein that regulates the expression of other genes during embryonic development. In family KE, the mutation changes an amino acid, leading to protein dysfunction. Lai and her colleagues determined the neural expression of FOXP2 during early brain development in humans, and the mouse version (foxp2), in mice (Lai *et al.* 2003) – mammalian "end points" separated by 75 million years of evolution (Mouse Genome Sequencing Consortium 2002). Other genetic studies shows that foxp2 in other mammals is expressed in the putamen as well as the caudate (Takahashi *et al.* 2003). The salient point here is that in mammalian brains the regulatory gene acts on the cortical-striatal-cortical circuits discussed above, as well as the inferior olives and cerebellum.

The FOXP2 gene provides an upper bound for the evolution of the human brain and the emergence of fully human speech capabilities. Despite the high degree of similarity there are distinctions between the mouse, chimpanzee, and human versions. The mouse and human versions are separated by three mutations; the chimpanzee and human versions by two mutations. Enard *et al.* (2002), using the techniques of molecular genetics, estimate that the human form appeared some-where in the last 200,000 to 100,000 years, in the time frame (Stringer 1998) associated with the emergence of hominids that appear to be the immediate precursors of modern humans. However, there is a debate concerning the time depth of the human form of FOXP2, as well as its significance. Krause *et al.* (2007) claim that the human form is shared with Neanderthals, which would place it back to 700,000 years, but Coop, Bullaughey, Luca and Przeworski (2008) dispute this, pointing out problems with the analysis and perhaps contamination of the Neanderthal bone samples with human DNA. However, we can set a lower bound, the most recent date for the appearance of modern human creative capacities from new insights on when fully human speech producing anatomy evolved.

Therapsids and us – dating the appearance of the human brain

The argument presented here has its roots in the manner by which therapsids, reptile-like mammals who lived in the Permian and Triassic eras (286 to 208 million years ago), are thought to have had a mammalian paeleocortex containing the anterior cingulated gyrus, which among other things directs a mother's attention to infants and controls the infant's "isolation" cry (MacLean and Newman 1988). Brains are not preserved in the fossil record; the anatomical feature that suggest that therapsids had a mammalian paleocortex is their mammalian middle ear bones. The three bones of the mammalian middle ear, absent in reptiles, act as an amplifier, increasing the likelihood of hearing a distressed infant's isolation call. The index for a brain capable of flexibly regulating the complex motor acts that underlie speech and conferring cognitive flexibility is the species-specific human supralaryngeal vocal tract.

The physiology of speech production

The vocal signals of all terrestrial mammals are generated by filtering a "source" of acoustic energy through an airway through which maximum energy passes at frequencies termed "formants" (Fant 1960). For phonated sounds the source is a quasi-periodic series of "puffs" of air generated by the larynx. The average fundamental frequency of phonation (F0), the rate at which these puffs of air occur, is perceived as the pitch of a person's voice. However, distinctions between different consonants and vowels are conveyed by formant frequency patterns, enhanced by durational cues (Hellwag 1781; Chiba and Kajiyama 1941; Fant 1960). As we speak, the airway above the larynx, the supralaryngeal vocal tract (SVT), continually changes, producing a time-varying formant frequency pattern. A given SVT shape will generate a set of particular formant frequencies. For example, the vowels [i] and [u] of the words "see" and "sue" can be produced with identical F0's, – different formant frequencies specify these vowels. The range of area functions and the overall length of the SVT determine the formant frequencies that it can generate. In the eighteenth and nineteenth centuries tubes were used to model the SVT. The reeds provided acoustic energy that was filtered by the tubes. Contemporary studies use computer-implemented models to determine the formant frequencies that particular SVT shapes can produce (e.g., Henke 1966; Stevens 1972; Baer *et al.* 1991; Story, Titze, and Hoffman 1996).

The species-specific adult-like human SVT has a tongue having an almost circular sagital (midline) contour forming two segments, a "horizontal" oral cavity (SVTh), and a vertical pharyngeal cavity (SVTv), having almost equal length (1:1 proportions), positioned at a right angle. Movements of the undistorted tongue in the space defined by the oral cavity and pharynx can produce the abrupt midpoint 10:1 area function discontinuities necessary to produce the formant frequency patterns of the "quantal" vowels [i], [u] and [a] (the vowel of *ma*), which have useful properties for both speech perception and production. Stevens (1972) showed that these vowels have perceptually salient acoustic "correlates" that can be produced while minimizing the need for precise motor control. Spectral peaks resulting from the convergence of two formant frequencies yield perceptual salience (Fant 1960). For [i] the second and third formants, F2 and F3, converge at a high frequency; for [a] F2 and F1 converge at the midpoint of the frequency spectrum; for [u] F1 and F2 converge at a low frequency. Using "quantal" vowels for vocal communication is analogous to communicating using flags that have brilliant saturated colors. Other vowels, the formants of which do not converge, produce formant patterns analogous to pastel colors.

Stevens also showed that, at the natural midpoint discontinuity resulting from junction between SVTh and SVTv, the human tongue can move as much as

1 cm back or forth without changing the formant frequencies appreciably. The exact position of the speaker's tongue with respect to the midpoint constriction for [i] does not have to be precise. Radiographic studies that track tongue movements confirm Steven's theory (Beckman, Jung, Lee and De Jong 1995). Carre, Lindblom, and MacNeilage (1995), using a different procedure, reached similar conclusions. Their SVT computer model "grew" a "vertical" pharyngeal portion (SVTv) that was equal in length to its "horizontal" oral cavity (SVTh) when directed at producing the full range of human vowels

In contrast, nonhuman primates, including the species studied by Fitch (1997, 2000b), have SVTs in which the tongue is almost entirely within their mouths. They inherently cannot produce quantal vowels because they cannot produce the necessary abrupt, midpoint area function discontinuities (Lieberman, Klatt, and Wilson 1969; Lieberman, Crelin, and Klatt 1972). Acoustic analyses of the vocalizations of non-human primates confirm the limited range of their formant frequencies (Lieberman 1968; Fitch 1997, 2000b).

Choking

The biological cost of the human SVT is an increased propensity for choking to death on food lodged in the larynx. As Darwin (1859) noted, "every particle of food and drink that we swallow has to pass over the orifice of the trachea, with some risk of falling into the lungs (1859: 191)." Palmer and his colleagues, reviewing studies of swallowing, note that in contrast to nonhuman mammals:

normal humans are at risk for inadvertently inhaling food particles both before and after swallowing. Indeed, obstruction of the airway by inhaled food is a significant cause of morbidity and mortality in otherwise healthy individuals. (Palmer *et al.* 1992)

Death resulting from a blocked larynx often is attributed to other causes, but tens of thousands of incidents of fatal choking have occurred (Feinberg and Ekberg 1990). About 500,000 Americans suffer from swallowing disorders (dysphagia), and deaths from choking are the fourth-largest cause of accidental deaths in the United States (www.nsc.org/library/report_injury_usa.htm). There would have been no reason for retaining the mutations that resulted in a human SVT, unless the neural mechanisms that confer the reiterative properties of speech were in place.

Who had a human SVT, who did not, and what does that say about language?

The details involved in inferring the presence of the soft tissue of the SVT from the skeletal remains of hominids who lived tens of thousands of years ago are complex and have been debated since the initial paper on that subject by

Lieberman and Crelin (1971). However, we can with certainty determine when a fossil hominid did not have a human SVT. The key is the length of the fossil's neck, which can in some cases be accurately estimated from preserved cervical vertebrae. McCarthy, Strait, Yates and Lieberman (forthcoming) found that the necks of Middle Paleolithic fossils who lived about 100,000 years ago were too short to have a pharyngeal SVTv that was equal in length to SVTh. A similar constraint rules out Neanderthals having a human SVT. Surprisingly, neck lengths that would support a fully human SVT are not apparent in the fossil record until the Upper Paleolithic, some 50,000 years ago, when a blossoming of complex tools and art appears in the archeological record – the "Cultural Revolution" noted by Klein (1999). Although elements of this ensemble of archeological evidence are evident earlier, the sudden appearance of an array of advanced artifacts has been taken to be a sign of cognitive advance. The appearance of the human SVT in the Upper Paleolithic supports this view. The presence of a human SVT in a fossil hominid can be regarded as an index for the reiterative neural substrate that makes voluntary speech possible. And that neural substrate also plays a critical role in making syntax, cognitive flexibility, and, yes, dancing possible. Speech, language, and some degree of cognitive flexibility surely were present earlier, but the presence of a SVT specialized for speech at the cost of choking places a date stamp on when brains like ours definitely existed.

I talk, therefore I am.

12 Genetics and the evolution of language: what genetic studies reveal about the evolution of language

Karin Stromswold[1]

In this paper, I discuss how genetic studies of language can inform discussions about the evolution of language. Depending on the results of genetic studies, the answer could be that genetic studies have nothing to add to such discussions. I take a more optimistic view and argue that genetic studies can and do provide insights about the evolution of language. The organization of this paper is as follows. I begin with a discussion of the relationship between genetics and the evolution of language, outlining some of the assumptions and limitations that exist about their relationship. I then summarize findings of published behavioral studies and our ongoing twin study of language. I end with a description of current theories about the evolution of language, discussing how results from genetic studies can inform and constrain theories about how human language evolved.

The relationship between the genetics and evolution of language

Variability and the heritability of language

Heritability (h^2) is an estimate of the extent to which genetic factors account for the observed (phenotypic) variance in a trait. Heritability estimates provide insight into the extent to which differences in language acquisition and proficiency are due to genetic factors. If these phenotypic differences are largely due to differences in people's genetic endowments, heritability estimates will be high. If these differences are random or are largely due to differences in people's environments, heritability estimates will be low. However, if people do not vary in linguistic ability, then heritability estimates for language will be zero, even if genetic factors are completely responsible for human language. Thus, the first question we must address is, do people vary linguistically?

Although the course of acquisition is remarkably similar for all normal children acquiring a given language (see Stromswold 2000), some children learn language more rapidly than others. For example, although normal English-speaking children tend to mispronounce the same phonemes in the same way (e.g., pronouncing the fricative /ð/ as its homorganic stop /d/) and to master the pronunciation of

English phonemes in the same order, some children achieve mastery before others (Sander 1972). Similarly, although children's first words are surprisingly similar, some normal twenty-four-month-olds say only a handful of words, whereas others say over 300 words (e.g. Fenson *et al.* 1994). This same pattern is seen for inflectional morphology. For example, Brown (1973) found that, although the three English-speaking children he studied acquired fourteen grammatical morphemes in the same order, they did so at very different ages. This same pattern – of remarkable similarity in the order of acquisition, but large differences in the rate of acquisition – is also seen for the acquisition of English questions, auxiliary verbs, subject-auxiliary inversion, verbal particle, datives, passives and other complex syntactic constructions (see Stromswold 2000).

People might eventually attain the same basic linguistic proficiency, albeit at different ages. Alternatively, some adults might be more linguistically proficient than others. Adults clearly differ in the size of their vocabularies, but do they also differ in grammatical knowledge (competence) or performance? Presumably all normal adults acquire the basic morphosyntax of their language, but perhaps some adults fail to master rare linguistic constructions (e.g., the English subjunctive, *if I were a plant, I would have chlorophyll rather than hemoglobin*). Even if adults all have the same grammatical competence, individual differences in performance factors (such as working memory) could affect the ease with which they produce and understand complex syntactic constructions such as center-embedded relative clauses (King and Just 1991). It appears that some adults are more linguistically adept than others. For example, individual differences have been reported in verbal fluency (Day 1979), in the interpretation of novel compound nouns (Gleitman and Gleitman 1970), and in the accuracy and speed of sentence processing (e.g., Bever *et al.* 1989; King and Just 1991), Indeed, given that people differ in their ability to acquire a second language as adults (see Dörnyei 2005), one could argue that the linguistic development of some people plateaus, whereas the linguistic development of others continues.

Genetic factors in language-impaired and linguistically normal people

About 5 percent of children are abnormally slow at learning language, with these delays being relatively specific to language (see Stromswold 1997). Approximately half of these children grow up to be language impaired, with language impairments tending to cluster in families (Stromswold 1998). Even if genetic factors play a role in the language of language-impaired people, they might play no role for linguistically normal people. Alternatively, genetic factors could affect both normal and language-impaired people, but different genetic factors might be involved for the two groups. Furthermore, even if the same genetic factors are involved, they might play a greater role for language-impaired people. If different genetic factors affect language-impaired and normal people, or if the same factors are involved but to different degrees, this suggests that the two populations are genetically distinct in some way(s) and, therefore, that the evolutionary history of normal and language–impaired people might have been somewhat different.

The genetics and evolution of language

Because genetic factors might have a greater impact for some components of language than others, one cannot merely determine the heritability for overall language, but one must do so for different components of language (syntax, phonology, etc.). One way genetics studies can inform theories about the evolution of language is by determining how heritable different language components are. If, for example, genetic factors currently account for none of the variance in the size of people's lexicons, this suggests that no trait that contributes to lexicon size was selected for. If genetic factors do account for some of the variance, this suggests that something related to lexicon size *might* have been selected for. However, it doesn't mean that something related to lexicon size actually was selected for, nor does it tell us what was selected for.

Genetic studies can also inform evolutionary theories by investigating the extent to which the genetic factors that affect language also affect other abilities. If the genetic factors that affect (some component of) language also affect a non-linguistic ability, this suggests that these linguistic and non-linguistic abilities have overlapping neural underpinnings, which in turn suggests that they may have co-evolved or that, evolutionarily speaking, one may have been parasitic on the other. For example, if there is substantial genetic overlap between the ability to speak clearly and the ability to chew and swallow, this might indicate that some of the same neural circuitry is necessary for efficient and accurate production of complex non-linguistic and linguistic oral movements. This in turn might indicate that these skills co-evolved or one was parasitic on the other. Similarly, if we find substantial genetic overlap for particular components of language (e.g., syntax and phonology), this could indicate overlap in the neural circuitry that subserve these components, which might indicate shared evolutionary history. However, the existence of genetic overlap between different abilities does not prove that the abilities share neural circuitry or evolutionary history. It could just be happenstance.

Genetics, reproductive fitness and the evolution of language

Given that only observable phenotypes (in this case linguistic performance) can be selected for, what is important from an evolutionary standpoint is that people differ in linguistic performance, not that they differ in underlying (unobservable) linguistic competence (i.e., universal grammar). Furthermore, even if people's linguistic performance differs, these differences may not affect reproductive success, just as eye color presumably does not affect reproductive success. In other words, even if we find significant heritability for language, it may tell us nothing about the evolution of language.

Although there is no way of knowing whether at some point in our evolutionary history there was a relationship between greater linguistic precociousness or proficiency and reproductive success, we can investigate whether such relationships currently exist. For example, at some point in human history, parents of a child with a frank language impairment might have had fewer subsequent children, a process that geneticists refer to as "stoppage." Consistent with stoppage occurring in the past, the one study I uncovered shows that first-born children and children with more siblings are less likely to be language-impaired than latter-born children or children with few siblings (Horwitz *et al.* 2003). Perhaps at some point in our evolutionary past, being linguistically precocious increased the likelihood of a child surviving to adulthood, at which point he or she could have children. I know of no study that investigates whether a relationship between linguistic precociousness and childhood survival currently exists. One might speculate that, at some point in human history, linguistically precocious children had more siblings because their parents waited less time before having another child (perhaps because it was easier to rear a child who they could talk to). Contrary to the reproductive success prediction, today, children's vocabulary, verbal SAT and IQ scores are inversely correlated with the number of siblings and spacing of siblings (Alwin 1991).

At some point in human history being more linguistically proficient as an adult might have improved reproductive fitness by increasing the number of offspring a person had or by decreasing the age at which the person had their first child. (Having children at an earlier age increases reproductive fitness independent of number of offspring because having children early results in more generations in a given time span.) In current times, people with even mild cases of schizophrenia, autism, and cerebral palsy have fewer children than normal people. I am unaware of any studies that have investigated whether this is true for people with written or spoken language impairments. I am also unaware of studies that have examined whether there is currently a relationship between normal adults' linguistic abilities and number of offspring or age of first child. However, contrary to the reproductive success prediction, in modern societies, women with more education (a possible proxy for linguistic ability) have fewer children and have their first child at a later age than women with little education (see Bledsoe *et al.* 1999).

Previous twin studies

The logic of twin studies

Putting aside the possibility of interactions and correlations between genetic and environmental factors (but see Stromswold 2005), the variability in linguistic abilities in a population (the phenotypic variance) is due to genetic variance and environmental variance.[2] The most common method used to tease apart the role of genetic and environmental factors is to determine whether monozygotic (MZ) cotwins are linguistically more similar to one another than dizygotic (DZ) cotwins. Because MZ and DZ cotwins share essentially the same pre- and postnatal environments, whereas MZ cotwins share 100 percent of their alleles and DZ cotwins share only 50 percent of their alleles (but see Stromswold 2001a; Stromswold 2006), we can obtain an estimate of the proportion of the variance in people's linguistic abilities that is due to genetic variance (i.e., h^2) by comparing the degree to which MZ cotwins are linguistically more similar to one another than DZ cotwins are.

Concordance rates for language disorders

One way to determine whether MZ cotwins are linguistically more similar than DZ cotwins is to compare the MZ and DZ concordance rates for language disorders. Twins are concordant for a language disorder if both cotwins are impaired, and discordant if only one cotwin is impaired. In ten twin studies of written or spoken language disorders, the concordance rates were greater for MZ than DZ twin pairs, with the differences being significant in all but one study (Stromswold 2001a). When the twin pairs from the five studies of spoken language disorders were pooled, the overall concordance rate for MZ twins (84 percent) was significantly greater than for DZ twins (50 percent). The overall concordance rate for the five studies of written language was also significantly greater for MZ twins (75 percent) than for DZ twins (43 percent). One can obtain an estimate of the role of heritable factors for a disorder by doubling the difference in MZ and DZ concordance rates for the disorder. Using this formula, these data suggest that approximately two-thirds of written and spoken language disorders are due to genetic factors.

Heritability estimates that are based on concordance rates have a number of limitations. First, they are only as valid as the diagnoses given to twins. If even a small percentage of non-impaired twins are incorrectly diagnosed as being language impaired or if some language-impaired twins are incorrectly deemed to be normal, this will dramatically affect heritability estimates. Second, heritability estimates are only as specific as the diagnoses twins receive. If some of twins' linguistic impairments are secondary to non-linguistic deficits, then the estimates obtained will not be good estimates of the heritability of linguistically specific impairments. A third limitation is that concordance-based estimates are estimates of broad-sense heritability, and as such include the influence of gene dominance, epistasis (interactions between genes) and interactions between genes and environment. A fourth limitation is that that concordance analyses take what is likely to be a continuous variable (linguistic ability) and artificially categorize people as either impaired or not impaired. Inevitably, there will be cases in which one twin scores just a few points higher than his or her cotwin, but this small difference is enough for one twin be labeled normal and the other impaired. Perhaps the most serious drawback of twin concordance studies is that they can only be used to study the heritability of language impairments, and not the heritability of normal linguistic function. This is important because it is becoming increasingly clear that there isn't perfect overlap in heritable factors that affect language development and proficiency in language-impaired and normal people (see Stromswold 2001a).

Univariate analyses of twins' linguistic abilities.

In cases where the data obtained are more or less continuous (e.g., scores on language tests) rather than dichotomous (e.g., presence or absence of a language disorder), one can address this last drawback by comparing the similarity of normal MZ and DZ cotwins' test scores. In univariate analyses, a twin's performance on test A is compared with his cotwin's performance on the same test. An estimate of the effect of heritable factors can be obtained by comparing the similarity of MZ and DZ cotwins' scores on the test. For example, Falconer's (1960) heritability estimate is calculated by doubling the difference between the MZ and DZ intra-twin correlation coefficients.

Meta-analyses of over 100 twin studies have revealed that about a third of the variance in vocabulary, two-thirds of the variance in phonemic awareness, and 15 percent of the variance in articulation is due to heritable factors (Stromswold 2001a). Due to the variability among the tests used in the twelve twin studies of morphosyntax, it was not possible to obtain a meta-analytic estimate of the role in genetic factors for morphosyntax. That said, for over 90 percent of the morphosyntactic tests, the MZ correlation coefficient was larger than the DZ correlation coefficient, with the difference being significant for a third of the tests. These meta-analyses also revealed that heritable factors accounted for a substantial amount of the variance in written language abilities (40 percent for reading and and 60 percent for spelling). In sum, univariate analyses of published data clearly indicate that heritable factors play a substantial role in the spoken and written linguistic abilities of normal people. However, like heritability estimates based on twin concordance, these estimates are estimates of broad sense heritability. A second limitation is that they do not reveal whether the heritable factors that affect language are specific to language. It is possible, for example, that the heritable factors that affect phonemic awareness also influence other cognitive, linguistic, or motor abilities.

Multivariate analyses of twins' linguistic abilities

Multivariate analyses can help determine how specific the genetic factors that influence language are (see de Jong 1999). In bivariate analyses, a twin's performance on test A is compared with his cotwin's performance on test B (covariance). Genetic influence on the phenotypic correlation between test A and B (bivariate heritability) is estimated by determining the extent to which the MZ cross-twin correlation is greater than the DZ cross-twin correlation. In contrast, the genetic correlation (R_G) estimates the extent to which the same genetic factors affect A and B, regardless of their contribution to the correlation between A and B. R_G may be high, yet bivariate heritability low and vice versa. For example, genetic factors might play a substantial role for both gross motor abilities and linguistic abilities, but if completely different genetic factors are responsible for gross motor and linguistic abilities, R_G will be zero. Conversely, genetic factors might play only a modest role for gross motor and linguistic abilities, but if the same genetic factors are responsible for both abilities, R_G will be high.

One limitation of multivariate analyses is that estimates of the R_G for two behavioral traits are only as good as the behavioral tests used to assess the two traits. For example, analyses of the Twins Early Development Study (TEDS) data suggest that no vocabulary- or syntax-specific genetic factors exist (Dale *et al.* 2000). However, this might reflect limitations in the way syntactic and lexical development were assessed. The TEDS study uses the MacArthur Communication Development Inventory vocabulary and syntax checklists (CDI, Fenson *et al.* 1994). For the vocabulary checklist, parents indicate whether their child has said 100 words. For the syntax checklist, parents choose which sentence in twelve pairs of sentences sounds more like something that their child would say (e.g. *baby crying* or *baby is crying*). It seems plausible that parents are fairly good at recalling whether their toddler has said particular words and, hence, that the CDI vocabulary measure is a reasonable measure of toddlers' lexical development. This may be less true for the CDI syntax measure. It is very unlikely that a child has said the exact sentences listed, so to complete the syntax checklist, parents must act as amateur developmental linguists. Furthermore, parents complete the syntax checklist immediately after completing the vocabulary checklist. Therefore, one worry is that the number of words parents check off may bias how often they select the "good" or "bad" sentences. If such a bias exists, it would explain the high R_G for vocabulary and syntax found in the TEDS study.

A second limitation of multivariate analyses is that they only allow one to determine the extent to which there is genetic overlap for the particular behavioral traits that one has assessed. For example, researchers involved in the TEDS study have used multivariate analyses to determine the specificity of genes that affect verbal and nonverbal abilities. In addition to heritable factors that influence both nonverbal cognitive abilities and verbal abilities, there appear to be genetic factors that influence verbal abilities but not non-verbal cognitive abilities (e.g., Price *et al.* 2000). It is possible, however, that these latter genetic factors affect more than just verbal abilities. For example, genetic factors that affect verbal abilities but not non-verbal cognitive abilities could nonetheless affect oral motor abilities, fine motor abilities, gross motor abilities, social-emotional abilities, etc. The only way to rule this out is to assess all of these abilities in the same group of subjects, and perform the appropriate analyses. Unfortunately, one must have data from a very large number of twins to do so.

The Perinatal Environment and Genetic Interaction (PEGI) study

Overview

In 2002, we began the PEGI study, a behavior genetic twin study that investigates how genetics, prenatal environment, neonatal environment, and postnatal environment affect development. Our study is unusual in two ways. First, we have data on a wide range of the twins' linguistic and non-linguistic abilities. Second, we have extensive information about the twins' perinatal periods. The results discussed in this paper are those obtained from the first 260-odd same-sex twin pairs who were between the ages of two and six when they were evaluated. It is clearly beyond the scope or goals of this paper to present in detail the analyses performed or the results obtained. (For a more details, see Stromswold 2005; Stromswold *et al.* 2005.) Rather, we only summarize those findings that are most likely to inform evolutionary theories of language.

Measures of linguistic and non-linguistic abilities

The PEGI twins' abilities were assessed in many ways. The twins' linguistic abilities were assessed using the parent-administered Ages and Stages (AS) communication test (Bricker and Squires 1999). In addition, twins who were less than three years old were given the CDI (see above, p. 182) and twins who were between three and six years old were given the Parent Assessment of Language (PAL, Stromswold 2001b) tests.[3] Parents also reported when their twins acquired four linguistic milestones (onset of babbling, first words, first multi-word utterances, and clear articulation) and how much speech-language therapy their twins had received. In addition to these linguistic measures, the PEGI study included gross motor measures (AS gross motor score, amount of physical therapy received, and onset of sitting, crawling, walking, running, and climbing stairs), fine motor measures (AS fine motor scores, amount of occupational therapy received, and onset of finger feeding, fork feeding and scribbling), oral motor measures (amount of feeding therapy received and onset of drinking from a cup), social measures (AS personal-social scores, onset of social smiling, and amount of psychological or behavioral therapy), and cognitive measures (AS problem-solving scores and amount of special educational services received).

Genetic factors in language-impaired and normal twins

Twins were classified as language-impaired if they had been diagnosed with a language impairment, or if they had received two or more years of speech-language therapy. Concordance analyses of twin pairs in which one or both twins were language-impaired revealed that genetic factors accounted for over 80 percent of the language disorders in our twins. Furthermore, non-additive (i.e., dominant) genetic factors only played a role in the linguistic abilities of language-impaired twins. That said, univariate analyses revealed the same general pattern of results for language-impaired and normal twins, with genetic factors playing a greater role for PAL articulation scores (70 percent and 31 percent respectively for language-impaired and normal twins) and PAL syntax scores (100 percent and 26 percent respectively for language-impaired and normal twins) than for PAL lexical scores (69 percent and 5 percent respectively for language-impaired and normal twins). Because we found the same basic pattern of results for the two groups, we combined data from all of the twins into a single group. Doing so gave us adequate statistical power to perform the bivariate analyses described below.

Heritability of linguistic and non-linguistic abilities

When we combined all the twins' data, genetic factors accounted for a significant percentage of scores on all sections of the PAL, with genetic factors accounting for 41 percent of the twins' phonological abilities and 60 percent of their syntactic abilities, but only 18 percent of their lexical abilities. Genetic factors also accounted for a significant portion of the variance for most of the non-linguistic abilities studied, with genetic factors accounting for about a third of the twins' fine motor abilities, half of their social abilities, two-thirds of their gross motor abilities and essentially all of their cognitive abilities. Indeed, non-linguistic oral motor ability was the only non-linguistic ability for which genetic factors did not play a substantial role. Post hoc analyses revealed that genetic factors played a greater role in the non-linguistic abilities of language-impaired twins than normal twins, with the difference being particularly striking for oral motor ability. This raises the possibility that some of the twins' language impairments were not linguistically specific, but rather were secondary to more general impairments.

Genetic overlap for linguistic and non-linguistic abilities

The genetic overlap between linguistic and non-linguistic abilities varied according to the non-linguistic ability considered. The genetic overlap was greatest for oral motor and linguistic abilities (more than 90 percent overlap for therapy measures) and fine motor and linguistic abilities (approximately 80 percent overlap for AS scores and 90 percent overlap for therapy measures) followed by social and linguistic abilities (approximately three-quarters overlap for AS scores and one-half overlap for therapy measures) followed by cognitive and linguistic abilities (approximately one-half overlap for AS scores and one-quarter overlap for therapy measures),[4] with considerably less genetic overlap between gross motor and linguistic abilities (approximately 10 percent for AS scores and 50 percent for therapy measures).

The high genetic overlap for language and oral motor skills and for language and fine motor skills could reflect shared neural circuitry for tasks that require complex motor control (perhaps involving the recruitment of the supplementary motor area). The high overlap between linguistic and social ability might reflect shared neural circuitry for social skills and social-pragmatic aspects of language. Indeed, this explanation is consistent with the results of post hoc analyses that showed little genetic overlap for our measures of social skill and our measures of more formal aspects of language (PAL phonology and syntax scores).

Genetic overlap for linguistic milestones

We found considerable genetic overlap for the onset of words and sentences, the onset of words and clear articulation, and the onset of sentences and clear articulation. In striking contrast, there was essentially no genetic overlap between the onset of babbling and any of the other three linguistic milestones. This suggests that different genetic factors may be involved in babbling than in the production of words, sentences and clearly articulated sentences. Indeed, it is possible that contrary to common belief, babbling is not a precursor to linguistic communication. Furthermore, if different genetic factors affect babbling, this could mean that the evolutionary history of babbling was different from that of other aspects of language.

Genetic overlap for parent-report measures of lexical and syntactic abilities

We found almost complete genetic overlap for CDI vocabulary and sentence scores and for word and sentence milestones. Although this could reflect some deep underlying property of words and sentences, we believe the high R_G's merely reflect the fact that CDI and milestone measures are parent-report measures. Analogous to the bias parents might have when completing the CDI word and sentence checklists (see p. 182), if parents remember that their child said his or her first word at an early age but they can't remember exactly when their child began saying sentences, parents might be biased to say he or she began producing sentences at an earlier age than s/he actually did.

Genetic overlap for PAL scores

Another possibility is that the high R_G's for children's CDI word and sentence scores and for children's word and sentence milestones are due to all four measures being production measures (i.e., they involve speaking). The PAL phonology and lexical tests are production tests, whereas the PAL syntax test is a comprehension test (see footnote 3). Thus, if the high word-sentence R_G's are due to the CDI and milestones involving language production, the R_G for PAL phonology and PAL lexical scores should be greater than the R_G for PAL syntax scores and either PAL phonology or PAL lexical scores. Contrary to this prediction, we found greater genetic overlap for syntax and phonology scores than for lexical scores and either syntax or articulation scores.

Possible causes of the phonology–syntax genetic overlap

Hauser, Chomsky, and Fitch (2002) argue that recursion is the only property that is specific to human language (i.e., what they call the faculty of language narrow, FLN). If Hauser, Chomsky, and Fitch (2002) are right and syntax is recursive but phonology is not, the genetic overlap between phonology and syntax cannot be a reflection of recursion. There are two ways of dealing with this. The first is to argue that Hauser, Chomsky, and Fitch (2002) are wrong and phonology is, in some sense, recursive. The second is to argue that some other property is shared by phonology and syntax. Depending on whether this property is specific to human language (i.e., a property that is not shared with any other non-linguistic human ability or with any ability of any nonhuman species), this property would be part of FLN or the broader set of abilities that are required for human language (what Hauser, Chomsky, and Fitch [2002] call the "Faculty of Language Broad").

Although we cannot know for sure, phonology and syntax share (at least) two properties that could account for their large genetic overlap. The first is that in both phonology and syntax, simple units combine together to form more complex units. In the case of phonology, the units are phonemes that combine to form syllables.[5] In syntax, words (or more precisely, morphemes) combine to form sentences (or more precisely, clauses). Thus, one possible explanation for the genetic overlap between syntax and phonology is that this overlap reflects the combinatoric nature of phonology and syntax. If this is the correct explanation, we would predict that if we tested people's ability to produce and/or comprehend derivational complex words (e.g., *teach+er*, *bird+bath*), we would find the genetic overlap between derivational morphology and syntax to be at least as great as the overlap between phonology and syntax.[6]

The second possible explanation for the genetic overlap between syntax and phonology is that phonology and syntax both have hierarchical, branching structures with higher nodes dominating intermediate nodes that in turn dominate atomic elements. In the case of phonology, the highest node in the hierarchy is the syllable, and the intermediate nodes are onsets and rimes. Rimes in turn are composed of nuclei and codas, and onsets, nuclei and codas are all composed of phonemes. In syntax, lexical and grammatical morphemes combine to form phrases that in turn combine to form clauses that combine to form sentences.

Phonological and syntax units are constrained in the ways in which they can be combined, and these constraints make reference to the hierarchical structure of phonology and syntax. To take a trivial example, in a syllable, the onset and coda may be null, but the nucleus cannot be. Further phonological constraints appear to exist across languages (e.g., the sonority hierarchy) and within languages. For example, within a language, although an onset may be comprised of more than one consonant, there are restrictions on which phonemes can form clusters and the order in which these phonemes must occur. For example, in English /st/ is a legitimate consonant cluster in onset position, but /ʃt/ is not. Furthermore, /st/ is allowed, but /ts/ is not. Lastly, certain consonant clusters are allowed as onsets but not codas. For example, /skw/ is licit as an onset (e.g., in the word *squirrel*), but not as a coda. Similarly, within a language, there are restrictions on the ways in which morphemes can combine to form phrases and how these phrases can combine to form clauses. For example, in Chomsky's (1986a) Principles-and-Parameters theory, this restriction is cached out by saying that the ordering of specifier and head and head and complement must be the same for all phrases in a given language.

Evolution of language

Theories about the evolution of language

The intent of this section is not to espouse a particular theory about the evolution of language. Rather, we will attempt to compare some recent evolutionary

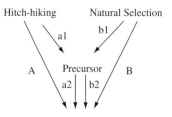

Figure 12.1 A schema for theories of language evolution

theories of language, many of which are described more fully in this volume. Broadly speaking, these theories can be characterized along three dimensions.[7] The first dimension is the process by which the genetic factors that currently subserve language came into existence. Some theorists (e.g., Pinker 1994; Pinker and Bloom 1990) argue that the genetic factors involved in language conferred a reproductive advantage on those who possessed them and therefore these factors were selected for (i.e., natural selection theories, the right side of figure 12.1). Other theorists (e.g., Chomsky 1987; Piattelli-Palmarini 1989) argue that the evolution of language was serendipitous, with the genes involved in language being passed on to subsequent generations because they happened to be near genes for other functions that were advantageous (i.e. hitch-hiking theories, the left side of figure 12.1). A second dimension along which evolutionary theories differ is whether *any* of the genetic factors that evolved (via whatever process) were specifically linguistic (language-specific theories, represented by *A* and *B* in figure 12.1) or whether all of the genetic factors also subserved some non-linguistic function (precursor theories, represented by lower case *a* and *b* in figure 12.1). The third dimension concerns what functions the genetic factors involved in language support.

For language-specific theorists, the question is how specific were the linguistically specific genetic factors? For example, did these genetic factors only affect some subcomponent(s) of language (e.g., syntax, Bickerton 1990; Newmeyer 1991), or did they support functions that were used in more than one component of language (perhaps hierarchical structures involved in phonology and syntax, see p. 187). In other words, what were the functions of the genetic factors represented by *A* and *B* in figure 12.1? For precursor theorists, the question is what non-verbal abilities were co-opted or underlay (some aspects or components of) linguistic abilities? Among the abilities that have been proposed are oral motor skill (e.g., Lieberman 1984), fine motor skill (e.g., object manipulation, tool creation or use, Bickerton 1990; Greenfield and Savage-Rumbaugh 1990; Greenfield 1991; Tobias 1994), non-verbal cognitive abilities (e.g., abstract mental representations, Gärdenfors 2003), social cognition (Knight 1998a; Worden 1998), theory of mind (Dunbar 1998), and mind reading (Origgi and Sperber 2000).

Evolutionary implications of genetic findings

The finding that genetic factors play a substantial role in all aspects of language means that evolutionary processes could have been involved in all aspects of language. The finding that genetic factors play a greater role for syntactic and phonological abilities than lexical abilities could indicate that syntax and phonology evolved together and somewhat separately from the lexicon. This could reflect that having a large vocabulary conferred less of an advantage than being syntactically or phonologically gifted, or that syntax and phonology both hitch-hiked on another ability that conferred reproductive success.

The finding that genetic factors play a greater role in the linguistic abilities of language-impaired people than normal people could mean that normal and language-impaired people's language involve somewhat different genetic processes. If this is true, it could reflect that somewhat different neural circuitry subserves language in language-impaired and normal people, which in turn could mean that, with respect to language, the evolutionary history of language-impaired and normal people may have differed. For example, selective pressure against very poor linguistic abilities (i.e., the type of stoppage described in above, p. 179) might have been greater than the selective pressure for slightly better linguistic abilities within the range of normal.

The high genetic overlap for linguistic and oral motor abilities provides support for theories that argue that language evolved from non-linguistic oral motor abilities (e.g., Lieberman 1984; Locke 1998; Ujhelyi 1998). Similarly, the finding that some of the same genetic factors affect linguistic and fine motor abilities is consistent with theories that argue that fine motor abilities were a precursor to language (e.g., Bickerton 1990; Greenfield and Savage-Rumbaugh 1990; Greenfield 1991; Tobias 1994).

If the genetic overlap for linguistic and social ability indicates that the neural underpinning for social cognition and language are partially shared, this means language could have (partially) evolved from social abilities, consistent with the theories of Knight (1998a), Worden (1998), Dunbar (1998), Origgi and Sperber (2000), and others. The greater genetic overlap for syntax and phonology than for either the lexicon and syntax or the lexicon and phonology suggests that the evolutionary history of syntax and phonology may have been more similar than the evolutionary history of the lexicon and either syntax or phonology. For example, it is possible that genetic factors coded for some function that allowed for the simultaneous development of phonology and syntax.

The more we know about the genetics of language, the more genetics can inform and constrain evolutionary theories of language. Unfortunately, there is much we do not know. No studies have investigated how genetic factors affect abilities involved in discourse-pragmatics, derivational morphology, or supra-segmental phonology, nor have studies investigated the genetic overlap between linguistic abilities and non-linguistic abilities such as sequencing, visual-spatial integration, drawing, and theory of mind.[8] In addition, only a handful of studies have performed multivariate analyses with more than two variables, and no studies have simultaneously investigated the genetic overlap among phonologic, syntactic, and lexical abilities. We are also unaware of studies that simultaneously investigate overlap among more than one component of language and any of the motor abilities assessed in the PEGI study. Without such studies, one cannot know how specific the genetic factors that affect (components of) language really are. As we learn the answers to these and other questions, we will be better equipped to develop and evaluate theories about the evolution of language.

In summary, results of genetic studies of language are most consistent with linguistic models and evolutionary theories of language that invoke both general and language-specific factors. Unfortunately, although current and future genetic studies of language may provide further insights into what linguistic and non-linguistic abilities co-evolved and, perhaps, insights into which abilities were precursors to language, they cannot tell us the process by which language evolved (i.e., natural selection vs. hitch-hiking or happenstance).

Part IV

Anthropological context

13 A putative role for language in the origin of human consciousness

Ian Tattersall

Introduction

As a paleontologist I have no particular expertise in the matter of precisely how language may have originated, or of its neural substrate, or even of how this most human of attributes might most accurately be defined or characterized. But as a student of evolution I may be in a position at least to suggest in what context language – or at least the potential to produce it – was discovered, and to point out the importance that this discovery may have had in releasing the extraordinary – and very generalized – human capacity that so clearly distinguishes our species *Homo sapiens* today.

Until rather recently, our hominid precursors were non-symbolic, non-linguistic creatures. That is, they almost certainly more closely resembled other primates than modern human beings in the ways in which they perceived, and communicated information about, the world around them. This is not meant to imply that earlier hominids were unsophisticated in their perceptive and communicative abilities, or even that they were necessarily inferior to us in those qualities. It is just to say that they were *different*, although that difference may well in the end have made them the losers in the grand competition for ecological space and economic resources that played out in Africa, Europe, and Asia toward the end of the last Ice Age.

Prior to the dramatic spread of modern *Homo sapiens* at some time in the period centering on around 50,000 years ago, it had been routine for several different species of hominid to coexist in some manner throughout the Old World (Tattersall 2000). But, in the few tens of millennia following the emergence of behaviorally modern *Homo sapiens*, all of our species' hominid competitors rapidly disappeared, in a process that certainly tells us more about the special nature of behaviorally modern *Homo sapiens* than it tells us about what it means to be a hominid in general. The abruptness and synchronicity of this Old World-wide elimination of competing hominid forms suggests that, whatever it was about *Homo sapiens* that suddenly positioned our species as the sole hominid on the planet, it cannot simply have been an extrapolation of pre-existing evolutionary trends in the human lineage (Tattersall 2004). Clearly, with the arrival of our species, something truly new had occurred within the hominid family. It thus seems worthwhile to look briefly at the patterns of both biological and technological innovation that prevailed in hominid history prior to the emergence of *Homo sapiens*, as background for understanding the nature, or at least the context, of that event. And it turns out that the observed pattern in this history, which is one of highly sporadic change, contrasts dramatically with the linear thinking that has dominated paleoanthropology since Ernst Mayr (1950) and Theodosius Dobzhansky (1955) brought the Evolutionary Synthesis to paleoanthropology around the midpoint of the last century.

The Synthesis, with its emphasis on gradual generation-by-generation change, viewed hominid history as in essence that of a single lineage gradually burnished to its current perfection (Mayr 1950; see discussion of the historical background in Tattersall 2009). And even though new discoveries over the past several decades have obliged paleoanthropologists to recognize that actual events were a lot more complex than this model admits, minimalist and pro-gressivist interpretations of hominid history still tend to dominate studies of hominid evolution, underpinned by a widespread perception that, for the past 2 million years at least, hominid history has largely been a story of steadily increasing brain size and behavioral complexity.

Patterns in hominid evolution

The origins of the hominid family itself are still somewhat mysterious, but recent finds have made it clear that the hominid family tree was bushy from the very start, some 7 million years ago (Gibbons 2006). In other words, the early history of Hominidae was pretty conventional, in the sense that the dominant signal emerging from the hominid fossil record, like that of other successful mammalian families, is consistently one of evolutionary experimentation rather than of linear refinement. New hominid species regularly came on the scene, did battle on the ecological stage, and more often than not went extinct. In a larger perspective these individual species dramas added up to a dynamic and ongoing exploration of the many ways that there evidently are to be hominid.

The one feature shared by all of the very early fossil hominids is less any defining morphology than the claim, sometimes made on rather slender grounds, that all were terrestrial bipeds (see Gibbons 2006). But the early form of bipedality of these and the other "bipedal apes" of the period from about 6 to 2 million years ago is not well characterized as "transitional" between ancestral arboreality and modern striding terrestriality. For this adaptation was actually a stable and highly successful one that, as far as we know, remained unchanged in its essentials for several million years, even as a host of ancient australopith species came and went. Almost throughout this long period of adaptive stasis, it is hard to demonstrate that our ancient precursors had acquired cognitive capacities significantly in advance of those of today's apes, for it was not until about 2.6 million years ago that the first appearance of stone tools gives us a material basis for making inferences about cognition (Schick and Toth 1993). Interestingly, while exactly which hominid made this fateful invention is unknown, it is virtually certain that the hominid concerned possessed an archaic body build and a brain not much larger than one would expect in an ape of similar size (Tattersall 2004). And if this is so we find, right at the beginning, evidence of a theme that we find repeated throughout hominid history: biological and technological advances do *not* go hand in hand. And this disconnect between anatomical and behavioral innovation actually makes eminent sense. For there is quite obviously no place that any innovation can arise, except *within* a species.

The earliest stone tools were crude but effective, and the toolmakers were evidently simply after an *attribute*: a sharp cutting edge (Schick and Toth 1993). It apparently made little difference what the sharp flake actually looked like. Still, the availability of cutting implements must have made an enormous difference to the economic lives of the first tool-makers, and this invention certainly signals a higher level of cognitive sophistication than we find in modern apes, which, even when intensively coached, are unable to grasp fully the concept of striking one stone with another at precisely the angle required to detach a sharp flake. What is more, the early tool-makers were capable of a degree of foresight and planning, for they carried suitable rocks for considerable distances before fracturing them into tools as required. Once invented, however, stone tools provide evidence of the other pervasive major theme in hominid evolution: that innovations, once established, have tended to persist for long periods of time. This is because it was not for another million years that any substantial innovation was made in stone tool-making (see discussion in Klein 1999).

At about 1.6 million years ago, an altogether new kind of tool was introduced: the so-called Acheulean handaxe, a larger implement consciously fashioned to a set and regular shape. Apparently, Acheulean toolmakers had started to make tools to a "mental template" that existed in their minds before tool-making began. This is indirect evidence of yet another cognitive advance, although it is impossible to know exactly how it reflects the tool-makers' subjective experience of the world around them.

Interestingly, though, hominids of an entirely new kind had been around for several hundred thousand years *before* this innovation was made. At a little under 2 million years ago, hominids of essentially modern body build appeared, and are best exemplified by the amazing 1.6 million-year-old "Turkana Boy" skeleton from northern Kenya (Walker and Leakey 1993). Often assigned to the species *Homo ergaster*, these early upright striders, with brains a little bigger than those of the bipedal apes but still little more than half the size of ours today, were the first hominids to be truly emancipated from the forest edge and woodland habitats to which their precursors had previously been confined. They rapidly spread far beyond their birth continent of Africa, as perhaps best documented at the extraordinary 1.8 million-year-old site of Dmanisi, in the Caucasus (e.g. Gabunia *et al.* 2000). Yet they did so in the absence of larger brains or of stone tool-working technologies any more sophisticated than those of their predecessors; and only a quarter-million years later did the invention of the Acheulean announce the "discovery" of a new cognitive potential that had presumably lain unexploited since the novel anatomical form had appeared hundreds of thousands of years earlier.

Once more, there is a then a long wait for the next technological innovation. This came in the form of core preparation, whereby a stone "core" was carefully shaped until a single blow would detach a more or less finished tool. And again, this invention came long after a new kind of hominid had shown up in the fossil record, at about 600,000 years ago in Africa and shortly thereafter in Eurasia. It was hominids of this new species *Homo heidelbergensis* that, some 200,000 years later, apparently introduced such important novelties as the building of shelters and the regular domestication of fire in hearths (e.g. Klein 1999). It is arguable whether or not the cranial base (the roof of the upper vocal tract) of these hominids shows evidence of any ability to produce the sounds associated today with speech (probably not); but there is certainly nothing in the archeological record left by these creatures that convincingly suggests symbolic activities (Tattersall 2004). By this time, hominids doubtless communicated vocally and gesturally in relatively sophisticated ways; but without evidence of symbolism it seems highly unlikely that they possessed anything resembling structured language.

Perhaps the most accomplished practitioners of prepared-core tool-making were the Neanderthals, *Homo neanderthalensis*. And it is this species, which flourished in Europe and western Asia following about 200,000 years ago, that provides us with the best mirror in which to see reflected the uniqueness of our own species, *Homo sapiens*. For while the Neanderthals had brains as large as ours, invented the burial of the dead, and clearly took care of disadvantaged members of society, they too left little behind them to suggest that they possessed symbolic consciousness (e.g. Klein 1999). They were, moreover, the hominids who were entirely evicted from their vast territory, in the dozen millennia or so following about 40,000 years ago, by arriving *Homo sapiens* whose existences were very clearly drenched in symbol (White 1989). These early European *Homo sapiens*, known as the Cro-Magnons, created astonishing art on the walls of caves. They carved exquisite figurines. They decorated everyday objects, and made notations on plaques of bone. They played music on bone flutes, and without question sang and danced as well. In short, they were *us*. And the material record they left behind is distinguished most notably from those of their non-African predecessors and contemporaries by its clear indications of a symbol-based mode of cognition.

Still, the Cro-Magnons were not the first creatures who *looked* just like us. The highly characteristic bony anatomy that distinguishes modern *Homo sapiens* may have had its roots in Africa as long as 160–200,000 years ago (White *et al*. 2003; McDougall, Brown, and Fleagle 2005), long before we find the earliest intimations of symbolic behaviors in that continent at perhaps about 100–80,000 years ago (Henshilwood *et al*. 2003). Similarly, while anatomically modern *Homo sapiens* shows up for the first time in the Levant at a little under 100,000 years ago, these early Levantine anatomical moderns were making stone tool kits that were virtually indistinguishable from those made by the Neanderthals with whom they apparently shared this region for upwards of 50,000 years, far longer than the period of cohabitation in Europe (Klein 1999). Interestingly, the final eviction of the Neanderthals from the Levant came right after the appearance there of stone tools equivalent to those the Cro-Magnons brought with them into Europe. And what this suggests, at least to me, is that cohabitation or alternation of some sort was possible as long as the behaviors of both *Homo neanderthalensis* and *Homo sapiens* could best be described as the most sophisticated extrapolations yet of the trends toward increasing brain size, and presumably of cognitive complexity, that had preceded them. But once *Homo sapiens* had begun to behave in a "modern" way, an entirely unanticipated phenomenon was on the scene. With its advent, the rules of the game changed entirely, and our species became an irresistable force in Nature, intolerant of competition and able to indulge that intolerance.

The origin of modern human cognition

So what happened to allow the apparently radical reorganization of hominid cognition implied by this event? To answer this question it is necessary to recognize that in evolution form has to precede function, if only because without form there can be no function. Indeed, there is a strong argument to be made that any novelty must arise as an "exaptation," a new variant arising independently of any novel function for which it might later be co-opted. If this is so, it is permissible to speculate that the neural substrate for our remarkable symbolic cognitive abilities initially arose as a byproduct, or at least co-product, of the extensive physical reorganization that we see so clearly reflected today in our unique osteology. And if this is correct, the *potential* for symbolic cognition offered by this substrate must have lain unexploited for some considerable lapse of time until it was "discovered" by its possessors. This discovery must have been made, and our symbolic potential unleashed, by some behavioral/cultural innovation. The most plausible candidate for this cultural stimulus is the invention of language, an activity that is virtually synonymous with our symbolic reasoning ability – and that would certainly be impossible in its absence. Language involves forming intangible symbols in the mind, and it allows us to recombine those symbols in new ways, and to pose the "what if?" questions that permit us to be creative and to perceive and to relate to the world around us in an entirely unique fashion. Importantly, by the time demonstrably symbolic behaviors began to be expressed, the structures that permit speech had already been in place for a considerable time – certainly since the emergence prior to 150,000 years ago of *Homo sapiens* as an anatomical entity – having initially been acquired in some other context entirely.

How and in what exact social context language was invented – by creatures obviously already possessing the potential to acquire it – is something beyond my expertise to speculate about. And I certainly do not wish to suggest that language as we know it today, with all of its complexities and subtleties, sprang into existence overnight. But the crucial components of object-naming (Geschwind 1965), and the creation of mental symbols for external objects and abstract ideas, must have been part of this initial leap if we are to explain the passage of an organism from a non-symbolic into a symbolic cognitive state. The crossing of this cognitive gulf is nothing short of mind-boggling from almost every point of view. But we know it happened; and although the result of the acquisition of the biological underpinnings of symbolic cognition was an astonishing one, as a category of phenomenon this acquisition needs no special explanation. Indeed, in evolutionary terms it is thoroughly mundane. Birds had feathers for many millions of years before they co-opted them for flight; and *Homo sapiens* very plausibly possessed a symbol-ready brain well before symbolic cognition was adopted. Feathers were not acquired for flight (indeed, nothing is acquired for anything); and the apomorphy of the human brain that makes it symbol-ready (whatever that uniqueness may be) was not acquired to suit it for symbolic cognition. In this perspective, it appears that the achievement of symbolic reasoning was an emergent event, rather than a simple extrapolation of pre-existing trends. For although our vaunted mental capacities are clearly based on earlier historical acquisitions, they were not *predicted* by them. Much as students of human structural and cognitive evolution have liked to think of our history as a linear progression from primitiveness to perfection, this is clearly an erroneous perspective. Remarkable as our species *Homo sapiens* undoubtedly is, it was not fine-tuned by evolution for symbolic cognition and language.

14   On two incompatible theories of language evolution

Derek Bickerton

The Hauser-Chomsky-Fitch position

A recent article by Hauser, Chomsky and Fitch (2002, henceforth HCF) sought to instruct workers in the field of language evolution as to how they should proceed with further research. The authors distinguished between FLB, the faculty of language in its broad sense (including all factors, whether language-specific, human-specific, or otherwise, that go to make up all that lay persons mean by the term "language") and FLN, the faculty of language in its narrow sense, limited to those aspects of FLB that are unique to both language and humans. In selecting their Hypothesis 3 over two alternative hypotheses, they wrote: "We propose in this hypothesis that FLN comprises only the core computational mechanisms of recursion as they appear in narrow syntax and the mapping to the interfaces" (HCF: 1573).[1]

Subsequent debate (Pinker and Jackendoff 2005; Jackendoff and Pinker 2005; Fitch, Hauser, and Chomsky 2005) has focused mainly on the correct line of division between FLN and FLB – a definitional rather than a substantive issue, though admittedly one with non-trivial implications – leaving aside some more general evolutionary implications of HCF. The position of HCF may be briefly summarized as follows: language is composed of many factors, possibly all but one of which either preexisted language (that is, occurred in some form in prehuman, alingual species) or arose among human ancestors for functions other than language. Each of these factors evolved separately and presumably through normal evolutionary processes. The uniquely linguistic factor, recursion (the capacity to create potentially infinite sentences by re-entering superordinate categories like "noun phrase" or "sentence" as subordinate categories of themselves) arose either from an unspecified mutation or a change of function in some other, preexisting, but yet-to-be-identified faculty (number, perhaps, or navigation, or social cognition). Recursion combined with the other faculties sufficed, in a manner never spelled out, to yield modern human language.

Surprisingly, for an article on language evolution, HCF contained very little about evolution. A great deal is now known about the evolution of the human species and its ancestors, from the last common ancestor we share with chimpanzees and bonobos – a species that cannot have had any form of language – to the rapid expansion of human culture beginning in Africa over 100,000 years ago, by which time we almost certainly had language in more or less its present form. However, HCF does not attempt to link any aspect of language, whether broadly or narrowly conceived, to the history of human evolution.

What it does, after making the FLB/FLN distinction, is to advocate a comparative, multi-disciplinary approach to problems of language evolution, and to suggest to researchers how and where they might look for precursors of particular FLB ingredients, including whatever antecedent capacity might have become, perhaps through change of a prior function, the recursive property of natural language. There is no suggestion of an answer, or even that answers might be required, to two of the most crucial questions one can ask about language evolution:

Question 1: If (as HFC suggests) language emerged from the integration of many disparate faculties, all (or all but one) of which evolved separately for non-linguistic purposes, how, where, when and why did this integration take place?
Question 2: Why, if so many ingredients of FLB were already present in other species, has no species but ours shown the least tendency to develop language (or anything remotely like it)?

Failure to address the first question highlights the extremely abstract model of language evolution we have to assume if we are to accept the argument of HCF – a model so abstract that any account of language evolution in terms of process is ruled out. That argument makes sense only if the emergence of language is *not* a process, but an instantaneous event, and indeed, as discussed below, the model described by Chomsky (2005) treats language evolution, like language acquisition, as instantaneous.

Failure to address the second question undercuts the emphasis on comparative studies that supports HCF's main thesis. If it is legitimate to determine what precursors of language can be found in other species, it is at least equally legitimate (and perhaps more revealing for our understanding of general evolutionary processes) to determine what prevented species equipped with such precursors from developing anything resembling language.

Lacking from HCF (and indeed, from much other work on language evolution) is any apparent awareness of the enormity of language in an evolutionary context. It is not enough to note language's uniqueness; many features – elephants' trunks, bats' sonar, the heat sensors of pit vipers – are equally unique. It is essential to understand the stark contrast between the fact that every other species that has ever inhabited the earth has managed its affairs and fulfilled its communicational needs, whatever they were, perfectly well without anything resembling language, and the fact that language gave the one species that developed it effective command and control over all other species. In other words, the emergence of language represents a unique TYPE of evolutionary process, one so extraordinary that only some equally unique combination of circumstances could have brought it to birth.

Chomsky's elaboration of the HCF model

The model implied by HCF is spelled out in somewhat more detail in Chomsky (2005). Summarizing this model, Chomsky states:

> In some small group from which we all descend, a rewiring of the brain took place yielding the operation of unbounded Merge, *applying to concepts of the kind I mentioned* ... The individual so rewired had many advantages: capacities for complex thought, planning, interpretation and so on. The capacity is transmitted to offspring, coming to predominate. *At that stage, there would be an advantage to externalization*, so the capacity might come to be linked as a secondary process to the sensorimotor system for externalization and interaction, including communication. (Emphasis added.)

Chomsky (in contrast to most investigators of the evolution of language) thus assumes that language came into existence first as a "language of thought." Consequently, recursion could, at first, operate not over words (which did not yet exist) but only over "concepts of the kind I mentioned," which he describes as follows:

> There do, however, seem to be some critical differences between human conceptual systems and symbolic systems of other animals. Even the simplest words and concepts of human language and thought lack the relation to mind-independent entities that has been reported for animal communication ... The symbols of human language and thought are quite different.

In other words, this "quite different," fully developed human conceptual system formed a necessary prerequisite for the emergence of recursion, which could not operate over a conceptual system the constituents of which were limited to a direct, one-to-one relationship with objects in the world. But a change from "symbolic systems of other animals" to "human conceptual systems" would represent a cognitive change unparalleled in evolution. How, when, and why could so momentous a development have taken place? Chomsky gives no answer, replacing the problem of how language evolved with another, equally challenging problem: how a typically human conceptual system evolved.

Chomsky has been trapped into this position by his own argument. He sees what is most typical and characteristic of language as its capacity to shape thought and planning – something very different from the capacity to evoke direct reactions to features of the physical environment that exhaustively accounts for the productions of animal communication systems (ACSs). This is true of language today, but not necessarily of language at earlier stages. It is necessarily true if and only if language had no earlier stages. If language was always the same, then it must have emerged abruptly in its modern form. If it emerged abruptly, and still required a modern human conceptual system, Chomsky is forced to assume that such a system preexisted language.

Chomsky's belief that language had no earlier stages has an interesting origin. In the study of language acquisition he has long held to the "idealization of instantaneity," claiming that the one-word, two-word, etc. stages through which most children pass are epiphenomenal, and that the underlying grammar of language is unchanged throughout the acquisition process. In his 2005 paper he explicitly links language evolution with language acquisition; in both, he claims, similar considerations apply, "unbounded Merge must at some point appear," and therefore "must have been there all along," even if it does not become apparent until later.

What Chomsky is claiming here is that events in the life of an individual organism can be equated with events in the life of a species – events taking place over a period involving unnumbered lives of human (and perhaps prehuman) individuals. Where individual, modern-human organisms are acquiring a pre-existing language, the idealization makes sense; recursion forms an established (and presumably, biologically supported) element of language, so there is a very real sense in which it must be present in the language-acquiring organism (even if it does not make itself manifest until later).[2] But since evolution involves a series of individuals (at least two, even if Chomsky is correct) where the last in the series fully possessed language, while the first lacked any trace of it, the "instantaneity" claim cannot be based on the assumption that recursion "was there all along", and would indeed be baseless were it not for the possibility that unbounded Merge represents the only means by which units of language can be concatenated to form larger, meaningful structures.

If this was the case, Chomsky's argument would be unanswerable, even for a series of individuals. There would then be only two possible states: one, characteristic of all nonhuman animals, where communicative units could not be assembled into larger wholes by any means whatsoever, and the other, characteristic of modern humans, where such wholes can be assembled without limit by repeated applications of Merge. Assume as the limiting case a series of individuals with only two members (e.g. parent and child); the first would lack Merge and therefore be unable to concatenate anything; the second would possess it and thus could (potentially at least – one would expect performance limitations) concatenate without limit.

But it is not the case that there is no means of concatenation other than unbounded Merge. Compare these two utterances:

1) Give orange me give eat orange me eat orange give me eat orange give me you.
2) The boy Bill asked to meet Mary thinks he is clever.

The first is by a trained chimpanzee, Nim Chimpski (Terrace 1979). It is not possible to determine any structural relationship between the units of (1). For example, it is impossible to determine whether the eleventh unit of (1), *me*, is the object of the preceding unit, *give*, or the subject of the following unit, *eat*. Yet the utterance as a whole is far removed from anything found in ACSs. It consists of units semantically similar to, if not identical with, human words (as opposed to units semantically resembling whole propositions, as in ACSs) and the proposition it asserts is interpretable not by grammatical but by semantic and pragmatic means: Nim wants someone to give him an orange so he can eat it. But, leaving semantics and pragmatics aside, the sequence is unified only by its linear structure, a "beads-on- a-string" sequence where all units remain separate and equidistant from U, the utterance head, and where there is no mechanism other than linear sequencing for determining relations such as "notional subject of," "notional object of," and so on.

(2), unlike (1), is structure-dependant. If (2) were constructed the same way (1) is constructed, and if relations were determined by linear distance, then *Mary* could be the subject of *thinks* (with which it agrees in person and number, as well as being contiguous) just as *me* could be the subject of *eat* in (1). For that matter, (2) could be decomposed into two fully grammatical sentences:

(3a)   The boy Bill asked to meet (with object focus).
(3b)   Mary thinks he is clever.

But as every English speaker knows, *Mary*, though linearly adjacent to *thinks*, is structurally quite distant from it, and in fact much closer to *Bill*, since it forms part of the real subject of *thinks*, i.e. *the boy Bill asked to meet Mary*. The difference between structural and non-structural forms of concatenation may be stated formally in terms of the modes by which each is assembled, as follows:

(4) Non-structural: A + B
             A + B + C
             A + B + C + D
             A + B + C + D + E ...

(5) Structural: A + B •• [AB]
             [AB] + C •• [[AB] C]
             D + E •• [DE]
             [[AB] C] + [DE] •• [[[AB] C] [DE]]

(5) clearly is produced by Merge: C is structurally closer to A, with which it has been merged to form the unit [[AB]C], than it is to D, which has been merged with E to form [ED], even though C and D are contiguous in the linear string. Conversely, in (4), where the only measure of closeness is linear, C is nearer to D than it is to A.

(4) represents a simpler, hence arguably more primitive, mode of concatenation than (5), and examples like (1) which (apart from its unusual length) is quite typical of "language"-trained ape production, strongly suggest that such a model lay within the cognitive scope of the last common ancestor of humans and chimpanzees.[3] Chomsky, although he has quite explicitly denied the existence of any concatenation mechanism other than unbounded Merge (personal communication, July 8, 2006), implicitly admits its existence when he remarks that "neither the phonological nor morphological elements [of words] have the 'beads-on-a-string' property required for computational analysis of a corpus" (Chomsky 2005). The "beads-on-a-string" property is, of course, precisely what characterizes (4) and distinguishes it from (5).

In fact, that property still exists in modern human language. However, it operates not between words but between sentences. Sentences, just like the units in (4), have no formal syntactic relationship with one another, as can be shown by the fact that grammatical relations (e.g. anaphora) that operate across clauses of the same sentence do not apply when such clauses take the form of distinct sentences:

> (6a)   Bill showed the photos to the boys. Every boy_i was surprised that his_i photos flattered him_i.
>
> (6b)   Bill showed the photos to the boys. Every boy_i was surprised. *His_i photos flattered him_i.

In (6a), *his* and *him* will naturally be interpreted as co-referent with *every boy*; interpreting them as co-referent with *Bill* is possible, but relatively unlikely. However, in the almost identical (6b), these items cannot be interpreted as co-referent with *every boy*, and will almost certainly be interpreted as referring to *Bill*. The only significant difference between (6a) and (6b) is that in (6a), the quantified noun occurs in the same sentence as the pronouns, while in (6b), noun and pronouns occur in different sentences. In other words, the anaphoric relation between quantified noun and pronoun results from the fact that a single sentence, produced by Merge, contains them both and contains them in a specific syntactic configuration.. Conversely, while each of the sentences in (6b) is produced by Merge, that operation is not used to link those sentences together.

This is not to suggest that discourse is unstructured; indeed, a large body of contemporary theory (see Grosz and Sidner 1990 and references therein) deals with the constraints that determine discourse coherence. But for that matter, even strings like (1) obey semantic and pragmatic constraints (try randomly inserting items like *apple* or *tickle* in (1)), hence represent much more than mere random stringing. However, it should be clear that the constraints operating on ape utterances and super-sentential human language (regardless of whether these are the same or different) are distinct from the constraints that operate within sentences, and that derive from the fact that intra-sentential processes involve Merge while other types of concatenation do not. In contrast, Chomsky's claim that unbounded Merge is the only concatenating mechanism for linguistic objects would force the conclusion, counter to fact, either that paragraphs are constructed by the same means as sentences, or that sentences cannot be concatenated to form narratives or arguments.

The fact that there are, even today, two means by which linguistic units can be concatenated into larger structures (one for words into sentences, another for sentences into discourse) removes the main justification for adopting a model of language evolution with only one step (from an alingual state to full language via recursion). Chomsky mentions (without citing) "many proposals involving precursors with Merge bounded: an operation to form two-word expressions from single words to reduce memory load for the lexicon, then another operation to form three-word expressions, etc." I know of no such proposals, but agree with Chomsky that if they exist they are misguided. The point he seemingly misses is that the mechanism of (4) – let us, to distinguish it from Merge, call it "Sequence" – is, in principle, just as unbounded as Merge, since sentences can accumulate without limit. (There is, perhaps unfortunately, no upper limit on the Longest Possible Scholarly Paper!)

What keeps Sequence more restricted than Merge when the former is used to create single propositions is exactly what keeps Merge from producing overly long sentences: performance factors. Those factors operate more stringently on Sequence than they do on Merge, and the reason can easily be seen by comparing examples (1) and (2). In Merge, relations between constituents are strictly determined, hence ambiguities are relatively rare, even in longer sentences. In Sequence, relations between constituents are controlled only by semantic and pragmatic considerations and other discourse-coherence factors. If Sequence is used in concert with Merge (as it is in normal human discourse) there is little consequent increase in ambiguity; however, if Sequence is used without Merge to create mono-propositional utterances (as in ape "language," pidgins, and perhaps the early utterances of children) ambiguities arising from undetermined structural relationships (such as arose when we tried to determine the grammatical/semantic function of *me* in (1)) multiply as utterance length increases, effectively limiting the unit length of Sequence utterances to low single-digit figures.

Chomsky concludes the summary of his model cited above by stating that "It is not easy to imagine an account of human evolution that does not assume at least this much, in one or another form." In fact, it is not at all difficult to produce an account that differs in almost every respect from Chomsky's – one that not only differs from it, but avoids the problems with instantaneity, Merge versus Sequence, and the prior conceptual system discussed above. The alternative model, too, is more consistent with, and can be more readily integrated into, biologically and paleontologically based accounts of the overall process of human evolution. The remainder of this paper will provide a necessarily brief sketch of one such account.

An alternative to Chomskyan evolution

The type of protolanguage originally envisaged for human ancestors in Bickerton (1990) consists of units comparable to, if probably not identical with, the lexical items of modern human language, These can be conjoined to form propositions by the operation of Sequence as in example (4) above. Since, as HCF is surely correct in arguing, most components of FLB evolved in other species, and since not only apes but a number of other species with relatively high brain-to-body ratios have been shown to be capable of acquiring similar forms of protolanguage under instruction (Gardner and Gardner 1969; Herman 2002; Pepperberg 1987; Schusterman and Krieger 1984, etc.), the last common ancestor of humans, chimpanzees, and bonobos probably required only two additional factors to achieve protolanguage. Those were, first, a selective pressure demanding something more than a typical ACS, and second, a development away from iconic and indexical devices founds in ACSs towards the type of symbolic unit represented by the words of modern human language (Deacon 1997).

At this stage we need to take account of one of the more helpful suggestions of HCF (p. 1572): "[C]urrent thinking in neuroscience, molecular biology, and developmental biology indicates that many aspects of neural and developmental function are highly conserved, encouraging the extension of the comparative method to all vertebrates *and perhaps beyond*" (emphasis added). If we begin by asking whether any ACS exhibits properties beyond those normally found in such systems, the answer does indeed take us beyond vertebrates. Displacement – the capacity to refer to objects not present in the here-and-now – is a feature normally found only in human language, due to the fact that truly symbolic units refer not directly to objects in the physical world, but indirectly through reference to the abstract categories to which such objects belong, which are not tied to specific manifestations of objects in the way that ACS units are. Outside language, we find displacement only in the ACSs of bees and ants.[4]

Bees (von Frisch 1967; Gould 1976; Dyer and Gould 1983) and ants (Wilson 1962; Hangartner 1969; Moglich and Holldobler 1975; Holldobler 1978) transfer information to nest-mates about food sources they have discovered which may be quite distant – certainly outside those nest-mates' sensory range. The main purpose of these transfers is recruitment: encouraging nest-mates to join in exploiting a source too large and/or too transient for individuals to exploit alone.

The term "recruitment" is sometimes used to include phenomena such as chimpanzee food calls or behaviors used by canids and other social predators to initiate a collective hunt of prey already in view. Here it will be used solely to refer to a transfer of information about objects outside both sender's and receiver's currently perceptible environment – in other words, a transfer of information that involves displacement.

The "language" of honey bees is devoted almost entirely to recruitment (except for a few dances that appear to be connected with swarming) and has been correspondingly elaborated in this direction, providing information to potential recruits for foraging expeditions on at least three parameters: direction of food source, distance to food source, and relative quality. Ant "language" varies from species to species, but often includes nest-mate recognition, alarm signals, and various sex pheromones. Though narrower in their range of foraging information than the communication of bees, recruitment mechanisms among ants fall into several classes: tandem running, where a single ant leads another ant towards food; light trail laying plus a waggle display, used to recruit groups; and the establishment of a semi-permanent chemical trail, sometimes varying in strength according to the quality of the food source, where the source is large and mass recruitment is required (Sudd and Franks 1987). In some cases, a recruitment mechanism such as tandem running is immediately preceded by presentation of a food sample (Moglich, Maschwitz, and Holldobler 1974); it may not seem unduly fanciful to suggest this as a primitive precursor of predication ("Come/get X-food").

Need for recruitment arises from the particular niches developed by ants and bees respectively: niches that have some obvious differences (bees forage aerially, ants terrestrially, for example) but have many more similarities than differences. By examining these similarities we can specify characteristics common to both species and niche that would select for an ACS designed for recruitment and therefore containing the essential feature of displacement.

A species that practices recruitment must be social and cooperative. It must engage in extractive foraging and cannot be an obligate carnivore or herbivore (living prey would have moved by the time its location was disclosed to recruits, while edible vegetation is normally ubiquitous enough to render recruitment unnecessary). Food sources must be scattered rather than contiguous, and unpredictable in place, duration, quantity, and quality. Given these characteristics, the larger and/or more transient the food source, the greater will be the pressure towards recruitment. A fission-fusion type of foraging strategy, a central place for food-collection and information-sharing, and provisioning for less mobile group members constitute further factors favoring recruitment strategies.

Now consider the situation of human ancestors approximately 2 million years ago. Climate change had turned large areas of their East African habitat from mosaic woodland to savannah (Reed 1997). Due to loss of previous foods such as nuts, fruit, etc, those ancestors had become low-end scavengers, using a crude toolkit to smash bones from previously scavenged carcasses and extract the highly nutritious marrow (Binford 1985). Potentially, however, the richest source of food lay in carcasses of megafauna, whose hides were often too thick and tough for teeth to penetrate until the expansion of internal gases ruptured them – a matter of many hours, maybe even days. It has been demonstrated experimentally that stone flakes formed in the production of Oldowan tools can cut through elephant hide (Schick and Toth 1993), thus affording hominids a narrow window of opportunity to shift to active scavenging and butchery (Bunn and Kroll 1986; Blumenschine 1987) and enabling them to access raw meat before it was available to any other species. That this window was indeed exploited is proved by frequent findings of bones more recent than 2 million years ago in which tooth-marks are superimposed on cut-marks, proving that by then hominids were indeed accessing carcasses before other carnivores (Monahan 1996).

Optimal foraging theory (Stephens and Krebs 1986), confirmed by studies on a wide variety of species (Irons, Anthony, and Estes 1986; Schmitz 1992; Velasco and Millan 1998, etc.), indicates that any species will select the food source that yields the highest calorific intake relative to the energy expended in obtaining it. However, exploiting carcasses of megafauna entailed significant risks. Almost all predators scavenge when opportunity offers, and at the time in question, numerous predatory species, including several now extinct and some much larger than modern predators, competed for carcasses (Lewis 1997, Treves and Naughton-Treves 1999). Hominids could succeed only if, in the words of a Confederate general, they "got there fustest with the mostest". O'Connell, Hawkes, and Blurton-Jones (1999: 478) provide a striking vignette of the circumstances under which recruitment might have occurred: "Neither would transport of parts to 'central places' be indicated … individuals or groups may simply have *called attention to* any carcass they encountered or acquired, just as do modern hunters … If the carcass had not yet been taken, *the crowd so drawn* could have done so, then consumed it on or near the spot, again just as modern hunters sometimes do" (emphasis added).

How could "individuals or groups" have "called attention" to such carcasses without some means, however crude or primitive, of indicating that a large carcass was available and distinguishing its species, with perhaps other infor-mation (such as size, or the strength of the competition)? Other groups and individuals each had their own affairs to attend to, which they would not abandon without substantial cause. Moreover, if the informants needed to continue searching for an adequate "crowd" before themselves returning to the carcass, they would have had to give some indication as to where and/or how far away the carcass was located. Note that, for displacement to be achieved, the units comprising the message did not (yet) have to be symbolic in themselves. While indexical units cannot displace, iconic units can; for many English-acquiring children, arbitrary *doggie* and iconic *bow-wow* are interchangeable. The history of sign language, a medium that naturally favors iconicity, contains ample evidence of how quickly iconic signs can become conventionalized and opaque in reference. Displacement and conventionalization form a bridge between presymbolic and symbolic utterances.

If recruitment was indeed the selective pressure that started protolanguage, it was one found, among primates, only in human ancestors. Other primates hunt on occasion, and consume the meat thereby obtained; however, they seldom scavenge, and certainly never attempt to access large carcasses, with or without the presence of competing scavengers. Pressure to recruit thus meets the unique-ness requirement that must be met by any selective pressure towards language.

Moreover, human ancestors from approximately 2 million years ago exhibit most of the recruitment-encouraging characteristics discussed above: sociality, cooperation, probably provisioning of less mobile members, and almost cer-tainly a fission-fusion strategy for extractive foraging of multiple food sources, many of them scattered, transient, non-contiguous, and unpredictable, including some (megafauna) too large and dangerous to be exploited by individuals or small groups.

In addition, the model sketched above satisfies three other criteria that present serious problems for alternative approaches: initial utility, credibility, and self-interest.

To become an established behavior, language had to show utility from its earliest stage. But when language first appeared there must have been only a handful of meaningful units. Very few functions – certainly not social (Humphrey 1976; Hurford, Studdert-Kennedy, and Knight 1998) or sexual (Miller 1999) ones – could have been discharged with a lexical inventory of a half-dozen or fewer items.[5] Information about large, rich, and transient food sources would, however, have been immediately adaptive no matter how small the number of referential units involved.

The second criterion arises from the fact that words are "cheap tokens" (Zahavi 1975) – since talk is energetically cheap, members of a species already capable of deception would have been reluctant to trust them. In a recruitment situation this problem does not arise; there either would or wouldn't be a dead hippopotamus on the other side of the hill, so verification would have been swift and effective.

With regard to the third criterion, language usually imparts information, but as Burling (2005: 193) notes, those with information "should keep it for themselves so that they can use it for their own advantage." However, to keep information about dead megafauna to oneself would be counterproductive, since the meat could only be accessed with the help of others.

The possibility that language emerged in the context of recruitment for active scavenging opens up a scenario for its subsequent evolution that differs sharply from Chomsky's (which has no subsequent evolution – language was perfect from birth). To describe that evolution here would take us too far afield. However, one final point should be made. HCF envisages that recursion could have first been utilized for some function other than language: navigation, number or social cognition. Presumably it evolved for such a function through natural selection. But if recursion could have been selected for other functions, where its utility is far from self-evident, why not for language, where its utility is obvious?

Compare these two accounts for plausibility. In one, recursion was selected for a non-linguistic function, presumably through normal evolutionary mechanisms. Later, a human conceptual system, with concepts ready to be labeled with words, emerged mysteriously in the mind. Recursion was then co-opted to sequence the units of this system, without any particular stimulus for this procedure. Only thereafter, when the "language of thought" was externalized, could the physical environment play a causative role or become involved in any way – that is, only when the main part of the procedure was already completed

In the other, language arose through selective pressure towards a type of communicative system capable of displacement that had already operated successfully in other species – a system designed for recruitment in order to fully exploit rich food sources. That pressure created an initially crude and primitive protolanguage, but in brains orders of magnitude larger than those of ants or bees such a system could not be limited to its initial function. Once established, protolanguage itself became a selective pressure for its own expansion, and for mechanisms that would then regularize, and thus automate and disambiguate, ever-lengthening propositions – mechanisms such as hierarchical structure and recursion. At the beginning of the process, human ancestors had only a standard primate conceptual system, but this co-evolved with language to gradually create the rich and complex system that characterizes language today.

One or other of these sharply differentiated scenarios must lie closer to the truth of how language evolved. Which will prove more correct is, of course, an empirical issue. It should, however, be noted that the first requires an additional component – an account of how typically human (i.e. symbolic) concepts evolved – whereas in the second, language and conceptual structure would have co-evolved through progressive abstraction of originally iconic elements.

15 On the evolution of language: implications of a new and general theory of human origins, properties, and history

Paul M. Bingham

Introduction

Human language apparently has the structure and properties expected of a device produced by natural selection (Jackendoff 2002: chap. 6; Pinker and Jackendoff 2005). However, we continue to lack a clear theoretical explanation of how or why language evolved uniquely in the human lineage. Equivalently, we have not understood the circumstances under which language might have become adaptive in human ancestors but not in any other of the many thousands of large animal species. Though many theories of language evolution have been proposed in the ca. 150 years since Darwin, none has answered these questions convincingly nor born the fruit expected of a robust theory.

I briefly summarize here a body of new theoretical work which predicts that elite language should evolve uniquely in the humen lineage. These predictions arise simply, parsimoniously. Moreover, they account economically for all elite human communicative behaviors, not merely speech. This theory also suggests new perspectives on the structure of language and of the mind.

The concept of *elite* capabilities introduced above is vital. Various constraints impose adaptive trade-offs, resulting in *elite* execution of one task at the expense of merely serviceable (or negligible) capacity for another. For example, dolphins and horses are both mammals that can swim. Dolphins are *elite* swimmers but horses are not. All animals can (ostensibly; below) exchange information using symbolic, combinatorially generated and parsed gestures (manual/physical or vocal). Humans have *elite* skill at such exchanges, while no other animals (apparently) do. The goal of this chapter is a coherent theory of the evolution of this elite human adaptive capability.

I outline this new theory in the first portion of the chapter and synopsize several of its implications in the second.

Nonhuman animal communication as a social behavior – prelude to language as an element of uniquely human social cooperation

Nonhuman animals exchange information – they communicate. For example, some moths use a sophisticated pheromone/receptor system to permit males to find females for mating. Further, for example, the members of a school of fish or flock of birds can move with such coordination that they produce an intense *gestalt* of a single "organism." Finally, young mammals receive elaborately detailed cultural traditions from their mothers as they grow to independence.[1]

What (if anything) is unique about human communication that might explain our evolution of language? I will argue that the answer is straightforward. Evolution of nonhuman animal communication is constrained by the same universal factor that limits all social cooperation in all animals at all times, *conflicts of interest*. Conflicts of interest are apparently as central to social behavior as gravity is to cosmology. Evolved social behavior, including the exchange of information, is apparently directly determined by conflicts of interest and their management.

In contrast to nonhuman animals, humans have evolved (uniquely) the capacity to manage these conflicts of interest, creating an entirely new opportunity for adaptive exchange of very large amounts of information. On this theory, uniquely human language (*sensu stricto*) is merely one subelement of the massive evolutionary redeployment of ancestral animal assets in response to this well-defined new opportunity for adaptive information exchange.

In the remainder of this section I will synopsize the extensive body of empirical evidence that conflicts of interest are, indeed, the *sole* limitation on the evolution of animal communication. This lays the vital groundwork for understanding the proposed, uniquely human solution to the universal conflict of interest problem and the implications of this solution to the evolution of human language.

The theory reviewed here is built on one of the approaches to genetic evolution widely accepted in one of contemporary evolutionary biology's major subcultures (Hamilton 1964 a, 1964 b; Williams 1966; Maynard Smith, 1982; Dawkins, 1976, 1986, 1996). The following is a brief review of the vital issues for those unaccustomed to thinking about the evolutionary logic of animal social behavior. (Biological sophisticates can skip to the last seven paragraphs of this section.)

Genetic design information builds organisms. Organisms replicate this design information by reproduction. The power of exponential population growth implicit in biological reproduction engenders intense competition (the Malthusian constraint) between members of the same species (conspecifics) for reproduction. Genetic design information that builds organisms who win this competition consistently over many generations lives on; alternative forms of design information are lost.

Genetic design information can "win" this Malthusian "game" in a variety of ways. It can build organisms that reproduce especially efficiently. Alternatively, design information can build organisms that assist in the reproduction of other conspecific organisms built by the same version of design information. In practice in the world of real animals, this second, alternative strategy almost always implies assisting close genetic kin (parents, siblings, offspring) in ways that support their reproduction. This assistance of close kin often includes the exchange of "cultural" information about the world (below).

Some individual members of some species use one or the other of these two alternative reproductive strategies exclusively. More commonly, individuals use a combination of the two strategies – personal reproduction and (sometimes) assistance of close kin in their efforts to reproduce.

As a result of this suite of strategic objectives/constraints, individual animals will normally behave *as if* the following statements about the world were true.

First, the "interests" of the design information that builds individual organisms (for the "purpose" of replicating that design information) are paramount. Of course, genetic design information (DNA sequence information) is "inanimate" and has no "consciousness" of "interests"; however, natural selection inevitably shapes this unconscious information so that it builds organisms that tend to behave exactly as they would *if* they were controlled by genetic design information that *did* have such conscious interests.

Second, the "interests" of distinct copies of genetic design information in different conspecific individuals are inevitably incompatible in a Malthusian world. Replication of one piece of design information generally occurs at the expense of the replication of a competing piece of conspecific design information. Equivalently, the interests of different pieces of conspecific design information are in "conflict."

Thus, as a result of the straightforward effects of natural selection, any two conspecific individuals who are not unambiguously, demonstrably built by the same design information will tend to behave *as if* they are serving these conflicting interests. In practice, close kin who share information recently inherited from common ancestors are the only conspecific individuals in which these conflicts of interest will be relatively attenuated.

More simply, we expect non-kin conspecific animals to behave *as if* they have intense conflicts of interest with one another. Though different biological subcultures take somewhat different views of some of the details of this problem (see Krebs and Davies 1993; Hauser 1996; Dugatkin 1997 for recent reviews), the fundamentals relating to communication are arguably straightforward, including the following.

The implications of this "conflict of interest problem" are vital to understanding nonhuman animal communication. Specifically, for example, we expect non-kin conspecifics to engage in "hostile manipulation" (Krebs and Dawkins 1984) – animal A will have an incentive to generate behavioral information influencing non-kin animal B in the interests of animal A and against the interests of animal B.

The effect of the prospect of hostile manipulation is that non-human animals are highly adapted to ignoring and resisting attempts at manipulation by non-kin conspecifics. In practice, therefore, conspecifics exchange information essentially exclusively under one of three conditions as follows.

First is hard-to-fake (intrinsically reliable) information. For example, this includes unambiguous physical signals of size and strength such as the roaring of a lion or chest pounding by a male gorilla.

Second is the exchange of information between non-kin conspecifics who happen to lack a significant conflict of interest in some particular, recurring context (typically narrow and briefly persisting). For example, male and female moths must find one another in order to mate and reproduce. At the moment of mating they have a nearly pure confluence of interest. Thus, the female's pheromone signal is reliable and the male follows it.

Third is exchange of information between close genetic kin (unambiguously built by many pieces of the same design information) who are otherwise relatively unlikely to come into competition. The simplest (and classic) example of this pattern is the mammalian mother/pup-cub-calf-baby pair. Mammalian maternity is never in doubt (unlike paternity) and thus the mother and her offspring are unambiguously close kin. Moreover, the typical mammalian life cycle means that the young are commonly forced to disperse (or to assist the mother) when they reach maturity – so that the prospect of future competitive threat to the mother (actually to her design information) is modest.

Thus, mammalian mothers are expected to provide relatively extensive amounts of reliable, culturally transmitted information to their offspring. The diverse mammalian cultural traditions passed from mother to offspring (hunting techniques in cheetahs and fruit preferences in orangutans, for example) are presumptive manifestations of this predicted pattern of communication.

Another example is especially relevant here. The waggle dance of some honeybees is frequently invoked in discussions of nonhuman animal communication and its relevance to human language. However, the full social implications of this case are sometimes missed. Hymenopteran social cooperation in cases like the honeybee involves close genetic kinship and, thus, a confluence of interest.[2] If the conflict of interest problem is what limits nonhuman animal communication, we would expect members of individual beehives to exchange information. The waggle dance is apparently an example of the expected exchange.

All the above cases contain crucial insights for the human language problem. Communication can be highly adaptive but the scope or horizon for this adaptation is apparently strictly and universally limited by the conflict of interest problem. This will be the essential issue for us here.

It is also useful to notice several additional details. Even nonhuman animal communication in the face of conflicts of interest (threat in defense of territory, say) requires the communication of intent through behavior. Clearly, the same is true for at least some (and perhaps all) cases of nonhuman communication under conditions of confluence of interest (the waggle dance, for example). As has long been recognized, the waggle dance arguably consists of abstract, symbolic communication. However, even "iconic" signaling (again, threat, for example) should probably be regarded as symbolic – the iconic mimicry of aggression "symbolizes" intent and intent is what is communicated.

Thus, we anticipate that nonhuman animals have all the capacities necessary for language, but on a scale more modest than elite human capabilities. Though the issue is intensely controversial among some professional linguists, there is considerable reason to believe that this is, in fact, the case. For example, nonhuman animals can apparently generate and comprehend simple (by elite human standards) combinatorial communicative gesture sets in either manual sign or vocal modes (see Patterson and Cohn 1999 and Pepperberg 1999, respectively).

The complexity of hierarchically nested combinatoriality ("recursion") in human language has been suggested to be a uniquely human property (Hauser, Chomsky, and Fitch 2002). However, there is reason to question this possibility. Nonhuman animals arguably parse highly dynamic, hierarchically nested combinatorial information sets of stupendous complexity (shifting "scenes") to allow their spectacularly precise adaptive responses to complex environments.[3] Further, elite nonhuman animal movement clearly implies the ability to generate complex, hierarchically nested, combinatorial movement sets (easily harnessed for symbolic gesture generation). On this biologically plausible view, humans and nonhumans do not differ in their capacity for elite "recursion," but merely in the specific tasks these elite capacities are adaptively committed to.

Collectively, these observations support several crucial general conclusions. Nonhuman animal individuals exchange information in precisely the way we would expect if the conflict of interest problem were the *sole* limitation on the exchange of such information. Moreover, the nonhuman animal evidence argues that *no other factor* than solution of the conflict of interest problem and *no new capability* (ability to generate and comprehend "combinatorial symbolism" or a new level of individual intelligence, for example) need precede evolution of elite, symbolic communication. If a hypothetical animal should evolve the capacity to manage individual conflicts of interest on a large new scale, communication on the corresponding large new scale will evolve *without the necessity to suppose any other pre-condition. This is the essential point to understand.* It is apparently impossible to discuss the evolution of language without grasping this issue.

If this argument is correct, it follows that humans must be a very specific new kind of animal – the first animal to manage the conflict of interest problem on a large scale. The next three sections bring us to precisely this same conclusion along a different and highly illuminating path.

Conflicts of interest, kinship-independent social cooperation and human uniqueness

Humans have a large array of unique properties in addition to speech. These include unprecedented ecological dominance, remarkable cognitive/adaptive virtuosity and elaborate, ostentatiously public ethical/political/religious behaviors, among others. Moreover, even in the specific domain of communication, speech is only one element of a suite of uniquely elite human capabilities. For example, we also display unprecedented virtuosity at acquiring new manual skills by observation/imitation.

All uniquely human properties, without exception, are well explained as either elements or consequences of a single underlying cause – adaptation to vastly expanded social cooperation independent of close genetic kinship (Alexander 1987; Bingham 1999, 2000; Bingham and Souza 2009). This uniquely human kinship-independent social cooperation, in turn, apparently has a single, simple underlying cause – unprecedented access to the capacity to coercively suppress/manage conflicts of interest inexpensively (Bingham 1999, 2000; Okada and Bingham 2008; Bingham and Souza 2009). These are, of course, the very same conflicts of interest that apparently determine the scope and properties of nonhuman animal communication (preceding section).

The following section develops the underlying logic of this new theory of the origins of human uniqueness.

Death from a distance – conflict of interest, competition, and cooperation

The game theoretic analyses of Okada and Bingham (2008) indicate that the following logic of evolution of kinship-independent social cooperation is coherent and compelling.[4] Moreover, alternative recent theories – including diverse group selection theories (reviewed in Sober and Wilson 1998; Gintis 2000) and an individual selection theory (Gardner and West 2004) – apparently lack adequate completeness and/or biological verisimilitude to be helpful to the language evolution problem.

On the theory we are reviewing here, the logic of animal social cooperation and the unique human expansion of that cooperation is as follows. Consider a set of non-kin individuals who cooperate to generate a gross individual benefit exceeding the costs of that cooperation – call them *cooperators*. In general, the benefits of such cooperative behaviors can also be commandeered by other individuals who failed to pay the initial cost of the cooperative enterprise – call these other individuals *free riders*. Moreover, individual free riders will do better adaptively than individual cooperators as a result of evading the costs of cooperation while partaking of its benefits. As a result, cooperation will not evolve where the opportunity for adaptive free riding exists. Equivalently, cooperation between individuals with conflicts of interest will not evolve. As we have already seen, this is precisely what we observe when we examine the communicative (and social) behavior of nonhuman animals.

This logic can be changed in one way – and, apparently, *only* in one way – as follows (Bingham 1999; Okada and Bingham 2008). Non-human animal social cooperation is dominated by the fact that individuals who pursue non-cooperative self-interest at the expense of possible future cooperative gain do better in short-term, head-to-head competition with individuals who make the opposite choice. The only way to alter this logic is to reverse the dictates of immediate, individual self-interest – rendering pursuit of cooperative gain the *individually* superior *short-term* adaptive choice.

This outcome can only be achieved when *individually self-interested* cooperators can impose a cost on non-cooperative individuals (free riders) that exceeds the benefit from free riding.[5] This can only occur, in turn, when imposing this cost on free riders is individually remunerative to self-interested cooperators. As far as we can tell from observation of human and nonhuman animal behavior, there is only a single viable way to impose such costs on a free rider – to inflict violence.[6]

These elementary theoretical and empirical constraints apparently allow only a single coherent solution (Okada and Bingham 2008). This solution has two parts. First, self-interested cooperators must directly recover the costs they incur (energy expended, time spent, risk of injury) while imposing costs, in turn, on would-be free riders. This implies that violence (and threat) must generally be directly remunerative. For example, ostracism might be preemptive, anticipatory – coercively forestalling free riding. Under these conditions, the costs of coercively ostracizing would-be free riders is recovered exclusively by active ostracizers when they retain the portion of the proceeds of cooperation that would otherwise have gone to the free rider. We refer to this logic in its most general form as *compensated coercion.*[7]

Second, for preemptive coercion to be adaptively viable the costs of imposing coercive violence on would-be free riders must be *less than* the returns from ostracizing the free rider. *This simple, transparent requirement appears to be the key to understanding human uniqueness.* This cost-benefit requirement can apparently *only* be met in an animal in which many conspecific cooperators can *simultaneously* (*synchronously*) project violence (and, thus, credible threat) on a target individual. Moreover, the only known strategy that permits efficient synchronous projection of threat is the ability to inflict injury and even kill (and, thus, credibly threaten) conspecific adults from a substantial distance – remote or "stand-off" threatening strategies. (Visualize the threat of gunfire for the moment. We will return to the original evolved ancestral remote threatening capability below.) Most animals cannot inflict injury "remotely" and, instead, attack through direct contact ("proximally"). Proximally threatening animals do not have access to cost-effective (adaptive) coercive ostracism (below).

The logic of this synchronous threat requirement is easily accessible intuitively and is described in detail in Bingham (1999, 2000) and Okada and Bingham (2008). The gist is as follows. In remote-threatening animals many individuals project potentially injurious action (again, visualize gunfire) simultaneously on a target individual. In contrast, in proximally threatening animals potential injury is projected alternatively by one or a small number of attackers in direct contact with the target. In both remote and proximal threateners each of n would-be coercive ostracizers absorbs (on average) $1/n$th of the target's return threat (injury and potential injury) during a coercive episode. However, for remote-threatening animals the target is absorbing in-coming threat n-times faster than for proximally threatening animals. This factor results in termination of the coercive episode (for example, by incapacitation of the target) n-times sooner.

As a consequence, the amount of cost (threat) to which each would-be *remote* ostracizing cooperator is (potentially) exposed is dramatically reduced (n-times). In turn, the *net* benefit from coercive ostracism is correspondingly (and dramatically) improved. This makes coercive ostracism instantaneously individually self-interested behavior in a remote-threatening animal but not in a proximally threatening one.

In actual practice, animals will evolve to anticipate costs and risks. Thus, each "rational player"[8] will usually elect to fight or stand down based on her (or his) anticipated costs and benefits. Full-blown violent episodes will be rare. Standing down for free riders means accepting ostracism. Standing down for cooperators means tolerating free riding.

The crucial point is that coercive ostracism in support of social cooperation is almost never a rational choice for a proximal threatener but is often a rational choice in a remote threatener. This is, of course, exactly what we see when we look for cooperation between nonhuman animals with conflicts of interest (including non-kin conspecifics). There is virtually none.

As we will see below, the original ancestral humans were apparently the first animals ever to evolve the capacity for elite projection of conspecific threat remotely. The magnitude of the reduction in costs of coercion for a remote-threatening animal is enormous (above). Thus, it is reasonable to propose that coercive suppression of conspecific conflicts of interest is the fundamental human adaptive strategy in the same sense that flight is the fundamental adaptive strategy of birds, for example (Bingham 1999, 2000; Okada and Bingham 2008).

Notice one point specifically. Our theory predicts that pursuit of individual self-interest will lead *inevitably* to the evolution of kinship-independent social cooperation in any animal that happens to evolve (for whatever reason) the capacity to credibly threaten adult conspecifics remotely.[9]

It is beyond the scope of this manuscript to review all the relevant empirical evidence (see following section); however, note that this theoretical approach appears to give us a complete theory of human origins and properties and also generalizes to a robust theory of history (Bingham 1999, 2000; Okada and Bingham 2008; Bingham and Souza 2009).

Finally, this theory predicts that we will engage in extensive mutual support among large sets of non-kin individuals, a pursuit we will subjectively experience as reflecting our (uniquely human) common humanity.

The fossil record of elite human throwing: the novel evolution of access to inexpensive conspecific coercion

Our theory predicts that the only animal in the history of our planet to evolve massive kinship-independent social cooperation should be precisely the only animal ever to have evolved the capacity for elite projection of threat against adult conspecifics remotely. Moreover, this one-of-a-kind animal should have evolved expanded kinship-independent social cooperation explosively after the evolution of elite remote threat.

Humans appear to be members of precisely this predicted animal lineage. We are the first animal ever to have evolved elite remote threat capability (in the form of uniquely human elite well-aimed, high-momentum throwing)[10] and the first ever to have evolved massive kinship-independent social cooperation. (Our uniquely massive contemporary cooperation is self-evident – as is its "policing" with remote-threatening projectile weapons. See below for an approach to recognizing the origin of our unique social cooperation in the ancient human past.)

Moreover, the paleoanthropological record clearly indicates that very late prehumans evolved elite throwing – followed very rapidly by the first symptoms of uniquely human social cooperation (earlier evidence is reviewed in Bingham 1999 and 2000; strong new evidence has been generated by the recent digs of early *Homo* remains in Dmanisi, Asian Georgia; excavations reviewed in Fischman 2005; reviewed in Bingham and Souza 2009).

In overview, this large body of fossil evidence strongly supports the picture our theory predicts and requires as follows. A late prehuman australopith was apparently presented with a new adaptive opportunity – "professional" hunting and/or power scavenging (systemically chasing dedicated hunters, like the big cats, off their kills, for example). This novel opportunity probably arose in local consequence of pervasive East African climate change encompassing the period at issue (Vrba 1995; Trauth *et al.* 2005).

As an animal with millions of years of history as a bipedal omnivore (and the body to match), this newly carnivorous late australopith was "forced to innovate" in quirky ways. These apparently included evolution of elite aimed throwing – as evidenced by the presence of missile-size stones (manuports) and by a series of radical alterations of the postcranial australopith skeleton to produce the characteristic *Homo* skeleton (reviewed in detail in Bingham 1999, 2000; Bingham and Souza 2009).

As expected, these skeletal redesigns for throwing are systematic and pervasive. For example, the human hand has apparently been redesigned relative to the ancestral australopith hand to support the precise gripping and release of a baseball-size projectile. Moreover, the shoulder, pelvis, and foot have also been redesigned as expected to support the quirky, explosively violent, whole-body torqueing motion of elite human throwing.

As predicted by our theory, the first indirect evidence for elite human throwing (fossil prey processed by hominids) is visible just before the first unambiguous members of *Homo* – beginning perhaps as early as 2.3 million years ago. The complete suite of human skeletal adaptations to elite throwing is clearly in place with the earliest full-blown members of *Homo* at ca. 1.8 million years ago.

This new elite-throwing animal did not remain merely another member of the extensive East African carnivore guild. Rather, very shortly after the evolution of elite throwing (around or shortly before 1.8 million years ago), this animal rapidly evolved an entirely new scale of social cooperation – as evidenced by brain enlargement and enhanced adaptive sophistication (as discussed below; also see Bingham 1999, 2000; Bingham and Souza 2009).

Again, this is precisely what our theory predicts. Elite throwing is expected to have an "unintended" consequence. It should open an unprecedented adaptive opportunity – individually self-interested, compensated ostracism producing (as a by-product) massively, uniquely expanded social cooperation.

With these insights in hand we can return to the evolution of human language with improved confidence.

Language in the land of elite information exchange

A longstanding evolutionary question has been, "If elite communication is such a good adaptive trick, why do only humans possess it?" We can now answer this question – directly and forcefully. *Conflicts of interest limit the adaptive scope of communication and humans are the first animal ever to be able to manage those conflicts of interest on a large scale.*

This chapter could end here. We arguably have the answer we need and can now confidently approach speech as an element of a sophisticated biological adaptation of known evolutionary history and adaptive purpose. However, it is useful to go a little further – to enrich our intuition about the details of elite communication as a component of uniquely human social cooperation and of human speech as one subcomponent of this elite communication. More specifically, it is vital to grasp that "speech" is not a free-standing adaptation, but rather merely one element of a diverse array of adaptations to strategic information exchange on a new scale. This status of speech is both a central, falsifiable prediction of our new theory and, arguably, an empirical fact.

We have extensive evidence that the behavioral sophistication of animals is limited by the amount of "cultural" information they have access to (Wrangham *et al.* 1994; Whiten *et al.* 1999; van Schaik *et al.* 2003). The amounts of *non-cultural* behavioral design information (genetic information and individual experience) available to an individual animal were apparently "maxed-out" several hundred million years ago. In contrast, cultural information can continue to grow in amount indefinitely (under well-defined circumstances; below).

As we have seen, cultural information transmission is expected to be limited by the conflict of interest problem. Thus, we anticipate that a mammal evolving the capacity to manage the conflict of interest problem will gain access to vastly expanded amounts of – adaptively priceless – culturally transmitted behavioral design information. This new mammal would now learn from *many* rather than just from *mom* (close kin). Such an animal should show brain expansion[11] and increased behavioral sophistication as a result.

Of course, from its very beginning ca. 1.8 million years ago, *Homo* displays brain expansion. Moreover, elite human stone tool manufacture and increased ecological range suggest improved behavioral sophistication from early-on. Indeed, the consequences of unprecedented human social cooperation and expanded sharing of culturally transmitted information are apparently the sources of uniquely human cognitive virtuosity. Again, notice that this feature of human uniqueness emerges coincidently with access to *cost-effective*, compensated ostracism (elite throwing; above), as required if our theory is correct.[12]

How would an enlarged stream of cultural information have been transmitted in the earliest members of *Homo*? Initially, it would likely have been passed on in the same way as cultural information is transmitted in other mammals. The details of this process are still an active, contentious area of research (reviewed in Hauser 1996; Hayes and Galef 1996; Hurley and Chater 2005), but we have a good grasp of some of the ways this is done. For example, cheetah mothers often hunt where their very young cubs can observe (from a tree perch, for example). As the cubs develop further, the mother will bring partially disabled live prey for them to practice on. Still later, she brings ever more healthy live practice prey until the cubs are ready to assume their adult roles as elite solitary speed hunters.

This mammalian pattern of cultural transmission presumably depends on diverse observational and learning skills. We don't yet know how best to parse this constellation of abilities in detail; however, capacities including "understanding intent" and "imitation" clearly play roles. Operationally, "facilitated" exposure and "guided" practice are also involved.

We predict that an animal that has new access to vastly increased amounts of cultural information (as a consequence of management of conflicts of interest) should develop this suite of skills on a new, more sophisticated level. Humans look just like such an animal, of course – arguably independently of language (sign or speech). For example, many humans can master a Mozart piano sonata (even the blind or non-speaking autistic savants) or scrimshaw (even the deaf) – but no nonhuman animal ever will.

There are many additional pieces of evidence that language is merely one element of a more complex "total package" of adaptations for uniquely human elite information exchange. One specific example will illustrate this general point – the social use of attention and the human eye. As Tomasello and others have emphasized (reviewed in Carpenter *et al.* 1998), humans have uniquely elite capacities for "joint" or "shared" attention – when two or more individuals focus by mutual consent on the same object or event. It is especially striking that the human eye has apparently been redesigned (with a bright white sclera) to make the human gaze direction easily detectable in support of its salience (Kobayashi and Koshima 2001).

Our new theoretical grasp also suggests new ways of thinking about emerging insights into the neurobiology of language. One example will illustrate this (reviewed in Corballis 2003; also see Rizzolatti, Fogassi, and Gallese 2000, and Arbib 2002). For reasons presumably including ease of co-development and efficiency of function, areas of the brain with especially closely related functions are often spatially juxtaposed. Classic examples are the sensory and motor cortical homunculi and the mapping of the retina onto the primary visual cortex.

Uniquely human voluntary control of speech apparently requires ostensibly phylogenetically novel structures in the vicinity of Broca's area. Moreover, other elements in this immediate area probably represent phylogenetically older structures allowing the understanding of "intent" and "goal directed behavior" in others.

This striking observation has been taken as evidence that speech "borrowed" machinery previously designed for communication based on manual gesture (reviewed in Corballis 2002). This suggestion may very well be correct. However, it might (also or alternatively) be the case that language and understanding manual intent map so closely because they are two subassemblies coordinately subserving the larger strategic objective of elite transmission of adaptively useful cultural information in all modalities.[13]

Lastly, Philip Tobias and Dean Falk originally proposed that human language-like behavior originated with the earliest members of *Homo* around or shortly before 1.8 million years ago (see Tobias 1987 for a review of the early history of this interpretation). This proposal is based on the emergence of a well-defined Broca's cap in fossil skull endocasts of the earliest members of *Homo*.

This view has been largely ignored by linguists. However, the new theory we are exploring here strongly suggests that Tobias and Falk were right about early emergence of elite language-like behavior.[14] Of course, we may never know whether the first enlargement of Broca's cap most directly supported elite cultural transmission by imitation, symbolic manual gesture, speech *sensu stricto* or some combination of these.

In summary, our theory accounts for human cognitive virtuosity and the evolution of elite communication in all modalities as direct consequences of the management of conflicts of interest for access to culturally transmitted information.[15] This adaptation is apparently part of the original, uniquely human suite emerging explosively at or shortly before 1.8 million years ago on this view. One last time for emphasis, note that human language appears to be merely one subelement of an array of predictable adaptations to exploitation of this new access to information, an element likely to have been present is some substantial form from the dawn of *Homo*.

How might new theory help us?

New theories are initially evaluated on the basis of logical coherence, fit with empirical evidence, parsimony, and scope. However, the real test of good theory is its ultimate fecundity. Earlier theories of language evolution have been notably sterile. It will be of interest to see if the theory reviewed here does better.

It is useful to consider several likely directions for progress. First, we discussed above elements of the evolutionary logic of animal and human communication and of its underlying neurobiology. These considerations plainly suggest that human language involves *no qualitatively new* elements or features. Rather, human language apparently looks precisely as it should if it was produced by merely enhancing and redeploying universal animal devices and properties.

It is important to be emphatic. On this theory there is no reason whatever to suppose that any qualitatively new neural/cognitive capability[16] was necessary to initiate the evolution of human language (or communication more generally). Indeed, such proposals are arbitrary and gratuitous on this view. The only qualitatively new, rate-limiting step in the evolution of human language was the management of the conflict of interest problem on our theory.

Second, the conclusion in the preceding paragraph has a potentially useful corollary. The structure of human language is unlikely to reflect the structure of any new peripheral add-on widgets. Rather, the structure of language is very likely to reflect the recruitment of the underlying structure of the ancient ancestral animal mind to the task of communication. From this perspective, linguistics can be viewed as one of the central approaches of the larger universal cognitive sciences enterprise, rather than as the domain of a small group of narrow specialists.

If this view of the origins of human language is correct, the labors of empirical vocal and sign linguists (see Pinker and Jackendoff 2005, and Aronoff *et al.* 2008, respectively) are likely to bear phenomenally rich fruits.

Notes

2 SOME SIMPLE EVO DEVO THESES: HOW TRUE MIGHT THEY BE FOR LANGUAGE?

1. Lewontin (1998), updating his pessimistic conclusions in an earlier edition.
2. Massino Piatelli, *A Debate on Bio-Linguistics*, Endicott House, Dedham MA, May 24–25, 1974; Centre Royaumont, Paris. Hauser, Chomsky, and Fitch (2002).
3. Sauerland and Gärtner (2007). For another formulation, see Hauser, Chomsky and Fitch (2002), taking FLN to be a computational system generating syntactic structures along with mappings to the two interfaces.
4. More accurately, it is generated in the underlying ("abstract") structure from which both (1) and (2) are derived, with slightly different lexical choices.
5. Derived, respectively, from structures analogous to "Mary met someone who walked to that bus station" and "Mary is too angry to meet someone who talked to Bill."
6. See Chomsky (1955; most of 1956 revision published by Plenum [1975a] and Chicago [1985]). On the inadequacy of the mode of word identification assumed there, adapted from a proposal of Zellig Harris intended for morpheme identification, see Yang (2004).
7. On Peirce's largely neglected proposals, their importance and flaws, see Chomsky (1968), chap. 3. Peirce was concerned with discovery in the sciences, but similar considerations hold for language acquisition, though in this case the process is virtually reflexive and beyond the level of consciousness, in essentials.
8. It was recently reported that "a specific change in control of gene expression – and not an actual gene – can produce a gross morphological change in a mammal," inducing bat-like characteristics in mice, extending earlier results on flies and worms, reported to be the first such case for mammals (*Science* 319, 18 January 2008, 263–264; summary of a study by Richard Behringer in *Genes and Development* [January 2008]).
9. Jacob and P&P, see Chomsky (1980: 67). Baker (2001).
10. Editor's comments in Joos (1957).
11. Gunther Stent, cited in Carroll (2005: 24).
12. See Leiber (2001).
13. Weinreich *et al.* (2006).
14. Sherman (2007).
15. Cited in Maynard Smith *et al.* (1985). Kauffman (1995).

16. Jacob (1982); Erwin (2003).
17. Or, perhaps, select a probability distribution over the attainable languages, with a small set becoming highly valued during the course of acquisition and most others reduced to negligible probability, in effect "unknown" by the language user. On this matter, see Yang (2002); "Three factors in language variation," forthcoming in *Lingua*.
18. Among other factors that would be expected to enter into the evolution, development, and functioning of language are properties of the brain, now unknown – not a great surprise. "The neuroscience of higher cognitive processes is only beginning" and even for vastly simpler organisms like insects, where invasive experimentation is unimpeded, "we clearly do not understand how the nervous system computes," or even "the foundations of its ability to compute," even for "the small set of arithmetic and logical operations that are fundamental to any computation." Kandel and Squire (2000). Gallistel (1997, 1998).
19. On some of the misunderstandings of the program and its backgrounds, see my contribution to the symposium on Margaret Boden, *Mind as Machine: A History of Cognitive Science*, Oxford, 2006 (Chomsky 2007), at www.sciencedirect.com; N. Chomsky, M. D. Hauser and W. T. Fitch, "Appendix: the Minimalist Program," at wjh.harvard.edu/%7Emnkylab/publications/recent/EvolAppendix.pdf.
20. Specifically, it bars phrase structure grammars (and earlier versions of transformational rules), as well as the technical devices introduced in other approaches. The empirical inadequacy of phrase structure rules (context-free grammars, etc.) was clear from the start, and from the 1960s it has been shown that the complex stipulations they introduce are unnecessary even for a restricted role, so that they apparently can be eliminated entirely. Transformational rules, while much simplified, have been more resilient, for reasons that appear directly.
21. Wallace (1889: 467).
22. Shipley, Smith, and Gleitman (1969: 322–342).
23. Jacob (1982). On precursors, see Chomsky (1966, third edition, edited by James McGilvray, with introduction, full translations and quotes from updated scholarly editions (Chomsky 2008), and McGilvray's introduction.
24. Note that postulation of an independent or prior "language of thought" LOT raises all the problems of evolution of language, but with the extra difficulty that we have almost no idea what LOT would be, independently of linguistic evidence.
25. Petitto (2005). Fitch (2006). Tattersall (1998, 2002: 167).
26. Hauser (2000). Cheney and Seyfarth (2007).
27. Gallistel, introduction, in Gallistel (1990). Goodall cited by Tattersall (2002).
28. On these matters, see among others reference of note 23 and Chomsky (2000). The technical concept of reference is unproblematic for the context for which it was invented: for formal systems, in which the relation of *reference* is stipulated, holding for example between numerals and numbers. Approaching it is a sensible normative ideal for science: we hope that such notions as *electron* and *verb phrase* pick out real things in the world. Similarly, no problem arises for model-theoretic approaches to semantics of natural language, as long as the individuals postulated are recognized to be internal syntactic entities, of particular significance for interpretation at the C-I interface, much as such syntactic entities as phonemes are particularly relevant to the SM interface. But the act of referring in human language and thought does not seem to involve *reference* in the technical sense, and endless confusion has resulted from failure to recognize the fact.

29. Tattersall (1998). Striedter (2006). He adds qualifications about the structural and functional properties of primate brains. Minor genetic changes with broad consequences are by now well attested.
30. Tattersall (1998). On emergence of intelligence, Tattersall (2005).
31. On these matters, and the implausibility of "trait-by-trait" evolution of human language, see Berwick (1997: 231–249).
32. Though it does play a role at the levels of cognitive processing where phonetic realization is integrated into interpretation; see pp. 24–5.
33. See, e.g., Cherniak, et al. (2004). On the role of general learning strategies, see particularly Yang (2002).
34. As stressed in the earliest work in generative grammar, there is a conceptual difference between considerations of "simplicity" (symmetry, non-redundancy, etc.) that are language-internal, hence part of UG, and those that enter into science-construction or that reduce to natural law. The conceptual distinction is clear, but where the chips fall remains murky.
35. Or, as noted, if it is recruited from some other capacity (as now seems unlikely), to account for the emergence of the "instruction" to employ it for the generative purpose at hand.

4 THREE MEANINGS OF "RECURSION": KEY DISTINCTIONS FOR BIOLINGUISTS

1. Here's an example of a recursive function, implementing the Fibbonaci number definition, that can't be optimized automatically to iteration:

```
define Fib(x) :
If x < 2 then
    return x
else
    return Fib(x-1) + Fib(x-2)
```

7 DID LANGUAGE EVOLVE BEFORE SPEECH?

1. Bickerton has since modified his view somewhat, arguing the roots of syntax might be traced to reciprocal altruism in primates, but he still appears to maintain that language in the genus *Homo* was essentially protolanguage, without syntax, until the emergence of *Homo sapiens* (Calvin and Bickerton 2000).

10 WHAT IS LANGUAGE, THAT IT MAY HAVE EVOLVED, AND WHAT IS EVOLUTION, THAT IT MAY APPLY TO LANGUAGE?

1. In our case, hyper-analyzed concepts such as *meaning, reference, representation, grammar, innateness,* etc.
2. Exemplary of this strategic choice today are, in a vast production, recent publications by Michael Tomasello, Michael Arbib, and Philip Lieberman, and the reinterpretations of data on specific language deficits by Annette Karmiloff-Smith and the late Elisabeth Bates.

3. Chomsky's assertion, in a lecture at MIT, that it is conceivable, in the abstract, that the brain machinery (whatever that is) supporting Narrow Syntax could, in another species, on Mars, be connected to, say, vision or motor control is perfectly compatible with the specificity of language in humans. Language is composed of Narrow Syntax plus the constraints imposed by the interfaces and there is hardly anything relevant we may derive from general cognition (whatever that may mean). Chomsky adds that, in a sense, *all* of what traditionally goes under the label of linguistic studies is to be reconceptualized *as* phenomena at the interfaces.

4. It is now used as a current acronym in pediatrics: IEMs.

5. Finding the best universal format for electronic dictionaries across different languages represents a serious theorctical challenge. Expert linguists and expert computer scientists have joined forces and obtained dedicated grants to solve this problem (one of the most advanced such programs has been coordinated by Terence Langendoen at the University of Arizona).

6. It's below contempt that opponents of this view should label us as "creationists" (Arbib 2005). Immunologists should also be labeled creationists under the same criterion.

7. Iteration is not recursion and the discovery that apes (allegedly) can group edible objects into heaps and then make heaps of heaps is surely no basis for a language primitive (contra Arbib 2005).

12 GENETICS AND THE EVOLUTION OF LANGUAGE: WHAT GENETIC STUDIES REVEAL ABOUT THE EVOLUTION OF LANGUAGE

1. This work was supported by the NSF (BCS-0446838), the Busch Biomedical Research Fund and the Bamford-Lahey Children's Foundation. I am grateful to the participants of the Morris Symposium on the Evolution of Language for their insightful comments. I am also indebted to the twins and their parents who have participated in the PEGI study.

2. Although most twin studies make a distinction between environmental factors that only one cotwin experiences and those that both cotwins experience, I do not do so because the distinction is irrelevant for the arguments I am making. When it comes to the evolution of language, all that matters is how much of the linguistic variance is due to genetic factors because only genetic factors could have been selected for.

3. The PAL articulation test is a twelve-item word repetition task. The PAL lexical access test is a timed rapid naming test. The PAL syntax test is a twelve-item comprehension test of semantically reversible sentences. In a study of 122 children, PAL scores were very highly correlated with standardized language test scores (correlation > .70), and PAL scores correctly categorized over 95 percent of children as language-impaired or normal (Stromswold *et al.* 2006).

4. The genetic overlap between speech-language therapy and special education services should be interpreted with caution because many PEGI twins were too young to have received special education services.

5. Alternatively, the atomic elements could be phonetic features. Either way, the logic is the same.

6. In many linguistic theories, inflectional morphology (e.g., the *-ing* and *-ed* in *walk-ing* and *walk-ed*) is considered part of syntax. Such theories would predict substantial

genetic overlap between inflectional morphology and syntax because both tap syntactic abilities. Indeed, in terms of genetic overlap, according to theories that combine inflectional morphology and syntax (e.g., Chomsky's minimalist program, Chomsky 1992/1993), we should find greater overlap between syntax and inflectional morphology than between syntax and phonology.
7. An earlier characterization of evolutionary theories along two dimensions appears in Ganger and Stromswold (1998).
8. We recently began collecting data on our twins' discourse-pragmatics, reading, spelling, handwriting, mathematical, visual-spatial integration, sequencing, drawing and interpersonal abilities. We are also collecting data on behavioral disorders (e.g., attention disorders, autistic spectrum disorders, anxiety disorders).

14 ON TWO INCOMPATIBLE THEORIES OF LANGUAGE EVOLUTION

1. It is perhaps worth noting that prior to HCF, at least two of its three coauthors differed radically both on whether language was continuous with ACSs and whether it resulted from natural selection. Hauser voted affirmatively on both issues, stating that language was "a communicative device that evolved from earlier forms," and that, while Chomsky "considers the theory of natural selection to be lacking as an account of either the design or function of the language organ," he himself "disagree[d] with this claim" (Hauser 1996: 32, 35). Chomsky, on the other hand, insisted repeatedly on the uniqueness of language, and stated that "in the case of such systems as language … it is not easy even to imagine a course of selection that might have given rise to them" (Chomsky 1988: 167). HCF, therefore, represents a compromise in which Hauser abandoned his insistence on the universality of natural selection and in return received confirmation that most of language (FLB) had animal antecedents, while Chomsky abandoned his insistence on the uniqueness of language and in return received confirmation of the special status of recursion and its freedom from natural selection. As in most compromises, many substantive issues had to be ignored or glossed over, as shown below.
2. Or even if it does not appear at all. The case of Pirahã, a language which according to Everett (1992) lacks overt recursion, and which has been used by some authors (e.g. Pinker and Jackendoff 2005; Parker 2006) to suggest that recursion may not form an essential part of language, is only a special and extreme case of this acquisitional delay, and should not be used as an argument against the universality of recursion unless it can be shown that Pirahã-speaking children are incapable of acquiring a recursive language.
3. While trained apes were taught individual lexical items, none of them seems to have been explicitly taught to string these together; the latter behavior appears to have developed spontaneously.
4. There may, of course, be other species whose modes of communication are not yet well understood. One intriguing case is that of ravens (Heinrich 1989). Immature ravens seem to be able to communicate to one another the locations of carcasses currently being exploited by older birds who can only be dispossessed by weight of numbers; somehow, in the course of nightly roosts, information is apparently exchanged, enabling those numbers to be recruited. However, the means by which this is done remains unknown.

5. Johansson (2005: 212) suggests that, as chimpanzees practice social manipulation even without language, "this removes most of the force from [Bickerton's] argument." To the contrary: the fact that chimpanzees are already so adept socially makes it implausible that a half-dozen or so lexical items would have added anything substantive to their repertoire, and suggests that motivation to improve their social skills would have been low to non-existent.

15 ON THE EVOLUTION OF LANGUAGE: IMPLICATIONS OF A NEW AND GENERAL THEORY OF HUMAN EVOLUTION, PROPERTIES, AND HISTORY

1. See Terkel (1996) for a particularly clear, unambiguous analysis of rodent cultural transmission.
2. See Hauser (1996) for a review of the waggle dance. A small level of coercive suppression of conflicts of interest through "worker policing" is probably also involved here (reviewed in Barron *et al.* 2001). The form of this policing is as follows. Each worker eats the eggs of other (mostly half-sister) workers because the half-nephews that would result from these eggs are less closely related to the non-laying half-sister than are the queen-laid male eggs (brothers to the workers). Each worker's best *available* adaptive choice is to raise brothers, rather than their own more closely related sons. Under these conditions, the bee colony remains stable over prolonged periods of time – producing the large-scale, cooperative enterprise we are familiar with. Conflicts of interest between individuals are trumped by their effective (and enforced) confluence of interest.
3. Nonhuman animals almost certainly parse their perceptual world in the same hierarchical, combinatorial fashion as humans do (Biederman 1987).
4. Notice that the logic described here is somewhat different than the logic of the adaptive game that human behavior actually solves (Okada and Bingham 2008). However, this discussion encompasses the essential intuitive issues of self-interest and cost in the management of conspecific conflicts of interest.
5. Readers inexperienced in thinking about the social cooperation problem might think that this is an unnecessarily narrow construal of the issues. One example will illustrate that this naïve intuition is mistaken. One might imagine that cooperative individuals would choose to avoid non-cooperative individuals and keep the proceeds of cooperation for themselves. Unfortunately, what can be shared can be stolen. Thus, free riders have a powerful incentive to aggressively invade any successful population of cooperators. They do not just "go away." Thus, free riders are a fact about the world that must be actively dealt with if cooperation is to evolve.
6. As animals quickly evolve to "understand" the threat of conspecific violence (reviewed in Maynard Smith 1982; Krebs and Davies 1993; Dugatkin 1997), in practice this involves mostly the day-to-day *threat* of violence, with occasional episodes of true violence to establish the credibility of the threat.
7. Policing information sharing can have the same underlying logic. For example, cooperators can be directly compensated for ostracizing hostile manipulators in various ways, including seizure of the free rider's "property" (Okada and Bingham 2008) – a human practice conserved in the form of "fines" through the present.
8. Of course, animals (human or nonhuman) are rarely, if ever, rational in the sense of having conscious access to the actual strategic logic of their behaviors, including

their social behaviors. Rather, natural selection produces proximate psychological devices that cause animals to react to recurrent local cues *as if* they were such strategically aware actors.

9. Though it is beyond the scope of this chapter to discuss them, there are additional strategic barriers to "cooperative" self-interested ostracism (beyond the simple cost/ benefit considerations discussed in the text) that apparently only remote killers can overcome (Okada and Bingham 2008). These considerations further increase our confidence that remote killing is the vital "first domino" in the evolution of uniquely human social cooperation.

10. We contemporary humans retain these ancestral human skills (think of American baseball) and they are unique to humans among all living animals and apparently to members of *Homo* among extinct animals (below). Though some primates occasionally throw in the wild, none approaches elite human skill – no chimp will ever pitch for the Yankees.

11. It is vital to understand that human brain expansion is almost certainly a clear fossil indicator of an increased scale of social cooperation as follows. Entirely independently of the informational arguments in the text, life history arguments are strong. Specifically, early *Homo* brain expansion is also associated with a substantial increase in body size. Both these changes (brain and body size) result from a rather dramatic redesign of human life history (Bogin 1999; Key 2000). This altered life history creates uniquely human prolonged-gestation adult females, helpless fetus-like "babies" and prematurely weaned "children" – all much more vulnerable than their non-human counterparts, all requiring the human "village" to survive and prosper. From the beginning of *Homo* it apparently took "a (cooperative) village to raise a (human) child", just as it continues to today.

12. Notice, especially, that brain expansion and cognitive virtuosity are *effects* on this theory, not primarily *causes*.

13. Another observation is potentially salient in this connection. The work on split-brain patients strongly suggests that a formal function (called the "interpreter") is intimately associated with these same (usually left-hemisphere) areas (see Gazzaniga 1985, for a review.) The interpreter produces social "justifications" and "rationalizations" of our actions (including confabulations). The perspective we are developing here would probably predict this intimate functional relationship between acquisition of praxis, language and ethical/social recruitment/self-justification.

14. Notice that it follows from this new perspective that views of language as a late addition to the human repertoire (at the behaviorally modern human revolution less than 100,000 years ago, for example) are extremely unlikely. The new theory proposed here has a very different interpretation of human adaptive revolutions like the behaviorally modern revolution (Bingham 1999, 2000; Bingham and Souza 2009).

15. In other words, we now have a credible theoretical explanation for why humans were the first and only animals to invade the "cognitive niche" (Tooby and DeVore 1987; Pinker and Bloom 1990).

16. "Recursion" mentioned above (Hauser, Chomsky, and Fitch 2002) is one example of such a proposed novel capability necessary (or causal) for the evolution of language; however, many others candidates have also been proposed over they years. On our theory, all members of this large class of proposals are highly doubtful.

References

Adcock, Greg J., Elizabeth S. Dennis, Simon Easteal, Gavin A. Huttley, Lars S. Jermiin, William J. Peacock, and Alan Thorne. 2001. Mitochondrial DNA sequences in ancient Australians: Implications for modern human origins. *Proceedings of the National Academy of Sciences* 98: 537–542.

Agrawal, Alka, Quinn Eastman and David Schatz. 1998. Implications of transposition mediated by V(D)J-recombination proteins RAG1 and RAG2 for origins of antigen-specific immunity. *Nature* 394: 744–751.

Aldridge, J. Wayne, Kent C. Berridge, Mark Herman and Lee Zimmer. 1993. Neuronal coding of serial order: Syntax of grooming in the neostratum. *Psychological Science* 4: 391–393.

Alexander, Garrett E. and Michael D. Crutcher. 1990. Functional architecture of basal ganglia circuits: Neural substitutes of parallel processing. *Trends in Neurosciences* 13: 266–271.

Alexander, Garrett E., Mahlon R. Delong, and Peter L Strick. 1986. Parallel organization of functionally segregated circuits linking basal ganglia and cortex. *Annual Revue of Neuroscience* 9: 357–381.

Alexander, Michael P., Margaret A. Naeser, and Carole L. Palumbo. 1987. Correlations of subcortical CT lesion sites and aphasia profiles. *Brain* 110: 961–991.

Alexander, Richard. D. 1987. *The Biology of Moral Systems*. Hawthorne, NY: A. de Gruyter.

Alwin, Duane F. 1991. Family of origin and cohort differences in verbal ability. *American Sociological Review* 56(5): 625–638.

Ambrose, Stanley H. 2001. Paleolithic technology and human evolution. *Science* 291: 1748–1752.

Arbib, Michael. 2002. The mirror system, imitation and the evolution of language. In *Imitation in Animals and Artifacts*, eds. Kerstin Dautenhahn and Chrystopher L. Nehaniv, 229–280. Cambridge, MA: MIT Press.

2005. From monkey-like action recognition to human language: An evolutionary framework for neurolinguistics. *Behavioral and Brain Sciences*, 28(2): 105–124.

Armstrong, David F. 1999. *Original Signs: Gesture, Sign, and the Source of Language*. Washington, DC: Gallaudet University Press.

Armstrong, David F., William C. Stokoe, and Sherman E. Wilcox. 1995. *Gesture and the Nature of Language*. Cambridge, UK: Cambridge University Press.

Armstrong, David F. and Sherman E. Wilcox. 2007. *The Gestural Origin of Language*. Oxford, UK: Oxford University Press.

Arnold, Kate and Klaus Zuberbuhler. 2006. Semantic combinations in primate calls. *Nature* 441: 303.

Aronoff, Mark, Irit Meir, Carol A. Padden, and Wendy Sandler. 2008. The roots of linguistic organization in a new language. *Interaction Studies* 9: 133–153.

Atlas, Jay. 2005. *Logic, Meaning, and Conversation: Semantical Underdeterminacy, Implicature, and Their Interface*. Oxford, UK: Oxford University Press.

Atran, Scott. 2002. *In Gods We Trust*. Oxford, UK: Oxford University Press.

Avital, Eytan and Eva Jablonka. 2000. *Animal Traditions: Behavioural Inheritance in Evolution*. Cambridge, UK: Cambridge University Press.

Baer, Thomas, John C. Gore, L. Carol Gracco, and Patrick W. Nye. 1991. Analysis of vocal tract shape and dimensions using magnetic resonance imaging: Vowels. *Journal of the Acoustical Society of America* 90: 799–828.

Baker, Mark C. 2001. *The Atoms of Language*. New York: Basic Books.

Bar-Hillel, Yehoshua. 1953a. On recursive definitions in empirical sciences. *Eleventh International Congress of Philosophy* 5: 160–165.

    1953b. A quasi-arithmetical notation for syntactic description. *Language* 29: 47–58.

    1954. Logical syntax and semantics. *Language* 30: 230–237.

Baron-Cohen, Simon, Helen Tager-Flusberg, and Donald Cohen. 2000. *Understanding Other Minds*. Second edition. New York: Oxford University Press.

Barron, Andrew B., Benjamin P. Oldroyd, and Francis L. W. Ratnieks. 2001. Worker reproduction in honey-bees (Apis) and the anarchic syndrome: A review. *Behavioral Ecology and Sociobiology* 50(3): 199–208.

Baum, Shari. R., Sheila. E. Blumstein, Margaret A. Naeser, and Carole L. Palumbo. 1990. Temporal dimensions of consonant and vowel production: An acoustic and CT scan analysis of aphasic speech. *Brain and Language* 39: 33–56.

Beckman, Mary E., Tzyy-Ping Jung, Sook-hyang Lee, Kenneth De Jong, Ashok K. Krishnamurthy, Stanley C. Ahalt, K. Bretonnel Cohen and Michael J. Collins. 1995. Variability in the production of quantal vowels revisited. *Journal of the Acoustical Society of America* 97: 471–489.

Benson, Donald F. and Norman Geschwind. 1985. Aphasia and related disorders: A clinical approach. In *Principles of Behavioral Neurology*, ed. M.-Marsel Mesulam, 193–228. Philadelphia, PA: F. A. Davis.

Berridge, Kent C. and Ian Q. Whitshaw. 1992. Cortex, striatum and cerebellum: Control of serial order in a grooming sequence. *Experimental Brain Research* 90: 275–290.

Berwick, Robert. 1997. Syntax facit saltum. *Journal of Neurolinguistics* 10(2/3): 231–249.

Bever, Thomas. C., Caroline Carrithers, Wayne Cowart, and David J. Townsend. 1989. Language processing and familial handedness. In *From Reading to Neurons: Issues in the Biology of Language and Cognition*, ed. Albert M. Galaburda, 331–357. Cambridge, MA: MIT Press.

Bickerton, Derek. 1981. *Roots of Language*. Ann Arbor, MI: Karoma Publishers.

    1990. *Language and Species*. Chicago, IL: Chicago University Press.

    1995. *Language and Human Behavior*. Seattle, WA: University of Washington Press.

    2000. How protolanguage became language. In *The Evolutionary Emergence of Language: Social Function and the Origins of Linguistic Form*, eds. Chris Knight, Michael Studdert-Kennedy and James R. Hurford, 264–284. Cambridge, UK: Cambridge University Press.

2002. Foraging versus social intelligence in the evolution of protolanguage. In *The Transition to Language*, ed. Alison Wray, 207–225. Oxford, UK: Oxford University Press.

2003. Symbol and structure: A comprehensive framework for language evolution. In *Language Evolution*, eds. Morton H. Christiansen and Simon Kirby, 77–93. Oxford, UK: Oxford University Press.

2007. Language evolution: A brief guide for linguists. *Lingua* 117: 510–526.

Biederman, Irving. 1987. Recognition-by-components: A theory of human image understanding. *Psychological Review* 94(2): 115–147.

Binford, Lewis S. 1985. Human ancestors: changing views of their behavior. *Journal of Anthropological Archaeology* 4: 292 327.

Bingham, Paul M. 1999. Human uniqueness: A general theory. *Quarterly Review of Biology* 74(2): 133–169.

2000. Human evolution and human history: A complete theory. *Evolutionary Anthropology* 9(6): 248–257.

Bingham, Paul M. and Joanne Souza. 2009. *Death from a Distance and the Birth of a Humane Universe*. Charleston, SC: BookSurge Press.

Bledsoe, Caroline H., John B. Casterline, Jennifer A. Johnson-Kuhn, and John G. Haaga (eds.). 1999. *Critical Perspectives on Schooling and Fertility in the Developing World*. Washington, DC: The National Academy Press.

Blumenschine, Robert J. 1987. Characteristics of an early hominid scavenging niche. *Current Anthropology* 28: 383–407.

Blumstein, Sheila E. 1994. The neurobiology of the sound structure of language. In *The Cognitive Neurosciences*, ed. Michael S. Gazzaniga, 915–929. Cambridge, MA: MIT Press.

1995. The neurobiology of language. In *Speech, Language and Communication*, eds. Joanne L. Miller and Peter D. Eimas, 339–370. San Diego, CA: Academic Press.

Blumstein, Sheila E., William E. Cooper, Harold Goodglass, Sheila Statlender, and Jonathan Gottlieb. 1980. Production deficits in aphasia: a voice-onset time analysis. *Brain and Language* 9: 153–170.

Bogin, Barry 1999. *Patterns of Human Growth*. Cambridge, UK: Cambridge University Press.

Bosinski, Gerhard C., Olaf Jöris, Marie-Antoinette de Lumley, Givi Majusuradze, and Aleksander Mouskhelishvili. 2000. Earliest Pleistocene hominid cranial remains from Dmanisi, Republic of Georgia: Taxonomy, geological setting and age. *Science* 288: 1019–1025.

Boutla, Mrim, Ted Supalla, Elizabeth L. Newport, and Daphne Bavelier. 2004. Short-term memory span: Insights from sign language. *Nature Neuroscience* 7: 997–1002.

Bradbury, Jack W. and Sandra L. Vehrencamp. 1998. *Principles of Animal Communication*. Oxford, UK: Blackwell.

Bricker, Dianne and Jane Squires. 1999. *Ages & Stages Questionnaire: A Parent-completed, Child-Monitoring System*. Second edition. Baltimore, MD: Paul H. Brookes Publishing Company.

Brinck, Ingar and Peter Gärdenfors. 2003. Cooperation and communication in apes and humans. *Mind and Language* 18: 484–501.

Briscoe, Ted. 2003. Grammatical assimilation. In *Language Evolution*, eds. Morton H. Christiansen and Simon Kirby, 295–316. Oxford, UK: Oxford University Press.

Broca, Paul. 1861. Remarques sur le siege de la faculté de la parole articulée, suivies d'une observation d'aphemie (perte de parole). *Bulletin de la Société d'Anatomie* (Paris) 36: 330–357.

Browman, Catherine P. and Louis F. Goldstein. 1995. Dynamics and articulatory phonology. In *Mind as Motion*, eds. Timothy van Gelder and Robert F. Port, 175–193. Cambridge, MA: MIT Press.

Brown, Roger. 1973. *A First Language: The Early Stages*. Cambridge, MA: Harvard University Press.

Bruner, Jerome. 1973. *Going Beyond the Information Given*. New York: Norton.

Bruner, Jerome, Jacqueline Goodnow, and George Austin. 1956. *A Study of Thinking*. New York: Wiley.

Bruner, Jerome and Leo Postman. 1949. On the perception of incongruity: A paradigm. *Journal of Personality* 18: 206–223.

Bunn, Henry and Ellen M. Kroll. 1986. Systematic butchery by Plio-Pleistocene hominids at Olduvai Gorge, Tanzania. *Current Anthropology* 27(5): 431–442.

Burling, Robbins. 2005. *The Talking Ape*. New York: Oxford University Press.

Bybee, Joan and James L. McClelland. 2005. Alternatives to the combinatorial paradigm of linguistic theory based on domain general principles of human cognition. *The Linguistic Review* 22: 381–410.

Byrne, Richard. 1995. *The Thinking Ape: Evolutionary Origins of Intelligence*. Oxford, UK: Oxford University Press.

Byrne, Richard and Andrew Whiten (eds.). 1988. *Machiavellian Intelligence: Social Expertise and Evolution of Intellect in Monkeys, Apes and Humans*. Oxford, UK: Oxford University Press.

Calvert, Gemma A. and Ruth Campbell. 2003. Reading speech from still and moving faces: The neural substrates of visible speech. *Journal of Cognitive Neuroscience* 15: 57–70.

Calvin, William H. and Derek Bickerton. 2000. *Lingua ex Machina: Reconciling Darwin and Chomsky with the Human Brain*. Cambridge, MA: MIT Press.

Carnie, Andrew. 2008. *Constituent Structure*. Oxford, UK, Oxford University Press.

Carpenter, Malinda, Katherine Nagell, Michael Tomasello, George Butterworth and Chris Moore. 1998. *Social Cognition, Joint Attention, and Communicative Competence from 9 to 15 Months of Age*. Chicago, IL: University of Chicago Press.

Carre, Rene, Bjorn Lindblom, and Peter MacNeilage. 1995. Acoustic factors in the evolution of the human vocal tract. *C. R. Académie des Sciences Paris*, 320(IIb), 471–476.

Carroll, Sean. 2005. *Endless Forms Most Beautiful: The New Science of Evo Devo and the Making of the Animal Kingdom*. New York: Norton.

Carruthers, Peter and Peter K. Smith (eds.). 1996. *Theories of Theories of Mind*. Cambridge, UK: Cambridge University Press.

Carston, Robyn. 2002. *Thoughts and Utterances: The Pragmatics of Explicit Communication*. Oxford, UK: Blackwell.

Chaitin, Gregory J. 2006. *Meta-Math!: The Quest for Omega*. New York: Vintage.

Changeux, Jean Pierre, Philippe Courrege and Antoine Danchin. 1973. Theory of epigenesis of neuronal networks by selective stabilization of synapses. *Proceedings of the National Academy of Sciences USA* 70: 2974–2978.

Cheney, Dorothy and Robert M. Seyfarth. 2005. Constraints and preadaptations in the earliest stages of language evolution. *Linguistic Review* 22: 135–159.

2007. *Baboon Metaphysics*. Chicago, IL: University of Chicago Press.

Cherniak, Christopher. 2009. Brain wiring optimization and non-genomic nativism. In *Of Minds and Language: The Basque Country Encounter with Noam Chomsky*, eds. Massimo Piattelli-Palmarini, Juan Uriagereka and Pello Salaburu, 108–119. Oxford, UK: Oxford University Press.

Cherniak, Christopher, Zekeria Mokhtarzada, Raul Rodriguez-Esteban, and Kelly Changizi. 2004. Global optimization of cerebral cortex layout. *Proceedings of the National Academy of Sciences of the United States of America* 101(4): 1081–1086.

Chiba, Tsutomu and Masato Kajiyama. 1941. *The Vowel: Its Nature and Structure*. Tokyo: Tokyo-Kaisckan.

Chimes, Gary. 2001. Factors associated with variation in overhand throwing performance by females. Ph.D. dissertation. Stony Brook University, NY.

Chomsky, Noam. 1955. *The Logical Structure of Linguistic Theory*. Cambridge, MA: The MIT Press.

1956. Three Models for the Description of Language. IRE Transactions on Information Theory IT-2(3): 113–124. Reprinted (1965, slightly emended) in *Readings in Mathematical Psychology*, eds. R. Duncan Luce, Robert R. Bush, and Eugene Galanter, 105–124. New York: John Wiley and Sons.

1957. *Syntactic Structures*. The Hague: Mouton.

1965. *Aspects of the Theory of Syntax*. Cambridge, MA: MIT Press.

1966. *Cartesian Linguistics: A Chapter in the History of Rationalist Thought*. New York: Harper & Row. New Zealand

1968. *Language and Mind*. New York: Harcourt Brace Jovanovich.

1972. Remarks on Nominalization. In *Studies on Semantics in Generative Grammar*, 11–61. The Hague: Mouton.

1975a. *Logical Structure of Linguistic Theory*. New York: Plenum. Excerpted from 1956 revision of 1955 ms., Harvard University and MIT., IL.

1975b. *Reflections on Language*. New York: Pantheon.

1980. *Rules and Representations*. New York: Columbia University Press.

1981. *Lectures on Government and Binding*. Dordrecht: Foris.

1985. *Logical Structure of Linguistic Theory*. Chicago, IL: Chicago University Press.

1986a. *Barriers*. Cambridge, MA: MIT Press.

1986b. *Knowledge of Language: Its Nature, Origin, and Use*. New York: Praeger Scientific.

1987. *Language and Problems of Knowledge: The Managua Lectures*. Cambridge, MA: MIT Press.

1988. *Language and Problems of Knowledge*. Cambridge, MA: MIT Press.

1992/1993. A minimalist program for linguistic theory. In *A View from Building 20: Essays in Linguistics in Honor of Sylvain Bromberger*, eds. Samuel Keyser and Kenneth Hale, 1–52. Cambridge, MA: MIT Press.

1995a. Language and nature. *Mind* 104: 1–61.

1995b. *The Minimalist Program*. Cambridge, MA: MIT Press.

2000. *New Horizons in the Study of Language and Mind*. Cambridge, UK: Cambridge University Press.

2002. *New Horizons in the Study of Language and Mind*. New York: Cambridge University Press.

2005. Some simple evo-devo theses: how true might they be for language? Paper presented at *the Morris Symposium on the Evolution of Language*, Stony Brook University, NY, October 2005.

2007. Symposium on Margaret Boden, *Mind as Machine: A History of Cognitive Science. Artificial Intelligence* 171: 1094–1103.

2008. *Cartesian Linguistics: A Chapter in the History of Rationalist Thought.* Third edition, ed. James McGilvray. Christchurch, New Zealand: Cybereditions Corp.

Chomsky, Noam, Marc Hauser, and Tecumseh Fitch. 2005. Appendix: The Minimalist Program. unpublished manuscript. http://wjh.harvard.edu/%7Emnkylab/publications/recent/EvolAppendix.pdf.

Condillac, Étienne B. de. 1971. *An Essay on the Origin of Human Knowledge.* T. Nugent (tr.), Gainesville, FL: Scholars Facsimiles and Reprints. (Originally published 1746.)

Cools, Roshan, Roger A. Barker, Barbara J. Sahakian, and Trevor W. Robbins. 2001. Mechanisms of cognitive set flexibility in Parkinson's disease. *Brain* 124: 2503–2512.

Coop, Graham, Kevin Bullaughey, Francesca Luca, and Molly Przeworski. 2008. The timing of selection at the human FOXP2 gene. *Molecular Biology and Evolution* 25: 1257–1259.

Corballis, Michael C. 2002. *From Hand to Mouth: The Origins of Language.* Princeton, NJ: Princeton University Press.

2003. From mouth to hand: Gesture, speech, and the evolution of right-handedness. *Behavioral and Brain Sciences* 26(2): 199–260.

2004a. FOXP2 and the mirror system. *Trends in Cognitive Sciences* 8(2): 95–96.

2004b. The origins of modernity: Was autonomous speech the critical factor? *Psychological Review* 111: 543–552.

Correia, Sérgio P. C., Anthony Dickinson, and Nicola S. Clayton. 2007. Western scrub-jays anticipate future needs independently of their current motivational state. *Current Biology* 17: 856–861.

Cretekos, Chris J., Ying Wang, Eric D. Green, NISC Comparative Sequencing Program, James F. Martin, John J. Rasweiler IV, and Richard R. Behringer. 2008. Regulatory divergence modifies limb length between mammals. *Genes and Development* 22: 141–151.

Critchley, MacDonald. 1975. *Silent Language.* London: Butterworth.

Crow, Timothy J. 2002. Sexual selection, timing, and an X-Y homologous gene: Did *Homo sapiens* speciate on the Y chromosome? In *The Speciation of Modern Homo Sapiens*, ed. Timothy J. Crow, 197–216. Oxford, UK: Oxford University Press.

Culicover, Peter W. and Ray Jackendoff. 2005. *Simpler Syntax.* Oxford: Oxford University Press.

Cummings, Jeffrey L. 1993. Frontal-Subcortical circuits and human behavior. *Archives of Neurology* 50: 873–880.

Cummings, Jeffrey L. and D. Frank Benson. 1984. Subcortical dementia: Review of an emerging concept. *Archives of Neurology* 41: 874–879.

Cutland, Nigel. 1980. *Computability: An Introduction to Recursive Function Theory.* Cambridge, UK: Cambridge University Press.

Dale, Philip S., Ginette Dionne, Thalia C. Eley, and Robert Plomin. 2000. Lexical and grammatical development: A behavioural genetic perspective. *Journal of Child Language* 27: 619–642.

Darwin, Charles. 1859. *On the Origin of Species*. Facsimile ed. 1964 Cambridge, MA: Harvard University Press.

Davis, Martin. 1958. *Computability and Unsolvability*. New York: McGraw-Hill.

Dawkins, Richard. 1976. *The Selfish Gene*. Oxford, UK: Oxford University Press.
   1986. *The Blind Watchmaker*. New York: Norton.
   1996. *Climbing Mount Improbable*. New York: Norton.

Day, Ruth S. 1979. Verbal fluency and the language-bound effect. In *Individual Differences in Language Ability and Language Behavior*, eds. Charles J. Fillmore, Daniel Kempler, and William S.-Y. Wang, 57–84. New York: Academic Press.

Deacon, Terrence William. 1997. *The Symbolic Species: The Co-evolution of Language and the Brain*. New York: W.W. Norton.

Decety, Jean, Julie Grèzes, Nicolas Costes, Daniela Perani, Marc Jeannerod, Emmanuel Procyk, Fabrizio Grassi, and Ferruccio Fazio. 1997. Brain activity during observation of actions. Influence of action content and subject's strategy. *Brain* 120: 1763–1777.

DeGraff, Michel (ed.). 1999. *Language Creation and Language Change: Creolization, Diachrony, and Development*. Cambridge, MA: MIT Press.

DeGusta, David, W. Henry Gilbert, and Scott P. Turner. 1999. Hypoglossal canal size and hominid speech. *Proceedings of the National Academy of Sciences* 96: 1800–1804.

De Heinzelin, Jean, Desmond J. Clark, Tim White, William Hart, Paul Renne, Giday WoldeGabriel, Yonas Beyene, and Elisabeth Vrba. 1999. Environment and behavior of 2.5-million-year-old bouri hominids. *Science* 284: 625–629.

de Jong, Peter F. 1999. Hierarchical regression analysis in structural equation modeling. *Structural Equation Modeling* 6: 198–211.

Delong, Mahlon R. 1993. Overview of basal ganglia function. In *Role of the Cerebellum and Basal Ganglia in Voluntary Movement*, eds. Noriichi Mano, Ikuma Hamada, and Mahlon R. DeLong, 65–70. Amsterdam: Excerpta Medica.

D'Esposito, Mark and Michael P. Alexander. 1995. Subcortical Aphasia: Distinct profiles following left putaminal hemorrhage. *Neurology* 45: 38–41.

Dessalles, Jean-Louis. 2000. *Aux origines du langage. Une histoire naturelle de la parole*. Paris: Hermès.
   2004. About the adaptiveness of syntactic recursion. *Coevolution of Language and Theory of Mind*. Interdisciplines: electronic conference.
   2007. *Why We Talk*. Oxford, UK: Oxford University Press.

Di Sciullo, Anna Maria and Edwin Williams. 1978. *Words*. Cambridge, MA: MIT Press.

Dobzhansky, Theodosius. 1955. *Evolution, Genetics, and Man*. New York: John Wiley & Sons.
   1973. Nothing in biology makes sense except in the light of evolution. *American Biology Teacher*. 35: 125–129.

Dor, Daniel and Eva Jablonka. 2000. From cultural selection to genetic selection: a framework for the evolution of language. *Selection* 1(1–3): 33–55.
   2001. How language changed the genes: Towards an explicit account of the evolution of language. In *New Essays on the Origin of Language*, eds. Jürgen Trabant and Sean Ward, 149–175. Berlin: Mouton.

2004. Culture and genes in the evolution of human language. In *Human Paleoecology in the Levantine Corridor*, eds. Naama Goren-Inbar and John D. Speth, 105–114. Oxford, UK: Oxbow Books.

Dörnyei, Zoltán. 2005. *The Psychology of the Language Learner: Individual Differences in Second Language Acquisition*. Mahwah, NJ: Lawrence Erlbaum.

Dronkers, Nina. F., Johnna K. Shapiro, Brenda Redfern, and Robert T. Knight. 1992 The role of Broca's area in Broca's aphasia. *Journal of Clinical and Experimental Neuropsychology* 14: 52–53.

Ducrot, Oswald 1972. *Dire et ne pas dire*. Paris: Hermann.

Dugatkin, Lee Alan. 1997. *Cooperation Among Animals: An Evolutionary Perspective*. New York: Oxford University Press.

Dunbar, Robin. 1996. *Grooming, Gossip and the Evolution of Language*: London: Faber & Faber.

   1998. Theory of mind and the evolution of language. In *Approaches to the Evolution of Language: Social and Cognitive Bases*, eds. James R. Hurford, Michael Studdert-Kennedy, and Chris Knight, 92–110. Cambridge, UK: Cambridge University Press.

Dyer, Fred C. and James L. Gould. 1983. Honey bee navigation. *American Scientist* 71: 587–597

Edelman, Gerald M. 1987. *Neural Darwinism: The Theory of Neuronal Group Selection*. New York: Basic Books.

Egnor, S. E. Roian, Carmen G. Iguina, and Marc D. Hauser. 2006. Perturbation of auditory feedback causes systematic perturbation in vocal structure in adult cotton-top tamarins. *Journal of Experimental Biology* 209: 3652–3663.

Egnor, S. E. Roian, Jeanette Graham Wickelgren, and Marc D. Hauser. 2007. Tracking silence: adjusting vocal production to avoid acoustic interference. *Journal of Comparative Physiology* 193: 477–483.

Ellen, Paul and Catherine Thinus-Blanc (eds.). 1987. *Cognitive Processes and Spatial Orientation in Animal and Man*, vol. I: *Experimental Animal Psychology and Ethology*. Leiden, The Netherlands: Martinus Nijhoff Publishers.

Enard, Wolfgang, Molly Przeworski, Simon E. Fisher, Cecilia S. L. Lai, Victor Wiebe, Takashi Kitano, and Svante Pääbo. 2002. Molecular evolution of FOXP2, a gene involved in speech and language. *Nature* 418: 869–871.

Epstein, Richard L. and Walter A. Carnielli. 2000. *Computability: Computable Functions, Logic, and the Foundations of Mathematics*. Second edition. London: Wadsworth/Thomson Learning.

Erwin, Douglas. 2003. The Goldilocks hypothesis. *Science* 302: 1682–1683.

Everett, Daniel L. 1986. Pirahã. In *Handbook of Amazonian Languages*, vol. I, eds. Desmond C. Derbyshire and Geoffrey K Pullum, 200. The Hague: Mouton.

   1991. *A Língua Pirahã e a Teoria da Sintaxe*. São Paulo: Unicamp.

   1992. A língua pirahã e a teoria da sintaxe: Descrição, perspectivas e teoria. Dissertation. Editora Unicamp.

   2005. Cultural constraints on grammar and cognition in Pirahã. *Current Anthropology* 46(4): 621–646.

Falconer, Douglas S. 1960. *Introduction to Quantitative Genetics*. New York: Ronald Press Company.

Fant, Gunnar. 1960. *Acoustic Theory of Speech Production*. The Hague: Mouton.

Feinberg, Michael J. and Olle Ekberg. 1990. Deglutition after near-fatal choking episode: radiologic evaluation. *Radiology* 176: 637–640.

Fenson, Larry, Philip S. Dale, J. Steven Reznick, Elizabeth Bates, Donna J. Thal, and Stephen J. Pethick. 1994. Variability in early communicative development. *Monographs of the Society for Research in Child Development* 59, Serial No. 242.

Fischman, Josh. 2005. The Pathfinders. *National Geographic* 207(4): 16–27.

Fisher, S. E., and G. F. Marcus. 2006. The eloquent ape: genes, brains and the evolution of language. *Nature Reviews, Genetics* 7: 9–19.

Fisher, Simon. E., Faraneh Vargha-Khadem, Kate E. Watkins, Anthony P. Monaco, and Marcus E. Pembry. 1998. Localization of a gene implicated in a severe speech and language disorder. *Nature Genetics* 18: 168–170.

Fitch, W. Tecumseh. 1997. Vocal tract length and formant frequency dispersion correlate with body size in macaque monkeys. *Journal of the Acoustical Society of America* 102: 1213–1222.

 2000a. The evolution of speech: A comparative review. *Trends in Cognitive Sciences* 4: 258–267.

 2000b. Skull dimensions in relation to body size in nonhuman mammals: The causal bases for acoustic allometry. *Zoology* 103: 40–58.

 2005. The evolution of language: A comparative review. *Biology and Philosophy* 20: 193–230.

 2006. Production of vocalizations in mammals. In Keith Brown, (ed.) *Encyclopedia of Language and Linguistics*, 115–121. Oxford, UK: Elsevier.

 in press. Prolegomena to a science of biolinguistics. In *Learning from Animals?: Examining the Nature of Human Uniqueness*, eds. Louise Roeska-Hardy and Eva M. Neumann-Held, 15–44. London: Psychology Press.

Fitch, W. Tecumseh and Marc D. Hauser. 2002. Unpacking honesty: generating and extracting information from acoustic signals. In *Acoustic Communication*, eds. Andrea Megala-Simmons and Arthur N. Popper, 65–137. New York: Springer.

 2004. Computational constraints on syntactic processing in a nonhuman primate. *Science* 303: 377–380.

Fitch, W. Tecumseh, Marc Hauser, and Noam Chomsky. 2005. The evolution of the language faculty: clarifications and implications. *Cognition* 97. 179–210.

Fitch, W. Tecumseh and David Reby. 2001. The descended larynx is not uniquely human. *Proceedings of the Royal Society of London* B 268: 1669–1675.

Flowers, Kenneth A. and Colin Robertson. 1985. The effects of Parkinson's disease on the ability to maintain a mental set. *Journal of Neurology, Neurosurgery, Psychiatry* 48: 517–529.

Fodor, Jerry. 2003. *Hume Variations*. New York: Oxford University Press.

Fodor, Jerry and Massimo Piattelli-Palmarini. in press. *What Darwin Got Wrong*. New York: Farrar, Straus and Giroux.

Foley, Robert. 1987. *Another Unique Species: Patterns in Human Evolutionary Ecology*. Harlow: Longman Scientific and Technical.

Fox, Danny and Howard Lasnik. 2003. Successive-cyclic movement and island repair: The difference between Sluicing and VP-ellipsis. *Linguistic Inquiry* 34(1): 143–154.

Friederici, Angela D. 2004. Processing local transitions versus long-distance syntactic hierarchies. *Trends in Cognitive Science* 8(5): 245–247.

Reference

Frisch, Karl von. 1967. Honeybees: Do they use direction and distance information provided by their dancers? *Science* 158: 1072–1076.

Gabunia, L., A. Vekua, D. Lordkipanidze, C. C. Swisher, R. Ferring, A. Justus, M. Nioradze, M. Tvalchrelidze, S. C. Anton, G. Bosinski, O. Jöris, M. A. Lumley, G. Majsuradze, and A. Mouskhelishvili. 2000. Earliest Pleistocene hominid cranial remains from Dmanisi, Republic of Georgia: Taxonomy, geological setting, and age. *Science* 288: 1019–1025.

Gabunia, Leo, Abesalom Vekua, David Lordkipanidze, Carl C. Swisher, Reid Ferring, Antje Justus, Medea Nioradze, Merab Tvalcrelidze, Susan Anton, and Charles Randy Gallistel. 1990. Representations in animal cognition: An introduction. *Cognition* 37: 1–22.

Gallistel, Charles Randy (ed.). 1990. *Animal Cognition, Cognition* (Special Issue), 37 (1–2).

——— 1997. Neurons and Behavior. In *Conversations in the Cognitive Neurosciences*, ed. Michael S. Gazzaniga, 71–89. Cambridge, MA: MIT Press.

——— 1998. Symbolic processes in the brain: the case of insect navigation. In *Invitation to Cognitive Science*, eds. Don Scarborough and Saul Sternberg vol. IV: *Methods, Models and Conceptual Issues*, 1–51. Cambridge, MA: MIT Press.

——— 2000. The replacement of general-purpose learning models with adaptively specialized learning modules. In *The New Cognitive Neuroscience*, Second edition, ed. Michael Gazzaniga, 1179–1191. Cambridge, MA: MIT Press.

——— 2002. Frequency, contingency and the information processing theory of conditioning. In *Frequency Processing and Cognition*, eds. Peter Sedlmeier and Tilmann Betsch, 153–171. Oxford, UK: Oxford University Press.

Ganger, Jennifer and Karin Stromswold. 1998. The innateness, evolution and genetics of language. *Human Biology* 70: 199–213.

Gärdenfors, Peter. 1996. Cued and detached representations in animal cognition. *Behavioural Processes* 36: 263–273.

——— 2003. *How Homo Became Sapiens: On the Evolution of Thinking*. Oxford, UK: Oxford University Press.

——— 2004. Cooperation and the evolution of symbolic communication. In *The Evolution of Communication Systems*, eds. D. Kimbrough Oller and Ulrike Griebel, 237–256. Cambridge, MA: MIT Press.

——— 2007. The cognitive and communicative demands of cooperation. *Hommage à Wlodek: Philosophical Papers Dedicated to Wlodek Rabinowicz* <http://www.fil.lu.se/hommageawlodek>.

Gardner, R. Allen and Beatrice T. Gardner. 1969. Teaching sign language to a chimpanzee. *Science* 165: 664–672.

——— 1980. Two comparative psychologists look at language acquisition. In *Children's Language*, vol. II., ed. Keith E. Nelson, 309–369. New York: Halsted.

Gardner, Andy and Stuart A. West. 2004. Cooperation and punishment, especially in humans. *American Naturalist* 164(6): 753–764.

Gazzaniga, Micheal S. 1985. *The Social Brain: Discovering the Networks of the Mind*. New York: Basic Books.

Gentilucci, Maurizio, Francesca Benuzzi, Massimo Gangitano and Silvia Grimaldi. 2001. Grasp with hand and mouth: A kinematic study on healthy subjects. *Journal of Neurophysiology* 86: 1685–1699.

Gentilucci, Maurizio and Michael C. Corballis. 2006. From manual gesture to speech: A gradual transition. *Neuroscience and Biobehavioral Reviews* 30: 949–960.

Gentner, Timothy Q., Kimberly M. Fenn, Daniel Margoliash, and Howard C. Nusbaum. 2006. Recursive syntactic pattern learning by songbirds. *Nature* 440: 1204–1207.

Gerardin, Emmanuel, Angela Sirigu, Stéphanie Lehéricy, Jean-Baptiste Poline, Bertrand Gaymard, Claude Marsault, Yves Agid, and Denis Le Bihan. 2000. Partially overlapping neural networks for real and imagined hand movements. *Cerebral Cortex* 10: 1093–1104.

Gerhart, John and Mark Kirschner. 1997. *Cells, Embryos, and Evolution: Towards a Cellular and Developmental Understanding of Phenotypic Variation and Evolutionary Adaptability.* Malden, MA: Blackwell.

Gersting, Judith L. 1999. *Mathematical Structures for Computer Science.* Fourth edition. New York: W. H. Freeman.

Geschwind, Norman. 1965. Disconnexion syndromes in animals and man: Part I. *Brain* 88: 237–294.

Gibbons, Ann. 2006. *The First Human: The Race to Discover Our Earliest Ancestors.* New York: Doubleday.

Gibbs, Wayt. 2003. The unseen genome: Beyond DNA. *Scientific American* December: 107–113.

Gibson, Kathleen R. and Stephen Jessee. 1999. Language evolution and expansions of multiple neurological processing areas. In *The Origins of Language: What Nonhuman Primates Can Tell Us*, ed. Barbara J. King, 189–227. Santa Fe, NM: School of American Research Press.

Gilbert, Daniel T. and Timothy D. Wilson. 2007. Prospection: Experiencing the future. *Science* 317: 1351–1354.

Gilbert, Scott F. 2003. The morphogenesis of evolutionary developmental biology. *International Journal of Developmental Biology* 47: 467–477.

Gintis, Herbert. 2000. Strong reciprocity and human sociality. *Journal of Theoretical Biology* 206(2): 169–179.

Gleitman, Henry and Lila Gleitman. 1970. *Phrase and Paraphrase.* New York: W. W. Norton.

Glenberg, Arthur M. 1997. What memory is for. *Behavioral and Brain Sciences* 20: 1–19.

Gold, Mark. 1967. Language identification in the limit. *Information and Control* 10: 447–474.

Goldberg, Adele E. 2003. Constructions: a new theoretical approach to language. *Trends in Cognitive Science* 7(5): 219–224.
    2005. *Constructions at Work: Constructionist Approaches in Context.* New York: Oxford University Press.

Goldin-Meadow, Susan and David McNeill 1999. The role of gesture and mimetic representation in making language the province of speech. In *The Descent of Mind*, eds. Michael C. Corballis and Stephen E. G. Lea, 155–172. Oxford, UK: Oxford University Press.

Goldstein, Kurt. 1948. *Language and Language Disturbances: Aphasic Symptom Complexes and Their Significance for Medicine and Theory of Language.* New York, Grune and Stratton.

Gomez, Juan Carlos. 2004. *Apes, Monkeys, Children, and the Growth of Mind.* Cambridge, MA: Harvard University Press.

Gould, James L. 1976. The dance-language controversy. *Quarterly Review of Biology* 51: 211–4

Gould, Stephen and Richard Lewontin. 1979. The spandrels of San Marco and the Panglossian paradigm: A critique of the adaptationist programme. *Proceedings of the Royal Society London B* 205: 581–598.

Graffi, Giorgio. 2001. *200 Years of Syntax: A Critical Survey.* Philadelphia, PA: John Benjamins Publishing Co.

Grafton, Scott T., Michael A. Arbib, Leonida Fadiga, and Giacomo Rizzolatti. 1996. Localization of grasp representations in humans by positron emission tomography. 2. Observation compared with imagination. *Experimental Brain Research* 112: 103–111.

Graybiel, Ann M. 1995. Building action repertoires: memory and learning functions of the basal ganglia. *Current Opinion in Neurobiology* 5: 733–741.

    1997. The basal ganglia and cognitive pattern generators. *Schizophrenia Bulletin* 23: 459–469.

    1998. The basal ganglia and chunking of action repertoires. *Neurobiology Memory Learning* 70: 119–136.

Greenberg, Benjamin D., Dennis L. Murphy, and Steven A. Rasmussen. 2000. Neuroanatomically based approaches to obsessive-compulsive disorder: Neurosurgery and transcranial magnetic stimulation. *Psychiatric Clinics of North America* 23: 671–685.

Greenfield, Patricia M. 1991. Language, tools and brain: The ontogeny and phylogeny of hierarchically organized sequential behavior. *Behavioral and Brain Sciences* 14: 531–595.

Greenfield, Patricia and E. Susan Savage-Rumbaugh. 1990. Grammatical combination in *Pan paniscus*: Process of learning and invention. In *Language and Intelligence in Monkeys and Apes: Comparative Developmental Perspectives*, eds. Sue Taylor Parker, and Kathleen Rita Gibson, 540–578. Cambridge, UK: Cambridge University Press.

Grewal, Shiv and Danesh Moazed. 2003. Heterochromatin and epigenetic control of gene expression. *Science* 301: 798–802.

Grice, Paul 1957. Meaning. *Philosophical Review* 66: 377–388.

    1989. *Studies in the Ways of Words*, Cambridge, MA: Harvard University Press.

Grossman, Murray, Susan Carvell, Stephen Gollomp, Matthew B. Stern, Gwyn Vernon, and Howard I. Hurtig. 1991. Sentence comprehension and praxis deficits in Parkinson's disease. *Neurology* 41: 1620–1628.

Grossman, Murray, Susan Carvell, Stephen Gollomp, Matthew B. Stern, Martin Reivich, Donald Morrison, Abass Alavi, and Howard L. Hurtig. 1993. Cognitive and physiological substrates of impaired sentence processing in Parkinson's disease. *Journal of Cognitive Neuroscience* 5: 480–498.

Grosz, Barbara J. and Candace Sidner. 1990. Plans for discourse. In *Intentions in Communications*, eds. Phillip Cohen, Jerry Morgan, and Martha Pollack, 417–444. Cambridge, MA: MIT Press.

Grush, Rick. 1997. The architecture of representation. *Philosophical Psychology* 10: 5–23.

Gulz, Agneta. 1991. *The Planning of Action as a Cognitive and Biological Phenomenon.* Lund, Sweden: Lund University Cognitive Studies 2.

Hale, Kenneth and Samuel Jay Keyser. 1993. On argument structure and the lexical representation of semantic relations. In *The View from Building 20*, eds. Samuel Jay Keyser and Kenneth Hale, 53–109. Cambridge, MA: MIT Press.

2002. *Prolegomenon to a Theory of Argument Structure*. Cambridge, MA: MIT Press.

Halle, Morris and Alec Marantz. 1993. Distributed morphology and the pieces of inflection. In *The View from Building 20*, eds. Samuel Keyser and Kenneth Hale, 111–176. Cambridge, MA: MIT Press.

Hamilton, William D. 1964a. Genetical evolution of social behaviour I. *Journal of Theoretical Biology* 7(1): 1–16.

1964b. Genetical evolution of social behaviour II. *Journal of Theoretical Biology* 7(1): 17–52.

1996. *Narrow Roads of Gene Land: the Collected Papers of W. D. Hamilton*. Oxford/ New York: W. H. Freeman/Spektrum.

Hanakawa, Takashi, Ilka Immisch, Keiichiro Toma, Michael A. Dimyan, Peter Van Gelderen, and Mark Hallett. 2003. Functional properties of brain areas associated with motor execution and imagery. *Journal of Neurophysiology* 89: 989–1002.

Hangartner, Walter. 1969. Trail-laying in the subterranean ant Acanthomyops interjectus. *Journal of Insect Physiology* 15: 1–4.

Hare, Brian, Josep Call and Michael Tomasello. 2001. Do chimpanzees know what conspecifics know? *Animal Behaviour* 61: 139–151.

Harris, Zelig. 1986/1951. *Structural Linguistics*. Chicago, IL: University of Chicago Press.

Hauser, Marc D. 1996. *The Evolution of Communication*. Cambridge, MA: MIT Press.

2000. *Wild Minds: How Animals Really Think*. New York: Henry Holt.

2001. What's so special about speech? In *Language, Brain, and Cognitive Development: Essays in Honor of Jacques Mehler*, ed. Emmanuel Dupoux, 417–434. Cambridge, MA: MIT Press.

2006. *Moral Minds: How Natured Designed a Universal Sense of Right and Wrong*. New York: HarperCollins/Ecco.

Hauser, Marc D., David Barner, and Tim J. O'Donnell. 2007. Evolutionary linguistics: a new look at an old landscape. *Language, Learning and Development* 3: 101–132.

Hauser, Marc D., Noam Chomsky, and W. Tecumseh Fitch. 2002. The faculty of language: What it is, who has it, and how did it evolve? *Science* 298: 1569–1579.

Hauser, Marc D. and W. Tecumseh Fitch. 2003. What are the uniquely human components of the language faculty? In *Language Evolution*, eds. Morton H. Christiansen and Simon Kirby, 158–181. Oxford, UK: Oxford University Press.

Hauser, Marc D. and Josh McDermott. 2003. The evolution of the music faculty: a comparative perspective. *Nature Neuroscience* 6: 663–668.

Hauser, Marc D., Elissa L. Newport, and Richard N. Aslin. 2001. Segmenting a continuous acoustic speech stream: Serial learning in cotton-top tamarin monkeys. *Cognition* 78: B53–B64.

Hayes, Catherine. 1952. *The Ape in Our House*. London: Gollancz.

Heinrich, Bernd. 1989. *Ravens in Winter*. New York: Summit Books.

Hellwag, Christoph. 1781. *De Formatione Loquelae*, Dissertation, Tübingen.

Henke, William L. 1966. Dynamic articulatory model of speech production using computer simulation. Ph.D. Dissertation. MIT.

Henshilwood, Christopher S., Francesco d'Errico, Curtis W. Marean, Richard G. Milo, and Royden Yates. 2001. An early bone tool industry from the Middle Stone Age at Blombos Cave, South Africa: Implications for the origins of modern human behaviour, symbolism and language. *Journal of Human Evolution* 41: 631–678.

Henshilwood, Christopher S., Francesco d'Errico, Royden Yates, Zenobia Jacobs, Chantal Tribolo, Geoff A. Duller, Norbert Mercier, Judith C. Sealy, Helene Valladas, Ian Watts, and Ann G. Wintle. 2003. Emergence of modern human behavior: Middle Stone Age engravings from South Africa. *Science* 295: 1278–1280.

Herman, Louis. M. 2002. Language learning. In *Encyclopedia of Marine Mammals*, eds. William F. Perrin, Bernd Wursig, and J. G. M. Hans Thewissen, 685–689. New York: Academic Press.

Hermisson, Joachim and Günter P. Wagner. 2004. The population genetic theory of hidden variation and genetic robustness. *Genetics* 168: 2271–2284.

Hewes, Gordon W. 1973. Primate communication and the gestural origins of language. *Current Anthropology* 14: 5–24.

Heyes, Cecilia M. and Bennett G. Galef. 1996. *Social Learning in Animals: The Roots of Culture*. San Diego, CA: Academic Press.

Hochstadt, Jesse. 2004. The Nature and causes of sentence comprehension deficits in Parkinson's disease: Insights from eye tracking during sentence picture matching. Ph.D. dissertation. Brown University.

Hockett, Charles F. 1960. Logical considerations in the study of animal communication. In *Animal Sounds and Communication*, eds. Wesley E. Lanyon and William N. Tavolga, 392–430. Washington, DC: American Institute of Biological Sciences.

  1960. The origin of speech. *Scientific American* 203(3): 88–96.

Hofstadter, Douglas R. 1979. *Gödel, Escher, Bach: An Eternal Golden Braid*. New York: Basic Books.

Holldobler, Bert. 1978. Ethological aspects of chemical communication in ants. *Advances in the Study of Behavior* 8: 75–115.

Hopcroft, John E., Rajeev Motwani, and Jeffrey D. Ullman. 2000. *Introduction to Automata Theory, Languages and Computation*. Second edition. Reading, MA: Addison-Wesley.

Horn, Laurence. 1989. *A Natural History of Negation*. Chicago: University of Chicago Press.

Horn, Laurence and Gregory Ward. 2004. *The Handbook of Pragmatics*. Oxford, UK: Blackwell.

Horwitz, Sarah Mccue, Julia R. Irwin, Margaret J. Briggs-Gowan, Joan M. Bosson Heenan, Jennifer Mendoza, and Alice S. Carter. 2003. Language delay in a community cohort of young children. *Journal of the American Academy of Child and Adolescent Psychiatry* 42: 932–940.

Hubel, David and Torsten Wiesel. 1959. Receptive fields of single neurons in the cat's striate cortex. *Journal of Physiology* 148: 574–591.

  1962. Receptive fields, binocular interaction and functional architecture in the cat's visual cortex. *Journal of Physiology* 160: 106–154.

Hughes, Claire, James Russell, and Trevor W. Robbins. 1994. Evidence for executive dysfunction in autism. *Neuropsychologia* 32: 477–492.

Humphrey, Nicholas K. 1976. The social function of intellect. In *Growing Points in Ethology*, eds. Paul P. G. Bateson and Robert A. Hinde, 303–317. Cambridge, UK: Cambridge University Press.

1993. *A History of the Mind*. London: Vintage Books.

Hurford, James R., Michael Studdert-Kennedy, and Chris Knight (eds.). 1998. *Approaches to the Evolution of Language*. Cambridge, UK: Cambridge University Press.

Hurley, Susan L. and Nick Chater. 2005. *Perspectives on Imitation: From Neuroscience to Social Science*. Cambridge, MA: MIT Press.

Ike-uchi, Masayuki. 2003. *Predication and Modification: A Minimalist Approach*. Tokyo: Liber Press.

Illes, Judy, E., Jeffrey Metter, William R. Hanson, and Shuji Iritani. 1988. Language production in Parkinson's disease: Acoustic and linguistic considerations. *Brain and Language* 33: 146–160.

Irons, David B., Robert G. Anthony, and James A. Estes. 1986. Foraging strategies of glaucous-winged gulls in a rocky intertidal community. *Ecology* 67: 1460–1474.

Isaac, Llywelyn Glynn. 1982. The earliest archaeological traces. In *Cambridge History of Africa*, vol. I, ed. J. Desmond Clark, 157–247. Cambridge, UK: Cambridge University Press.

1984. The archaeology of human origins: Studies of the lower Pleistocene in East Africa 1971–1981. *Advances in World Archaeology* 3: 1–87.

Iverson, Jana M. and Susan Goldin-Meadow 2005. Gesture paves the way for language development. *Psychological Science* 16: 367–371.

Jablonka, Eva and Marion J. Lamb. 1995. *Epigenetic Inheritance and Evolution: The Lamarckian Dimension*. Oxford, UK: Oxford University Press.

Jablonka, Eva and Geva Rechav. 1996. The evolution of language in light of the evolution of literacy. In *Origins of Language (Collegium Budapest Workshop Series No.2)*, ed. Jürgen Trabant, 70–88. Budapest: Collegium Budapest.

Jackendoff, Ray. 2002. *Foundations of Language: Brain, Meaning, Grammar, Evolution*. Oxford, UK: Oxford University Press.

2007. *Language, Consciousness, Culture: Essays on Mental Structure*. Cambridge, MA: MIT Press.

Jackendoff, Ray and Fred Lerdahl. 2006. The capacity for music: What's special about it? *Cognition* 100: 33–72.

Jackendoff, Ray and Steven Pinker. 2005. The nature of the language faculty and its implications for the evolution of language (Reply to Fitch, Hauser, and Chomsky). *Cognition* 97: 211–225.

Jacob, François. 1982. *The Possible and the Actual*. New York: Pantheon Books.

Jaenisch, Rudolf and Adrian Bird. 2003. Epigenetic regulation of gene expression: How the genome integrates intrinsic and environmental signals. *Nature Genetics* 33: 245–254.

Jellinger, Kurt A. 1990. New developments in the pathology of Parkinson's disease. In *Advances in Neurology, vol. LIII: Parkinson's Disease: Anatomy, Pathology and Therapy*, ed. Max B. Streifler, 1–15. New York: Raven Press.

Johansson, Sverker. 2005. *Origins of Language: Constraints on Hypotheses*. Amsterdam: John Benjamins.

Johansson, Sverker, Jordan Zlatev, and Peter Gärdenfors. 2006. Why don't chimps talk and humans sing like canaries? *Behavioral and Brain Sciences* 29(3): 287–288.

Joos, Martin (ed.). 1957. *Readings in Linguistics: The Development of Descriptive Linguistics in America since 1925*. Washington, DC: American Council of Learned Societies.

Joshi, Aravind K., K. Vijay-Shanker, and David J. Weir. 1991. The convergence of Mildly Context-Sensitive formalisms. In *Processing of Linguistic Structure*, eds. Peter Sells, Stuart M. Shieber, and Thomas Wasow, 31–81. Cambridge, MA: MIT Press.

Judson, Horace F. 1979. *The Eighth Day of Creation: Makers of the Revolution in Biology*, Plainview, NY: Cold Spring Harbor Laboratory Press. (New expanded edition 1996.) New York: Simon and Schuster.

Just, Marcel A., Patricia A. Carpenter, Timothy A. Keller, William F. Eddy, and Keith R. Thulborn. 1996. Brain activation modulated by sentence comprehension. *Science* 274: 114–116.

Kahneman, Daniel. 2003. A perspective on judgment and choice: mapping bounded rationality (Nobel Lecture). *American Psychologist* 58(9): 697–720.

Kamp, Yves and Martin Hasler. 1990. *Recursive Neural Networks for Associative Memory*. New York: John Wiley & Sons.

Kandel, Eric R. and Larry R. Squire. 2000. Neuroscience: Breaking down scientific barriers to the study of brain and mind. *Science* 290: 1113–1120.

Kaplan, Hillard, Kim Hill, Jane Lancaster, and Magdalena Hurtado. 2000. A theory of human life history evolution: Diet, intelligence, and longevity. *Evolutionary Anthropology* 9: 156–185.

Kauffman, Stuart. 1993. *The Origins of Order*. New York: Oxford University Press.
　1995. *At Home in the Universe: The Search for Laws of Self-organization and Complexity*. New York: Oxford University Press.

Kay, Richard F., Matt Cartmill, and Michelle Barlow. 1998. The hypoglossal canal and the origin of human vocal behavior. *Proceedings of the National Academy of Sciences (USA)* 95: 5417–5419.

Keeley, H. Lawrence and Nicholas Toth. 1981. Microwear polishes on early stone tools from Koobi Fora, Kenya. *Nature* 293: 464–465.

Kegl, Judy, Anne Senghas and Maria Coppola. 1999. Creations through contact: Sign language emergence and sign language change in Nicaragua. In *Language Creation and Language Change: Creolization, Diachrony, and Development*, ed. Michel DeGraff, 179–237. Cambridge, MA: MIT Press.

Key, Catherine A. 2000. The evolution of human life history. *World Archaeology* 31(3): 329–350.

King, Jonathan and Marcel A. Just. 1991. Individual differences in syntactic processing: The role of working memory. *Journal of Memory and Language* 30: 580–602.

Kirby, Simon. 1999. *Function, Selection and Innateness: The Emergence of Language Universals*. Oxford, UK: Oxford University Press.
　2002. Natural language from artificial life. *Artificial Life* 8(2): 185–215.

Kirschner, Marc W. and John C. Gerhart. 2005. *The Plausibility of Life: Resolving Darwin's Dilemma*. New Haven, CT: Yale University Press.

Klein, Denise, Robert J. Zatorre, Brenda Milner, Ernst Meyer, and Alan C. Evans. 1994. Left putaminal activation when speaking a second language: Evidence from PET. *NeuroReport* 5: 2295–2297.

Klein, Richard G. 1999. *The Human Career*. Second edition. Chicago: Chicago University Press.

Klein, Richard G., Graham Avery, Kathryn Cruz-Uribe, David Halkett, John E. Parkington, Teresa Steele, Thomas P. Volman, and Royden Yates. 2004. The Ysterfontein 1 Middle Stone Age site, South Africa, and early human exploitation of coastal resources. *Proceedings of the National Academy of Sciences* 101: 5708–5715.

Knight, Chris. 1998a. Introduction: Grounding language function in social cognition. In *Approaches to the Evolution of Language: Social and Cognitive Bases*, eds. James R. Hurford, Michael Studdert-Kennedy, and Chris Knight, 9–16. Cambridge, UK: Cambridge University Press.

1998b. Ritual/speech coevolution: A solution to the problem of deception. In *Approaches to the Evolution of Language: Social and Cognitive Bases*, eds. J. R. Hurford, M. Studdert-Kennedy, and C. Knight, 68–91. Cambridge, UK: Cambridge University Press.

Knuth, Donald E. 1973. *The Art of Computer Programming: Fundamental Algorithms*. Second edition. London: Addison Wesley.

Kobayashi, Hiromi and Shiro Kohshima. 2001. Unique morphology of the human eye and its adaptive meaning: comparative studies on external morphology of the primate eye. *Journal of Human Evolution* 40(5): 419–435.

Kohler, Evelyne, Christian Keysers, M. Allessandra Umiltà, Leonardo Fogassi, Vittorio Gallese, and Giacomo Rizzolatti. 2002. Hearing sounds, understanding actions: Action representation in mirror neurons. *Science* 297: 846–848.

Köhler, Wolfgang. 1921. Zur Psychologie des Schimpansen. *Psychologische Forschung* 1: 2–46.

1925. *The mentality of apes*, London: Routledge and Kegan Paul.

Komarova, Natalia and Martin Nowak. 2001. Natural selection of the critical period for language acquisition. *Proceedings of the Royal Society London B* 268: 1189–1196.

Konner, Melvin. 1982. *The Tangled Wing: Biological Constraints on the Human Spirit*. New York: Harper.

Kotz, Sonja. A., Martin Meyer, Kai Alter, Mireilli Besson, D. Yves Von Cramon, and Angela D. Frederici. 2003 On the lateralization of emotional prosody: An fMRI investigation. *Brain and Language*, 96: 366–376.

Krause, Johannes, Carles Lalueza-Fox, Ludovic Orlando, Wolfgang Enard, Richard E. Green, Hernan A. Burbano, Jean-Jacques Hublin, Catherine Hänni, Javier Fortea, Marco de la Rasilla, Jaime Bertranpetit, Antonio Rosas, and Svante Pääbo. 2007. The derived FOXP2 variant of modern humans was shared with Neanderthals. *Current Biology* 17: 1908–1912.

Krebs, John R. and Nicholas B. Davies. 1993. *An Introduction to Behavioural Ecology*. Oxford, UK/Cambridge, MA: Blackwell Scientific Publications.

Krebs, John R. and Richard Dawkins. 1984. Animal signals: mind reading and *manipulation*. In *Behavioral Ecology: An Evolutionary Approach*, eds. John R. Krebs and Nicholas B. Davies, 380–402. Sunderland, MA: Sinauer Associates.

Lai, Cecilia S. L., Simon. E. Fisher, Jane A. Hurst, Faraneh Vargha-Khadem, and Anthony P. Monaco. 2001. A forkhead-domain gene is mutated in a severe speech and language disorder. *Nature* 413: 519–523.

Lai, Cecilia S. L., Dianne Gerrelli, Anthony P. Monaco, Simon E. Fisher, and Andrew J. Copp. 2003. FOXP2 expression during brain development coincides with adult sites of pathology in a severe speech and language disorder. *Brain* 126: 2455–2462.

Lange, Klaus W., Trevor W. Robbins, C. David Marsden, M. James, Adrian M. Owen, and Geraldine M. Paul. 1992. L-Dopa withdrawal in Parkinson's disease selectively impairs cognitive performance in tests sensitive to frontal lobe dysfunction. *Psychopharmacology* 107: 394–404.

Larson, Richard K. 1991. The projection of DP (and DegP). Syntax Colloquium Series. University of Indiana – Bloomington.

Larson, Richard K. and Hiroko Yamakido. 2008. Ezafe and the deep position of nominal modifiers. In *Adjectives and Adverbs: Syntax, Semantics, and Discourse*, eds. Louise McNally and Christopher Kennedy, 43–70. Oxford, UK: Oxford University Press.

Larson, Susan 2007. Evolutionary transformation of the hominin shoulder. *Evolutionary Anthropology* 16: 172–187.

Lashley, Karl S. 1951. The problem of serial order in behavior. In *Cerebral Mechanisms in Behavior*, ed. Lloyd A. Jefress, 112–146. New York: Wiley.

Lasnik, Howard, Juan Uriagereka, and Cedric Boeckx. 2005. *A Course In Minimalist Syntax: Foundations and Prospects (Generative Syntax)*. Oxford, UK: Blackwell.

Lehericy, Stephanie, Mathieu Ducros, Pierre-Francois Van de Moortele, Chantal Francois, Lionel Thivard, Cyril Poupon, Nick Swindale, Kamil Ugerbil, and Dae-Shik Kim. 2004. Diffusion tensor tracking shows distinct corticostriatal circuits in humans. *Annals of Neurology* 55: 522–529.

Leiber, Justin. 2001. Turing and the fragility and insubstantiality of evolutionary explanations. *Philosophical Psychology* 14.1: 83–94.

Leonard, William and L. Marcia Robertson. 1997. Comparative primate energetics and hominind evolution. *American Journal of Physical Anthropology* 102: 265–281.

2000. Ecological correlates for home range variation in primates: Implications for human evolution. In *On the Move: How and Why Animals Travel in Groups*, eds. S. Boinski and P. A. Garber, 628–648. Chicago, IL: University of Chicago Press.

Lerdahl, Fred and Ray Jackendoff. 1983. *A Generative Theory of Tonal Music*. Cambridge, MA: MIT Press.

Leslie, Alan. M., Ori Friedman, and Tamsin P. German. 2004. Core mechanisms in "theory of mind." *Trends in Cognitive Sciences* 8: 528–533.

Lettvin, Jerome, Humberto Maturana, Warren McCulloch, and Walter Pitts. 1959. What the frog's eye tells the frog's brain. *Proceedings of the Institute of Radio Engineers* 47: 1940–1951.

Levinson, Stephen C. 1983. *Pragmatics*. Cambridge, UK: Cambridge University Press.

2000. *Presumptive Meanings: The Theory of Generalized Conversational Implicature*. Cambridge, MA: MIT Press.

Lewis, Mark E. 1997. Carnivorean paleoguilds of Africa: Implications for hominid food procurement strategies. *Journal of Human Evolution* 32: 257–258

Lewontin, Richard. 1998. The evolution of cognition: Questions we will never answer. In *Invitation to Cognitive Science*, eds. Don Scarborough and Saul Sternberg Vol. IV: *Methods, Models and Conceptual Issues*, 107–132. Cambridge, MA: MIT Press.

Liberman, Alvin M., Franklin S. Cooper, Donald P. Shankweiler, and Michael Studdert-Kennedy. 1967. Perception of the speech code. *Psychological Review* 74: 431–461.

Lichtheim, Ludwig. 1885. On aphasia. *Brain* 7: 433–484.

Lieberman, Daniel E. 1998. Sphenoid shortening and the evolution of modern cranial shape. *Nature* 393: 158–162.

Lieberman, Daniel E., Brandeis M. McBratney and Gail Krovitz. 2002. The evolution and development of cranial form in Homo sapiens. *Proceedings of the National Academy of Sciences* 99: 1134–1139.

Lieberman, Daniel E., Callum F. Ross, and Matthew J. Ravosa. 2000. The primate cranial base: Ontogeny, function and integration. *Yearbook of Physical Anthropology* 43: 117–169.

Lieberman, Philip. 1968. Primate vocalizations and human linguistic ability. *Journal of the Acoustical Society of America* 44: 1157–1164.

    1984. *The Biology and Evolution of Language*. Cambridge, MA: Harvard University Press.

    1998. *Eve Spoke: Human Language and Human Evolution*. New York: W. W. Norton.

    2000. *Human Language and Our Reptilian Brain: The Subcortical Bases of Speech, Syntax, and Thought*. Cambridge, MA: Harvard University Press.

    2002. On the nature and evolution of the neural bases of human language. *Yearbook of Physical Anthropology* 45: 36–62.

    2006. *Toward an Evolutionary Biology of Language*. Cambridge, MA: Harvard University Press.

Lieberman, Philip and Edmund S. Crelin. 1971. On the speech of Neanderthal man. *Linguistic Inquiry* 2: 203–222.

Lieberman, Philip, Edmund S. Crelin, and Dennis H. Klatt. 1972. Phonetic ability and related anatomy of the newborn, adult human, Neanderthal man, and the chimpanzee. *American Anthropologist* 74: 287–307.

Lieberman, Philip, Joseph Friedman and Lianne S. Feldman. 1990. Syntactic deficits in Parkinson's disease. *Journal of Nervous and Mental Disease* 178: 360–365.

Lieberman, Philip, Edward T. Kako, Joseph Friedman, Gary Tajchman, Lianne S. Feldman, and Eleonora B. Jiminez. 1992. Speech production, syntax comprehension, and cognitive deficits in Parkinson's disease. *Brain and Language* 43: 169–189.

Lieberman, Philip, Dennis H. Klatt and William H. Wilson. 1969. Vocal tract limitations on the vowel repertoires of rhesus monkey and other nonhuman primates. *Science* 164: 1185–1187.

Lieberman, Philip, Angie Morey, Jesse Hochstadt, Mara Larson, and Sandra Mather. 2005. Mount Everest: A space-analog for speech monitoring of cognitive deficits and stress. *Aviation, Space and Environmental Medicine* 76: 198–207.

Liégeois, Frédérique, Torsten Baldeweg, Alan Connelly, David G. Gadian, Mortimer Mishkin, and Faraneh Vargha-Khadem. 2003. Language fMRI abnormalities associated with FOXP2 gene mutation. *Nature Neuroscience* 6: 1230–1237.

Lightfoot, David. 2000. The spandrels of the linguistic genotype. In *The Evolutionary Emergence of Language*, eds. Chris Knight, Michael Studdert-Kennedy, and James R. Hurford, 231–247. Cambridge, UK: Cambridge University Press.

Linz, Peter. 2001. *An Introduction to Formal Languages and Automata*. Sudbury, MA: Jones & Bartlett.

Lisker, Leigh and Arthur S. Abramson. 1964. A cross language study of voicing in initial stops: acoustical measurements. *Word* 20: 384–442.

Locke, John F. 1998. Social sound-making as a precursor to spoken language. In *Approaches to the Evolution of Language: Social and Cognitive Bases*, eds.

James R. Hurford, Michael Studdert-Kennedy, and Chris Knight, 190–201. Cambridge, UK: Cambridge University Press.

Lotka, Alfred J. 1956/1924. *Elements of Mathematical Biology*. New York: Dover.

MacLarnon, Ann and Gwen Hewitt. 2004. Increased breathing control: Another factor in the evolution of human language. *Evolutionary Anthropology* 13: 181–197.

MacLean, Paul D. and Joseph D. Newman. 1988. Role of midline frontolimbic cortex in the production of the isolation call of squirrel monkeys. *Brain Research* 450: 111–123.

MacSwan, Jeff. 2005. Codeswitching and generative grammar: A critique of the MLF model and some remarks on "modified minimalism." *Bilingualism: Language and Cognition* 8(1): 1–22.

Marantz, Alec. 1997. No escape from syntax: don't try morphological analysis in the privacy of your own lexicon. In *Proceedings of the 21st Annual Penn Linguistics Colloquium*, eds. Alexis Dimitriadis, Laura Siegel, Clarissa Surek-Clark, and Alexander Williams, 201–225. Philadelphia, PA: The University of Pennsylvania Working Papers in Linguistics.

Marín, Oscar, Wilhelmus J. A. J. Smeets, and Agustín González. 1998. Evolution of the basal ganglia in tetrapods: A new perspective based on recent studies in amphibians. *Trends in Neurosciences* 21: 487–494.

Marr, David. 1982. *Vision*. San Francisco: Freeman.

Marsden, C. David and Jose A. Obeso. 1994. The functions of the basal ganglia and the paradox of sterotaxic surgery in Parkinson's disease. *Brain* 117: 877–897.

Maynard Smith, John. 1982. *Evolution and the Theory of Games*. Cambridge, UK: Cambridge University Press.

Maynard Smith, John, R. Burian, S. Kauffman, P. Alberch, J. Campbell, B. Goodwin, R. Lande, D. Raup, and L. Wolpert. 1985. Developmental constraints and evolution. *The Quarterly Review of Biology* 60.3: 265–287.

Maynard Smith, John and Eörs Szathmáry. 1995. *The Major Transitions in Evolution*. Oxford, UK: Oxford University Press.

Mayr, Ernst. 1950. Taxonomic categories in fossil hominids. *Cold Spring Harbor Symposium on Quantitative Biology* 15: 109–118.

McBrearty, Sally and Alison S. Brooks. 2000. The revolution that wasn't: A new interpretation of the origin of modern human behavior. *Journal of Human Evolution* 39: 453–563.

McCarthy, Robert C., David S. Strait, Fredrich Yates, and Philip Lieberman. forthcoming. *The Recent Origin of Human Speech*.

McCulloch, Warren, and Walter Pitts. 1943. A logical calculus of the ideas immanent in nervous activity. *Bulletin of Mathematical Biophysics* 5: 115–133.

McDougall, Ian, Francis H. Brown, John G. Fleagle. 2005. Stratigraphic placement and age of modern humans from Kibish, Ethiopia. *Nature* 433: 733–736.

McGurk, Harry and John MacDonald. 1976. Hearing lips and seeing voices. *Nature* 264: 746–748.

Medsker, Larry R. and Lakhmi C. Jain (eds.). 2000. *Recurrent Neural Networks: Design and Applications*. Boca Raton, FL: CRC Press.

Mellars, Paul A. 2006. Going east: New genetic and archaeological perspectives on the modern human colonization of Eurasia. *Science* 313: 796–800.

Mellars, Paul A. and Chris B. Stringer (eds.). 1989. *The human revolution: Behavioural and Biological Perspectives on the Origins of Modern Humans*. Princeton, NJ: Princeton University Press.

Merchant, Jason. 2001. *The Syntax of Silence: Sluicing, Islands, and the Theory of Ellipsis*. Oxford, UK: Oxford University Press.

Merchant, Jason. 2004. Fragments and ellipsis. *Linguistics and Philosophy* 27: 661–738.

Middleton, Frank A. and Peter L. Strick. 1994. Anatomical evidence for cerebellar and basal ganglia involvement in higher cognition. *Science* 266: 458–461.

Miller, Cory T., Elizabeth Dibble, and Marc D. Hauser. 2001. Amodal completion of acoustic signals in a nonhuman primate. *Nature Neuroscience* 4: 783–784.

Miller, Cory T., Carmen Gloria Iguina and Marc D. Hauser. 2005 Processing vocal signals for recognition during antiphonal calling in tamarins. *Animal Behaviour* 69: 1387–1398.

Miller, Geoffrey F. 1999. Sexual selection for cultural displays. In *The Evolution of Culture*, eds. Robin I. M. Dunbar, Chris Knight and Camilla Power, 71–91. Edinburgh: Edinburgh University Press.

Minsky, Marvin. 1986. *The Society of Mind*. New York: Simon and Schuster.

Mirenowicz, Jacques and Wolfram Schultz. 1996. Preferential activation of midbrain dopamine neurons by appetitive rather than aversive stimuli. *Nature* 379: 449–451.

Moglich, Michael and Bert Holldobler. 1975. Communication and orientation during foraging and emigration in the ant *Formica fusca*. *Journal of Comparative Physiology* 101: 275–88.

Moglich, Michael, Ulrich Maschwitz, and Bert Holldobler. 1974. Tandem calling: A new kind of signal in ant communication. *Science* 186: 1046–1047.

Monahan, Christopher M. 1996. New zooarchaeological data from Bed II, Olduvai Gorge, Tanzania: Implications for hominid behavior in the early Pleistocene. *Journal of Human Evolution* 31: 93–128.

Monchi, Oury, Michael Petrides, Valentina Petre, Keith Worsley, and Alain Dagher. 2001. Wisconsin Card Sorting Revisited: Distinct neural circuits participating in different stages of the task identified by event-related functional magnetic resonance imaging. *Journal of Neuroscience* 21: 7733–7741.

Mouse Genome Sequencing Consortium. 2002. Initial sequencing and comparative analysis of the mouse genome. *Nature* 420: 520–562.

Mulcahy, Nicholas J. and Josep Call. 2006. Apes save tools for future use. *Science* 312: 1038–1040.

Musso, Mariacristina, Andrea Moro, Volkmar Glauche, Michel Rijntjes, Jürgen Reichenbach, Christian Büchel, and Cornelius Weiller. 2003. Broca's area and the language instinct. *Nature Neuroscience* 6(7): 774–781.

Nadel, Lynn and Massimo Piattelli-Palmarini. 2003. What is cognitive science? In *Encyclopedia of Cognitive Science*, vol. I, ed. Lynn Nadel, xiii–xli. London, UK: Macmillan.

Naeser, Margaret A., Michael P. Alexander, Nancy Helms-Estabrooks, Harvey L. Levine, Susan A. Laughlin, and Norman Geschwind. 1982. Aphasia with predominantly subcortical lesion sites: Description of three capsular/putaminal aphasia syndromes. *Archives of Neurology* 39: 2–14.

Nance, Water E. and Michael J. Kearsey. 2004. Relevance of connexin deafness (DFNB1) to human evolution. *American Journal of Human Genetics* 74: 1081–1087.

Natsopoulos, Demetrios, George Grouios, Sevasti Bostantzopoulou, Georges Mentenopoulos, Zoe Katsarou, and John Logothetis. 1993. Algorithmic and heuristic strategies in comprehension of complement clauses by patients with Parkinson's disease. *Neuropsychologia* 31: 951–964.

Nevins, Andrew, David Pesetsky, and Cilene Rodrigues. 2007. Piraha? exceptionality: A reassessment [electronic version]. *LingBuzz* 1–58. http://129.242.176.75:9091/lingbuzz/@wrsYmjShqyDRdYVI/6Fc Retrieved 8 March 2007.

Newmeyer, Frederick. 1991. Functional explanation in linguistics and the origins of language. *Language and Communications* 11: 3–28.

Nowak, Martin, Natalia Komarova, and Partha Niyogi. 2001. Evolution of universal grammar. *Science* 291: 114–118.

Nowak, Martin, Natalia Komarova and Partha Niyogi. 2002. Computational and evolutionary aspects of language. *Nature* 417: 611–617.

Nowak, Martin, Joshua Plotkin, and Vincent Jansen. 2000. The evolution of syntactic communication. *Nature* 404: 495–498.

O'Connell, James F., Kristen Hawkes, and Nicholas. G. Blurton-Jones. 1999. Grandmothering and the evolution of Homo erectus. *Journal of Human Evolution* 36: 461–85.

O'Donnell, Tim J., Marc D. Hauser, and W. Tecumseh Fitch. 2005. Using mathematical models of language experimentally. *Trends in Cognitive Science* 9: 284–289.

Okada, Daijiro and Paul M. Bingham. 2008. Human uniqueness-self-interest and social cooperation. *Journal of Theoretical Biology* 253: 261–70.

Oppenheimer, Stephen. 2003. *Out of Eden: The Peopling of the World*. London: Constable.

Origgi, Gloria. 2001. Interpretare il linguaggio e interpretare gli altri: una o due teorie? *Sistemi Intelligenti* 13: 171–188.

Origgi, Gloria and Dan Sperber. 2000. Evolution, communication and the proper function of language. In *Evolution and the Human Mind: Language, Modularity and Meta-cognition*, eds. Peter Carruthers and Andrew Chamberlain, 140–169. Cambridge, UK: Cambridge University Press.

Osvath, Mathias. 2009a. In the search of inner worlds: Are humans alone in the mental world of possible futures? In *Human Characteristics: Evolutionary Perspectives on Human Mind and Kind*, eds. Henrik Høgh-Olesen, Jan Tønnesvang, and Preben Bertelsen, 44–64. Cambridge University Scholars.

2009b. Spontaneous planning for future stone throwing in a male chimpanzee. *Current Biology* 19(5): R190–191.

Osvath, Mathias and Peter Gärdenfors. 2005. Oldowan culture and the evolution of anticipatory cognition. *Lund University Cognitive Studies* 122.

2007. What are the evolutionary causes of mental time travel? *Behavioral and Brain Sciences* 30: 329–330.

Osvath, Mathias and Helena Osvath. 2008. Chimpanzee (*Pan troglodytes*) and orangutan (*Pongo abelii*) forethought: Self-control and pre-experience in the face of future tool use. *Animal Cognition* 11(4): 661–674(14).

Palleroni, Alberto, Cory T. Miller, Marc D. Hauser, and Peter Marler. 2005. Prey plumage adaptation against falcon attack. *Nature* 434: 973–974.

Palmer, Jeffrey B., Nathan J. Rudin, Gustavo Lara, and Alfred W. Crompton. 1992. Coordination of mastication and swallowing. *Dysphagia* 7: 187–200.

Parent, Andre. 1986. *Comparative Neurobiology of the Basal Ganglia*. New York: John Wiley & Sons.

Parker, Anna R. 2006. Evolving the narrow language faculty: Was recursion the pivotal step? Paper presented at the 6th International Conference on the Evolution of Language, Rome, April 2006.

Patterson, Francine and Ronald H. Cohn. 1999. *Koko-love!: Conversations with a Signing Gorilla*. New York: Dutton Children's Books.

Patterson, Nick, Daniel J. Richter, Sante Gnerre, Eric S. Lander, and David Reich. 2006. Genetic evidence for complex speciation of humans and chimpanzees. *Nature* 441: 1103–1108.

Peirce, Charles Saunders. 1931–1935. *The Collected Papers of Charles Sanders Peirce*. vols. I–IV. Cambridge, MA: Harvard University Press.

Penrose, Roger. 1989. *The Emperor's New Mind*. London: Penguin.

Pepperberg, Irene M. 1987. Acquisition of the same/different concept by an African Grey parrot. *Animal Behavior and Learning* 15: 423–432.

    1999. *The Alex Studies: Cognitive and Communicative Abilities of Grey Parrots*. Cambridge, MA: Harvard University Press.

Perruchet, Pierre and Arnaud Rey. 2005. Does the mastery of center-embedded linguistic structures distinguish humans from nonhuman primates? *Psychonomic Bulletin and Review* 12: 307–313.

Petitto, Laura-Ann. 2005. How brain begets language: On the neural tissue underlying human language acquisition. In *The Cambridge Companion to Chomsky*, ed. James McGilvray, 84–101. Cambridge, UK: Cambridge University Press.

Petraglia, Michael, Ravi Korisettar, Nicole Boivin, Christopher Clarkson, Peter Ditchfield, Sacha Jones, Jinu Koshy, Marta Mirazón Lahr, Clive Oppenheimer, David Pyle, Richard Roberts, Jean-Luc Schwenninger, Lee Arnold, and Kevin White. 2007. Middle Paleolithic assemblages from the Indian subcontinent before and after the Toba super-eruption. *Science* 317: 114–116.

Petrides, Michael, Geneviève Cadoret, and Scott Mackey. 2005. Orofacial somatomotor responses in the macaque monkey homologue of Broca's area. *Nature* 435: 1235–1238.

Petronis, Arturas. 2001. Human morbid genetics revisited: Relevance of epigenetics. *Trends in Genetics* 17(3): 142–146.

Piattelli-Palmarini, Massimo (ed.). 1980. *Language and Learning: The Debate between Jean Piaget and Noam Chomsky*. Cambridge, MA: Harvard University Press.

    1981. Equilibria, crystals, programs, energetic models and organizational models. In *Italian Studies in the Philosophy of Science*, ed. Maria Luisa Dalla Chiara, 341–359. Dordrecht, Holland: Reidel.

    1989. Evolution, selection and cognition: From "learning" to parameter setting in biology and in the study of language. *Cognition* 31: 1–44.

    2008. Novel tools at the service of old ideas. *Biolinguistics* 2(2): 237–246.

Piattelli-Palmarini, Massimo and Juan Uriagereka. 2004. The immune syntax: The evolution of the language virus. In *Variations and Universals in Biolinguistics*, ed. Lyle Jenkins, 341–377. Amsterdam: Elsevier.

    2005. The evolution of the narrow faculty of language: The skeptical view and a reasonable conjecture. *Lingue e Linguaggio* 4(1): 27–79.

    2008. Still a bridge too far? Biolinguistic questions for grounding language on brains. *Physics of Life Reviews* 5(4): 207–224.

in press. A geneticist's dream, a linguist's nightmare: The case of FOXP2. In *Biolinguistics Investigations*, eds. Anna Maria Di Sciullo and Cedric Boeckx. Oxford, UK: Oxford University Press.

Pietroski, Paul M. 2005. Meaning before truth. In *Contextualism in Philosophy: Knowledge, Meaning and Truth*, eds. Gerhard Preyer and Georg Peter, 255–302. Oxford, UK: Oxford University Press.

Pinker, Steven. 1979. Formal models of language learning. *Cognition* 7: 217–283.

1984. *Language Learnability and Language Development*. Cambridge, MA: Harvard University Press.

1994. *The Language Instinct: How the Mind Creates Language*. New York: William Morrow.

2003. Language as an adaptation to the cognitive niche. In *Language Evolution*, eds. Morton H. Christiansen and Simon Kirby, 16–37. Oxford, UK: Oxford University Press.

Pinker, Steven and Paul Bloom. 1990. Natural language and natural selection. *Behavioral and Brain Sciences* 13: 707–784.

Pinker, Steven and Ray Jackendoff. 2005. The faculty of language: What's special about it? *Cognition* 95: 201–236.

Ploog, Detlev. 2002. Is the neural basis of vocalisation different in non-human primates and *Homo sapiens*? In *The Speciation of Modern Homo Sapiens*, ed. Timothy J. Crow, 121–135. Oxford, UK: Oxford University Press.

Plummer, Thomas. 2004. Flaked stones and old bones: Biological and cultural evolution at the dawn of the dawn of technology. *Yearbook of Physical Anthropology* 47: 118–164.

Premack, David. 2004. Is language the key to human intelligence? *Science* 303: 318–320.

2007. Human and animal cognition: Continuity and discontinuity. *Proceedings of the National Academy of Sciences* 104: 13861–13867.

Polit, Andres and Emil Bizzi. 1978. Processes controlling arm movements in monkeys. *Science* 201: 1235–1237.

Povinelli, Daniel. 2000. *Folk Physics for Apes*. Oxford, UK: Oxford University Press.

Pray, Leslie. 2004. Epigenetics: Genome, meet your environment. *The Scientist* 18(13): 1–10.

Price, Thomas S., Thalia C. Eley, Philip S. Dale, Jim Stevenson, Kim Saudino, and Robert Plomin. 2000. Genetic and environmental covariation between verbal and nonverbal cognitive development in infancy. *Child Development* 71: 948–959.

Pylkkänen, L. and A. Marantz. 2003. Tracking the time course of word recognition with MEG. *Trends in Cogntive Science* 7(5): 187–189.

Raby, Caroline, Dean Alexis, Anthony Dickinson, and Nicola. S. Clayton. 2007. Planning for the future by western scrub-jays. *Nature* 445: 919–921.

Ramus, Franck, Marc D. Hauser, Cory T. Miller, Dylan Morris, and Jacques Mehler. 2000. Language discrimination by human newborns and cotton-top tamarins. *Science* 288: 349–351.

Raymond, Eric Steven. 2004. *The Art of Unix Programming*. Boston, MA: Addison-Wesley.

Recanati, François. 2004. *Literal Meaning*. Cambridge, UK: Cambridge University Press.

Reed, Kaye E. 1997. Early hominid evolution and ecological change through the African Plio-Pleistocene. *Journal of Human Evolution* 32: 289–322.

Rhodes, Jill and Steven Churchill. 2008. Throwing in the middle and upper Paleolithic: Inferences from an analysis of humeral retroversion. *Journal of Human Evolution* 30: 1–11.

Rissman, J., J. C. Eliasesen, and S. E. Blumstein. 2003. Am event-related fMRI study of implicit semantic priming. *Journal of Cognitive Neuroscience*.15: 1160–1175.

2003. An event-related fMRI study of implicit semantic priming. *Journal of Cognitive Neuroscience* 15: 1160–1175.

Rizzolatti, Giacomo and Michael A. Arbib. 1998. Language within our grasp. *Trends in Cognitive Sciences* 21: 188–194.

Rizzolatti, Giacomo, Roselino Camarda, Leonardo Fogassi, Maurizio Gentilucci, Giuseppi Luppino and Massimo Matelli. 1988. Functional organization of inferior area 6 in the macaque monkey. II. Area F5 and the control of distal movements. *Experimental Brain Research* 71: 491–507.

Rizzolatti, Giacomo L., Leonardo Fogassi and Vittorio Gallese. 2000. Mirror neurons: Intentionality detectors? *International Journal of Psychology* 35(3–4): 205–205.

Roberts, A., William. 2002." Are animals stuck in time?" *Psychological Bulletin* 128: 473–489.

2006. The questions of temporal and spatial displacement in animal cognition. In *Comparative Cognition: Experimental Explorations of Animal Intelligence*, eds. Edward A. Wasserman and Thomas R. Zentall, 145–163. New York: Oxford University Press.

Rogers, James, Geoffrey K. Pullum, and Marc D. Hauser. In review. Evolving linguistic computation. *Trends in Cognitive Science*.

Rohl, Jeffrey S. 1984. *Recursion via Pascal*. Cambridge, MA: Cambridge University Press.

Roitblat, Herbert L. 1982. The meaning of representation in animal memory. *Behavioral and Brain Sciences* 5: 353–372.

Ronshaugen, Matthew, Nadine McGinnis, and William McGinnis. 2002. Hox protein mutation and macroevolution of the insect body plan. *Nature* 415: 914–917.

Russell, Bridget A., Frank J. Cerny, and Elaine T. Stathopoulos. 1998. Effects of varied vocal intensity on ventilation and energy expenditure in women and men. *Journal of Speech, Language, and Hearing Research* 41: 239–248.

Sander, Erik K. 1972. When are speech sounds learned? *Journal of Speech and Hearing Disorders* 37: 55–63.

Sandler, Wendy, Irit Meir, Carol Padden, and Mark Aronoff. 2005. The emergence of grammar: Systematic structure in a new language. *Proceedings of the National Academy of Sciences* 102: 2661–2665.

Sanes, Jerome N, John P. Donoghue, Venkatesan Thangaraj, Robert R. Edelman, and Steven Warach. 1995. Shared neural substrates controlling hand movements in human motor cortex. *Science*. 268: 1775–1777.

Sauerland, Uli, and Hans-Martin Gärtner (eds.). 2007. *Interfaces + Recursion = Language?* Berlin: Mouton de Gruyter.

Savage-Rumbaugh, E. Sue. 1994. Hominid evolution: Looking to modern apes for clues. In *Hominid Culture in Primate Perspective*, eds. Duane Quiatt and Junichiro Itani, 7–49. Niwot, CO: University Press of Colorado.

Savage-Rumbaugh, E. Sue, Kelly McDonald, Rose A. Sevcik, William D. Hopkins, and Elizabeth Rubert. 1986. Spontaneous symbol acquisition and use by pygmy chimpanzees (*Pan panicus*). *Journal of Experimental Psychology: General* 115: 211–235.

Savage-Rumbaugh, E. Sue, Stuart G. Shanker, and Talbot J. Taylor. 1998. *Apes, Language and the Human Mind*. New York: Oxford University Press.

Schick, Kathy D. and Nicholas Toth. 1993. *Making Silent Stones Speak: Human Evolution and the Dawn of Technology*. New York: Simon and Schuster.

Schmitz, Oswald J. 1992. Optimal diet selection by white-tailed deer: Balancing reproduction with starvation risk. *Evolutionary Ecology* 6: 125–141.

Schusterman, Ronald J. and Kathy Krieger. 1984. California sea lions are capable of semantic interpretation. *The Psychological Record* 34: 3–23.

Schutzemberger, Marco. 1961. On the definition of a family of automata. *Information and Control* 4: 245–270.

Searcy, William A. and Stephen Nowicki. 2005. *The Evolution of Animal Communication: Reliability and Deception in Signaling Systems*. Princeton, NJ: Princeton University Press.

Semaw, Sileshi, Paul R. Renne, John W. K. Harris, Craig S. Feibel, Raymond L. Bernor, N. Fesseha, and Ken Mowbray. 1997. 2.5-million-year-old stone tools from Gona, Ethiopia. *Nature* 385: 333–336.

Semaw, Sileshi, Michael, J. Rogers, Jay Quade, Paul Renne, Robert Butler, Manuel Domínguez-Rodrigo, Dietrich Stout, William Hart, Travis Pickering, and Scott Simpson. 2003. 2.6-Million-year-old stone tools and associated bones from OGS-6 and OGS-7, Gona, Afar, Ethiopia. *Journal of Human Evolution* 45: 169–177.

Seyfarth, Robert and Dorothy Cheney. 2003. The structure of social knowledge in monkeys. In *Animal Social Complexity: Intelligence, Culture, and Individualized Societies*, eds. F. de Waal and P. Tyack, 207–229. Cambridge, MA: Harvard University Press.

Sherman, Michael Y. 2007. Universal genome in the origin of metazoa. *Cell Cycle* 6.15: 1873–1877.

Shipley, Elizabeth, Carlota Smith, and Lila Gleitman. 1969. A study in the acquisition of Language. *Language* 45: 322–342.

Simeone, Antonio, Dario Acampora, Massimo Gulisano, Anna Stornaiuolo and Edoardo Boncinelli. 1992. Nested expression domains of four homeobox genes in developing rostral brain. *Nature* 358: 687–690.

Sipser, Michael. 1997. *Introduction to the Theory of Computation*. Boston, MA: PWS Publishing.

Skiena, Steven S. 1998. *The Algorithm Design Manual*. New York: Springer Verlag.

Soare, Robert I. 1996. Computability and Recursion. *The Bulletin of Symbolic Logic* 2: 284–321.

Sober, Elliot and David Sloan Wilson. 1998. *Unto Others: The Evolution and Psychology of Unselfish Behavior*. Cambridge, MA: Harvard University Press.

Sperber, Dan 2000. Metarepresentations in an Evolutionary Perspective. In *Metarepresentations: A Multidisciplinary Perspective*, ed. Dan Sperber, 117–137. Oxford, UK: Oxford University Press.

Sperber, Dan and Deirdre Wilson. 1986. *Relevance Communication and Cognition*. Second edition. Oxford, UK: Blackwell. Second revised edition 1995.

2002. Pragmatics, Modularity and Mind-reading. *Mind and Language* 17: 3–23.

Spurzheim, Johann Gaspar. 1815. *The Physiognomical System of Drs. Gall and Spurzheim: Founded on an Anatomical and Physiological Examination of the Nervous System in General, and of the Brain in Particular, and Indicating the Dispositions and Manifestations of the Mind*. London: Baldwin, Cradock and Joy.

Stabler, Edward P. 2004. Varieties of crossing dependencies: Structure dependence and mild context sensitivity. *Cognitive Science* 28: 699–720.

2009. Computational models of language universals: Expressiveness, learnability and consequences. In *Language Universals*, eds. Morten Christiansen, Christopher Collins, and Shimon Edelman. Oxford, UK: Oxford University Press.

Stalnaker, Robert. 1999. *Context and Content: Essays on Intentionality in Speech and Thought*. Oxford, UK: Oxford University Press.

Stephens, David W. and John R. Krebs. 1986. *Foraging Theory*. Princeton, NJ: Princeton University Press.

Stevens, Kenneth N. 1972. Quantal nature of speech. In *Human Communication: A Unified View*, eds. Edward E. David and Peter B. Denes, 51–66. New York: McGraw Hill.

Stoianov, Ivelin. 2000. Recurrent autoassociative networks: Developing distributed representation of hierarchically structured sequences by autoassociation. In *Recurrent Neural Networks: Design and Applications*, eds. Larry R. Medsker and Lakhmi C. Jain, 205–241. Boca Raton, FL: CRC Press.

Story, Brad H., Ingo R. Titze, and Eric A. Hoffman. 1996. Vocal tract area functions from magnetic resonance imaging. *Journal of the Acoustical Society of America* 100: 537–554.

Stowe, Laurie A., Anne M. J. Paans, Albertus A. Wijers, and Frans Zwarts. 2004. Activation of "motor" and other non-language structures during sentence comprehension. *Brain and Language* 89: 290–299.

Striedter, Georg. 2006. Précis and multiple book review of *Principles of Brain Evolution*. *Behavioral and Brain Sciences* 29: 1–36.

Stringer, Christopher. B. 1998. Chronological and biogeographic perspectives on later human evolution. In *Neanderthals and Modern Humans in Western Asia*, eds. Takeru Akazawa, Kenichi Aoki, and Ofer Bar-Yosef, 29–38. New York: Plenum.

Stromswold, Karin. 1997. Specific language impairments. In *Behavioral Neurology and Neuropsychology*, eds. Todd E. Feinberg and Martha J. Farah, 755–772. New York: McGraw Hill.

1998. The genetics of spoken language disorders. *Human Biology* 70: 297–324.

2000. The cognitive neuroscience of language acquisition. In *The New Cognitive Neurosciences*, Second edition, ed. Michael Gazzaniga, 909–932. Cambridge, MA: MIT Press.

2001a. The heritability of language: A review and meta-analysis of twin, adoption and linkage studies. *Language* 77: 647–723.

2001b. *The Parent Assessment of Language (PAL) Tests*. unpublished ms.

2005. Genetic specificity of linguistic heritability. In *Twenty-first Century Psycholinguistics: Four Cornerstones*, ed. Anne Cutler, 121–139. Mahwah, NJ: Lawrence Erlbaum Associates.

2006. Why aren't identical twins linguistically identical? Genetic, prenatal and postnatal factors. *Cognition* 101: 333–384.

Stromswold, Karin, Kathleen Schramm, Diane Molnar, Scott Holodak, and Ellyn Sheffield. 2005. *The role of specific and non-specific genetic factors in language development*. Paper presented at the Society for Research in Child Development, Atlanta, GA.

Stromswold, Karin, Ellyn Sheffield, Debra Truit, and Diane Molnar. 2006. Parents can test preschool children's language: The Parent Assessment of Language (PAL) test. *Rutgers University Center for Cognitive Science Technical Report* 84: 1–31.

Studdert-Kennedy, Michael. 1998. The particulate origins of language generativity: From syllable to gesture. In *Approaches to the Evolution of Language*, eds. James R. Hurford, Michael Studdert-Kennedy, and Chris Knight, 169–176. Cambridge, UK: Cambridge University Press.

Stuss, Donald T. and D. Frank Benson. 1986. *The Frontal Lobes*. New York: Raven Press.

Suc, Jean-Pierre, Adele Bertini, Suzanne A. G. Leroy, and Danica Suballyova 1997. Towards the lowering of the Pliocene/Pleistocene boundary to the Gauss-Matuyama reversal. *Quaternary International* 40: 37–42.

Sudd, John H. and Nigel R. Franks. 1987. *The Behavioral Ecology of Ants*. New York: Chapman & Hall.

Suddendorf, Thomas and Michael C. Corballis. 1997. Mental time travel and the evolution of human mind. *Genetic, Social and General Psychology Monographs* 123: 133–167.

2007. The evolution of foresight: What is mental time travel and is it unique to humans? *Behavioral and Brain Sciences* 30(3): 299–313.

Szabó, Zoltan (ed.). 2005. *Semantics versus Pragmatics*. Oxford, UK: Oxford University Press.

Takahashi, Kaoru, Fu-Chin Liu, Katsuiku Hirokawa and Hiroshi Takahashi. 2003. Expression of FoxP2, a gene involved in speech and language in the developing and adult striatum. *Journal of Neuroscience Research* 73: 62–72.

Tattersall, Ian. 2009. *The Fossil Trail: How We Know What We Think We Know About Human Evolution*. Second edition. New York: Oxford University Press.

1998. *The Origin of the Human Capacity*. New York: The American Museum of Natural History.

2000. Once we were not alone. *Sci American* 282(1): 56–62.

2002. *The Monkey in the Mirror: Essays on the Science of What Makes Us Human*. New York: Harcourt.

2004. What happened in the origin of human consciousness? *The Anatomical Record. Part B, New Anatomist* 276B: 19–26.

2005. Patterns of innovation in human evolution. *Nova Acta Leopoldinia* 93: 145–157.

Terkel, Joseph. 1996. Cultural transmission of feeding behavior in the black rat. In *Social Learning in Animals: The Roots of Culture*, eds. Cecilia M. Heyes and Bennett G. Galef, 17–47. San Diego, CA: Academic Press.

Terrace, Herbert S. 1979. *Nim*. New York: Knopf.

Thompson, D'Arcy and John Bonner. 1917/1992. *On Growth and Form*. Cambridge, UK: Cambridge University Press.

Tobias, Philip V. 1987. The brain of *Homo habilis*: A new level of organization in cerebral evolution. *Journal of Human Evolution* 16: 741–761.

1994. The evolution of early hominids. In *Companion Encyclopedia of Anthropology*, ed. Tim Ingold, 33–78. London, UK: Routledge.

Tomasello, Michael. 1999. *The Cultural Origins of Human Cognition*. Cambridge, MA: Harvard Unversity Press.

2000. Acquiring syntax is not what you think. In *Speech and Language Impairments in Children: Causes, Characteristics, Intervention, and Outcome*, eds. Dorothy V. M. Bishop and Laurence Leonard, 1–15. Hove, UK: Psychology Press.

2003. On the different origins of symbols and grammar. In *Language Evolution*, eds. Morton H. Christiansen and Simon Kirby, 94–110. Oxford, UK: Oxford University Press.

2004. What kind of evidence could refute the UG hypothesis? Commentary on Wunderlich. *Studies in Language* 28: 642–645.

2005. Beyond formalities: The case of language acquisition. *The Linguistic Review* 22: 183–198.

Tomasello, Michael, Malinda Carpenter, Josep Call, Tanva Behne and Henrike Moll. 2005. Understanding and sharing intentions: The origins of cultural cognition. *Behavioral and Brain Sciences* 28: 675–691.

Tooby, John and Leda Cosmides. 2000. Toward mapping the evolved functional organization of mind and brain. In *The New Cognitive Neurosciences*, ed. Michael Gazzaniga, 1167–1178. Cambridge, MA: MIT Press.

Tooby, John and Irving DeVore. 1987. The reconstruction of hominid evolution through strategic modeling. *In The Evolution of Human Behavior: Primate Models*, ed. Warren G. Kinzey, 183–238. Albany, NY: State University of New York Press.

Toro, Juan M. and Josep B. Trobalon. 2005. Statistical computations over a speech stream in a rodent. *Perception and Psychophysics* 67: 867–875.

Toro, Juan M. and Josep B. Trobalon and Núria Sebastian-Galles. 2003. The use of prosodic cues in language discrimination tasks by rats. *Animal Cognition* 6: 131–136.

2005. Effects of backward speech and speaker variability in language discrimination by rats. *Journal of Experimental Psychology: Animal Behavior Processes* 31: 95–100.

Toth, Nicholas. 1985. The Oldowan reassessed: A close look at early stone artifacts. *Journal of Archeological Science* 12: 101–120.

Trauth, Martin H., Mark A. Maslin, Alain Deino, and Manfred R. Strecker. 2005. Late Cenozoic moisture history of East Africa. *Science* 309: 2051–2053.

Treves, Adrian and Lisa Naughton-Treves. 1999. Risk and opportunity for humans co-existing with large carnivores. *Journal of Human Evolution* 36: 275–282.

Treves, Alessandro. 2005. Frontal latching networks: A possible neural basis for infinite recursion. *Cognitive Neuropsychology* 22(3–4): 276–291.

True, Heather, Ilana Berlin, and Susan Lindquist. 2004. Epigenetic regulation of translation reveals hidden genetic variation to produce complex traits. *Nature* 431: 184–189.

Tulving, Endel. 2005. Episodic memory and autonoesis: Uniquely human? In *The Missing Link in Cognition: Evolution of Self-Knowing Consciousness*, eds. Herbert Terrace and Janet Metcalfe, 3–56. New York: Oxford University Press.

Ujhelyi, Mária. 1998. Long call structure in apes as a possible precursor for language. In *Approaches to the Evolution of Language: Social and Cognitive Bases*, eds. James R. Hurford, Michael Studdert-Kennedy, and Chris Knight, 171–189. Cambridge, UK: Cambridge University Press.

Uriagereka, Juan. 1998. *Rhyme and Reason: An Introduction to Minimalist Syntax*. Cambridge, MA: MIT Press.

van Gelderen, Elly and Jeff MacSwan. 2008. Interface conditions and code-switching: Pronouns, lexical DPs, and checking theory. *Lingua* 118(6): 765–776.

Vanhaeren, Marian, Francesco d'Errico, Chris Stringer, Sarah L. James, Jonathan A. Todd, and Henk K. Mienis. 2006. Middle Paleolithic shell beads in Israel and Algeria. *Science* 312: 1785–1788.

van Schaik, Carel P., Marc Ancrenaz, Gwendolyn Borgen, Birute Galdikas, Cheryl D. Knott, Ian Singleton, Akira Suzuki, Sri Suci Utamia, and Michelle Merrill. 2003. Orangutan cultures and the evolution of material culture. *Science* 299(5603): 102–105.

Vargha-Khadem, Faraneh, Kate E. Watkins, Katherine J. Alcock, Paul Fletcher, and Richard Passingham. 1995. Praxic and nonverbal cognitive deficits in a large family with a genetically transmitted speech and language disorder. *Proceedings of the National Academy of Sciences USA* 92: 930–933.

Vargha-Khadem, Fararneh, Kate E. Watkins, Cathy J. Price, John Ashbruner, Karl J. Friston, Richard S. J. Frackowiak, Mortimer Mishkin, David G. Gadian, and Richard E. Passingham. 1998. Neural basis of an inherited speech and language disorder. *Proceedings of the National Academy of Sciences USA* 95: 12695–12700.

Vauclair, Jacques. 1990. Primate cognition: From representation to language. In *"Language" and Intelligence in Monkeys and Apes*, eds. Sue Taylor Parker and Kathleen Rita Gibson, 312–329. Cambridge, UK: Cambridge University Press.

Velasco, Juan and Andres Millan. 1998. Feeding habits of two large insects from a desert stream: *Abedus herberti (Hemiptera: Belostomatidae) and Thermonectus marmoratus (Coleoptera: Dytiscidae). Aquatic Insects* 20: 85–96.

Vouloumanos, Athena and Janet F. Werker. 2004. Tuned to the signal: The privileged status of speech for young infants. *Developmental Science* 7: 270–276.

Vrba, Elizabeth S. 1995. *Paleoclimate and Evolution, with Emphasis on Human Origins.* New Haven, CT: Yale University Press.

Wagner, Günter P. 2000. What is the promise of developmental evolution? Part I: why is developmental biology necessary to explain evolutionary innovations? *Journal of Experimental Zoology Part A: Ecological Genetics and Physiology* 288: 95–98.

Walker, Alan and Richard E. F. Leakey (eds.). 1993. The Nariokotome *Homo erectus skeleton.* Cambridge MA: Harvard University Press.

Wallace, Alfred Russel. 1889. *Darwinism: An Exposition of the Theory of Natural Selection, with Some of Its Applications.* London, UK: Macmillan.

Watanabe, Shigeru, Eriko Yamamoto, and Midori Uozumi. 2006. Language discrimination by java sparrows. *Behavioural Processes* 73: 114–116.

Watkins, Kate E., Nina F. Dronkers, and Faraneh Vargha-Khadem. 2002. Behavioural analysis of an inherited speech and language disorder: Comparison with acquired aphasia. *Brain* 125: 452–464.

Watkins, Kate E., Antonio P. Strafella, and Tomas Paus. 2003. Seeing and hearing speech excites the motor system involved in speech production. *Neuropsychologia* 41: 989–994.

Watkins, Kate E., Faraneh Vargha-Khadem, John Ashbruner, Richard E. Passingham, Alan Connelly, Karl J. Friston, Richard S. J. Frackowiak, Mortimer Mishkin, and David G. Gadian. 2002. MRI analysis of an inherited speech and language disorder: Structural brain abnormalities. *Brain* 125: 465–478.

Weinreich, Daniel M., Nigel F. Delaney, Mark A. DePristo, and Daniel L. Hartl. 2006. Darwinian evolution can follow only very few mutational paths to fitter proteins. *Science* 312: 111–114.

Wernicke, Carl. 1874/1967. The aphasic symptom complex: A psychological study on a neurological basis. *In Proceedings of the Boston Colloquium for the Philosophy of Science*, vol. IV, eds. Robert S. Cohen and Marx W. Wartofsky, 34–97. Dordrecht: Reidel.

West-Eberhard, Mary Jane. 2003. *Developmental Plasticity and Evolution*. Oxford, UK: Oxford University Press.

Wexler, Kenneth and Peter Culicover. 1980. *Formal Principles of Language Acquisition*. Cambridge, MA: MIT Press.

White, Randall. 1989. Visual thingking in the Ice Age. *Scientific American* 260(7): 92–99.

White, Timothy D., Berhane Asfaw, David DeGusta, Henry Gilbert, Gary D. Richards, Gen Suwa, and F. Clark Howell. 2003. Pleistocene *Homo sapiens* from Middle Awash, Ethiopia. *Nature* 423: 742–747.

Whiten, Andrew. 2002. The imitator's representation of the imitated: Ape and child. In *The Imitative Mind: Development, Evolution, and Brain Bases*, eds. Andrew N. Meltzoff and Wolfgang Prinz, 98–121. Cambridge, UK: Cambridge University Press.

Whiten, Andrew and Richard W. Byrne (eds.). 1997. *Machiavellian Intelligence II: Evaluations and Extensions*. Cambridge, UK: Cambridge University Press.

Whiten, Andrew, Jane Goodall, William C. McGrew, Toshisada Nishida, Vernon Reynolds, Yukimaru Sugiyama, Caroline E. G. Tutin, Richard W. Wrangham, and Christopher Boesch. 1999. Cultures in chimpanzees. *Nature* 399(6737): 682–685.

Williams, George C. 1966. *Adaptation and Natural Selection: A Critique of Some Current Evolutionary Thought*. Princeton, NJ: Princeton University Press.

Wilson, Edward O. 1962. Chemical communication in the fire ant Solenopsis Saevissima. *Animal Behavior* 10: 134–164.

Wolpert, Daniel M., Kenji Doya, and Mitsuo Kawato. 2003. A unifying computational framework for motor control and social interaction. *Philosophical Transactions of the Royal Society, London, B* 358: 593–602.

Wood, Bernard J. 2002. Hominid revelations from Chad. *Nature* 418: 134–135.

Wood, Bernard and Mark Collard. 1999. The human genus. *Science* 284: 65–71.

Worden, Robert. 1998. The evolution of language from social intelligence. In *Approaches to the Evolution of Language: Social and Cognitive Bases*, eds. James R. Hurford, Michael Studdert-Kennedy, and Chris Knight, 148–166. Cambridge, UK: Cambridge University Press.

Wrangham, Richard W., William C. McGrew, Frans B. M. de Waal, and Paul Heltne. 1994. *Chimpanzee Cultures*. Cambridge, MA: Harvard University Press (in cooperation with the Chicago Academy of Sciences)

Wundt, Wilhelm M. 1921. *Elements of Folk Psychology*. New York: Macmillan.

Yang, Charles. 2002. *Knowledge and Learning in Natural Language*. Oxford, UK: Oxford University Press.

2004. Universal Grammar, statistics, or both. *Trends in Cognitive Sciences* 6 (10): 451–456.

forthcoming Three factors in language variation. *Lingua*.

Yip, Moira. 2006. The search for phonology in other species. *Trends in Cognitive Science* 10: 442–446.

Zahavi, Amotz. 1975. Mate selection – a selection for a handicap. *Journal of Theoretical Biology* 53: 205–214.

Zlatev, Jordan, Tomas Persson, and Peter Gärdenfors. 2005. Bodily mimesis as the "missing link" in human cognitive evolution. *Lund University Cognitive Studies* 121.

Index

abductive principle 49
abstraction 149
  abstract neural modeling 153
acquisition of language 2, 4, 32, 46, 59, 60, 63,
  66, 163, 202
  hereditability of language 176–177
    twin studies 180–187
  perinatal environment and genetic interaction
    (PEGI) study 183–187
  genetic factors in language-impaired and
    normal twins 184
  genetic overlap for linguistic and non-
    linguistic abilities 185
  genetic overlap for linguistic milestones 185
  genetic overlap for PAL scores 186
  genetic overlap for parent-report measures
    of lexical and syntactic abilities 186
  hereditability of linguistic and non-
    linguistic abilities 184–185
  measures of linguistic and non-linguistic
    abilities 183–184
  overview 183
  possible causes of the phonology–syntax
    genetic overlap 186–187
  see also learning
adaptationism 13, 92–93
Alexander, Michael P. 166
analogies 21
animals
  collaboration by 110
  communication systems 16, 21, 23, 24, 57,
    66, 72, 74, 93, 95, 96, 98, 163, 201
  birdsong 22, 28, 87, 88
  code model 127
  conceptual-intentional systems of non-
    linguistic animals 29–32
  discrete infinity and constraints on learning
    32–37
  imitation 28–29
  numbers 33–34
  physiology of speech production 173–174
  recruitment 207

sign languages 119, 137
  as social behaviour 212–216
  specialness of speech 26–29
  planning 106–107
anthropological context 11–13
aphasia 10, 166
Arbib, Michael 66
architecture of language 5–7
  parallel 67, 68, 70–71
  syntactical 67, 68, 69, 70, 71
Aristotle 57
arithmetic 53
articulatory phonology 120
assimilate-stretch principle 143
asymmetry 55, 56, 60
attention 222
automata 153

Bach, Johann Sebastian 82, 83–85
Baker, Mark 49
ban on investigations into origins of language 1
behavioral theories 153
  developmental-behavioral plasticity
    136–140
  genetic assimilation 142–144
Bickerton, Derek 71, 92, 117
big bang theory 117
biolinguistics 45
biological foundations 9–11, 16, 50
  age of specificity in biology 155–156
  evo devo (evolutionary developmental
    biology) theses 9, 45, 50, 51, 135–136,
    146–147
    co-evolutionary spiral 145–146
    developmental-behavioral plasticity
      136–140
  genetics *see* genetics
birdsong 22, 28, 87, 88
Bloom, Paul 146, 147
bodily ornamentation 122
Bow Wow theory 2
Boysen, Sarah T. 34

brain development and structure 58, 59, 64, 116, 117, 118, 164, 221, 222
  aphasia 10, 166
  dating appearance of human brain 172–175
  electrophysiologic studies 169–170
  FOXP2 gene and 10, 170–172
  imaging studies 10, 169–170
  local basal ganglia operations 169–170
  neural circuits 166–169
    cortical-striatal-cortical circuits 167–168
    neurodegenerative diseases 10, 168–169
Broca-Wernicke model 165–166
Burling, Robbins 119
Bybee, Joan 66

canalization 9, 138–139
capacity for language 56, 58, 63, 64–65, 71
Carroll, Sean 50
categorical perception 21
childcare 109
choking risk 174
Chomsky, Noam 1, 2, 3, 4, 5, 66, 69, 73, 94, 117, 146, 149, 151, 161, 163, 164, 186, 199, 201–206
Chomsky hierarchy 86–88, 97, 153
code model of communication 125, 127–128
codeswitching 159
coercion 217–220
co-evolutionary spiral 145–146
cognition 7, 11
  age of specificity in 153–155
  deficits 165
  origin of 193–194, 197–198
    patterns in hominid evolution 11, 194–197
  prospective see prospective cognition
collaboration 12, 216–219
  animal communication and 212–216
  for future goals 110–111, 113
    need for symbols in communication 111–113
  kinship-dependent social cooperation 216
communication 93
  animal systems 16, 21, 23, 24, 57, 66, 71, 74, 93, 95, 96, 98, 163, 201
  birdsong 22, 28, 87, 88
  code model 127
  conceptual-intentional systems of non-linguistic animals 29–32
  discrete infinity and constraints on learning 32–37
  imitation 28–29
  numbers 33–34
  physiology of speech production 173–174
  recruitment 207
  sign languages 119, 137

  as social behaviour 212–216
  specialness of speech 26–29
code model 125, 127–128
  elite information exchange 220–223
  inferential model 125, 126–127, 128–131
  symbolic 111–113
comparative approach to evolution of language 19–22, 26–37, 65
  conceptual-intentional systems of non-linguistic animals 29–32
  discrete infinity and constraints on learning 32–37
  specialness of speech 26–29
competition 216–219
complexity 66
computer science interpretation of recursion 76–78
conflicts 141, 144
  of interests 212, 213, 214, 216–219, 221
consciousness see cognition
constraints on learning 32–37
context-free languages (CFLs) 153
continuity hypothesis 26
contracts 111, 113
cooperation see collaboration
creative capacity of language 163–164
  Broca-Wernicke model 165–166
  dating appearance of human brain 172–175
  local basal ganglia operations 169–170
  neural circuits 166–169
    cortical-striatal-cortical circuits 167–168
    neurodegenerative diseases 10, 168–169
  reiteration 163, 164–165
  FOXP2 and 170–172
Cro-Magnon people 196
Crow, Timothy J. 117
cued representation 104
Culicover, Peter W. 69
culture
  cultural information 221–222
  evolution of languages and 9, 140–141, 146
    co-evolutionary spiral 145–146
    evolution of speakers 142–144
  language and 63, 66
  Oldowan culture 8, 107–110, 114, 115, 208
Cuvier, Georges 50

Darwin, Charles 20, 50, 51, 170
Deacon, Terrence 66, 110, 146, 147
Descartes, René 2, 19
detached representation 104–105
developmental neurobiology 153
developmental-behavioral plasticity 136–140
Diamond, Jared 58
discourse 12, 204

discrete infinity 32–37
diseases and disorders
    concordance rate for language disorders
        180–181
    neurodegenerative diseases 10, 168–169
displacement 206
DNA 14, 155, 213
Dobzhansky, Theodosius 11, 170

ecology
    origin of language and 103
elite information exchange 220–223
elite throwing 13, 219–220
energy use 122, 209
epigenetics 156
Everett, Daniel 88
evolingo 96
evolution 156–157, 170, 199
    dating appearance of human brain 172–175
    evo devo (evolutionary developmental
        biology) theses 9, 45, 50, 51, 135–136,
        146–147
        co-evolutionary spiral 145–146
        developmental-behavioural plasticity
            136–140
    of language see origins and evolution of
        language
    patterns in hominid evolution 11, 194–197
exploration 137–138
externalist philosophy 57, 60, 61
eyes 222

faculty of language 14–19, 37–38, 46, 91
    broad sense (FLB) 14, 17, 19, 23, 24, 25, 37,
        74, 95–96, 186, 199, 200
    comparative evidence 26–37
        conceptual-intentional systems of non-
            linguistic animals 29–32
        discrete infinity and constraints on learning
            32–37
        specialness of speech 26–29
    narrow sense (FLN) 4, 11, 14, 17, 18–19,
        23–24, 25, 37, 74, 95–96, 163, 186,
        199, 200
    testing hypotheses about 22–25
finite-state grammar 34
finite-state languages 153
Fitch, W. Tecumseh 1, 2, 4, 5, 36, 66, 69, 73, 86,
    87, 163, 164, 186, 199
Fodor, Jerry 162
foraging 207–209
FOXP2 gene 10, 11, 118, 122, 123, 156, 170–172
fragments 158–159
free riders 217, 218
functionalism 158

Galileo Galilei 19
Gallistel, C. R. 57
game theory 216
Garrod, Archibald E. 155
generative grammar 48, 149, 164
genetics 64, 135, 156–157
    design information 212
    evolution of language and 176, 178
        evolutionary implications of genetic
            findings 189–190
        genetic factors in language-impaired
            and linguistically normal people
            177–178
        perinatal environment and genetic
            interaction (PEGI) study 183–187
        reproductive fitness 178–179
        theories 187–188
        twin studies 11, 180–187
        variability and hereditability of language
            176–177
    FOXP2 gene 10, 11, 118, 122, 123, 156,
        170–172
    genetic accommodation 142
    genetic assimilation 142–144
    PAX6 genetic system 157
Gentner, Timothy Q. 88
gestural theory 118–119
Goethe, Johann Wolfgang von 51
Gold, Mark 33
Goldberg, Adele 66
Goldstein, Kurt 165
Goodall, Jane 57
Gould, Steven 50, 51
government binding theory 67
grammar 45, 97, 129, 160
    finite-state 34
    generative 48, 149, 164
    phrasal constituents 150–151, 162
    phrase-structure 36
    universal 3, 33, 50, 51, 60, 61, 64, 65
Grice, Paul 125

Hauser, Marc D. 1, 2, 4, 5, 36, 66, 69, 73, 86, 87,
    163, 164, 186, 199
HCF theory 199–201
    alternative to 206–210
    Chomsky's elaboration 201–206
hereditability of language 176–177
    twin studies 180–183
        concordance rate for language disorders
            180–181
        multivariate analysis of twins' linguistic
            abilities 182–183
        perinatal environment and genetic
            interaction (PEGI) study 183–187

hereditability of language (cont.)
　univariate analysis of twins' linguistic
　　abilities 181–182
Hockett, Charles F. 105
homologous traits 21
homoplasies 21
Humboldt, Wilhelm von 19
Hume, David 57, 60
Huxley, Thomas 51
hypoglossal nerve 117

iconic miming 112
idioms 159
I-language 9
imagination 105
　inner worlds 105
imitation 28–29
　iconic miming 112
indexical communication 112
inferential model of communication 125,
　　126–127, 128–131
infinity
　discrete 32–37
information exchange 220–223
inner worlds 105
instantaneity 202
interests
　conflicts of 212, 213, 214, 216–219, 221
interface systems 8–9, 36, 46, 67

Jackendoff, Ray 66, 69
Jacob, François 3, 49, 55, 59

Kant, Immanuel 162
kinship-dependent social cooperation 216

language
　acquisition see acquisition of language
　definitions 63
　notion of 149
　origins see origins and evolution of
　　language
larynx 26, 74, 118, 173
　choking risk 174
Lashley, Karl 164
learning 51, 60, 63, 138, 222
　constraints on 32–37
　evolution of language and 146
　general learning mechanism 33
　genetic assimilation and 144
Lerdahl, Fred 65
lexicalism 160
lexicon 72
Liberman, Alvin M. 17
Lieberman, D. E. 118

limits admissible hypotheses 49
linguistic interpretation of recursion 78–83
　empirical tests 80–81
　meaning as empirical indicator of structure
　　81–83
linguistics 149–150
Lingusitics Society of Paris 1
Lotka, Alfred J. 152
Luria, Salvador 55, 59

McGurk effect 26
Marr, David 66
marriage 111
Marsden, C. David 169
Marshack, Alexander 56, 58
mathematics
　arithmetic 53
　mathematical biology 151
　meta-mathematical interpretation of
　　recursion 82, 83–85
Matsuzawa, Tetsuro 34
meaning as empirical indicator of structure
　　81–83
memory 95, 96, 161
Merge mechanism 4, 6, 12, 52–54, 55, 59, 61,
　　62, 201, 202, 204
meta-mathematical interpretation of recursion
　　82, 83–85
migration from Africa 122
miming
　iconic 112
mind
　theory of 8, 31, 65, 74, 125
minimalism in linguistic theorizing 3–4, 51, 52,
　　59, 60, 94–95, 154, 160, 164
mirror neurons 29
Move mechanism 54
music 65, 74, 82, 122
　birdsong 22, 28, 87, 88

Neanderthal people 11, 117, 118, 196
neurological foundations 9–11
　developmental neurobiology 153
　local basal ganglia operations 169–170
　mirror neurons 29
　neural circuits 166–169
　　cortical-striatal-cortical circuits
　　　167–168
　　neurodegenerative diseases 10, 168–169
new ideas
　communication of 112
　cultural evolution of languages and
　　140–141
Nowak, Martin 33
numbers 33–34

Obeso, Jose A. 169
obsessive-compulsive disorder 167
Oldowan culture 8, 107–110, 114, 115, 208
origins and evolution of language 1, 2, 5, 15–16,
    45, 58, 61, 64, 66, 157–158, 161–162,
    211, 223–224
  adaptationism 13, 92–93
  anthropological context 11–13
  architecture of language 5–7
    parallel 67, 68, 70–71
    syntactical 67, 68, 69, 70, 71
  ban on investigations into 1
  biological foundations see biological
    foundations
  Broca-Wernicke model 165–166
  cognition and 193–194, 197–198
    patterns in hominid evolution 11, 194–197
  communication as social behaviour 212–216
  comparative approach 19–22, 26–37, 65
    conceptual-intentional systems of non-
      linguistic animals 29–32
    discrete infinity and constraints on learning
      32–37
    specialness of speech 26–29
  cultural evolution 9, 140–141, 146
    co-evolutionary spiral 145–146
    evolution of speakers 142–144
  elite information exchange 220–223
  evo devo (evolutionary developmental
    biology) theses 9, 45, 50, 51, 135–136,
    146–147
    co-evolutionary spiral 145–146
    developmental-behavioral plasticity
      136–140
  faculty of language see faculty of language
  forces behind 103–104
  genetics and 176, 178
    evolutionary implications of genetic
      findings 189–190
    genetic factors in language-impaired and
      linguistically normal people 177–178
    perinatal environment and genetic
      interaction (PEGI) study 183–187
    reproductive fitness 178–179
    theories 187–188
    twin studies 11, 180–187
    variability and hereditability of language
      176–177
  HCF theory 199–201
    alternative to 206–210
    Chomsky's elaboration 201–206
  interface systems 8–9, 36, 46, 68
  language before speech 8, 115–116
    early scenario 116
    evolutionary scenario 121–123

    gestural theory 118–119
    gradual switch 119–121
    late scenario 117–118
  minimalism in linguistic theorizing 3–4, 51,
    52, 59, 60, 94–95, 154, 160, 164
  neurological foundations see neurological
    foundations
  phases 151–152, 162
  pragmatic perspective 124, 131
    evolution of language and the two models
      of communication 127–131
    two models of communication 125–127
  principles and parameters model 2–3, 4,
    49–50, 51
  prospective cognition 104–107, 109, 113
    collaboration for future goals 110–111, 113
    need for symbols in communication about
      future goals 111–113
    Oldowan culture 8, 107–110, 114

parallel architecture 67, 68, 70–71
Parkinson's disease 10, 168
PAX6 genetic system 157
Peirce, Charles Sanders 49, 61, 112
perinatal environment and genetic interaction
    (PEGI) study 183–187
  genetic factors in language-impaired and
    normal twins 184
  genetic overlap for linguistic and non-
    linguistic abilities 185
  genetic overlap for linguistic milestones 185
  genetic overlap for PAL scores 186
  genetic overlap for parent-report measures of
    lexical and syntactic abilities 186
  hereditability of linguistic and non-linguistic
    abilities 184–185
  measures of linguistic and non-linguistic
    abilities 183–184
  overview 183
  possible causes of the phonology–syntax
    genetic overlap 186–187
Petitto, Laura 56
phases 151–152, 162
phonology 66–67, 69
  articulatory 120
  phonology–syntax genetic overlap 186–187
phrases 150–151, 162
  phrase-structure grammar 36
phrenology 165
physiology of speech production 11, 173–174
Piattelli-Palmarini, Massimo 45
pidgin languages 71
Pinker, Steven 69, 146, 147
Pirahã language 88
planning 105–107

plasticity
  developmental-behavioral 136–140
Pooh Pooh theory 2
population dynamics 152
pragmatic perspective on evolution of language
      124, 131
  two models of communication 125–127
    evolution of language and 127–131
preadaptations 26, 69
Premack, David 86
prepositions 160
principles and parameters model 2–3, 4,
      49–50, 51
probabilities
  computation of 35
prospective cognition 8, 104–107, 109, 113
  collaboration for future goals 110–111, 113
  need for symbols in communication about
        future goals 111–113
  Oldowan culture 8, 107–110, 114
protolanguage 12, 71, 89–90, 115, 129, 206
  fallacy of subtraction and 10, 160–161

recruitment 207, 209, 210
recurrence 85–86
recursion 6, 7, 52, 62, 69, 73–75, 94, 164–165,
      201, 210, 215
  Chomsky hierarchy and 86–88
  importance of 89–90
  interpretations 75–76
    computer science interpretation 76–78
    linguistic interpretation 78–83
    meta-mathematical interpretation 82,
        83–85
  languages lacking recursion 88–89
  recurrence and 85–86
  recursive function theory 82, 83–85
reference relation 57
reiteration 10, 163, 164–165
  FOXP2 and 170–172
relevance theory 125
representation 104
  cued 104
  detached 104–105
reproductive fitness 178–179
reverse engineering 7, 65, 72, 159
rigidity principle 47
Rizzi, Luigi 53
RNA 155

St. Hilaire, Geoffroy 50
San people 122
schizophrenia 167
secrecy 141
selective stabilization mechanisms 137–138

self-interest 217
sensory-motor system 94
sentences 19, 32, 204
sequence 12, 205
sexual division of labour 109
Sherman, Michael 50, 51
sign languages 56, 209
  animals 119, 137
  language before speech 8, 115–116
    early scenario 116
    evolutionary scenario 121–123
    gestural theory 118–119
    gradual switch 119–121
    late scenario 117–118
social interaction 189
  animal communication as 212–216
  kinship-dependent 216
  origin of language and 103
spandrels 25, 156
specificity
  age of 152
  in biology 155–156
  in cognition 153–155
speech 56, 222
  language before speech 8, 115–116
    early scenario 116
    evolutionary scenario 121–123
    gestural theory 118–119
    gradual switch 119–121
    late scenario 117–118
  phonology 66–67, 69
  physiology of speech production 11,
        173–174
  specialness of 26–29
sphenoid bone 118
spinal cord 117
statistical inferences 33, 34
stoppage 179, 189
stratification in languages 141
Striedter, George 58, 59
string theory 148, 149
structuralism 149
structure of language 63, 65
  meaning as empirical indicator of structure
        81–83
subtraction
  fallacy of 10, 160–161
symbolic language 6, 111–113
syntax 4, 9, 10, 67, 68, 69, 70, 71, 103, 121,
      145, 158
  phonology–syntax genetic overlap 186–187

Tattersall, Ian 56, 58
technology see tool-making
telegraphic stage 54

theory construction 46
Thompson, D'Arcy 50, 151
thought
    language of 55
throwing 13, 219–220
Tomasello, Michael 112
tool-making 122, 195, 196
    Oldowan culture 8, 107–110, 114, 115, 208
    throwing 13, 219–220
tracer studies 167
triadic miming 112
Turing, Alan 50
twin studies 11, 180–183
    concordance rate for language disorders
        180–181
    multivariate analysis of twins' linguistic
        abilities 182–183
    perinatal environment and genetic interaction
        (PEGI) study 183–187
        genetic factors in language-impaired and
            normal twins 184
        genetic overlap for linguistic and
            non-linguistic abilities 185
        genetic overlap for linguistic milestones
            185

genetic overlap for PAL scores 186
genetic overlap for parent-report measures
    of lexical and syntactic abilities 186
hereditability of linguistic and non-
    linguistic abilities 184–185
measures of linguistic and non-linguistic
    abilities 183–184
overview 183
possible causes of the phonology–syntax
    genetic overlap 186–187
univariate analysis of twins' linguistic
    abilities 181–182

universal grammar 3, 33, 50, 51, 60, 61, 64, 65

Veneziano, Gabriele 148
verbs 160
voice-onset-time (VOT) 168
Volterra, Vito 152

Wallace, Alfred Russell 53, 58
Weber's law 33, 34
West-Eberhardt, Mary Jane 135

Yo He Hoo theory 2